STUDIES IN WELSH HISTORY

Editors

RALPH A. GRIFFITHS   KENNETH O. MORGAN
GLANMOR WILLIAMS

1

THE MONASTIC ORDER
IN SOUTH WALES, 1066–1349

Abergavenny Priory: wooden effigy of the patron, John de Hastings, d. 1313, or his son of the same name, d. 1325.

THE MONASTIC ORDER IN SOUTH WALES, 1066—1349

by

F. G. COWLEY

*Published on behalf of the
History and Law Committee
of the Board of Celtic Studies*

CARDIFF
UNIVERSITY OF WALES PRESS
1977

© University of Wales, 1977

First edition 1977
Paperback edition 1986

British Library Cataloguing in Publication Data

Cowley, F. G.
   The monastic order in South Wales,
   1066–1349.
   1. Monasticism and religious order—
   Wales, South—History
   I. Title
   271'.009429'4   BX2603

   ISBN 0-7083-0942-9

Printed at The Bath Press, Avon

IN MEMORY OF
MY MOTHER AND FATHER

EDITORS' FOREWORD

Since the Second World War, Welsh history has attracted considerable scholarly attention and enjoyed a vigorous popularity. Not only have the approaches, both traditional and new, to the study of history in general been successfully applied to Wales's past, but the number of scholars engaged in this enterprise has multiplied during these years. These advances have been especially marked in the University of Wales.

In order to make more widely available the conclusions of recent research, much of it of limited accessibility in postgraduate dissertations and theses, the History and Law Committee of the Board of Celtic Studies has inaugurated this new series of monographs, *Studies in Welsh History*. It is anticipated that many of the volumes will have originated in research conducted in the University of Wales or under the auspices of the Board of Celtic Studies. But the series will not exclude significant contributions made by researchers in other Universities and elsewhere. Its primary aim is to serve historical scholarship and to encourage the study of Welsh history.

PREFACE

This work is substantially the text of a thesis which was accepted by the University of Wales for the degree of Ph.D. in 1965. It attempts to outline the development of the monastic order and to record the activities of the monks in the two dioceses of St. David's and Llandaff over a period of nearly three centuries, from the time when the Normans first entered south Wales until the effects of the Black Death first began to be felt in the area.

These geographical and chronological limits have not been rigidly adhered to. In dealing with the question of attendance at the Cistercian General Chapter, for example, it was considered better to treat the Welsh province as a whole and not to omit reference to the houses of north Wales. Similarly Monmouth Priory has been included, although until the nineteenth century Monmouth fell within the diocese of Hereford. Occasionally material later than the chosen terminal date of this study has been included, especially when such evidence throws valuable light on earlier developments, as in the case of the unique Tintern Abbey account rolls. The term 'monastic order' has, however, been strictly interpreted. It includes the monastic orders proper and only those orders of regular canons whose way of life was hardly distinguishable from that of the monks. The non-monastic orders of friars, knights templar and hospitallers, already treated in monographs and articles, have been excluded from this study.

The form of Welsh place-names always presents difficulties. I have tried to be consistent and have been guided by Elwyn Davies, *A Gazetteer of Welsh Place-Names* (3rd ed. Cardiff, 1969), and Melville Richards, *Welsh Administrative and Territorial Units* (Cardiff, 1969).

In collecting material for this study and in writing it, I owe many debts of gratitude. At its inception, dearth of evidence—the spectre which looms over every historian who works on medieval Wales—made me doubt whether such a study was worthwhile or even possible. In these early stages of research Professor D. B. Quinn and Miss Marion Gibbs, under whose supervision the work was first undertaken, gave invaluable help, encouragement and advice. Dr. Glyn Ashton and Mr. Ceri Lewis, my former colleagues at the University College of South

Wales, Cardiff, drew my attention to sources of information which I would otherwise have missed and gave generous assistance with materials written in Welsh. Chance meetings with fellow-researchers, archivists and librarians are always potentially useful and in my own case two such meetings were particularly fruitful. Mr. W. R. B. Robinson first drew my attention to the valuable collection of manuscripts relating to Tintern Abbey which are to be found in the Badminton collection at the National Library of Wales. I am grateful to His Grace the Duke of Beaufort for permission to use these manuscripts. Mr. W. L. Collett, then Borough Librarian of Newport, in a chance encounter at a conference devoted to other matters, made me aware of the very useful collection of transcripts relating to Tintern Abbey which were gathered together by the antiquarian, Mr. J. G. Wood, and are now deposited at Newport Public Library. I have been saved from a number of errors of fact and infelicities of style by my colleagues Dr. D. G. Walker, Dr. R. A. Griffiths and Mr. Neville Masterman. They have read the manuscript more than once over the years and offered suggestions which have been gratefully accepted. I have benefited greatly, too, from the advice and assistance given by Dr. Brinley Jones, former Director of the University of Wales Press, and by the present Director, Mr. John Rhys, and his assistant, Mr. Alun Treharne.

It was a great privilege to have had the manuscript read by the late Professor David Knowles, who generously found time to read it during a very busy retirement. The influence of his writings on my own work was already very apparent but his searching criticisms have greatly improved the text.

To my friend and former teacher and director of studies, Professor Glanmor Williams, I owe a special debt of gratitude. His patience in reading and criticising the chapters as they were written and his encouragement at every stage of writing, helped to bring to a speedier completion a work upon which I had been engaged for many years.

Finally, I owe an inestimable debt of gratitude to my wife for her patience, assistance and constant encouragement.

F. G. Cowley

University College of Swansea
October 1975

CONTENTS

ABBREVIATIONS

AMC. Pembroke etc.	*Inventories of the Royal Commission on Ancient Monuments for Welsh Counties.*
Arch. Camb.	*Archaeologia Cambrensis.*
BBCS.	*Bulletin of the Board of Celtic Studies.*
BIHR.	*Bulletin of the Institute of Historical Research.*
Brec. Cart.	*Cartularium Prioratus S. Johannis Evangelistae de Brecon,* ed. by R. W. Banks (London, 1884).
Cal. Doc. Fr.	*Calendar of Documents Preserved in France,* ed. by J. H. Round (London, 1899).
Cal. Inq. Misc.	*Calendar of Inquisitions Miscellaneous.*
Cal. Inq. Post Mortem.	*Calendar of Inquisitions Post Mortem.*
Canivez, *Statuta*	*Statuta Capitulorum Generalium Ordinis Cisterciensis,* ed. by J. M. Canivez (7 vols., Louvain, 1933–39).
Carm. Cart.	*Cartularium S. Johannis Baptistae de Carmarthen,* ed. by Thomas Philipps (Cheltenham, 1865).
CCR.	*Calendar of Close Rolls.*
C.Ch.R.	*Calendar of Charter Rolls.*
CFR.	*Calendar of Fine Rolls.*
Clark, *Cartae*	*Cartae et Alia Munimenta quae ad Dominium de Glamorgan Pertinent* (2nd ed., 6 vols., Cardiff, 1910).
CPL.	*Calendar of Papal Letters.*
C.P.Pets.	*Calendar of Papal Petitions.*
CPR.	*Calendar of Patent Rolls.*
DNB.	*Dictionary of National Biography.*
Dugdale	Dugdale, W., *Monasticon Anglicanum,* ed. J. Caley (6 vols., London, 1846).
Ec.H.R.	*Economic History Review.*
EHR.	*English Historical Review.*
Episc. Acts	*Episcopal Acts and Cognate Documents relating to Welsh Dioceses, 1066–1272,* ed. J. Conway Davies (2 vols., Cardiff, 1946–8).
Episc. Reg. St. David's	*The Episcopal Registers of St. David's, 1397–1518,* ed. R. F. Isaacson (3 vols. London, 1917–20).
Gir. Camb.	Giraldus Cambrensis.
Hist. et Cart. Gloucester	*Historia et Cartularium Monasterii Sancti Petri, Gloucestriae,* ed. W. H. Hart (3 vols., London, Rolls Series, 1863–67).
JHSCW.	*Journal of the Historical Society of the Church in Wales.*
Jnl. Brit. Arch. Assoc.	*Journal of the British Archaeological Association.*
Mont. Coll.	*Montgomeryshire Collections.*
N.L.W.	National Library of Wales.
NLWJ.	*National Library of Wales Journal.*
P.R.O.	Public Record Office.

R.S. Rolls Series.

Rot. Parl. *Rotuli Parliamentorum* (7 vols. London, 1783–1832).

Taxatio *Taxatio Ecclesiastica Angliae et Walliae . . . P. Nicholai IV,* ed. S. Ayscough and J. Caley (London, Record Commission, 1802).

Trans. Cymm. *Transactions of the Honourable Society of Cymmrodorion.*

TRHS. *Transactions of the Royal Historical Society.*

Valor *Valor Ecclesiasticus temp. Henr. VIII . . .,* ed. J. Caley (6 vols., Record Commission, 1810–34).

VCH. *Victoria County History of England.*

LIST OF ILLUSTRATIONS

Abergavenny Priory: wooden effigy of the patron, John de Hastings, d. 1313, or his son of the same name, d. 1325.   *frontispiece*

PLATES

COPYRIGHT

Acknowledgements are due to the following for illustrations and permission to reproduce them:

Frontispiece, Plates I and III: Royal Commission on Ancient and Historical Monuments in Wales.

Plate II: H. Holloway, L.R.P.S.

Plate IV: Cambridge University Collection.

I

THE ELEVENTH-CENTURY BACKGROUND

To the Normans who entered south Wales as conquerors and colonists at the end of the eleventh century, the Welsh church must have appeared as a curious medley of archaic practice, material poverty and spiritual decadence.[1] The diocese in the sense of a clearly-defined territorial unit, divided into archdeaconries, deaneries and parishes was only slowly emerging and a bishop still tended to exercise jurisdiction over a number of individual churches rather than over a territorial, administrative area. The Welsh church had no synod for common action nor a recognized head to enforce uniformity and discipline. Though its orthodoxy could not be doubted, its relations with the see of Rome were tenuous and ineffectual. Clerical celibacy was the exception rather than the rule and hereditary succession to ecclesiastical office was well established. The churches which served the community were small, austere and primitive, exhibiting nothing of the scale and grandeur of the Romanesque churches which were rising in England and northern France.[2] Compared with the confident optimism of the Norman chroniclers, the prevailing tone of the fragmentary survivals of Welsh ecclesiastical literature is one of demoralization if not of despair. 'Why have the blind fates not let us die?', wrote Rhigyfarch as the Normans poured into his native Ceredigion:

> Now the labours of earlier days lie despised; the people and the priest are despised by the word, heart, and work of the Normans. For they increase our taxes and burn our properties . . . The honest man's hand is branded by burning metals. A woman now lacks her nose, a man his genitals . . . Serfdom is brought

---

[1] For a fuller treatment than can be given here, see Lloyd, *History of Wales*, i, pp. 202–28, ii, pp. 447–61; J. Conway Davies, *Episcopal Acts relating to Welsh Dioceses, 1066–1272*, i, pp. 2–76, ii, pp. 443–594, and C. Brooke, 'The Church and the Welsh Border in the Tenth and Eleventh Centuries', *Flintshire Historical Society Journal*, xxi (1964), pp. 32–45.

[2] D. B. Hague, 'Some Welsh Evidence [for Buildings of Ecclesiastical and Related Type]', *Scot. Archaeol. Forum*, v (1973), pp. 17–35.

to the neck with a meat-hook, and learns that nothing can be had at will . . . O unhappy and lamentable fate; slothful in seeking peace, slothful in taking up arms. O Wales you are afflicted and dying . . . An alien crowd speaks of you as hateful . . . O country deserted by God . . . What is now left for you but to weep excessively . . .[3]

The *Lives* of the Welsh saints composed during the period are themselves eloquent testimony to a church on the defensive. In the face of a formidable enemy, Welsh clerics began to turn to the traditions and achievements of the past in the hope of justifying and vindicating their rights in the present.

The sense of inertia and weakness apparent in the secular church is also reflected in the condition of Welsh monastic institutions. This was to be expected, for from the sixth century onwards the secular church and the monastic church had something in the nature of a common history. Much that appears anomalous in the organization of the church in Wales in the eleventh and twelfth centuries can be traced directly to the dominant role played by the monasteries in the life of the church in earlier centuries. In the sixth century sons of tribal chieftains forsook the world and with the help of family and clan founded monasteries. From these monasteries went forth missionary monks who proceeded to establish oratories, hermitages and churches in outlying districts.[4] In this way Wales became covered with a network of mother and daughter churches. The prestige, power and influence of certain of the mother churches gave them a vague but real superiority over the others. Sometimes the heads of these more important foundations combined in their persons the titles of both bishop and abbot. In Wales, however, the title and dignity of bishop was not eclipsed, as it was in Ireland, by the prestige enjoyed by an abbot. There was therefore an opportunity for real episcopal power to develop from origins primarily monastic. By the end of the eleventh century circumstances had combined to give two bishops an ascendancy and pre-eminence in south Wales: the bishop of St. David's and the bishop of

[3] The translation of Rhigyfarch's *Lament*, slightly modified, is taken from M. Lapidge, 'The Welsh-Latin Poetry of Sulien's Family', *Studia Celtica*, viii/ix (1973–4), pp. 89–93.

[4] Lloyd, *History of Wales*, i, pp. 124–59; E. G. Bowen, *Settlements of the Celtic Saints in Wales*, pp. 14–86.

Glamorgan. Both these bishops still exercised a jurisdiction over areas which had not been clearly defined but tended to fluctuate with the ebb and flow of princely power now in the west, now in the east.

In the meantime, however, what had happened to the original monastic foundations which had done so much to mould the life of the church in earlier centuries? The late Professor Knowles noted 'the tendency common in every country and century of the early middle ages, for the monastic life to lose its regular character, and for houses to become merely clerical establishments or to fall wholly under lay control'.[5] This had occurred in Wales, as it had in England. In Wales the communities of monks had become by the eleventh century collegiate communities of *claswyr* or canons.[6] Unlike England, Wales did not acquire for any length of time that degree of political cohesion and unity which enabled Dunstan, during the reign of King Edgar, to restore to the older foundations the regular monastic character they had lost. In Wales geographical barriers were too formidable and provincial loyalties too strong. Even at the beginning of the tenth century, however, there are signs that earlier traditions of scholarship, if not of spirituality, still commanded respect and imitation. Welsh scriptoria, with those of Brittany and Ireland, were providing books for the library of Glastonbury Abbey, the cradle of the monastic reform movement in England.[7]

Whatever advances had been made in the direction of monastic reform in Wales were brought to naught by the Norse raids which began in the second half of the tenth century. The richer monasteries along the coast were repeatedly plundered. St. David's was attacked in 982 and again in 988, together with Llanbadarn Fawr, Llandudoch (St. Dogmaels), Llancarfan and Llanilltud Fawr. In the fourth recorded attack on St. David's in 999, the raiders slew Bishop Morgeneu.[8] In the time

[5] Knowles, *Monastic Order*, p. 23.

[6] Lloyd, *History of Wales*, i, pp. 213–6.

[7] Unfortunately for the present argument, one of the texts which is certainly the product of a Welsh *scriptorium* is that of the first book of Ovid's *Ars Amatoria*, a work which we know deeply influenced Dunstan but was unlikely to trigger off a monastic revival; see *St. Dunstan's Classbook from Glastonbury* (Umbrae Codicum Occidentalium, iv, Amsterdam, 1961) and the introduction by R. W. Hunt.

[8] B. G. Charles, *Old Norse Relations with Wales*, pp. 24–9.

of Gerald of Wales the bishop's death was regarded as a form of divine retribution, since he was the first bishop of St. David's to break the austere customs of his monastery by eating flesh meat. Over seventy years later the see of St. David's was held by the learned Sulien. The leisurely scholarship of Sulien and his family in Ceredigion, though it revealed the still vigorous potentialities of the Celtic church, held out little promise of monastic reform.[9]

The *Lives* of St. Cadog and St. Illtud, written by native clerics when the Norman penetration of south Wales was at its height, are particularly valuable for their descriptions of the religious institutions which had grown out of the Celtic monasteries of the sixth century. Both authors attempt, rather unsuccessfully, to ascribe to the founder-saints conditions which in fact obtained at Llancarfan and Llanilltud Fawr in the eleventh century. Lifris, the author of *Vita Sancti Cadoci*, for example, records how St. Cadog

> appointed thirty-six canons, who should continuously and by their rule serve Nantcarfan church . . . and as many courts, in which the canons might have their buildings, and as many shares of arable land, wherein there were eighty acres, which were called from ancient times the possessions of the courts . . . and moreover as many homesteads, wherefrom they had necessaries of raiment and food.

Lifris then proceeds to describe in greater detail the various properties and the way they were shared between the abbot, the doctor and the *clerici*.[10] As a statement of sixth-century custom, the account has obvious anachronisms and contradictions. The Celtic monks of the sixth century emphasized the ideal of poverty with the same vigour as did St. Benedict in his Rule. The conception of shares and prebends would have been alien to them.[11] Moreover, the whole passage presupposes that the process of endowment had been completed before Cadog's death. Four hundred years or more of gradual consolidation of a monastery's estate have been telescoped into one lifetime. It seems evident that Lifris was describing

---

[9] For Sulien and his family, see J. Conway Davies, *Episc. Acts*, ii, pp. 493–506, and more recently Nora K. Chadwick in *Studies in the Early British Church*, pp. 121–82.

[10] *Vitae Sanctorum Britanniae et Genealogiae*, ed. A. W. Wade-Evans, pp. 120–2.

[11] L. Gougaud, *Christianity in Celtic Lands*, p. 81.

and attempting to justify the rights and privileges of the *clas* of Llancarfan as it had existed in his own day, or at least within living memory.

A similar body of *claswyr* is described by the unknown author of *Vita Sancti Iltudi* (written *circa* 1140). Illtud, according to the author

> appointed fifty canons, who at suitable times and fixed hours visited the church, having each of them his prebend, to wit, each his own homestead with profits, which were given by the people to keep in memory their souls. Yearly rents were paid to the abbot; what was paid was divided by common custom.[12]

Here again we have a justification of the developments which had transformed the former monastery into the *clas* of Llanilltud Fawr.

Conditions in these two Glamorgan houses were perhaps typical of similar large foundations elsewhere. At St. David's, which in the sixth century had been noted for the austerity of its monastic life, the community of monks had long since given place to a body of *claswyr*. Bernard, when he became bishop of St. David's in 1115, found the church 'thoroughly rude and unordered. For the clergy of the place who were called *Glaswir* . . . governed by barbarous rites, without order and rule, had wickedly taken possession of the goods of the church'.[13]

While the abbots of Llancarfan and Llanilltud Fawr appear to have been in clerical orders, the same cannot be said of the titular heads of some of the houses in mid-Wales. The circumstances in which Morfran, the abbot of Towyn, was involved in 1147 as defender of the castle of Cynfael do not suggest that he was a cleric.[14] At the end of the twelfth century, Gerald of Wales tells the story of a Breton visitor to Llanbadarn Fawr in the reign of Stephen. The visitor was present at the church on a feast day and saw the 'abbot' arrive carrying a spear and accompanied by a band of armed men.[15] Such a lay abbot had doubtless appropriated to himself the major part of the church's revenue, but fulfilled no clerical function.

---

[12] *Vitae Sanctorum Britanniae et Genealogiae*, pp. 210–11.

[13] Giraldus Cambrensis, *Opera*, iii, pp. 153–4, transl. from J. Conway Davies, *Episc. Acts*, i, p. 269.

[14] *Brut y Tywysogyon, Peniarth 20*, ed. Thomas Jones, pp. 56, 176–7. Cf. Lloyd, *History of Wales*, ii, p. 490 & note 14.

[15] Gir. Camb., *Opera*, vi, pp. 120–1.

In most, if not all, of the monasteries which in the 'Age of the Saints' had been centres conspicuous for missionary zeal and a rigorous monastic régime, a wholesale depression in monastic discipline had taken place. Signs of regular life, of monks living in community and bound by rule, do not appear. This general picture is confirmed by the implications contained in the *Life* of St. Caradog, a native hermit who lived to see the establishment of Norman control in south Wales. The record of his wanderings from Llandaff to Gower and thence to Dyfed give no indication of a regular community life in any part of south Wales.[16]

The spiritual and moral values of a society cannot, however, be judged solely by the efficiency of its organized, ecclesiastical institutions. While the larger foundations were in decay and their inmates leading a life alien to the spirit and ideals of their founders, one should not underestimate the value and potentialities of the native eremitical life of the eleventh and twelfth centuries. The life of Caradog has already been mentioned. He was born in Brycheiniog and became a courtier of Rhys ap Tewdwr. His negligence in losing two of his master's dogs brought down upon him the anger of Rhys and he was driven from court. He made his way to Llandaff and was there tonsured by Bishop Herewald. His *Vita* gives little indication of the periods of time he spent at the various places he visited, but he is next found at Llangenydd, where he restored the deserted and overgrown shrine of St. Cenydd and built himself an oratory.[17] Thence he proceeded to St. David's, and after being ordained a priest, he withdrew to the isle of Arry (probably Barry Isle, Llanrian, Pembs.). Pirate raids, however, forced him to relinquish his home there, and in 1105 he retired to a place near Haroldston in Rhos, only to be constantly harassed again by the Flemings who had recently settled there, and by one Tankard, the castellan of Haverford. Caradog died in 1124.[18]

The significance of Caradog in the religious history of his

---

[16] *Nova Legenda Anglie*, ed. C. Horstman, i, pp. 174–6.

[17] This may have been on Burry Holm, where in 1967 Mr. Douglas Hague uncovered the post holes of a wooden oratory below the remains of the stone medieval church; see F. G. Cowley, 'Llangenydd and its Priory', *Glamorgan Historian*, v (1968), p. 228 and plan.

[18] Lloyd, *History of Wales*, ii, pp. 591–3.

time has hardly been fully realized. His life and work are the first recorded indications of a renewed interest in monastic institutions in eleventh-century south Wales.[19] While his life as a hermit has been stressed by all authorities, it is not always mentioned that he had companions who shared his austere existence, and that he probably founded a community of hermits. He was in contact, too, with the hermits of Bardsey Island in north Wales.[20]. It is of interest that Llangenydd, where Caradog resided for a time, was chosen as the site of an alien cell many years before his death.

Caradog and his companions were not isolated representatives of the eremitical life in Wales. In the latter part of the twelfth century there were communities of hermits of long standing at Bardsey, Priestholm and Beddgelert. They were subject to no monastic or canonical order and owed nothing to Norman influence. We have it on the authority of the much-travelled Gerald of Wales that the eremitical life of Wales possessed an intensity and vitality which could not be rivalled in any part of Europe.[21]

Whether the native eremitical life of the time held out promise, with episcopal help and encouragement, of a revival and reform of monastic institutions under native auspices, comparable to that which had taken place elsewhere in Europe and was to take place in Ireland under Malachy, is a debatable question on which it is idle to speculate. For with the successful invasion of south Wales by the Normans, the initiative passed from the native Welsh into the hands of men who were already closely associated with the work of monastic foundation and reform on the continent and in England.

At first there was every indication that north Wales would be the first to fall to Norman arms. Appearances were deceptive, however, and the area was destined to retain its independence for another two centuries. It was the south which first succumbed. The attack, vigorous at first, but

---

[19] For a mention of Caradog as *monk* at Llangenydd, see *Book of Llan Dâv*, ed. J. G. Evans, p. 279.

[20] Lloyd, ii, p. 593, does not mention his companions and refers to a solitary warfare with the evil one 'drawing no support from a common monastic life'. The *Vita* shows clearly, however, that he was not alone (*Nova Legenda Anglie*, i, pp. 174–5).

[21] Gir. Camb., *Opera*, iv, pp. 167–8, vi, pp. 124, 131, 204.

checked by the death of William fitz Osbern and the circumstances following the revolt of his son, was revived during
Rufus's reign. The death of Rhys ap Tewdwr in 1093 gave
the signal for a number of concerted attacks on south Wales
from several directions. By 1135, almost the whole of south
Wales had come under Norman control. The area lay open to
all the new influences which the invaders had brought from
their native provinces of Normandy, Anjou, Maine and
Brittany. In the areas where the invaders settled, a feudal
organization was established. The castle became a familiar
feature of the landscape and with it the Benedictine priory,
Wales's first real contact with Latin monasticism.[22]

[22] The Rule of St. Benedict, though it had been adopted in Anglo-Saxon
England, did not pass thence to Wales. The text may have been known to Welsh
clerics. St. Benedict's Rule was certainly known in Ireland (L. Gougaud,
Christianity in Celtic Lands, pp. 405–6). It is significant, however, that when an
educated cleric like Rhigyfarch wished to describe the monastic life in its ideal
form he turned not to the Rule, but to the *Institutes* of Cassian. On this, see Owen
Chadwick, *John Cassian*, appendix 'Cassian and the Celts', pp. 201–3.

II

THE INTRODUCTION OF
LATIN MONASTICISM INTO SOUTH WALES

1. THE BENEDICTINE PRIORIES

The barons and knights who entered Wales at the end of the eleventh century belonged to a society in which the foundation and endowment of a monastery had become a conventional act of piety. Such an act in itself was a recognized means of atoning for past misdeeds, for 'just as water extinguishes fire, so alms extinguish sin'.[1] A founder or benefactor acted in the sure knowledge that the monks to whom he had given his patronage would pray for his material welfare in this world and his spiritual welfare in the next. The foundation of a monastery could at the same time be an investment of a different kind: a means of giving concrete form to a family's sense of pride and achievement. Even when the legislation of a reforming papacy had succeeded in greatly curtailing the proprietary rights of patrons, a baron or knight could still speak of 'my abbey' and 'my monks'.

Some of the greatest of the Norman barons already had an impressive record of foundation and benefaction to their credit before they entered Wales. William fitz Osbern, earl of Hereford, had founded in his native Normandy the abbeys of Lire (c. 1046) and Cormeilles (c. 1060).[2] Roger of Montgomery, earl of Shrewsbury, had instituted monks in the former collegiate church of Troarn and had also restored and amply endowed the abbey of St. Martin's, Séez. The latter abbey provided Roger with a community for his new foundation at Shrewsbury (f. 1083–90) and also attracted gifts from his two sons, Roger, the founder of Lancaster Priory, and Arnulf, the future earl of Pembroke and founder of Pembroke Priory.[3]

---

[1] *Cartulaire de l'Abbaye de Saint-Vincent du Mans*, ed. R. Charles et M. D.'Elbenne, no. 828, p. 467.
[2] *Complete Peerage*, vi, pp. 447–9; for the dates, see Knowles, *Monastic Order*, p. 701.
[3] *Complete Peerage*, xi, pp. 683–7; C. H. Haskins, *Norman Institutions*, p. 70.

It is difficult to describe briefly the type of monasticism with which the invaders were familiar. But some such attempt must be made, even at the risk of simplification, if subsequent developments are to be understood. However much they might differ in the details of their observance, there was a basic similarity between all the greater abbeys of Normandy in the kind of life lived within their walls. It was a life broadly based on the Rule of St. Benedict. The saint had legislated for a self-contained community whose members were bound by the vows of poverty, obedience and stability. Their day was to be occupied in liturgical prayer (about four hours), in meditative reading or private prayer (about four hours) and in manual work of a domestic kind (about six hours).[4] By the eleventh century custom and tradition had sanctioned considerable modifications in this régime. In the process much of the simplicity and balance which characterized Benedict's legislation was lost. Under the influence of the great abbey of Cluny, the liturgical prayers—the *Opus Dei*—had been so elaborated and lengthened that their recitation in choir took up the greater part of the monks' time. Domestic manual work had been virtually abandoned and relegated to paid lay servants. The place allotted to meditative reading (*lectio divina*) had undergone a subtle but inevitable change. *Lectio divina* had been envisaged by St. Benedict as reading directed towards the spiritual perfection of the monk. The works studied would normally consist of the Scriptures, literature on the monastic life, and the Fathers of the Church. It was but a short step from reading of this kind to intellectual study of wider range undertaken for its own sake. During the eleventh century the abbeys of Normandy came under the influence of a succession of talented men who had imbibed something of the intellectual renaissance which was taking place in northern Italy: William of Dijon, Jean of Fécamp, Lanfranc and Anselm. Under their influence a number of Norman abbeys—Bec particularly—became centres of learning which could provide a training for a monk in a variety of subjects not directly connected with the religious life.[5]

---

[4] Knowles, *Monastic Order*, pp. 3–15.
[5] Ibid., pp. 16–82, 83–89.

Despite modifications of the Rule, the standards of monastic observance and discipline tended to be high; 'in all the Norman monasteries', writes Professor Knowles, 'there was a spirit of enthusiasm and expansion, and in a few cases the highest levels of zeal and holiness were found'.[6]

Despite its youthful vigour, Norman monasticism was a sponsored monasticism which owed much to the individual initiative of the duke and his barons, a monasticism which was closely knit with the feudal fabric of the Norman state. After the conquest of England, the Conqueror looked to the Norman abbeys for personnel to revive monastic life in the older English abbeys. The monks who responded to his invitation were to exercise a potent influence on the life of the English church. However, few of the Norman abbeys were anxious to send colonies of monks to establish independent communities on English soil.[7] Their close feudal loyalties and sense of *esprit de corps* precluded that evangelical spirit which threatened two generations later to turn the whole monastic world Cistercian. Well into the reign of Henry I, the majority of the barons, too, still regarded Normandy as their homeland and Norman monasteries had chief claim on their patronage. As a result of these attitudes the number of new autonomous foundations in England was small. Between the years 1066 and 1102 only seven new Benedictine houses came into existence: Battle (1067), Selby (*c.* 1070), Shrewsbury (1083), Chester (1093), Spalding (1074), Colchester (1095), and Tewkesbury (1102).[8]

In direct contrast to this, and of particular significance for understanding developments in south Wales, are the scores of grants of churches, lands and tithes in England which were being made by barons and knights during the same period to favoured abbeys in Normandy and adjoining provinces. The Gregorian decrees against proprietary churches may have accelerated this movement, prompting laymen 'to divest themselves of a responsibility which was becoming an em-

[6] Ibid., p. 94.
[7] Some of the Norman abbeys preferred to establish cells rather than dependent conventual priories even within the Norman duchy itself; see the interesting example in *Calendar of Documents Preserved in France*, ed. J. H. Round, no. 1115, pp. 398–9.
[8] Knowles and Hadcock, *Medieval Religious Houses, England and Wales* (2nd ed. 1971), pp. 52–8.

barrassment'.[9] Most of the abbeys which benefited regarded these newly-acquired estates not as endowments for the establishment of new monasteries but as 'extensions of their domain on Anglo-Norman territory'.[10] The most economical method of administering them was to send a small group of monks, rarely more than three, to reside at a convenient centre and collect the rents for the abbey. In this way a dependent priory cell was formed. This practice, new to England, was soon adopted by English abbeys when they were granted small estates in outlying areas. By the end of the twelfth century some two hundred priories of this kind had come into existence.[11]

The granting of churches, lands and tithes in Wales to abbeys in England, Normandy, Maine and Anjou by the invaders of south Wales must be regarded as a natural extension of a movement which was already proceeding rapidly and on more ambitious lines in England. Grants began to be made soon after the conquest of Gwent and became more frequent after 1093 with the conquest of the Welsh 'kingdoms' of Brycheiniog, Morgannwg, Ystrad Tywi, Dyfed, and Ceredigion. As a result, nineteen dependent Benedictine priories were established in south Wales.[12]

Most of these priories remained mere cells and it would be fruitless to seek foundation charters for them. Their effective foundation dated from the time when churches and lands had been granted to the mother abbey. Seven of the priories, however, acquired the status of conventual priories: Chepstow, Monmouth, Abergavenny, Pembroke, Brecon, Goldcliff, and Ewenni. In such houses an attempt was made to secure the residence of monks in sufficient numbers to ensure an orderly and dignified performance of the liturgical prayers.[13] At the end of the eleventh century there was no general agreement as to what should constitute the minimum number of monks necessary for discharging these functions. It was probably due to the influence exercised by the newer orders, particularly the

---

[9] C. H. Holdsworth's review of D. Matthew, *Norman Monasteries and their English Possessions*, in *History*, xlix (1964), p. 56; cf. Knowles, *Monastic Order*, p. 135.
[10] D. Matthew, *Norman Monasteries and their English Possessions*, pp. 14, 28–9.
[11] Knowles, *Monastic Order*, p. 134.
[12] See Appendix I.
[13] Du Cange, *Glossarium Mediae et Infimae Latinitatis*, ii, p. 546, under *conventualis locus*.

Cistercian, that it became generally accepted that a fully conventual establishment should contain at least twelve monks apart from an abbot or prior.[14] In the thirteenth century this was certainly the norm to which episcopal visitors of monasteries constantly referred.

The process by which priory cells acquired conventual status is difficult to trace even for priories whose cartularies are still extant. The time taken for the transition to be made varied from house to house. At Abergavenny, for example, we find that during the reign of William II, Hamelin of Ballon gave to the abbey of St. Vincent, Le Mans, the chapel of his castle at Abergavenny and

> land for making a principal church in which they should serve God, and land for their own dwellings, and gardens, and orchards and vineyards, . . . a bourg also and an oven of their own, with water for a mill and fishing in his waters . . . He also gave them elsewhere one church with all its appurtenances and land for ten ploughs

Between 1100 and 1106 Hamelin and his brother Winibald made further grants to the abbey of St. Vincent of churches and tithes both in Gwent Uwchcoed and in England.[15] As a result of these grants, a priory cell came into existence. Although the monks of Abergavenny, when compiling the genealogies of their house, were to name Hamelin as the founder,[16] the priory does not appear to have acquired conventual status until the reign of Henry II. At some time before Henry II's death in 1189, William de Breos confirmed the gifts of his predecessors and made a number of additional grants to the priory:

> By this condition and tenor, that the abbot of St. Vincent . . . should make a convent in the same church which should beg unceasingly the mercy of God for the safety and soul of myself and all who are mentioned above. If I die before I fulfil these things, my heir will fulfil and do them.[17]

As far as Brecon was concerned, the two charters of Bernard Neufmarché, its acknowledged founder, give no indication of an intention to found a conventual priory,[18] but the priory

[14] C. J. Holdsworth in *History*, xlix (1964), p. 56.

[15] *Cal. Doc. Fr.*, pp. 367–9.

[16] Dugdale, iv, p. 615.

[17] Ibid., p. 616. The charter of H. de Bellocampo which pre-dates William's charter is witnessed by eight monks.

[18] *Brec. Cart.*, pp. 69–71. As Lloyd pointed out (*History of Wales*, ii, p. 436), the 'secunda carta' is actually the first.

probably acquired a quasi-conventual status before his death *circa* 1125. The chronicler of the mother house of Battle relates that Bernard, at the persistent entreaty of Roger, a monk of Battle who happened to be staying with him, gave to the abbey the church of St. John the Evangelist which lay outside the *munitio* of his castle, together with a territory called *Vetus Villa*. Roger restored the church from its foundations and, with the assistance of another Battle monk, Walter, he constructed domestic buildings there. Meanwhile, Roger acquired from men in the neighbourhood endowments of land and tithes and was able to report to his abbey that the small possession entrusted to him had greatly increased. In the process of time, Agnes, the wife of Bernard, prompted perhaps by illness, made a grant from her dower land of the small vill of Berrington in Herefordshire. Thus the possessions of the church in lands, mills, churches and tithes were gradually increased. With the assent of the king and of Bernard, the enriched establishment was made a dependency of Battle Abbey. Walter was made prior, and monks were called from Battle 'who as servants of God were to unite in performing the divine offices according to the rule'. In recognition of its subjection, the new priory was to pay 20*s.* annually to Battle Abbey.[19]

At Monmouth, too, the process appears to have been gradual and is difficult to trace. Wihenoc, the lord of Monmouth, was a Breton noble who held lands in the vicinity of Dol. Between 1074 and 1086, he granted lands, churches and tithes in the vicinity of Monmouth to the abbey of St. Florent près Saumur with the intention of founding a religious house. The monks stayed at first in the ancient church of St. Cadog near the castle while their church of St. Mary was being constructed. Though the church was completed by 1101 or 1102, when it was dedicated by Hervé, bishop of Bangor, the extant charters provide no definite evidence of when the priory became conventual. One charter of Baderon of Monmouth (d. 1176) gives the impression that the priory then contained only three monks. Like Abergavenny, Monmouth may not have become conventual in the accepted

[19] *Chronicon Monasterii de Bello*, ed. J. S. Brewer, p. 34. The chronicler was writing *c.* 1170.

sense of the term until the latter part of the twelfth century.[20] Monmouth was unique among the Benedictine priories in south Wales in that its monks were, from the first, familiar with the ecclesiastical traditions of the area in which they settled. The mother abbey of St. Florent had been founded in the fifth century near the border of Brittany, where the missionary activities of the Celtic saints were remembered with reverence. Even after the abbey was moved to Anjou, Breton influence upon it remained strong. Rhiwallon, lord of Dol, had two sons who became monks in the abbey and one of them, John, became abbot in 1070. Later Wihenoc, the founder of Monmouth, himself took the habit of monk in the abbey.[21]

The effective foundation of Goldcliff and Ewenni as conventual priories can be dated with greater precision. Robert de Chandos granted to the abbey of Bec the church of St. Mary Magdalen of Goldcliff, with the lands and tithes pertaining to it and the chapel *de Fraxino* with its appurtenances 'in order that a convent of monks may be set up therein for serving God and the glorious servant of Christ, Mary Magdalen, and for praying for ever for their benefactors'. His grant was confirmed by Henry I in 1113. The priory became the largest and richest of the Benedictine priories in south Wales.[22]

The church of St. Michael's, Ewenni, probably rebuilt on the site of an earlier church, was dedicated during the episcopate of Urban, bishop of Glamorgan (1107–34). A letter of Gilbert Foliot, abbot of Gloucester, which records the dedication, seems to imply that the church had already been given to Gloucester Abbey at this period.[23] In the 'List of Donations' in the Gloucester cartulary, it is recorded that Robert, earl of Gloucester made the priory of Ewenni quit of toll throughout all his land during the abbacy of Walter de

---

[20] Dugdale, iv, pp. 596–7; R. Graham, 'Four Alien Priories of Monmouthshire', *Jnl. Brit. Arch. Assoc.*, xxxv (1929–30), p. 103.
[21] S. M. Harris, 'The Kalendar of the *Vitae Sanctorum Wallensium*', *JHSCW.*, iii, no. 8 (1953), pp. 6–7, 10–12; Rose Graham, op. cit., p. 103.
[22] Dugdale, vi, p. 1022; *Regesta Regum Anglo-Normannorum*, ii (1100–1135), ed. C. Johnson and H. A. Cronne, no. 1014, pp. 106–7.
[23] The pre-Norman stones found on the site suggest the existence of an earlier church; see C. A. Ralegh Radford, *Ewenny Priory* (1952, rev. ed. 1970), pp. 22–3; *Letters and Charters of Gilbert Foliot*, ed. Adrian Morey and C. N. L. Brooke, no. 45, p. 82, and *Episc. Acts*, ii, pp. 638–9.

Lacy, that is, between 1130 and 1139.[24] If practice elsewhere provides any guide, it would seem that a priory cell of a few monks was established at Ewenni before 1141. In that year Maurice de Londres raised the cell to conventual status. He granted to God, Blessed Michael and the most holy Brigid, 'for maintaining my priory of Ewenni, to my prior of *Hoggemora* and the brethren devotedly serving God in the said priory', a number of specified lands and churches. The grant was made on condition that when the churches granted had been appropriated to the priory 'there shall be therein a convent of at least thirteen monks of the order of Gloucester'. Maurice's charter was the effective foundation charter of the conventual priory.[25]

Why did some priories attain conventual status and others remain cells? Location was obviously of some importance. A priory cell situated near an important castle which controlled a lordship intensively settled by the Anglo-Normans was more likely to attract benefactions on a scale necessary for the maintenance of a convent rather than one situated away from the main centres of power. Location, however, was not all important. The decisive factor was usually the attitude of the lay patron. Left to themselves, most abbeys were not interested in establishing dependent conventual priories. It certainly involved a financial risk and may also have involved a financial sacrifice. The initiative in most cases, therefore, lay with the patron of the priory cell. Here a variety of motives may have been present. The desire of 'new' men with insufficient resources to found an independent house, but anxious to have a miniature *Eigenkloster* on their lands, would prompt them to come to some arrangement with a large independent abbey for the establishment of a dependent conventual priory.[26] Such was certainly one of the reasons which must have moved Maurice de Londres to transform Ewenni into a conventual house. Again, most barons and knights were sensitive to monastic sanctity and were more likely to attempt to obtain conventual status for a cell which belonged to an abbey where

[24] *Hist. et Cart. Gloucester,* i, p. 117.
[25] Ibid., i, pp. 75–6, for the date, and Clark, *Cartae,* vi, pp. 2265–6, for the text of the charter.
[26] Knowles, *Monastic Order,* p. 135.

standards of discipline and observance were high.[27] Most of them realized, too, that prayers for themselves and their families were more likely to be punctiliously recited by a convent of monks than by a cell of two or three monks.

When a conventual dependent priory was established, the mother house usually protected its own interests by requiring the dependency to pay an annual sum of money as a token of its subjection. Brecon Priory, as we have seen, paid Battle Abbey 20s. Monmouth paid £6 13s. 4d. to St. Florent; Abergavenny, £5 7s. 0d. to St. Vincent, Le Mans; Chepstow, £3 13s. 4d. to Cormeilles; and Goldcliff, £1 to Bec.[28]

II. THE NEW ORDERS

While Norman monasticism was growing to maturity and making its influence felt in England and, to a lesser extent, in south Wales through the foundation of dependent priories, there was in many quarters a growing dissatisfaction with the monastic régime of existing Benedictine abbeys.[29] Many who had experienced life in these abbeys, and many of the secular clergy who were attracted to the religious vocation, began to withdraw to deserted places in search of a life of greater simplicity and austerity than could be found in existing institutions. In the last quarter of the eleventh century two centres of this eremitical life in France were important for the future history of the monastic order. One lay in the woodland of Colan, near Langres in northern Burgundy; the other in and around the Craon forest, a wild region on the borders of Brittany and Maine.

A group of hermits living in the woods of Colan invited Robert, abbot of St. Michael de Tonnerre, to become their leader and obtained letters from Pope Alexander II (1061–73) appointing him abbot. About 1075 he took his new community to Molesme where they settled in primitive huts made from the branches of trees. As with so many experiments of this kind the primitive simplicity did not last. Molesme grew rich

[27] See Bishop Uchtryd's confirmation of Maurice de Londres's grants to Ewenni, where the excellent observance of the Gloucester monks is especially noted, in C. E. Welch, 'An Early Charter of Ewenny Priory', NLWJ., x (1957–8), pp. 415–6.

[28] Rose Graham, op. cit., p. 107.

[29] For much of what follows, see Knowles, Monastic Order, pp. 191–226.

and adopted the customs and uses of neighbouring monasteries. Growing affluence and the abandonment of earlier ideals produced a rift in the community. Alberic, the prior (one of the original hermits of Colan), and Stephen Harding, the subprior, urged a move to found a new house where the Rule of St. Benedict would be observed literally. They were not successful in persuading the whole community to join them, but in 1098 twenty monks left Molesme to follow their Abbot Robert into the forest of Cîteaux. Robert was soon forced by papal mandate to return to Molesme. His place as abbot of Cîteaux was taken by Alberic, and Stephen Harding was appointed prior. During the abbacy of Alberic (1099–1109), a habit of grey-white was adopted, the accretions to the liturgical prayers sanctioned by Cluniac practice were dropped, manual work became a prominent part of the monk's life, and papal approval for the new foundation was secured. Despite these achievements and the election to the abbacy in 1109 of Stephen Harding, an Englishman of vision and constructive genius, numbers dwindled and the collapse of the new house seemed imminent. The turning point came with the arrival at Cîteaux in 1112 of Bernard with thirty companions. Thenceforward, expansion was rapid. The four elder daughter houses of Cîteaux were founded within three years: La Ferté in 1113, Pontigny in 1114, Clairvaux (with Bernard as abbot) and Morimund in 1115.

This assurance of future expansion probably prompted Stephen Harding to draw up the *Carta Caritatis*,[30] a carefully balanced constitution which regulated the relationship between Cistercian abbeys and provided machinery for maintaining uniformity of observance and a high level of discipline by means of annual visitation and attendance at General Chapter. The *Carta* attempted, with some success as events showed, to solve the perennial problem of all government: to reconcile the conflict between authority and liberty. By making the abbot of Cîteaux subject in the last resort to the corrective powers of the abbots of the four elder daughter houses, it avoided the dangers of the monarchical form of government as exemplified

[30] There are useful translations in *English Historical Documents, 1042–1189*, ed. D. C. Douglas and G. W. Greenaway, pp. 687–91, and L. J. Lekai, *The White Monks*, pp. 267–73.

by the congregation of Cluny. By its provisions for annual visitation of all houses and the institution of an annual General Chapter, it attempted to provide a guarantee against the decline of fervour and the gradual flagging of discipline and observance which was frequently the experience of the autonomous Benedictine abbeys. The *Carta* provided, for the first time in European history, a constitution for a supranational congregation within the church with members in every country of Europe.[31]

The second centre of the eremitical life which was destined to produce a number of founders of reformed monasteries lay in the Craon forest. In this region in the last decade of the eleventh century, large congregations of hermits were living a life of strict austerity. They were loosely organized into cells which were supervised by leaders and masters. Among these leaders, only two need concern us here: Bernard of Tiron and Vitalis of Mortain. Bernard, after a varied career as abbot of St. Cyprian, Poitiers, as a wandering preacher and as a hermit at Craon and at Chaussey on the Normandy coast, emerged with a band of disciples in 1109 and founded the abbey of Tiron in the diocese of Chartres. The new monastery soon became the mother of a numerous family of abbeys. Vitalis of Mortain, another of the many hermit leaders of Craon, had been a secular clerk in the retinue of Robert of Normandy. About 1105 he left Craon to seek greater solitude in the forest of Savigny. He founded a hermitage and was soon joined by disciples to whom he gave a rule of life. The abbey of Savigny was founded between 1112 and 1115,[32] and within thirty years it had become the head of a congregation numbering some thirty-three houses.

Mainly because of their location on or near lands controlled by Henry I, Tiron and Savigny made their influence felt across the English Channel earlier than did Cîteaux. Tironian influence in England was never strong. Between 1113 and 1115, however, Robert fitz Martin, lord of Cemais in west

---

[31] Recent work has shown that a number of additions to, and revisions of, the text of the *Carta* were made after its official approval by Pope Calixtus II in 1119. For a summary of this research, see Knowles, *Monastic Order* (2nd ed. 1963). pp. 752–3.

[32] B. D. Hill, *English Cistercian Monasteries and their Patrons in the Twelfth Century*, pp. 84–5.

Wales, brought thirteen monks from Tiron and founded a Tironian priory on or near the site of the ancient *clas* church of Llandudoch.[33] Subsequently, he obtained an additional thirteen monks from Tiron and permission to raise the priory to abbey status. The abbey seems to have been established on 10 September 1120, when Fulchard, the first abbot, was formally enthroned by Bernard, bishop of St. David's.[34] Although St. Dogmaels, as the new abbey came to be known, belonged to a reformed congregation, in one respect at least it followed the practice of the traditional Benedictine abbeys. Caldy Island, given to the monks by Geva, the founder's mother, became a dependent priory cell. Substantial domestic buildings and a church with choir space for a conventual number of monks still remain on the island.[35] Yet it is doubtful if Caldy ever maintained a permanent convent. The priory was ranked by Gerald of Wales with Cardigan, St. Clears and Llangenydd as places occupied by lone monks in defiance of the decrees of the Lateran Council of 1179.[36] In 1291 its income (£1 10s. 0d.) was clearly insufficient to maintain a conventual establishment and was valued with that of the mother house.[37] A second dependency of St. Dogmaels was founded at Pill about 1200 by Adam de Roche.[38] Dedicated to St. Mary and St. Budoc, the new priory was sufficiently well endowed by the founder and his men to acquire conventual status. Yet a third dependency of St. Dogmaels came into existence about the same time at Glascarrig in Wexford, Ireland. The exact date of its foundation and much of its later history are obscure.[39]

Savigny exercised a more powerful influence in England and Wales than Tiron mainly because the abbey lay within the

---

[33] 'Vita B. Bernardi Tironiensis' in Migne, *Patrologiae*, clxxii, col. 1426. Symeon of Durham gives 1113 as the date of the entry of Tironian monks into England, but it is not clear whether he is referring to the settlement at St. Dogmaels or Selkirk (*Opera*, ii, p. 247; cf. D. E. Easson, *Medieval Religious Houses, Scotland*, p. 60). The early charters of St. Dogmaels are given in *Cal. Doc. Fr.*, pp. 352–5, and Dugdale, iv, p. 130. For Llandudoch and St. Dogmaels, see A. W. Wade-Evans, 'Pembrokeshire Notes', *Arch. Camb.*, 1935, pp. 129–30.

[34] *Cal. Doc. Fr.*, pp. 353–4; Dugdale, iv, p. 130.

[35] *AMC. Pembroke*, pp. 37–9.

[36] Gir. Camb., *Opera*, i, p. 324.

[37] *Taxatio*, p. 276.

[38] Lloyd, *History of Wales*, ii, p. 660 note 27.

[39] E. M. Pritchard, *History of St. Dogmaels Abbey*, pp. 158–67; A. Gwynn and R. Neville Hadcock, *Medieval Religious Houses, Ireland*, pp. 112–13, gives +1190.

Norman duchy. Neath Abbey was the second of her eight
immediate daughter houses in England and Wales.[40] In 1130
Richard de Granville granted to the monks of Savigny an
area of waste land between the rivers Neath and Tawe and
rents and lands in Glamorgan and Devon 'on condition that
the abbot of the church of Savigny and the convent of the
same should institute in the same a convent of monks to reside
therein for ever under an abbot'. The convent appears to have
taken up residence on 25 October 1130.[41]

III. THE CISTERCIAN PLANTATION IN WALES

The year following the foundation of Neath saw the establishment at Tintern of the first Cistercian house on Welsh soil.
The colony came from the house of L'Aumône in the diocese
of Chartres, and land for founding an abbey was given to them
by Walter fitz Richard, lord of Chepstow.[42] Tintern grew in
numbers and in the course of the twelfth century was able to
found two daughter houses, the first at Kingswood (Glouc.)
in 1139 and the second at Tintern Minor (Co. Wexford,
Ireland) in 1200. The main impetus which resulted in the
colonization of Wales, however, proceeded not from L'Aumône
nor from her daughter house at Tintern but direct from
Clairvaux.

The circumstances surrounding the entry of monks from
Clairvaux into south Wales are shrouded in obscurity. Neither
the available letters of St. Bernard, who presided over Clairvaux
between 1115 and 1153, nor the diminutive annals of the house
mention the colonization.[43] Nor has there survived any
historia fundationis of a Welsh Cistercian house such as those
which exist for some of the Yorkshire abbeys. Even the south
Wales chroniclers are disappointingly reticent in noting the
beginnings of a movement which was to exert such an important
influence on the spiritual, social, economic and political life of
medieval Wales.

---

[40] Knowles, *Monastic Order*, p. 725.
[41] Dugdale, v, p. 259; Clark, *Cartae*, i, pp. 74–5; L. Janauschek, *Originum
Cisterciensium*, i, p. 98; 'Annales de Margan' in *Annales Monastici*, i, p. 13.
[42] Janauschek, op. cit., p. 10; cf. *Annales Cambriae*, p. 39. The terms of the
foundation charter exist only in *inspeximus* charters.
[43] B. S. James, *Letters of St. Bernard of Clairvaux*; 'Chronicon Clarevallense,
1147–92' in Migne, *Patrologiae*, clxxxv, cols. 1247–51.

St. Bernard had doubtless become familiar with the contemporary Welsh scene through the wide range of his contacts
with the feudal nobility and with distinguished ecclesiastics.
His friendship with St. Malachy, whose life he was later to
write and who was responsible for the introduction of the
Cistercian order into Ireland in 1142, also provided him with
some knowledge of the organization and traditions of the
Celtic church. Wales as a possible field for further colonization
was not therefore an 'ultima Thule' to the Cistercian authorities
during these years.

During the reign of Stephen, there were in south Wales two
capable men of affairs whose positions gave them unrivalled
opportunities for gathering knowledge from, and making
contacts with, the superiors of the Cistercian order. They were
Bernard, bishop of St. David's, and Robert, earl of Gloucester.
Bernard was a *curialis* and had served Henry I as a chancery
clerk and his queen as chaplain. Even after his election as
bishop he retained an influential position at court, advising
the king in chancery and acting as his emissary abroad. He
appears to have been on terms of familiarity with William
Giffard, who was responsible for the first Cistercian foundation
in England (that of Waverley in 1128), and with Thurstan,
archbishop of York, who played such an active role in the
expansion of the order in Yorkshire. It is not surprising,
therefore, that Bishop Bernard is the first person recorded as
having associated himself with the first colony of monks from
Clairvaux to enter Wales. The community established itself
on 16 September 1140 and in 1144 was given what turned out
to be a temporary home at Little Trefgarn near Haverfordwest.
Here it remained until it found a more suitable site at Whitland.
The site was granted by a certain John of Torrington and the
monks took possession probably in 1151.[44]

In south-east Wales, it was Robert, earl of Gloucester, who
provided a site for the second colony of monks from Clairvaux.
Robert, the bastard son of Henry I, inherited the estates of
Robert fitz Hamon by marrying his daughter, Mabel; he was
created earl of Gloucester about 1122. As a protagonist of

---

[44] Janauschek, op. cit., p. 62; *Annales Cambriae*, p. 43; Dugdale, vi, p. 590.
I have followed Lloyd, *History of Wales*, ii, pp. 593–4, for the sequence of events
and in allowing John of Torrington as the founder. The arguments put forward
by the compilers of *AMC. Carmarthen*, pp. 152–3, are not convincing.

Matilda's claim to the English throne, he played a prominent part in the upheaval of Stephen's reign. A man of integrity, a benefactor of monasteries and a patron of literature, Earl Robert was an obvious person for the white monks to approach for material aid in establishing a permanent home for the new community.[45] During these troubled years Bishop Bernard of St. David's shared with Robert, earl of Gloucester a common bond of loyalty. 'Bishop Bernard of St. David's', wrote Sir John Lloyd, 'was one of the few prelates in constant attendance upon Matilda.'[46] He might have acted as an intermediary between the earl and the monks who eventually found their home at Margam.

The solemn ceremony of endowment took place at Bristol at some time before Robert's death on 31 October 1147. Robert, accompanied by his two sons, Hamo and Roger, and a number of his feudal dependants, symbolically handed over to Nivard, a brother of St. Bernard, all the land between the Kenfig and Afan rivers from the brow of the mountains to the sea coast and his fisheries of Afan for the purpose of founding an abbey. The colony of monks from Clairvaux under their abbot, William of Clairvaux, took possession and established themselves at Margam on 23 November 1147.[47] In the same year, the abbeys of the order of Savigny were incorporated into the order of Cîteaux and assigned to the affiliation of Clairvaux.[48] Thus, Neath Abbey became the sister of the neighbouring and newly-founded abbey of Margam.

In the decade or so after the foundation of their house at Margam, the monks attempted to found a daughter house at Pendar in Blaenau Morgannwg.[49] They engaged the services and assistance of a hermit called Meilyr to act as an intermediary between themselves and the men of the Welsh hill lordships. Griffin, son of Ifor granted to Margam abbey, 'by the hand of brother Meiler *Awenet*', land in the region of Gelli-gaer and Llanfabon in the lordship of Senghennydd for

[45] *DNB.*, xlviii, pp. 356–8, and *Complete Peerage*, v, pp. 683–6.
[46] Lloyd, *History of Wales*, ii, p. 478.
[47] The foundation charter survives in an *inspeximus* of Hugh Despenser (Clark, *Cartae*, iii, pp. 1213–14); Janauschek, op. cit., p. 292; cf. 'Annales de Margan' in *Annales Monastici*, i, p. 14.
[48] Knowles, *Monastic Order*, pp. 250–1.
[49] F. G. Cowley, 'Margam and Pendar: a Reassessment of the Evidence', *JHSCW.* (forthcoming).

the purpose of founding a hermitage or abbey. At about the same time or somewhat later, Caradoc Verbeis gave to God, the Cistercian order, brother Meilyr and the brethren of Pendar a parcel of land in the parish of Llanwynno near Ynys-y-bŵl in the lordship of Meisgyn. Philip, son of Griffin was another donor to Margam, 'by the hand of brother Meiler', of land in the same region, and his grant, too, mentions the brethren of Pendar.[50]

Despite the co-operation and assistance of Meilyr, Margam's embryonic foundation in the hills was an abortive one. The lands acquired were lost and later in the century seem to have passed to the abbey of Caerleon, a daughter house of Strata Florida.

The failure of Margam, Neath and Tintern to found a daughter house in Wales raises a question of wider importance: why was Cistercian expansion directed exclusively from Whitland and her daughter houses rather than from the abbeys of south-east Wales? Geographical and cultural factors were of obvious importance. In south-west Wales the configuration of the mountain ranges and river valleys made communication with the north and north-east comparatively easy. South-east Wales, on the other hand, was effectively sealed off from the rest of Wales by the formidable barrier of the Brecon Beacons and Black Mountains. The kingdoms of Morgannwg and Gwent had formed political and cultural entities distinct from other parts of Wales from early times. Their proximity to the Anglo-Saxon kingdoms made them more susceptible to influences from the east and less amenable to the attempts occasionally made by native princes in the north to incorporate them into a unified Wales.

The immediate causes of the success of Whitland and the failure of houses in south-east Wales, however, are to be found in the political environment in which the respective abbeys found themselves in the second half of the twelfth century. Neath, Margam and Tintern were founded by Anglo-Norman lords, and the patronage of these abbeys continued throughout their existence to remain in the hands of Anglo-Normans. The community at Margam in the first century or so of its existence was predominantly Anglo-Norman and tended naturally to

[50] Clark, *Cartae*, i, pp. 148–9; ii, pp. 346–7; i, pp. 127–8.

side with its patron against the Welsh lords of the Blaenau. These lords, the heirs of Iestyn ap Gwrgant, were in frequent revolt against the abbey's patrons, the lords of Glamorgan. Mainly because of this political struggle, Margam failed to acquire the permanent goodwill of the Welsh of the hill lordships which was so necessary for the successful foundation of a daughter house in the region. Even if the abbey had done so, it seems unlikely that these inhospitable and dangerous regions would have been able to support a convent for long.

Whitland, also an Anglo-Norman foundation, seems to have experienced similar difficulty in its first attempt to found a daughter house. If the Cistercian lists used by Janauschek are correct, the first foundation at Cwm-hir took place on 22 July 1143, before the mother house had found a permanent home.[51] The foundation was an abortive one. On 1 June 1164, however, Robert fitz Stephen, lord of Pennardd in the Clare lordship of Ceredigion, drew a colony of monks from Whitland to found the abbey of Strata Florida at *yr hen fynachlog* on the banks of the River Fflur.[52] The foundation was a modest one,[53] and thus it might have remained had not events wrought a radical change in the political situation. In 1165 the abbey's founder and patron was captured by Rhys ap Gruffydd. In the years following, Rhys succeeded by statesmanship, hard fighting and good fortune in welding into some form of unity a number of Welsh cantrefs and commotes many of which had previously been under Norman control. In the process, he acquired for himself the patronage of the abbeys of Whitland and Strata Florida, and both abbeys began to receive postulants from the native Welsh in large numbers. Rhys took particular pride in the attention he had devoted to Strata Florida.[54] Though not technically the founder, he was certainly the effective founder of the abbey's fortunes. At some time before the end of the twelfth century, the monks of Strata Florida, enriched by Rhys's patronage, moved to a new site a mile and a half north-east of *yr hen fynachlog*. The building of the new

[51] Janauschek, op. cit., pp. 74–5; Lloyd, *History of Wales*, ii, p. 594.
[52] Gir. Camb., *Opera*, iv, p. 152; Janauschek, pp. 151 and 295; *Brut y Tywysogyon, Peniarth 20*, transl. and ed. Thomas Jones, p. 64.
[53] The church was about 126 feet long and 42 feet wide; see S. W. Williams, *The Cistercian Abbey of Strata Florida*, p. 21.
[54] For his charter to the abbey dated 1184, see Dugdale, v, pp. 632–3, and translation in S. W. Williams, op. cit., appendix pp. x-xiii.

church was sufficiently advanced in 1201 for the monks to make use of the choir.[55]

Hitherto, the hostility of the Welsh towards the Norman invader had made it difficult for them to found a house which they knew would be controlled by a mother house under Norman patronage. The rise of Rhys to a position of pre-eminence in south-west Wales removed this difficulty. His Welsh blood, his territorial power and the powerful influence he wielded outside the lands immediately under his control, enabled the Cistercian order to expand naturally from centres in south-west and central Wales unhindered by the political strife which limited the order's expansion from the south-east.

A colony from Whitland was established at Strata Marcella in 1170[56] and in 1176 another colony was sent to Cwm-hir. This abbey was re-founded on 1 August with an endowment provided probably by Cadwallon ap Madog, prince of Ceri and Maelienydd.[57] The abbeys of Strata Florida, Strata Marcella and Cwm-hir provided further colonies of monks for the establishment of houses at Cymer, Caerleon, Aberconwy and Valle Crucis.

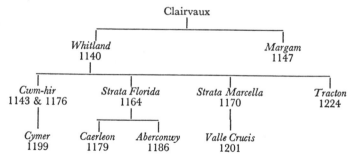

In 1179 Strata Florida sent a colony into south-east Wales to establish its first daughter house at Nant-teyrnon near Caerleon, with an endowment provided by Hywel ab Iorwerth, lord of Caerleon.[58] The exact location of the first site is not

---

[55] T. Jones Pierce, 'Strata Florida Abbey', *Ceredigion*, i (1950), p. 25; *Brut y Tywysogyon, Peniarth 20*, ed. Thomas Jones, p. 81.

[56] Lloyd, *History of Wales*, ii, p. 599.

[57] Janauschek, p. 74; Lloyd, ii, p. 600 and notes.

[58] *Brut y Tywysogyon, Peniarth 20*, p. 72. The date here provided by the chronicle of the mother house is to be preferred to that given by Janauschek, pp. 190, 298, i.e. 22 July 1189; Lloyd, ii. p. 600 and notes.

known, but the monks eventually built their abbey on a piece of land between two streams about two miles north-west of Caerleon.[59] The abbey was to be known by a variety of names. The versions of the *Brut* give Nant-teyrnon, Dewma and Caerleon.[60] In 1273 the Cistercian General Chapter decreed that the name *Lanterna*, rather than *Vallium*, should be entered in the official lists.[61] In the later middle ages, both Caerleon and Llantarnam were in frequent use, but the latter name gradually gained a wider currency.

Caerleon was from the first a house of the native Welsh and thus had an advantage over the rival house of Margam in acquiring gifts from the Welsh of the eastern part of Blaenau Morgannwg. The early stages of the contest between the two abbeys cannot be traced, but at an early date 'spheres of influence' were marked out. In one such area between the Taff and the Dowlais, Margam Abbey was to acquire what it could from the French and English, and Caerleon what it could from the Welsh.[62] By the beginning of the thirteenth century it seems clear that Caerleon had won from Margam much of the land around Pendar, the scene of Margam's earlier and unsuccessful attempt to found a daughter house.[63]

The prolonged negotiations which preceded the foundation of the last house on Welsh soil, that of Grace Dieu, are fairly well documented in the records of the Cistercian General Chapter. John of Monmouth first made known his intention of founding an abbey in 1217. His petition came before the General Chapter, and the abbot of Morimund was ordered to appoint discreet men to look into the matter and report their findings to the Chapter in the following year.[64] A long delay followed and it was not until 24 April 1226 that a convent of monks from Dore was eventually despatched to the new house of Grace Dieu.[65] Subsequent events show that the nine years'

[59] That a change of site took place is indicated by the reference in 1291 to land 'apud veterem Abbathiam' (*Taxatio*, p. 281b).
[60] *Brut y Tywysogyon*, *Peniarth 20*, p. 72 and note on p. 187.
[61] Canivez, *Statuta*, ii, p. 115.
[62] Clark, *Cartae*, ii, pp. 589–90.
[63] See the texts of the agreements between the two abbeys in Clark, *Cartae*, ii, pp. 289–90 (1203) and pp. 606–8 (1253).
[64] Canivez, *Statuta*, i, p. 481, and for subsequent references to the proposed house, ibid., ii, pp. 11, 19, 27, 43.
[65] Not from Waverley as most authorities state; see 'Annales Dorenses' in *Monumenta Germaniae Historica*, *Scriptores*, xxvii, p. 527.

delay probably owed as much to Welsh unrest in the area as to the lukewarmness of the would-be founder. In 1233 when John of Monmouth was waging war against Richard, earl of Pembroke, the Welsh burnt down the newly-founded abbey, alleging that it had been founded on territory which had been seized from them.[66] In the following year the General Chapter learnt that the abbey had been founded in an area rife with litigation. The abbots of Bruern and Kingswood were ordered to induce the founder to make peace with his adversaries and confer another site on the monks.[67] Meanwhile, the depredations of the Welsh continued and the abbey lands were stripped of their corn.[68] Possibly because of the local unrest, the abbots of Bruern and Kingswood failed to honour their commission.[69] By 1236, however, John of Monmouth had managed to secure another site for the monks and the father abbot was ordered to despatch a convent thither without delay.[70] Later in the century Grace Dieu may have moved yet a third time. In 1276 the abbots of Thame and Neath were ordered to inspect the site to which *Haymo comes Companiae*, brother of the king of England, intended to transfer the abbey of Grace Dieu.[71] The final site of the abbey lay on the banks of the River Trothy, four miles west of Monmouth.[72]

IV. THE REGULAR CANONS

The ideal which inspired clerics attached to a major church to live a common life, renouncing the pleasures and responsibilities of marriage and private property, had a long history even by the eleventh century.[73] Apologists for the regular canons in the twelfth century found authority for such a life in the lives led by the apostles of the early church.[74] The rapid growth in the number and importance of communities intent

[66] 'Annales de Waverleia', *Annales Monastici*, ii, p. 312.
[67] Canivez, *Statuta*, ii, p. 137.
[68] *CCR.*, *1231–34*, p. 445.
[69] Canivez, *Statuta*, ii, p. 147.
[70] Ibid., p. 155.
[71] Ibid., iii, p. 161.
[72] For the scant remains, see C. J. O. Evans, *Monmouthshire*, pp. 293–4, and more recently D. Williams, 'Grace Dieu Abbey: an Exploratory Excavation', *Monmouthshire Antiquary*, iii (1970–71), pp. 55–8.
[73] For the precursors of the Augustinian canons and for much of what follows, see J. C. Dickinson, *Origins of the Austin Canons and their Introduction into England*.
[74] *Acts of the Apostles*, ii, 42–7.

on practising the ideal in the second half of the eleventh century was essentially, however, the product of the Gregorian reform movement. Anxious to combat the degeneration of clerical morals and the secularization of church property, the leaders of the movement saw the new communities as useful allies and valuable instruments for the promotion of their policy of reform. To ensure a recognized place for such communities within the organization of the church, it became increasingly urgent in an age of growing legalism for them to adopt a patron of recognized fame and sanctity, and a rule of life which would command respect. After the pontificate of Urban II (d. 1099), communities in growing numbers began to adopt St. Augustine as their patron and his so-called 'Rule'[75] as the basis of their way of life.

The brevity of the 'Rule' gave it a flexibility which enabled it to be adopted by communities of varying background and origin. In the twelfth and thirteenth centuries the 'Rule' was successfully adopted not only by groups of hermits and secular canons in areas which had long been under the influence of Latin monasticism, but by communities of culdees and *claswyr* in Celtic lands.[76] The flexibility of the 'Rule' also enabled communities who adopted it to develop along highly individualistic lines. Initially, communities of regular canons were regarded as an effective means of making good the deficiencies of a notoriously lax and poorly educated secular clergy. They were placed in important churches to revive standards of worship either by performing the services themselves or by supervising the administrations of the secular clergy. By the beginning of the twelfth century, however, a number of the new communities were being influenced by the way of life of the newer reformed monasteries. A number of Augustinian houses were founded on sites far removed from centres of population where opportunities for parochial work were extremely limited. Some, too, resembled the newer orders in that the nucleus of the community derived from an

---

[75] For the text and textual history of the 'Rule', see Dickinson, op. cit., pp. 255–79.
[76] D. E. Easson, *Medieval Religious Houses, Scotland*, pp. 74–85; C. N. Johns, 'The Celtic Monasteries of North Wales', *Trans. Caern. Hist. Soc.*, xxi (1960), pp. 14–43, and 'Postscript', ibid., xxiii (1962), pp. 129–31.

earlier community of hermits. In such houses the contem-
plative element tended to be strong and there was probably
no intention, initially at least, of diverting these energies
outside the cloister by engaging in parochial work.

The progress of the Augustinian order in England during the
reign of Henry I owed much to royal and episcopal patronage
and encouragement. Such factors also influenced the establishment of Llanthony, the first Augustinian house on Welsh
soil. In the last years of the eleventh century, William, a
knight of Hugh de Lacy, abandoned his profession of arms and
with a few companions established a hermitage in the Llanthony valley.[77] William was joined in 1103 by Ernisius, who
had lived as a hermit at Edgarsley, near Cannock forest.
Ernisius was a man of some learning who had formerly been
chaplain to Queen Maud, a noted patroness of the Augustinians
in England. William and Ernisius built themselves a church
which was consecrated in 1108 by Urban, bishop of Glamorgan,
and Reinhelm, bishop of Hereford, and dedicated to St. John
the Baptist. Hugh de Lacy became the patron and benefactor
of the community, and Payn fitz John and Miles the constable
also appear to have played a prominent part in the endowment.[78] On the advice of Archbishop Anselm (d. 1109), a
community of regular canons was established and Ernisius was
elected the first prior. Since canons from Merton (founded
1114) as well as from Holy Trinity, Aldgate, and Colchester
were invited to instruct them in the 'Rule' of St. Augustine, it
seems unlikely that the new community was on a sound footing
until after 1114. 'Possibly the establishment of the priory at
Llanthony', writes J. C. Dickinson, 'though mooted or begun
in Anselm's time, was not finally accomplished until about
1118.'[79]

During the reign of Henry I, Llanthony acquired widespread
fame as a centre of the canonical life in its most austere form.

[77] What follows is based mainly on the *Historia Fundationis* in Dugdale, vi,
pp. 128–34, translated in G. Roberts, *Some Account of Llanthony Priory*, pp. 47–63;
Gir. Camb., *Opera*, vi, pp. 37–47, and the *Life* of Robert de Bethune, a former
prior, in H. Wharton, *Anglia Sacra*, ii, pp. 293–321.

[78] Henry de Lacy is described as founder in a bull of Innocent II dated 1131;
see *Papsturkunden in England*, ed. W. Holtzmann, i, no. 16, pp. 239–40. For Payn
fitz John and Miles, see ibid., and *Anglia Sacra*, ii, p. 304.

[79] Dickinson, op. cit., p. 112; cf. E. W. Lovegrove, 'Llanthony Priory', *Arch.
Camb.*, 1942–3, p. 218.

Henry I was himself a benefactor to the house, and his queen, Maud, made a gift of money to William the hermit for the adornment of the church. Roger of Salisbury visited the community and later described to his royal master in metaphorical terms the 'cloister' of mountains which the whole treasure of the king and his kingdom would be insufficient to purchase.[80]

On the death of Henry I, the rebellion of the Welsh almost put an end to the new foundation. Most of the canons fled for protection and shelter to their former prior, Robert de Bethune bishop of Hereford. A new site was prepared for them just outside Gloucester, later to be known as Lanthony Secunda, and the community took up residence soon after the consecration of the church there in May 1137.[81] However, the traditions attaching to the old site died hard. In 1135 a number of canons had refused to leave the house of their first profession and 'so it came to pass by Divine mercy, that at no time the church of Lanthony was wholly deprived of the residence of some of the religious'.[82]

Initially it was intended that Lanthony Secunda should be a daughter house or cell of the Welsh house. This was clearly recognized when Pope Eugenius III confirmed the possessions of both houses in 1146.[83] It was intended, too, that when peaceful conditions were restored most of the community should return to their old home. As the years passed, however, the canons of Lanthony Secunda became increasingly reluctant to return to their mother house of Llanthony Prima. Meanwhile, the latter house went through a period of obscurity and neglect, administered, it would seem, by priors who spent the greater part of their time at the daughter house of Lanthony Secunda. The books, vestments, relics, muniments, and even the bells of the older house were carried to Gloucester; it became a home of the old, the infirm and the factious, 'a dungeon and a banishment for criminals'. Prior Clement attempted to entice his canons back to the Welsh house by making it compulsory for the whole community to stay there

---

[80] *Episc. Acts*, i, p. 247; Dugdale, vi, p. 131; Gir. Camb., *Opera*, vi, pp. 39–40.
[81] *VCH. Glouc.*, ii, p. 87; Lovegrove, op. cit., p. 222.
[82] Roberts, op. cit., p. 57.
[83] *VCH. Glouc.*, ii, 88.

for some part of the year. The experiment was not a success and was soon abandoned. 'We shall all go to hell for the sake of St. John', Clement was accustomed to tell his canons.[84]

An unexpected revival in the fortunes of the Welsh house occurred with the Anglo-Norman conquest of Ireland. At the end of the twelfth and beginning of the thirteenth century, Hugh de Lacy and his son Walter began to make grants of lands and churches in Meath which were addressed specifically to the Welsh house.[85] These grants were matched by similar ones by different benefactors to the Gloucester house, and perhaps served to bring to a head the frequently disputed but unresolved question of the relative status of the two priories. In 1205 the two priories were formally separated and were henceforward to be autonomous, each having its own prior and convent.[86] Arrangements were also made to solve a more complex problem: the equal division of the possessions, much of which had been granted jointly to both houses by previous benefactors. So widespread were the interests of the two priories by this date, in England, Wales and Ireland, that a satisfactory division was not reached until as late as 1213.[87] Llanthony Prima remained an autonomous house until 1481, when it was granted to, and made a cell of, Lanthony Secunda by Edward IV.[88]

The community of regular canons at Carmarthen owed its origin to the initiative of Bernard, bishop of St. David's (1115–48). About 1110, Henry I had granted the church of St. Peter's, Carmarthen, the ancient *clas* church of Llan-deulyddog and land at Pentewi to Battle Abbey, and a dependent priory was established.[89] The chronicler of Battle records that in the course of time,

> Bernard, bishop of the same province, attracted by the charm of the place, strove with ardent desire to bring the same church under his own control.

He and his adherents made frequent pleas at the royal court until at length, on the election of Abbot Warner (1125), the

[84] Roberts, op. cit., pp. 60–3.
[85] Lovegrove, op. cit., pp. 214–5, 225–7.
[86] *VCH. Glouc.*, ii, p. 88.
[87] *Irish Cartularies of Llanthony Prima and Secunda*, ed. Eric St. John Brooks, pp. vii–viii, 205–12.
[88] Dugdale, vi, p. 139; Roberts, op. cit., pp. 77–9.
[89] *Chronicon de Monasterio de Bello*, ed. J. S. Brewer, pp. 55–6.

place was given to Bernard by the king and the monks of
Battle were compensated with land elsewhere.[90] Neither the
chronicler of Battle, nor a royal charter in which the grant to
Bernard is mentioned, states that Bernard planned to found
a house of canons. There is little reason to challenge J. E.
Lloyd's inference, however, that this was Bernard's intention.[91]
Bernard had ample opportunity for perceiving the virtues of
the new order not only from his acquaintance with Queen
Maud, a noted patroness of the Augustinians whom he had
served as chaplain, but from a number of his episcopal
colleagues who had founded such houses. The new community
at Carmarthen was certainly in existence before Henry I's
death in 1135,[92] and the texts of two of Bernard's deeds bear
witness to his interest in the foundation.[93] The 'Rule' of St.
Augustine was probably adopted as soon as the community
was established.[94] The priory church and domestic buildings
were constructed on or near the site of the old *clas* church of
Llandeulyddog.[95]

The only piece of evidence which gives a clue to the foundation date of the priory of Haverfordwest is contained in a
royal charter dated 1331 which confirms the grants which
Robert son of Richard son of Tancard 'made by his charter to
God, St. Mary and St. Thomas the Martyr of Haverford and
the canons serving God there'. From this it has been inferred
that Robert fitz Richard, lord of Haverford (d. 1213) was the
founder.[96] The memory of the hermit Caradog may have
inspired the founder in his enterprise. Caradog, when he
was driven from Barry Isle (Pembs.) by pirates about 1105,
was granted the *monasterium* of St. Ismael near Haverfordwest.
Here he was to be persecuted by Tancard (Robert's grand-
father) and patronized by Richard fitz Tancard (Robert's

[90] Ibid., pp. 61–2.
[91] *Ancient Charters*, ed. J. H. Round, p. 27; Lloyd, *History of Wales*, ii, p. 432.
[92] *Carm. Cart.*, no. 33, p. 10, for Henry I's charter to 'the canons of St. John of
Carmarthen'; cf. *Episc. Acts.*, i, p. 254.
[93] *Carm. Cart.*, no. 26, p. 8, no. 35, p. 10.
[94] The earliest recorded prior was appropriately named Augustine; see *Episc.
Acts*, i, p. 268.
[95] *AMC. Carmarthen*, pp. 257–8.
[96] Dugdale, vi, pp. 444–5; Lloyd, *History of Wales*, ii, p. 633.

father).[97] Unfortunately it is not known if Caradog's companions joined him at St. Ismael to form some sort of community such as existed later in the century at Priestholm and Beddgelert. The *cultus* of Caradog was certainly flourishing in 1200. It may be significant that the priory church of St. Thomas was erected not far from the site marked by tradition as his hermitage and that the church of St. Ismael was numbered among the priory's possessions in 1535.[98]

St. Kynemark's near Chepstow was the last and the smallest of the Augustinian foundations in Wales. It was founded probably after 1254 but certainly before 1271. In 1254 St. Kynemark was treated by officials charged with the Norwich valuation as a church belonging to the bishop and chapter of Llandaff and no mention was made of the priory.[99] In 1271 the prior of St. Kynemark makes, as far as is known, his earliest appearance in the records as a member of a jury summoned to Chepstow Castle.[100] The low figure at which the priory's temporal and spiritual possessions were assessed in 1291 (£11 7s. 4d.) and in 1535 (£8 4s. 8d.) indicates that the endowments were not intended to support more than a few canons.[101]

The name of the priory is itself a misnomer. The priory was dedicated to St. John the Baptist and was situated not in, but near, St. Kynemark's church. A papal mandate of 1355 refers to an apostate, 'Richard de Tudenham, Augustinian canon of St. John Baptist's near St. Kynemark, in the diocese of Llandaff, who had left his monastery and several times broken out of prison, and now wishes to be reconciled to his order'. This mandate provides the only evidence known to me of the affiliation of the priory.[102]

One can do little more than speculate as to the circumstances which prompted the foundation. In 1291 the prior was

---

[97] *Nova Legenda Anglie*, ed. C. Horstman, i, p. 175; Lloyd, op. cit., pp. 592; S. Baring-Gould and F. Fisher, *Lives of the British Saints*, ii, p. 77.
[98] *Valor*, iv, p. 389.
[99] W. E. Hunt, *Valuation of Norwich*, p. 319.
[100] J. A. Bradney, *History of Monmouthshire*, vol. iv, part 1, p. 146.
[101] *Taxatio*, pp. 278b, 282, 285b; *Valor*, iv, p. 372.
[102] *CPL.*, iii (1342–62), p. 575. Since this was written, fuller evidence has been brought together by L. A. S. Butler in 'The Augustinian Priory of St. Kinmark', *JHSCW.*, xv (1965), pp. 9–19, and 'St. Kynemark's Priory, Chepstow', *Monmouthshire Antiquary*, ii (1965), pp. 33–41.

rector of St. Kynemark, St. Arvans and Porthcaseg. These churches were perilously near large granges belonging to the Cistercians of Tintern. The Cistercians had gained a reputation for ruthlessness in the treatment of small churches. It is just conceivable, therefore, that the priory owed its foundation to the bishop and chapter of Llandaff and that the three churches, long associated with the see of Llandaff,[103] were deliberately appropriated to the priory as a legal safeguard against their possible destruction by the Cistercians of Tintern.

Like most of their counterparts in England, the Augustinian houses of south Wales were virtually autonomous. Though they were subject to the authority of the diocesan, they did not belong to a 'congregation' whose executives could enforce uniformity of observance. Nor, until after 1215, did they possess a chapter for the discussion of common problems or machinery whereby their houses could be officially visited by members of their own profession.

Before his death in 1197, and most probably between 1184 and 1189, Rhys ap Gruffydd founded at Talley a house of regular canons which belonged to the order of Prémontré.[104] Prémontré, in the diocese of Laon, was founded by St. Norbert in 1120 and the 'Rule' of St. Augustine was adopted within a year of the foundation. The subsequent development of the Premonstratensian order, however, owed less to its founder than to the first abbot of Prémontré, Hugh de Fosses. Between 1131 and 1134, probably in response to the growing number of daughter houses colonized from Prémontré, statutes were drawn up which made Prémontré the head of an order closely organized on the Cistercian model. Particular emphasis was placed on uniformity of observance with regard to service books, diet and dress. The statutes of the new order followed those of Cîteaux, too, in stressing the need for seclusion from the world and forbidding the possession of 'altars to which a cure of souls pertains'. No provision at all was made for preaching. Parts of the 'Rule' of St. Augustine were abandoned and the new order soon acquired a strong monastic character. An annual General Chapter was established and the Cistercian

---

[103] *Book of Llan Dâv*, pp. 150, 165, 322.
[104] J. Beverley Smith and B. H. St. J. O'Neil, *Talley Abbey*, p. 4.

method of attaching a new foundation to a mother house for purposes of visitation was also adopted.[105]

After the foundation of Newhouse (Lincolnshire) in 1143, the number of Premonstratensian houses in England rapidly increased. More than twenty houses had been founded before 1188. Family connections played an important part in the spread of the order, with the result, possibly, that the founders formed a fairly homogeneous class. Most of them were not men of great wealth. They were new men, *curiales* who were consolidating their power and influence as itinerant justices and sheriffs in the service of Henry II. They were attracted to the new order partly because of its stricter observance and partly, perhaps, because the foundation of a Premonstratensian house required a less heavy outlay of material resources than that of a traditional Benedictine abbey. There is little evidence to show that they 'expected them to fulfil a function in the life of the church essentially different from that which they associated with the Cistercians and Benedictines'.[106]

Either by conscious imitation or instinctively as a man at ease with the conventions of his age, Rhys ap Gruffydd shared many of the traits which characterized his fellow magnates. He was proud yet sensitive and courteous. He was also particularly susceptible to the superstitious fears common to most warrior magnates. Despite his liberal benefactions to religious houses of all orders, he had not as yet actually *founded* any house of note within the territories under his rule. This, combined with his decision, delayed for three weeks, not to take the cross, may have spurred him to make the modest compensatory act which resulted in the foundation of Talley.[107] Personal acquaintance with some of the founders and benefactors of Premonstratensian houses in England— men like Ranulph Glanville with whom Rhys had frequently dined—was probably responsible for his choice of the order to which the new house would belong. Family connections may also have been important. Sometime before 1189, Rhys's eldest son Gruffydd had married Matilda, daughter of William

---

[105] H. M. Colvin, *The White Canons in England*, pp. 1–25.
[106] Ibid., p. 30.
[107] He was dissuaded from taking the cross by his wife; see Gir. Camb., *Opera*, vi, p. 15.

de Breos, who was an early benefactor of the new abbey.[108]
More puzzling is the affiliation of Talley. It was originally a
daughter of St. Jean of Amiens, a house which had no connections with the order in England.[109]

It remains debatable whether Rhys was inspired by a
motive more altruistic than that of endowing prayers for his
soul. It has been suggested that Rhys's foundation of the new
house and its endowment with older *clas* churches 'may have
been an attempt to revive the waning spirit of the *clas* through
the medium of a new religious order peculiarly fitted for the
purpose'.[110] Unfortunately, there is no evidence for the
manner in which the churches appropriated to Talley were
served in the late-twelfth and during the thirteenth century.
Nor is there any literary or archaeological evidence to connect
the site of the new foundation with an earlier community of
claswyr, though the abbey did acquire property which had
formerly belonged to the *clas* church of Llandeilo.[111] The
absence of pre-Norman Christian memorial stones at, or in
the immediate vicinity of, the abbey suggests that the new
community settled on virgin soil. As Gerald of Wales noted,
the house was meanly endowed, and it is unlikely that the
community was ever large enough for it to undertake parochial
work on a wide scale.[112]

V. THE NUNNERIES

More than one historian of the religious houses has drawn
attention to the inadequate provision made for women
attracted to the religious vocation in medieval England.[113] The
status of women and current conceptions of their role in
society doubtless weighted any scale of priorities in favour of
foundations for men. In Wales, where the legal status of women
was possibly higher than in England, less provision was made

---

[108] Lloyd, *History of Wales*, ii, p. 577; *Arch. Camb.*, 1893, p. 44.
[109] *Collectanea Anglo-Premonstratensia*, ed. F. A. Gasquet, iii, no. 574, pp. 121–2.
[110] T. Jones Pierce, 'Strata Florida Abbey', *Ceredigion*, i (1950), pp. 21–2.
[111] Melville Richards, 'The Carmarthenshire Possessions of Talyllychau',
Carmarthenshire Studies: Essays Presented to Major Francis Jones, pp. 110–21.
[112] Gir. Camb., *Opera*, iv, p. 143. The earliest reference to the number of canons
at Talley relates to 1371, when there were only six canons; see J. C. Russell,
British Medieval Population, p. 329.
[113] Knowles, *Monastic Order*, p. 136; J. C. Dickinson, *Monastic Life in Medieval
England*, p. 84.

than in comparable areas elsewhere.[114] Throughout the whole
of the middle ages only four religious houses for women were
established in Wales. All of them were small and one of them
scarcely existed for more than a year or so. Llanllŷr in the
Aeron valley, Ceredigion, was founded before 1197 by the
Lord Rhys and placed under the tutelage of Strata Florida.[115]
Llanllugan was founded before 1236 by Maredudd ap
Rhotpert, lord of Cydewain.[116] Llansanffraid in Elfael was
founded between 1170 and 1174 under the auspices of Strata
Marcella. Enoch, the abbot of Strata Marcella who supervised
the foundation, eloped with one of the nuns, and despite his
subsequent repentance it is unlikely that the foundation
survived the scandal.[117] The Benedictine priory of Usk was
founded before 1236 by one of the Clare lords of Usk.[118]

VI. ABORTIVE FOUNDATIONS

A number of priories and abbeys were founded in south
Wales between 1066 and 1226 which for one reason or another
failed to take root. Attention has already been directed to
three such abortive foundations.[119] Between 1116 and 1117
Gilbert fitz Richard granted the rich and ancient *clas* of
Llanbadarn Fawr to Gloucester Abbey for the foundation of
a priory.[120] Soon after the death of Henry I, however, the
Welsh regained control in Ceredigion and the monks of
Gloucester were driven out. They never succeeded in recovering
the church.[121] The priory of Llandovery came into existence
as a result of a grant to Great Malvern by Richard fitz Pons
of the church of the castle of Llandovery and two carucates of
land.[122] The vicious life of the three or four monks there

[114] Ireland had over 40 (A. Gwynn and R. N. Hadcock, *Medieval Religious
Houses, Ireland*, pp. 310–11) and Scotland at least 15 (D. E. Easson, *Medieval
Religious Houses, Scotland, passim*).
[115] Gir. Camb., *Opera*, iv, p. 152; Lloyd, *History of Wales*, ii, p. 603.
[116] Ibid. and p. 648 note 182.
[117] Gir. Camb., *Opera*, ii, p. 248, iv, pp. 168–9, vi, p. 59; Lloyd, ii, pp. 599–600.
[118] Dugdale, iv, p. 591. At the Dissolution the nuns regarded Richard de Clare
and Gilbert his son as their founders. They have not been satisfactorily identified;
see E. Owen, *Catalogue of Manuscripts Relating to Wales in the British Museum*, part
iii, pp. 660–65.
[119] For Cwm-hir, Carmarthen and Llansanffraid, see above pp. 25, 32–3, 38.
[120] *Hist. et Cart. Gloucester*, i, pp. 73–9, 106.
[121] Gir. Camb., *Opera*, vi, p. 121; cf. Lloyd, *History of Wales*, ii, pp. 432–3.
[122] Dugdale, iii, pp. 447–8; *CPR., 1374–77*, p. 282. Great Malvern also acquired
the church and manor of Llansbyddid. It formed the 'cell in the parts of Brecon
subject to Great Malvern' mentioned by Gerald of Wales (*Opera*, iv, p. 102).

resulted in their ejection *circa* 1185 by Rhys ap Gruffydd and the bishop of St. David's.[123]

Walter de Lacy took the unusual step of attempting to found a priory dependent on Monmouth Priory. He gave to the abbey of St. Florent and the convent of St. Mary, Monmouth, five carucates of land at *Radebanc*, stipulating that monks and a prior should reside there. On the death of a prior, a new one was to be supplied from the abbey of St. Florent or the priory of Monmouth and elected by Walter himself or by his heirs. The abbot of St. Florent was to have an ounce of gold as a pension. Nothing more is heard of the foundation.[124]

A number of proposed Cistercian houses also came to grief. In 1203 the General Chapter heard a petition from a 'king of Wales', presumably Llywelyn the Great, for the construction of an abbey.[125] No new house was founded. In the following year the General Chapter heard the petition of William de Breos, who wished to found an abbey in Wales.[126] The Coggeshall chronicler records that William had already constructed an abbey in Wales and handed it over to the house of Cîteaux.[127] Again, nothing more is heard of the foundation.

---

[123] Ibid., p. 100.
[124] P.R.O., Ancient Deed, E 210/D7221. I have not succeeded in dating the deed. The grant was made with the consent of his wife M., for the souls of his father and mother and R. his brother. The first three witnesses are *Willelmo de Laci, Ricardo de tut, Willelmo parvo.*
[125] Canivez, *Statuta*, i, p. 294.
[126] Ibid., p. 305. The name is given as William Brabox.
[127] *Radulphi de Coggeshalle Chronicon Anglicanum*, p. 147.

III

MONASTIC RECRUITMENT AND POPULATION

The majority of the monks who manned the Benedictine priories of south Wales during the twelfth and thirteenth centuries were drawn from their respective mother houses in England and France. It was the abbot and convent of the mother house who appointed the prior of a dependency and decided on the number of monks it was expedient for it to support.[1] It was the abbot and convent of the mother house, too, who gave their consent to a limited recruitment of novices from the locality in which the dependency was situated. This local recruitment does not appear to have been very frequent in the twelfth century. In the houses dependent on abbeys in Normandy it became less frequent after the loss of the duchy by the English crown in 1204. It then became important to the interests of the foreign abbeys to see that the core of convents in their dependencies should be formed from their own professed monks.

A policy of local recruitment was obviously out of the question for the numerous small cells which were scattered over south Wales. Such cells as Basaleg, Cardiff, Cardigan, Kidwelly, Malpas, St. Clears, Llangenydd and Llangua were never intended to attract recruits to the monastic life. The one, two or three monks who manned them were little more than custodians, intent only on sending the small revenue they collected to the mother abbey.

In the conventual priories a certain amount of local recruitment took place. These local recruits were either members of locally prominent Anglo-Norman families who had connections with the priory as patrons or benefactors, or sons of local burgesses with influential backers. In either case the monk-to-be often brought with him some material benefit to the priory. In the early-twelfth century, for example, Philip Alis gave land to Abergavenny Priory on behalf of his brother

---

[1] A prior of Brecon, charged in the last quarter of the thirteenth century with not keeping the required number of monks, replied that the matter did not rest with him but with the lord abbot; see *Brec. Cart.*, p. 137.

Ralph when he became a monk there. Walter of Malvenon gave land to the same priory when he himself took the habit there. Sometime before 1175 Robert of Baskerville granted a piece of land to Brecon Priory when his son James became a monk there. He and his wife received the privileges of fraternity and of burial at the priory. Both William de Breos and his wife interceded for James's reception before the arrangement was made. When Henry of Hereford, the king's constable, granted 3s. annually to buy lights for the priory church of Brecon, he made the grant in order that Godfrey *cocus*, who had honourably served him and his ancestors, might be made a monk there.[2]

Between the years 1216 and 1230 Peter fitz Herbert, lord of Blaenllyfni, made an agreement with Brecon Priory whereby he and his heirs might present to the priory as monks two suitable clerks who were to say masses for their souls. When these two died or were ejected from the house for a just cause, the prior and convent were to receive another two presented in the same way.[3] Such an agreement had its dangers, especially as the century wore on and a distinct class of chantry priests made their appearance. Were the presentees at Brecon to be considered as monks or as chantry priests? Trouble broke out in 1283 when Archbishop Pecham undertook a visitation of Battle Abbey. Pecham took disciplinary action against John de la Mere and Roger, two of Reginald fitz Peter's presentees, and recalled them to Battle Abbey. Reginald fitz Peter alleged that this was done without his consent and 'to his prejudice' and immediately embarked on a full-scale vendetta against the priory. A number of the monks' men were slain, their cattle impounded, and their corn and horses seized.[4] The outcome of the dispute during Reginald's lifetime is not known, but sometime after his death in 1286 the arrangement of presenting two clerks as monks was modified. In an agreement with the priory, Reginald's son, John, waived the right of presentation and gave the monks the right of choosing two of their own number to carry out the services hitherto performed by the presentees.[5]

[2] Dugdale, iv, p. 616; *Brec. Cart.*, pp. 80, 88–90.
[3] Ibid., pp. 94–5.
[4] *Registrum Epistolarum Johannis Peckham*, ii, p. 581, iii, pp. 810, 831–2.
[5] *Brec. Cart.*, pp. 23–4.

Of the seven recognized conventual Benedictine priories of south Wales,[6] it is doubtful if more than one expanded very much beyond the conventual number of twelve monks and a prior, except perhaps during the period of peak numbers which occurred at the end of the twelfth and beginning of the thirteenth centuries. Goldcliff Priory, the richest Benedictine house in south Wales, was exceptional, therefore, with its complement of twenty-five monks in 1295. In 1296 five were removed 'for lack of sustenance' and in 1297, five more, leaving fifteen monks.[7] At this period numbers in some of the other houses were tending to fall below even the conventual number. At Brecon *circa* 1283 there were only eight monks and a prior.[8] Despite a fairly comfortable income, Brecon's numbers never appear to have risen higher than this in the later middle ages. If the need arose Brecon could defend its deficiency by appealing to a charter which Roger, earl of Hereford, granted to the priory between 1143 and 1154. It stipulated that there should be a convent of at least six monks at Brecon.[9] The evidence for the fourteenth, fifteenth, and early-sixteenth centuries suggests that the priory obeyed this charter almost to the letter.[10]

Although Ewenni Priory was founded for twelve monks and a prior, the number appears to have dropped below this by the time of Archbishop Pecham's visitation in 1284. In his injunctions he enjoined that the bishop of Llandaff 'make careful provision to bring up to standard and even increase the number of monks according to the ancient custom, if your goods are sufficient for an increase in the number of the servants of God'.[11]

---

[6] Abergavenny, Brecon, Chepstow, Ewenni, Goldcliff, Monmouth and Pembroke.

[7] Rose Graham, 'Four Alien Priories of Monmouthshire', *Jnl. Brit. Arch. Assoc.*, xxxv (1929), p. 112.

[8] *Brec. Cart.*, p. 137: *quod deficiunt eis quatuor monachi de debito numero.* I have assumed the *debitus numerus* to be twelve.

[9] Ibid., pp. 71–3.

[10] There were six monks in 1377 (Russell, *British Medieval Population*, p. 329), four monks and a prior in 1401 (*Episc. Reg. St. David's*, i, p. 235), five monks during a vacancy in 1435 (*Brec. Cart.*, p. 140), five monks when Warham visited the priory in 1504 (G. Williams, *Welsh Church*, p. 559), and five monks and the prior made acknowledgement of the king's supremacy in 1534 (*Deputy Keeper's Reports*, vii (1846) p. 281).

[11] *Registrum Epistolarum*, iii, pp. 799–800.

At Abergavenny Priory in 1319 there were only five monks, and a year later Adam de Orleton, bishop of Hereford, reported that 'usually five monks, sometimes four and sometimes six but rarely seven or eight were found in the past to be professed therein and many at the desire of their abbot were frequently recalled to their own monastery'. Here the annual income of the priory had been about 240 marks sterling for forty years or more, and, as Orleston pointed out, amply sufficient to maintain thirteen or more monks.[12]

Michael Hurtaut, a monk of St. Florent près Saumur, reported *circa* 1271 that 'in the priory of Monmouth we have twelve monks together with a prior'. In 1315, however, the priory was so impoverished that the abbot of St. Florent was doubtful about its ability to support a convent and was experiencing difficulty in finding a monk willing to take over the priorate.[13]

Unfortunately there is no evidence for the numbers of monks at Chepstow and Pembroke during this time. What is known of their income makes it unlikely that figures differed much from those recorded for Brecon and Abergavenny.[14]

The three Augustinian houses of south Wales were autonomous and, once their communities had been established, were forced to recruit the larger part of their canons locally or within a reasonable distance of the respective priory. There is little evidence, however, that their communities differed radically in their racial composition from those of Benedictine houses dependent on English abbeys. Llanthony Prima drew part of its original community, as we have seen, from the Augustinian houses of Merton, Holy Trinity, London, and St. Botolph's, Colchester. It is hardly likely that it would have made a general policy of recruiting canons from the native Welsh, for after the Welsh revolt of 1135, which disrupted the religious life at Llanthony, the priory appears to have harboured a traditional grudge against the Welsh. They were, writes a chronicler of the house at the beginning of the thirteenth century, 'savage, without any religion, vagabonds, and delighted

---

[12] *CPL.*, ii, pp. 186, 211; *Registrum Ade de Orleton*, pp. 151–2, 191.
[13] Paul Marchegay, *Les Prieurés Anglais de Saint-Florent près Saumur*, pp. 16, 23.
[14] The earliest figure I have discovered for Chepstow is for 1370, when there were only 4 monks including the prior (P.R.O., Clerical Subsidy, Bundle 33/1).

in stealth; they had no settled abode, but removed as wind and weather inclined them'.[15] The names of the priors and canons which have survived incidentally in the records of the twelfth and thirteenth centuries are all Anglo-Norman.[16] The canons appear to have been recruited from Anglo-Norman families in the Welsh March, from the border counties and occasionally even further afield. Llanthony Prima remained a predominantly Anglo-Norman house throughout the fourteenth century.

The racial composition of Carmarthen Priory's community appears to have fluctuated with the vicissitudes of royal power in the area. At the beginning of the thirteenth century, the priory came for a while under the control of the Welsh. How this infiltration of Welsh canons occurred is not known for certain but may, perhaps, be attributed to 'the removal of the strong hand' of Henry II and to the disorder which followed.[17] In 1208 Cadifor was prior and attempts were being made to oust him by a group of canons sent from Lanthony by Gloucester. King John made a temporary arrangement with the prior that he should hold his priory for a fine of ten marks and William de Londres was ordered not to molest him. The bishop of St. David's was 'to cause the said canons of Lantoni, Gloucester, to depart from the priory of Kaermerdin—until the king should send anew thereon and to maintain the said priory in his possession'.[18] The reassertion and growth of royal power in Carmarthen during the reign of Henry III put an end to Welsh influence in the priory. During vacancies, the canons had to ask the king for licence to elect and candidates for the priorate were scrutinized by the king himself. Thenceforward, the priory became predominantly Anglo-Norman in its personnel and sympathies. Robert de Kermerdin was elected prior in 1246, and Walter de Haverford in 1253; William de Wycomb was prior in 1276, John Edrich in 1281,

---

[15] Dugdale, vi, p. 128. The translation is from Robert Atkyns, *Ancient and Present State of Gloucestershire*, p. 263.

[16] For the names of priors, see E. W. Lovegrove, 'Llanthony Priory', *Arch. Camb.*, 1942–3, *passim* and p. 229. Names of canons occur occasionally in the chancery enrolments; see *CPR.*, *1272–81*, p. 49; *CPR.*, *1281–92*, pp. 118, 130, 379; *CPR.*, *1292–1301*, p. 141.

[17] Lloyd, *History of Wales*, ii, pp. 573 *seq.* It is interesting to note that most authorities attribute the transcription of the *Black Book of Carmarthen* to this 'Welsh' period. For a discussion of this question, see below p. 156.

[18] J. Conway Davies, *Episc. Acts*, i, p. 334, citing *Rot. Fin.*, *1199–1216*, p. 434.

John de Chaundos in 1324, and John Wynter in 1333.[19] The priors were frequently employed as royal agents in the second half of the thirteenth and first half of the fourteenth centuries. This increasing association of the priory with the growth of the royal power made it a legitimate target for attack by the Welsh in time of war. A poem written by one of the canons, Simon of Carmarthen, in the middle of the thirteenth century bears eloquent testimony to the milieu in which the canons worked and prayed.[20] Written in Old French, the language of the castle, it represents a far cry from the ancient Welsh verses which the Welsh canons were presumably transcribing into the *Black Book* a generation or so earlier.

There is hardly any evidence as to the number of canons in the Augustinian houses before the Black Death. It is only possible, therefore, to make approximate guesses based on what is known of the financial condition of the three houses. The meagre income enjoyed by Haverfordwest and Carmarthen in the thirteenth and early-fourteenth centuries, for example, makes it unlikely that their communities rose much above the conventual number of twelve canons. Llanthony Prima in its early days before the Welsh revolt of 1135 had a community of forty canons or more.[21] The dislocation caused by the moving of the community and the establishment of a new site near Gloucester must have reduced the community at Llanthony Prima to a mere handful. Some recovery can be detected, however, in the formal division of the property of the houses of Llanthony Prima and Secunda in 1213 and in the charters granted to the former house in the two decades before this date.[22] By the middle of the thirteenth century it seems possible that the priory had recovered sufficiently to support perhaps double the conventual number.[23]

---

[19] *CPR., 1232–47*, p. 492; *CCR., 1251–55*, pp. 369–70; *CCR., 1272–79*, p. 427; *CPR., 1272–81*, p. 437; *CPR., 1324–27*, p. 37; *CCR., 1333–37*, p. 21.

[20] The text is in E. Stengel, 'Handschriftliches aus Oxford', *Zeitschrift für französische Sprache und Litterâtur*, xiv (1892), pp. 141–51. For a discussion of this poem, see below pp. 152–3.

[21] G. Roberts, *Some Account of Llanthony Priory*, p. 54.

[22] *V.C.H. Glouc.*, ii, p. 88; E. W. Lovegrove, 'Llanthony Priory', *Arch. Camb.*, 1942–3, pp. 214–5.

[23] Pecham's very full injunctions for Llanthony Prima (*Registrum*, iii, pp. 800–5) do not refer to a deficiency of canons. Even after the trials of the fourteenth century the priory was still supporting 13 canons in 1377 (Russell, *British Medieval Population*, p. 329 note 28).

Before the advent of the Cistercians into the heart of Wales in the 'forties of the twelfth century, there were very few opportunities open to Welshmen who were attracted to the monastic vocation. Some Welshmen, favoured by birth or brilliance, could, it is true, find admittance to one of the larger abbeys along the border. Nicholas ap Gwrgant, a member of an important ecclesiastical family in Glamorgan, spent thirty years as a monk of Gloucester before his election as bishop of Llandaff in 1148.[24] A few Welshmen may have been recruited by the Tironian abbey of St. Dogmaels and the Savigniac abbey of Neath. Such men were among the favoured few. In an age when the monastic vocation fulfilled a real social need, there was for the vast majority of Welshmen no community where they could become postulants. The Benedictine houses and the new Augustinian foundation at Llanthony were closed to them. The collegiate bodies of *claswyr* in south Wales, where they had survived the impact of the Norman conquest, could offer little in the way of an ordered monastic life. Membership of such communities was in any case regulated by a rigid caste system dependent on family connection.

This lack of organized monastic institutions open to the native Welsh explains in large measure the initial success of the Cistercian order and the rapidity of its expansion from the abbey of Whitland in south-west Wales. Welshmen flocked in large numbers to the abbeys founded on Welsh soil. Apart from a genuine religious desire for monastic expansion, it seems probable that many new houses were founded to relieve pressure on an overcrowded mother house. Whitland, founded in 1140, sent out three colonies of monks to found three new abbeys within thirty years of its foundation, and a fifteenth-century report states (with perhaps some exaggeration) that the abbey at its foundation supported a hundred monks in addition to servants.[25] Leland says that Cwm-hir was founded for sixty monks,[26] and the large monastic church, projected at the end of the twelfth century but never completed, shows that

[24] *Hist. et Cart. Glouc.*, ii, pp. 173–4, and J. Conway Davies, *Episc. Acts*, ii, p. 655. For his connection with the Llancarfan family, see ibid., p. 521.
[25] *CPR., 1436–41*, p. 380.
[26] Leland, *Itinerary in Wales*, ed. L. T. Smith, p. 52.

the abbey administration was optimistic about the availability of recruits.[27] In 1226, when the abbots of Cwm-hir and Strata Marcella met to settle a dispute, they were accompanied by about fifty of the senior advisers of their respective houses, which seems to suggest that the communities of both houses were fairly large.[28]

The Cistercians who entered Wales were tied by no political attachments. It soon became apparent, however, that they could not remain uncommitted in the racial and political struggles that were going on around them. A patron could make or break a community and it was inevitable, therefore, that the politics of the patron should be reflected in the racial composition of the communities he patronized. Whitland in the first generation of its growth became a predominantly Welsh house, partly because of its location but mainly, as we have seen, because of the rise to power in south-west Wales of the Lord Rhys, who acquired the patronage of both Whitland and Strata Florida by force of arms. The incomplete *fasti* of the abbots of Whitland show a succession of Welshmen from Cynan, who died in 1176, to Llywelyn, who occurs in 1279. A similar succession of Welsh abbots is recorded for Strata Florida.[29] The very remoteness of abbeys such as Strata Florida and Cwm-hir ensured that their communities would be predominantly if not exclusively Welsh. Caerleon Abbey, though it acquired an Anglo-Norman patron in the thirteenth century and was situated in an area of Anglo-Norman influence, maintained its Welshness because of its affiliation to the abbey of Strata Florida, a potent factor which could often over-ride other considerations.

From what social classes did the abbeys of Welsh Wales recruit their monks? Direct evidence is scarce; but remembering the close alignment of these abbeys with the native Welsh princes in their struggle for independence, it seems reasonable to infer that a large number of the monks were younger sons of the leading Welsh families of both north and south Wales.[30]

---

[27] See the plan in *AMC. Radnor*, p. 6.
[28] *Arch. Camb.*, 1888, p. 210.
[29] D. H. Williams, 'Fasti Cistercienses Cambrenses', *BBCS.*, xxiv (1971), pp. 190–1.
[30] Thus Knowles, *Monastic Order*, p. 347.

Another substantial group was formed by sons of married priests. Cadwgan, successively abbot of Strata Florida and Whitland, who became bishop of Bangor in 1215, was, according to Gerald of Wales, the son of an Irish priest and a Welsh mother and had a brother who was a monk at the abbey of Caerleon.[31] Peter, one of Cadwgan's predecessors as abbot of Whitland, was also, according to Gerald, the son of a priest and had himself been a canon of St. David's before taking the Cistercian habit.[32] In the twelfth century the Welsh Cistercians differed little in this respect from their brethren in the north of England. Ailred of Rievaulx, perhaps the most celebrated of the English Cistercians, was himself the son of an hereditary priest of Hexham.[33]

Clerical marriage persisted in Wales throughout the middle ages and it was natural that some of the sons of the clergy should become monks. A number of papal dispensations issued a century after Gerald wrote shows that sons of priests still formed a substantial group in Cistercian communities in west and north Wales. In 1307 a dispensation was issued to 'Lewellin Abyenan' (rect. ab Ieuan?), a monk of Whitland, to enable him to be promoted to any administration of his order because he was the son of a priest. In the same year, David 'de Launyan', another Whitland monk, was given a dispensation to allow him to fill any office except abbot 'notwithstanding that he is the son of a priest'.[34]

While it seems unlikely that an Anglo-Norman postulant would seek admission or even be accepted in a monastery such as Strata Florida or Cwm-hir, or a Welsh postulant in the abbeys of Tintern or Grace Dieu, there were two Cistercian houses in the lordship of Glamorgan which, although under Anglo-Norman patronage, were open to the native Welsh to a limited extent. The abbeys of Neath and Margam were patronized by the earls of Gloucester in their capacity as lords of Glamorgan. But both abbeys were situated near the

---

[31] For the identification of the bishop pilloried by Gerald of Wales (*Opera*, iv, pp. 161–7) as Cadwgan, see Lloyd, ii, p. 688, note 201. Cadwgan claimed kinship with Llywelyn the Great. For a fuller account of his career, see below, pp. 122–3.

[32] *Autobiography of Giraldus Cambrensis*, ed. H. E. Butler, pp. 196, 214.

[33] Knowles, *Monastic Order*, p. 241.

[34] *CPL.*, ii, p. 29.

Welsh member lordship of Afan, whose lords remained a thorn in the side of the lords of Glamorgan at least until 1276, when Morgan Fychan married the daughter and heiress of Walter de Sully.[35] The maintenance of a large number of Anglo-Norman monks in both of those 'frontier' monasteries may have been a matter of policy for the lords of Glamorgan from the time of their foundation.

The fullest evidence available is for the house of Margam. Of the thirteen abbots whose names are known for the period 1147–1349, all but one appear to have been of French or Anglo-Norman stock. Conan (or Cynan), who was abbot before 1166 and probably as late as 1190, had a name which was fashionable among the Welsh during the twelfth century and it is just possible that he was a Welshman. The name was also popular with the Bretons. It is, therefore, equally possible that Conan was a descendant of one of the many Breton families which had established themselves along the border at the end of the eleventh century.

The names of about seventy Margam monks have survived as witnesses to charters and in documents between the years 1147 and 1270. Eight of the seventy came from Anglo-Norman boroughs in south Wales: two from Cardiff, two from Haverford, two from Kenfig, one from Carmarthen, and one from Swansea. Thirteen came from outside Wales: two from Bedington, four from Bristol, one from Lichfield, one from Dublin, one from Biu(?), one from Chipstaple, one from Selby, one from Kirkstead and one from Furness. Some of the monks belonged to notable Anglo-Norman families who held land in Glamorgan, among them William de Regni, John de la Mara, Robert Poynz, and Walter Luvel, while a few were members of undistinguished families in the neighbourhood of the abbey, like Herbert de Avene, Walter Bagelan and John of Newton. The remainder are known only by their Anglo-Norman Christian names and nothing is known of their background or provenance. What is significant is that not one of the monks whose names we know during this period bore an unmistakably Welsh name.[36]

[35] J. Beverley Smith, 'The Lordship of Glamorgan', *Morgannwg*, ii (1958), p. 34.
[36] F. G. Cowley and N. Lloyd, 'An Old Welsh *Englyn* in Harley Charter 75 C 38', *BBCS.*, xxv (1974), pp. 411–13.

Even though there was a limited movement of monks from one abbey to another for disciplinary purposes, the analysis shows that Margam recruited from a fairly wide area. The evidence shows, too, that the Margam community was a predominantly Anglo-Norman one during the period before the Black Death, with Anglo-Norman literary interests and Anglo-Norman political sympathies. Even so, some allowance must be made for the presence of Welsh monks in both Neath and Margam. Some Welsh monks undoubtedly shelter under Anglo-Norman Christian names, such as the Clement, prior of Neath, referred to by Gerald of Wales; Clement was the brother of the Welshman and scholar, Master Maurice of Llangeinor.[37]

In addition to choir monks, there were in Cistercian abbeys, at least before the middle of the fourteenth century, large bodies of lay-brothers. Figures available for English Cistercian houses show that in the hey-day of Cistercian farming they outnumbered the choir monks by two and sometimes three to one. The evidence for Wales is disappointingly meagre. The names of about forty lay-brothers are recorded as witnesses in Margam charters. Although only twelve have names that are unmistakably Welsh, it seems likely that Margam Abbey recruited the majority of its lay-brethren from the native Welsh. Some of the lay-brothers had been fairly substantial landowners who joined the order late in life as corrodists rather than active workers. Such were men like Geoffrey Sturmi, an Anglo-Norman who gave his name to the present-day Stormy Down and whose estate of 200 acres or so eventually passed to the abbey. Canaythen, a tribesman of Morgan ap Caradog who had been blinded while a political hostage, gave Resolven to the abbey before becoming a lay-brother there. Gille Seis granted the abbey twenty-four acres of land. The abbey received him into full fraternity and promised to accept him as a lay-brother whenever he wished, 'provided their order can receive me, that is, if I do not have a wife or am not burdened with excessive debt'.[38]

By the beginning of the fourteenth century, the Cistercian abbeys of Wales were finding it increasingly difficult either to attract or maintain the large communities they had formerly

[37] Gir. Camb., *Opera*, viii, p. 310. See also Clark, *Cartae*, ii, pp. 227, 246.
[38] Clark, *Cartae*, i, p. 114, ii, pp. 347–8, 410–11.

housed. Apart from the attraction exerted by the new orders of friars and by alternative careers in the canon and civil law, financial difficulties were forcing abbeys to set limits to the number of monks they recruited. After the Welsh wars it is unlikely that Whitland, Strata Florida and Cwm-hir were wealthy enough to support the large communities they once housed.[39] Even in the abbeys of south-east Wales which were not directly involved in the main conflict, the decline in numbers is marked. In 1317 the abbey of Caerleon had only twenty monks where a generation earlier there had been sixty.[40] In 1336 Margam Abbey was maintaining with difficulty thirty-eight monks and forty lay-brothers. It seems clear that the decline in numbers had begun well before the Black Death.[41]

Although the Cistercian abbeys doubtless recruited as choir monks and lay-brothers many who would otherwise have turned to the solitary life, the hermit still retained his traditional place in Welsh religious life, unaffected by the waxing and waning of organized institutions.[42] Records of their activities are rare and the prevalence of their way of life is attested by place names and tributes to the hermit ideal in Welsh poetry rather than by formal accounts of their work. The available evidence indicates that the hermits were a heterogeneous group of varied backgrounds and intellectual attainments. Some lived in groups like the hermit Helyas whom Walter Map describes. 'A man of eminent faith and approved life', writes Map, . . . 'He had with him his brother Walenfreit and a number of others, in the forest which is called Dean.' Others, like the anchorite of Newgale and Wechelen, the hermit of Llowes in Elfael (both friends of Gerald of Wales),

[39] J. C. Russell, *British Medieval Population*, gives 7 monks for Whitland in 1381 and 8 monks for Cwm-hir in 1377.
[40] P.R.O., Ancient Petition 8368, translated in Bradney, *History of Monmouth-shire*, vol. 3, part ii, pp. 224–5.
[41] Clark, *Cartae*, iv, p. 1199. This trend is also apparent in north Wales. Basingwerk had only 20 monks and an abbot in 1347 (J. G. Edwards, *Calendar of Ancient Correspondence Concerning Wales*, p. 185). The earliest record of numbers at Tintern occurs in the year 1395, when 14 monks and an abbot witnessed a document (British Museum, Additional Charter 7488); for this, see Edward Owen, *A Catalogue of the Manuscripts Relating to Wales in the British Museum*, part iii, p. 680.
[42] For the Welsh 'meudwy' and the 'gwr ystafellog' (chambered man) in the Welsh laws, see Lloyd, i, p. 203 note 37 and p. 218.

lived alone but had frequent contacts with visitors who valued them for their spiritual counsel and their powers of healing and prophecy. Wechelen was semi-literate, but seems to have been able to speak and write a sort of pigeon-Latin using undeclined nouns and only the infinitives of verbs. The recluse of Newgale was a priest and presumably had some formal education. The anonymous anchorite of Llanddewibrefi (*fl.* 1346) was a man of wide culture; he is known solely by his 'Book', a compendium in Welsh of religious and philosophical texts.[43]

This eremitical life was not confined to men. The inadequate provision of organized religious institutions for women in Wales has been noted on an earlier page. For most women intent on following a religious vocation, the solitary life provided the one means of fulfilling it. Women recluses were numerous enough in pre-Norman Wales to find mention in the Laws[44] and, like their counterparts in England, continued to exist throughout the middle ages. They were generally to be found in close proximity to churches great and small. Gerald of Wales refers to a nun attached to a church belonging to the priory of Great Malvern in the Brecon region,[45] and also to a nun named Ewedus whose days and nights were spent in prayer in the cathedral church of St. David's.[46]

In the later middle ages, when monastic fervour had cooled and a spirit of secularism had infiltrated even into the cloisters of the Cistercians, the hermit in Wales continued to uphold the ascetic ideal as practised by the Celtic monks of the sixth century. In Gower the real memory of St. Cenydd, the hermit, was kept alive not by the alien prior and his colleague at Llangenydd Church, where a reputed relic of his skull was kept, but on the off-shore island of Burry Holm, where a succession of hermits in the fourteenth and fifteenth centuries followed his way of life.[47]

[43] Walter Map, *De Nugis Curialium*, pp. 76–7; Gir. Camb., *Opera*, i, pp. 89–93, 175, 178–81; *Autobiography of Giraldus Cambrensis*, ed. H. E. Butler, pp. 123–7; I. Foster, 'The Book of the Anchorite', *Proc. Brit. Acad.*, xxxvi (1950), pp. 197–226.
[44] Lloyd, *History of Wales*, i, p. 218.
[45] Gir. Camb., *Opera*, iv, p. 102.
[46] Ibid., i, p. 157.
[47] Birch, *Descriptive Catalogue of Penrice and Margam MSS.*, 4th series, part ii, p. 714; *CPR., 1396–99*, p. 382; ibid., *1422–29*, p. 523; ibid., *1476–85*, p. 296. For the ecclesiastical settlement on the island excavated by Mr. Douglas Hague, see the references in F. G. Cowley, 'Llangenydd and its Priory', *Glamorgan Historian*, v (1968), pp. 220–27.

IV

THE MONASTIC ECONOMY

The Wales which Gerald described at the end of the twelfth century, though increasing in population and prosperity, was still a relatively undeveloped country whose riches lay mainly in its herds and flocks and in the products of river, woodland and forest. Since agriculture in the strict sense of the term played a subsidiary role in the economy, Wales was compelled throughout the middle ages to import large quantities of wheat from Ireland and from adjacent English counties. Salt, iron and cloth were also imported. In exchange Wales could offer dairy produce, wool, skins and hides.[1]

Despite a general poverty, the coastal lowlands and the river valleys of the interior were sufficiently fertile to attract, after the Anglo-Norman conquest of south Wales, colonists who were prepared to settle permanently on the land, cultivate it and, if need be, fight for it. Apart from the higher military aristocracy who held large estates in England and rarely visited Wales except to exploit or defend their lordships, the new colonists were a group of diverse origin but prompted by a common hunger for land and a livelihood. Some were younger sons of families already well established in the western counties of England who had followed their lords into south Wales. Others had come from as far afield as Normandy, Anjou, Maine, Brittany and Flanders.

A century of such colonization in south Wales had resulted in significant changes both in the landscape and in social conditions. The fertile lowlands were more intensively settled and a good deal more land came under the plough. At the more important centres, the primitive wooden castles of an earlier age had been, or were being, replaced by more elaborate stone structures. The small trading communities which

---

[1] For the medieval Welsh economy, see E. A. Lewis, 'The Development of Industry and Commerce in Wales during the Middle Ages', *TRHS.*, xvii (1903), pp. 121–73, and 'A Contribution to the Commercial History of Medieval Wales', *Cymmrodor*, xxiv (1913), pp. 86–188.

gathered around their walls, intended primarily to provide provisions for their garrison, were gradually acquiring the status of commercial centres in their own right.

The scale and rapidity of such changes should not be exaggerated. Since the total population of the two southern dioceses can hardly have exceeded 100,000 and may have been considerably less,[2] progress in exploiting the land and in developing commerce must have been slow. The Welsh boroughs were never large centres of commerce and trade, and their populations rarely numbered more than 1,000. Wales throughout the medieval period could never boast of a York, a Lincoln or a Bristol.[3]

Much the same was true of the monasteries established in south Wales. They, too, were moulded to a large extent by their environment. Not one could compare in economic or political influence with such abbeys as Fountains, Gloucester, Bury, Peterborough or Ely. When seen in their local setting, however, it seems clear that they exercised a profound influence on economic life. It is important at the outset to define the nature of this influence. At one time or another extravagant claims have been made for the monks as pioneers in almost every sphere of economic activity. Record evidence is seldom available for testing such claims. While it is true that Margam was granted rights to mine coal, lead and iron in the first half of the thirteenth century, and that Monmouth, Tintern and Grace Dieu shared to some extent in the iron industry of the forest of Dean, there is nothing to suggest that these activities contributed much in the way of profits to the houses concerned.[4] They may safely be relegated to a secondary place in any general account of the monastic economy of the south Wales houses and of the influence of these houses on the Welsh economy.[5]

---

[2] Gerald of Wales's estimate that payment of Peter's Pence by every Welsh household would yield an income of 200 marks or more (*Opera*, iii, p.55) would, using a multiplier of 5, give a total Welsh population of 160,000.

[3] Only Cardiff appears to have had a population of over 2,000 (Corbett, *Glamorgan*, pp. 162–3). Estimates for other Welsh boroughs are given in J. C. Russell, *British Medieval Population*, pp. 337–51.

[4] Clark, *Cartae*, ii, pp. 564, 592, 605; Dugdale, iv, p. 596; *C.Ch.R.*, iii, p. 88; *Taxatio*, p. 172.

[5] For monastic coal mines in south Wales at the Dissolution, see J. U. Nef, *Rise of the British Coal Industry*, ii, p. 439.

Generally speaking, the monasteries of all the orders established in south Wales, whatever their geographical location, reinforced the economic influences which emanated from the castles, the boroughs and the Anglo-Norman settlements. Their establishment created a demand for more sophisticated products which only an organized system of commerce could satisfy. Wine was needed in abundance not only for the guest house table but for the 'blessed mutter of the Mass' which was celebrated at numerous altars in conventual churches. Cloth of superior quality than was manufactured locally was needed for the liturgical vestments. There were also basic dietary needs common to all large households living in a predominantly pastoral society. Corn was often needed in greater quantities than could be produced on the monastic estates to satisfy the needs of concentrated communities of monks, lay-brothers, servants and guests. Salt, never plentiful in Wales, was also needed in large quantities as a flesh preservative when cattle were slaughtered for the winter.[6]

The monastic churches which were being erected in south Wales at the end of the twelfth and beginning of the thirteenth century were on a scale hitherto unseen in Wales and hardly rivalled since. Their building created local employment first for unskilled and semi-skilled labourers, but later in the thirteenth century for skilled masons of native origin.[7] Greater and more intensive use was made of local quarries. Margam and Ewenni appear to have made frequent use of the Sutton stone quarries in the region of Southerndown. Tintern Abbey was working quarries in the Wye valley, and Llanthony Prima obtained its freestone from outcrops which occurred in the surrounding hills. Other abbeys were less fortunately placed. Strata Florida was built mainly from slate rubble quarried locally; but according to a nineteenth-century tradition, the freestone was shipped from Somerset and thence transported across Tregaron marsh to the monastery site. Cwm-hir appears to have obtained its freestone from the Grinshill quarries near Shrewsbury.[8]

[6] For a ship belonging to the abbot of Margam loaded with salt purchased in Devon, see *CCR., 1227–31*, p. 203.

[7] E. W. Lovegrove, 'Valle Crucis', *Arch. Camb.*, 1936, pp. 8–11; 'Llanthony Priory', *Arch. Camb.*, 1946–7, p. 69.

[8] *C.Ch.R.*, iii, p. 103; Gir. Camb., *Opera*, vi, pp. 44–5; T. Jones Pierce, *Ceredigion*, i (1950), p. 30; S. W. Williams, *Strata Florida Abbey*, pp. 106–7; 'The Cistercian Abbey of Cwmhir, Radnorshire', *Trans. Cymm.*, 1894–5, pp. 92–3.

Perhaps the most important effect of monastic settlement was that it resulted in a more intensive exploitation of the soil. Even at the end of the thirteenth century, when some monasteries were finding it expedient to lease or let lands at farm, monastic landowners in south Wales still had well over 40,000 acres under the plough. The Cistercians especially were eager to accept, purchase or obtain on lease marginal lands which required constant supervision. Such, for example, were the low-lying coastal lands which Margam possessed at the river mouths of the Afan and Ely,[9] Tintern on the Caldicot level,[10] and Neath adjoining the Loughor estuary.[11] These lands were drained, embanked against the sea, and cultivated. It should be added that this was no 'pious exercise of the energetic monks'. They were not committed to any programme of social improvement. For many of the monasteries, as for the humblest of peasants, the choice was unequivocal: 'plough or perish, dig or die'.

While the general influences exerted by the monasteries of all orders on the native economy were similar, there were marked variations in the endowments enjoyed by individual houses. There were, too, significant differences in the type of endowment enjoyed by houses of different orders and in the methods by which they were exploited. A clearer idea of these differences in size and methods of exploitation may be gained by treating the economies of the main orders represented in south Wales separately.

I. THE BENEDICTINE ECONOMY

All sixteen of the Benedictine priories which took root in south Wales after the conquest were situated in the more fertile lowland which had been settled by the Anglo-Normans. Only eight of them attained the status of conventual priories: Chepstow, Monmouth, Abergavenny, Pembroke, Brecon, Goldcliff, Ewenni, and the nunnery of Usk. In the generation or so after their foundation these houses were granted a variety

---

[9] These lands were exploited from the granges of Melis and More. The latter is now the Cardiff suburb of Grangetown. For drainage works at Meles, see Clark, *Cartae*, ii, pp. 255–6, 590–91.

[10] For Tintern's drainage works at More grange, see *C.Ch.R., 1300–1326*, p. 104.

[11] F. V. Emery, 'Cwrt-y-Carne Grange', *South Wales Evening Post*, 16 Nov. 1956.

of income and sources of income: lands, rents, tithes, villeins, burgesses, mills, fisheries, forges and churches. The early charters addressed to them, couched in the specialized terminology of a society in which personal and corporate income was often an ill-defined amalgam of services and payments in kind, provide no clear picture of the monastic economy. It seems probable that many of the earliest endowments were merely makeshift measures, designed to provide a temporary maintenance for the monks while their buildings were being completed. It is not until the thirteenth century, when the mist clears a little, that one is able to see more clearly the pattern of the estates of the Benedictine houses and evaluate the main sources of their income. By this date, some of the earlier endowments had been lost or alienated. It seems probable, too, that many of the earlier grants of tithes of produce and food rents had been commuted into money payments.

In comparison with the extensive grange lands of the Cistercians, the landed estates of the Benedictine houses in south Wales were small.[12] The arable estates of all but one of the houses for which figures are available were less than 500 acres in extent. Monmouth Priory had 480 acres of arable land, Abergavenny 240 acres, and Chepstow 201 acres of arable, 28½ acres of meadow and 82 acres of waste and pasture. Two of the Benedictine cells had lands which equalled these in extent. Llangua, a cell of the Norman abbey of Lire, had 480 acres of arable land and Cardigan Priory, a cell of Chertsey Abbey, 240 acres. Much smaller in extent was the arable held by cells like Llangenydd (120 acres) and St. Clears (12 acres) and the nunnery of Usk (24 acres). For the Benedictine houses in south Wales, the extent of Goldcliff's estate was exceptional. It had 1,221 acres of arable and 125 acres of meadow on its estates in south-east Wales alone. In Somerset the priory possessed the manors of Membury, Preston and Monksilver,

---

[12] The acreages given below and in the tables in Appendix II are to be treated solely as approximations. They are based on figures given in the *Taxatio* of 1291, where the extent of land is frequently reckoned in carucates. There were wide variations in the size of the carucate even in south Wales. For comparative purposes I have assumed a stable carucate of 120 acres, as does J. S. Donnelly, 'Changes in the Grange Economy of English and Welsh Cistercian Abbeys', *Traditio*, x (1954), pp. 399–458. Cf. also W. Rees, *South Wales and the March*, p. 280.

the size of which is unrecorded. In the early-fourteenth century they were worth at least £50 per annum.[13]

Despite their limited size, the Benedictine estates were situated on richer soils than those of the Cistercians. They were also fully developed estates in the sense that they contained free and unfree tenants who owed rents and services, ground their corn at the priory mills, and owed suit at the prior's courts. Leaving aside the profits from demesne farming which cannot be determined in the absence of account rolls, the Benedictine priories were therefore the recipients of a substantial and fairly predictable fixed income. In 1291 assised rents, together with curial income, formed a major item in the temporal income of all Benedictine houses. At Goldcliff Priory assised rents amounted to £23 13s. 8d., and pleas, perquisites, fines, and market tolls to £13 6s. 8d. At Monmouth assised rents came to £14 6s. 8d. and curial revenue to 10s. At Abergavenny assised rents were valued at £7 2s. 2½d. and curial income at 13s. 4d. Even the very much poorer house of Chepstow drew £7 7s. 2d. from assised rents and 6s. 8d. from its courts.

Not all the income from assised rents came from tenants on the land. Many of the Benedictine priories were borough communities occupying major churches and sheltering beneath the walls of important castles. Around these castles, small boroughs were already coming into existence at the end of the eleventh century. It was natural, therefore, that the priories should acquire interests in borough property. Wihenoc and William fitz Baderon granted to Monmouth Priory 'seven burgesses in their market',[14] and Bernard Neufmarché similarly granted to Brecon Priory five burgesses in his castlewick.[15] At this period the grant of a person means little more than the grant of a person's services, free or unfree. In these grants lay the origin of the borough rents and jurisdictional rights enjoyed by most Benedictine priories in south Wales throughout the middle ages. Even the smaller priories drew income from this source. In 1291 the prior of Llangua was drawing £1 from assised rents in Abergavenny.[16] In 1305 the prior of

[13] CCR., 1337–39, p. 175.
[14] P. Marchegay, Les Prieurés Anglais de Saint-Florent Près Saumur, p. 26.
[15] Similar grants were being made by his son; see Brec. Cart., p. 69.
[16] Taxatio, p. 282.

St. Clears received 32s. annually from 32 burgages in the adjoining borough and 5s. from 12 'chensarii'.[17] By this time most of the conventual priories had attracted to themselves quasi-urban settlements of their own.[18]

With these manorial and burghal types of revenue should also be classed the revenues in cash and kind derived from the mills which the Benedictine priories had acquired. Brecon Priory had a number of valuable mills on the Honddu and Usk rivers. When these were burned in the Welsh wars the prior denuded his wood of Monkton in order to repair them. 'It was necessary', he claimed, 'to cut from their own timber in order that the mills, on which the greater part of their sustenance depends, should not lie idle.'[19] Goldcliff Priory had eight mills on its south Wales estates, Monmouth Priory three, and Abergavenny two. Even the smallest cells could usually boast of one mill.[20]

Livestock played a comparatively minor role in the economy of the Benedictine priories of south Wales and in most cases appears to have been reared to fulfil domestic requirements alone. Figures are available for only four houses, but they may be taken as representative of houses of similar size. Goldcliff, the richest house, heads the list with 120 sheep, 64 cows and 4 mares on its estates in the diocese of Llandaff. Monmouth Priory had a flock of 40 sheep and a herd of 7 cows. The small cells of Kidwelly and Llangenydd had only 5 and 6 cows respectively.[21] In the second half of the thirteenth century Brecon had a small flock of sheep, from whose milk the convent was accustomed to make two cheeses a day, and a sufficiency of horses and oxen to make small gifts to the patron and benefactors of the priory and to the abbot of Battle.[22] But it seems fairly clear that the Benedictine houses did not engage in sheep farming on a large scale as the Cistercians did and that the profits from livestock formed but a small item of total income.

[17] P.R.O., E.106/4/19. This income had almost doubled by 1377; see P.R.O., E.106/11/1, and British Museum, Add. MS.6164, pages 352-3 (pencil pagination).
[18] Hence the occasional adoption of the place name Monkton, as at Pembroke and Brecon. The layout of these settlements can best be seen in the pictorial town maps of Speed.
[19] Brec. Cart., p. 138.
[20] Taxatio, pp. 281b, 171b, 283, 282 (Llangua), 276b (Llangenydd).
[21] Ibid., pp. 284, 174b, 276b.
[22] Brec. Cart., p. 139.

Of equal, and occasionally of greater, importance than manorial and burghal revenue, was the spiritual income enjoyed by the Benedictine priories. Churches had formed part of the original endowments of all the Benedictine priories. Initially the income to be derived from them was not large. The religious merely appointed the parson and drew a pension from him as a token of the priory's patronage and *dominium* over the church. At the end of the twelfth and beginning of the thirteenth centuries, however, it became customary for religious houses to obtain episcopal licence to appropriate churches within their gift. It then became possible for the religious as rectors to draw the rectorial tithes. These usually accounted for about two-thirds of a church's revenue. By the latter part of the thirteenth century spiritual income probably formed the largest single item of income enjoyed by the Benedictine houses, whatever their size. Monmouth Priory was rector of four churches in Hereford diocese (Monmouth, Dixton, Goodrich Castle, and Llanrothal), three churches in Worcester diocese (Taddington, Stretton Asperton and Long-hope) and three churches in Llandaff diocese (Rockfield, Wonastow and Llangatwg Feibion Afel), besides drawing portions from eight other churches.[23] In 1291 this spiritual income was assessed at £62 19s. 2d., nearly three times the assessed figure of the priory's temporalities. Goldcliff Priory was rector of six churches, three in the diocese of Llandaff (Goldcliff, Christchurch and Peterston) and three in the diocese of Bath and Wells (Puriton, Woolverton and Nether Stowey), spiritualities which were extented at £72 16s. 0d., nearly half the figure for the house's total assessment. Appropriated churches within the diocese of St. David's are not noted with any consistency in the 1291 valuation. Brecon Priory, however, is known to have held five churches in the diocese whose values are noted in the valuation: Brecon (£20), Hay (£14), Llanigon (£10), Talgarth (£18) and Llan-gors (£8). The priory was also rector of Bodenham church in Hereford diocese (£13 6s. 8d.) and was drawing portions from the churches of Humber (£1), Brinsop (£1 13s. 4d.) and Hopton Wafers (6s. 8d.).[24] The total assessment of Brecon's

[23] *Taxatio, passim;* cf. also *Registrum Edmundi Lacy,* pp. 75–6.
[24] All the figures for individual churches are from the *Taxatio.*

spiritual income amounted to £86 6s. 8d., over twice the amount of its assessment for temporalities (£36 3s. 4d.) An even greater dependence on spiritual income is shown by a detailed extent of Pembroke Priory's property made in 1378. The priory held three appropriated churches (Castlemartin, St. Nicholas, Monkton and St. Michaels, Pembroke) and drew pensions and portions from seventeen other churches. Spiritual income accounted for just over 75 per cent of the priory's total income.[25]

The income of the conventual houses of south Wales was not centrally administered by a single officer like the Cistercian cellarer. The four main departmental offices of cellarer, chamberlain, sacristan, and almoner found in every Benedictine abbey were reproduced in their conventual dependencies, even when, as frequently occurred, the number of monks had fallen below the conventual number of twelve. In the second half of the thirteenth century, there were at Brecon, besides the prior, five administrative officers out of a total of only eight monks: a sub-prior, a cellarer, a chamberlain, a sacrist and an almoner.[26] To these officers was allocated specific income from manors and churches to enable them to fulfil their functions. It would be out of place here to trace the origin and growth of the obedientiary system.[27] It will suffice to note that the system owed much of its continuing strength to the donations which benefactors made to religious houses for specific purposes. Thus, at the beginning of the thirteenth century Alice de Putangle gave six acres of land to Brecon Priory 'for the maintenance of the poor'.[28] At about the same time, Mahel le Brec granted a rent of 12d. to Brecon for maintaining the lights of the church.[29] At the end of the century, Joan, countess of Pembroke, granted to Pembroke Priory, in return for an obit, a quitclaim of rent and other services from which food was to be distributed to thirteen poor people.[30] Land and income which accrued from such special donations were allocated to the relevant obedientiaries

[25] Dugdale, iv, p. 321.
[26] Brec. Cart., pp. 18, 138, 140.
[27] For the main offices and the obedientiary system generally, see Knowles, Monastic Order, pp. 427–39.
[28] Brec. Cart., p. 27.
[29] Ibid., pp. 44–5.
[30] CPR., 1330–34, pp. 67–8.

—in the cases quoted, to the almoner and sacristan. For the smaller houses, at least, the obedientiary system resulted in a fragmentation of income which made long-term planning and co-ordination difficult, if not impossible. Pecham was fully aware of this when he ordered the setting up of central treasuries of receipt in the houses of Ewenni, Goldcliff and Usk, into which all moneys were to be paid. 'By no other means', he wrote, 'can one accurately estimate the value of the goods of the house, and by this means is the door to theft, private ownership and sacrilege closed to everyone.'[31]

As far as external administration was concerned, the Benedictine estates were run in much the same way as lay estates. At the end of the twelfth century, and for the greater part of the thirteenth, it generally profited a landowner to take an active administrative part in the farming of the manorial demesne and to exploit it directly through a bailiff. This was a period of high farming when grain was being produced not merely for consumption within the manor but also for cash sale in neighbouring markets. At the beginning of the thirteenth century Brecon Priory was increasing its demesne in Welsh Talgarth by assarting land.[32] Even in the second half of the century the priory was directly exploiting through a bailiff its glebe and demesne land in Bodenham and Berrington.[33] Though evidence for other Welsh houses is not forthcoming, it would seem that the practice of direct exploitation was fairly general on the estates of other priories, at least during the first half of the thirteenth century. Much would depend, however, on the location of the monastic estates. Leasing and letting land at farm were not uncommon practices during the twelfth and thirteenth centuries and it would be wrong to regard them as peculiar to the later middle ages. In 1221 the priory of Cardiff was let to farm for an indefinite term and its monks returned to Tewkesbury Abbey. In 1233, when a prior had apparently returned to administer the property, the priory weir on the Taff was leased out for five years.[34] Spiritual

[31] *Registrum Epistolarum*, iii, pp. 798–800, 805–6.
[32] *Brec. Cart.*, p. 26.
[33] Ibid., pp. 134–5. The same record also mentions one Dodinus who kept a grange for the priory (probably Battle Grange) and rendered his accounts to the prior—another indication of direct exploitation.
[34] W. Rees, 'The Priory of Cardiff and Other Possessions of the Abbey of Tewkesbury in Glamorgan', *S. Wales and Mon. Rec. Soc.*, ii (1950), p. 150.

income was also being farmed at this period, although the practice was contrary to canon law. Between 1230 and 1240 the abbot of Glastonbury granted the endowments of his priory cell of Basaleg (the greater part of which consisted of spiritual income) to Elias, bishop of Llandaff, 'to hold by a perpetual farm of thirty five marks'.[35] Tewkesbury Abbey's Glamorgan churches of Kenfig and St. Leonard's, Newcastle, were being farmed by Margam Abbey.[36] These were acts of expediency rather than desperation, however. In the second half of the thirteenth century and the beginning of the fourteenth century leasing and letting of lands at farm assume a deeper significance.[37]

The sole representatives of the Tironian order in Wales, the abbey of St. Dogmaels, and its two dependencies of Pill and Caldy, deserve a brief separate treatment because they owed their origin to a reformed monastery which had close affinities with Cîteaux. Much of the landed endowment of St. Dogmaels had been built up during the lifetime of its founder, Robert fitz Martin who died *circa* 1159.[38] It consisted of a fairly large block of territory in the northern extremity of the lordship of Cemais and a smaller compact holding, later known as Mynachlog-ddu, on the south-eastern fringe of the lordship.[39] Outside the lordship of Cemais, Robert had also granted to the abbey his Devonshire manor of Rattery, and his mother gave the island of Caldy.[40] In the thirteenth century, the only major addition to the landed estate was made by William of Cantinton, who granted the abbey all his land at Fishguard.[41] At the end of the thirteenth century St. Dogmaels had upwards of 720 acres of arable land on its Pembrokeshire estates.[42]

Pill's lands lay in small scattered groups in the rich cantref of Rhos and the greater part of them was acquired during the thirteenth century. The acreage figures given in the two main

[35] *Episc. Acts*, ii, p. 719.
[36] Clark, *Cartae*, ii, pp. 277-8, 673-7.
[37] See below Chapter IX.
[38] *Complete Peerage*, viii, p. 531.
[39] Pritchard, *St. Dogmaels Abbey*, pp. 46-7.
[40] Ibid., p. 47.
[41] Ibid., pp. 50-52. The grant appears to have been made when Nicholas fitz Martin held the lordship, that is, between *c.* 1231 and 1282 (*Complete Peerage*, viii, pp. 533-5), not shortly after 1138, as Pritchard infers.
[42] *Taxatio*, p. 276.

charters which survive in an *inspeximus* show that the priory estate was well over 1,300 acres in extent; but how much was held in demesne, rented or otherwise alienated cannot be determined.[43] Unfortunately, no acreage figures are available for Pill in the 1291 valuation. Its temporalities were assessed at £21 4s. 10d.; the temporalities of St. Dogmaels at £52 11s. 4d.[44] As we have already seen,[45] Caldy remained a cell, at least from the beginning of the thirteenth century, and for the purposes of the 1291 assessment the carucate of land attached to the monastic church there was included in the valuation for St. Dogmaels.

Neither St. Dogmaels nor Pill had been loath to accept gifts of churches. Not long after its foundation St. Dogmaels had been granted the church of *Tregent* (East Brent?), *Wadtre* (Rattery?) and the chapel of Cockington in Devonshire.[46] During the episcopate of Bernard, the abbey had acquired 'all the land of Llys Prawst with the church'.[47] The founder of Pill had also granted the priory all the churches of his land.[48] Though both houses derived an important income from churches at the Dissolution, in the absence of episcopal deeds of appropriation, it is impossible to determine how soon they acquired the rectorial tithes of the churches granted to them.

Despite the affinities of the early Tironian order with that of the Cistercians, there is little to suggest that the economy of St. Dogmaels and its dependencies differed much from that of the Benedictine houses of south Wales.[49] The abbey lands on Mynydd Presely and the example of the Flemings of Rhos may have prompted St. Dogmaels to take a greater interest than the Benedictines in stock rearing, but no figures for livestock are available. As regards the lay-brethren mentioned in connection with St. Dogmaels in a record of a visitation of the abbey in 1402, it is worth remembering that 'lay brothers

[43] Dugdale, iv, pp. 502–5; Pritchard, op. cit., pp. 126–9. The acreage figures, where they are given in the *Valor* of 1535, also indicate an estate of over 1,000 acres.

[44] *Taxatio*, pp. 277b, 153b, 276.

[45] See above p. 20.

[46] Pritchard, *St. Dogmaels Abbey*, p. 40.

[47] *Episc. Acts*, i, p. 268.

[48] Pritchard, op. cit., p. 126.

[49] Pill, at least, had come within the jurisdiction of the black monk chapters by the fifteenth century; see *Chapters of the English Black Monks*, ed. W. A. Pantin, p. 358.

were not an original part of the economy' of the Tironian order.[50] The context in which they are mentioned indicates that they were either late vocations who did not intend to proceed to the priesthood or were recruited to alleviate the labour shortages caused by the fourteenth-century pestilences.[51]

II. THE ECONOMY OF THE REGULAR CANONS

At the Dissolution of the monasteries the evidence available for the regular canons of Wales presents a fairly uniform picture of houses with only small demesne farms, very heavily dependent for their livelihood on spiritual income and considerably less on rents in cash and kind.[52] The evidence for the twelfth and thirteenth centuries, meagre as it is, presents a less uniform pattern and shows for a number of houses a more diversified economy and for at least one house a more evenly balanced ratio of spiritual and temporal income.

The Augustinian houses of Carmarthen and Haverford were urban communities in so far as such a term can be used of the *rus in urbe* atmosphere which prevailed at these centres. Carmarthen since its foundation had been in possession of the 'Old Town' over whose burgesses it exercised a jurisdiction separate from that exercised by the royal officers in the New Town.[53] By the thirteenth century the priory had become an important burgage owner in both the old and the new settlements.[54] Haverford occupied a subsidiary suburban settlement about half a mile south of the main town at *Parva Haverford*. The landed property of both houses was less scattered than that of the Benedictine priories or of the Cistercians. Though little is known of the pattern of Haverford's estates in the cantref of Rhos,[55] all of Carmarthen's possessions were situated in the eastern commotes of Cantref Gwarthaf. The priory possessed

---

[50] Knowles, *Monastic Order*, p. 201.

[51] *Episc. Reg. St. David's*, i, pp. 248–9. For the role of the non-Cistercian *conversi*, see Knowles, pp. 419–20, 439, 719–20.

[52] One estimate puts the ratio of spiritual to temporal income enjoyed by the Welsh regular canons as a whole at four to one; see Glanmor Williams, *Welsh Church*, p. 348. A typical example is Carmarthen, for which see G. D. Owen, 'The Extent and Distribution of the Lands of St. John's at Carmarthen', *Carmarthen Antiquary*, i (1941), p. 21.

[53] *Carm. Cart.*, pp. 57–9.

[54] Ibid., pp. 1–4.

[55] Apart from a charter of the founder printed in Dugdale, vi, pp. 444–5, little survives to throw light on the priory's history during the thirteenth century.

four carucates of land at Newchurch (Eglwys Newydd),[56] two carucates at *Cwmoernant*(?),[57] one carucate in Manorgayn or Llangain (Eglwys Keyn)[58] and one carucate at Pentowyn (Pentewi).[59] In all, the arable land amounted to about 960 acres.[60]

In contrast to Carmarthen and Haverford, Llanthony and Talley occupied sites which were typically Cistercian. In the twelfth and thirteenth centuries Llanthony Prima was an oasis in a wild and barren valley. Its well laid-out gardens, orchards and well-stocked fishponds contrasted sharply with the heavily forested and rugged valley which was its setting.[61] Within the bounds of the valley and throughout its lands in Ewyas the canons enjoyed a far-reaching jurisdiction over their men which extended to capital offences affecting life and limb.[62] The bulk of Llanthony's landed wealth, however, lay beyond the Hatterall Hills in the diocese of Hereford, where at the end of the thirteenth century the priory held three demesne farms, four mills, and a very valuable weir and fishery.[63] The extent of the priory's arable demesne amounted to 1,080 acres. Llanthony's Herefordshire property consisted of fully manorialized units. The priory utilized the labour services of its tenantry, held courts, and drew appreciable sums from assised rents.[64] Llanthony's affinities with Cîteaux are therefore more apparent than real.

Not so Talley; it belonged to the order of Prémontré which 'was strictly organized from the start on Cistercian lines'.[65] It was situated, writes Gerald of Wales, 'in a rough and sterile

---

[56] *Carm. Cart.*, p. 10.

[57] I have assumed this to be the *Kennur, Kennuy, Comua* or *Kommev* mentioned in the charters printed in *Carm. Cart.*, pp. 8–9. Cf. *Episc. Acts*, i, p. 267.

[58] *Carm. Cart.*, p. 10; *Episc. Acts*, i, p. 281.

[59] *Carm. Cart.*, p. 10.

[60] The extent of the lands given in Henry II's confirmation charters (*Episc. Acts*, i, pp. 283, 290) agrees exactly with the figures given in the 1291 *Taxatio*, p. 277.

[61] See the interesting details given in a letter to William of Wycombe, printed by C. H. Talbot, 'William of Wycumbe, Fourth Prior of Llanthony', *Trans. Brist. and Glouc. Arch. Soc.*, lxxvi (1957), pp. 62–9. Remains of the fishponds and columbarium still survive; see C. J. O. Evans, *Monmouthshire*, p. 361.

[62] G. Roberts, *Some Account of Llanthony Priory*, pp. 75–6.

[63] *Taxatio*, p. 170.

[64] The priory drew £15 13s. 10d. in assised rents from its Herefordshire lands alone. This figure may be compared with the figures for assised rents on Cistercian estates in south-east Wales; see below pp. 239–41.

[65] Knowles, *Monastic Order*, p. 205.

spot, surrounded by woods on every side and beyond measure inaccessible and sufficiently meanly endowed'.[66] In the first half of the thirteenth century the abbey acquired vast tracts of mountain land together with a number of estates of very much smaller extent along the river valleys of the Teifi and Towy and as far afield as Abergavenny. These lands were exploited from granges in the Cistercian manner and presumably worked by lay-brethren and hired labourers during the first half of the thirteenth century. In 1291, however, Talley's arable lands were small in extent even when one makes allowances for lands leased and let to farm. There were two carucates at the granges of Maenor Frwnws and *Dolhenwel*, and one carucate apiece at the granges of Traethnelgan and Brechfa.[67]

On general grounds, it would seem likely that the regular canons took a greater interest in livestock farming than did the conventual Benedictine priories. Haverford held all her lands in the cantref of Rhos, where a strong Flemish colony was well-versed in sheep farming. Talley held extensive highland pastures ideal for sheep and providing rough grazing for cattle.[68] The hills around Llanthony, as its chronicler noted, contained 'very fruitful pastures . . . and rich meadows for feeding cattle which did compensate for the barrenness of other parts, and made amends for the want of corn'.[69] Carmarthen held rich pastures in the lordship of Llanstephan.[70] In spite of this, no figures for livestock appear in the 1291 valuation for Talley, Haverford or the Welsh lands of Llanthony. It is perhaps significant that the impoverished house of Carmarthen had 180 sheep, more than Goldcliff, the richest of the Benedictine houses.[71] Llanthony had 50 yearling sheep on its Herefordshire estates.[72] A few incidental records of the last

[66] E. Owen, 'A Contribution to the History of the Premonstratensian Abbey of Talley', *Arch. Camb.*, 1893, p. 122.
[67] Ibid., pp. 39–46; M. Richards, 'The Carmarthenshire Possessions of Tallyllychau', *Carmarthenshire Studies*, pp. 110–21; *Taxatio*, pp. 216b, 277, 283.
[68] See the charter of William de Breos granting land to Talley between Crickhowell and Abergavenny. He confirmed also their 'pasture of Telari for the needs of the animals of their brethren who reside in the aforesaid land of Gwent', *Arch. Camb.*, 1893, p. 44.
[69] G. Roberts, *Some Account of Llanthony Priory*, p. 48.
[70] *Carm. Cart.*, p. 10.
[71] *Taxatio*, p. 277.
[72] Ibid., p. 173b.

quarter of the thirteenth century show that the priory was engaged in livestock farming on a more ambitious scale nearer home. In the lordship of Ewyas, the priory had cattle, oxen, a stud for horse breeding and was also producing wool for the market. [73]

The importance of spiritual income in the economy of the regular canons varied from house to house. By the middle of the thirteenth century Llanthony had acquired in Ireland the rectorial tithes of 14 churches in addition to a valuable portion (20 marks) in a church. [74] By the beginning of the fourteenth century these were valued at £71. [75] The priory was even richer in churches in the diocese of Hereford, where it held the rectorial tithes of nine churches and portions in four others. In the 1291 valuation these churches were valued at over £96. [76] No monastic house in Wales could compare with Llanthony in the richness of its spiritual income. About three-quarters of its total was derived from this source. [77] Owing to omissions in the valuation of 1291, no statistically valid evidence can be deduced for the houses of Haverford and Talley. The former house had been granted the churches of St. Thomas, St. Mary and St. Martin, Haverford, by its founder, [78] and these churches had certainly been appropriated by the middle of the thirteenth century. However, only one of these churches—St. Martin's— is mentioned in the 1291 valuation. [79] By 1271 Talley had obtained interests in at least nine churches and sixteen chapels in the diocese of St. David's; but one should be on one's guard against regarding all these as appropriated to the abbey. [80] Rhys Fychan in his charter was careful to confirm these churches *in proprios usus quantum ad Dominium fundi pertinebat*. The qualifying phrase is significant, for later evidence

---

[73] *Cal. Inq. Misc.*, i, pp. 337–8; Roberts, *Llanthony Priory*, pp. 76–7; *CPR.*, *1272–81*, p. 350; *CPR.*, *1292–1301*, pp. 465–6.

[74] *Irish Cartularies of Llanthony Prima and Secunda*, ed. Eric St. John Brooks, *passim*.

[75] Ibid., p. 146. This valuation is not dated but was probably made in response to a papal mandate issued in 1326; see *CPL.*, ii (1305–42), p. 255.

[76] *Registrum Edmundi Lacy*, p. 73. This is merely a convenient transcript of the 1291 valuation for Hereford diocese arranged under religious houses.

[77] If one includes the rather late, conservative estimate of Llanthony's Irish property at £4 6s. 8d. (*Irish Cartularies*, p. 146), Llanthony's total temporalities were valued at £64 5s. 4d.

[78] Dugdale, vi, pp. 444–5.

[79] *Taxatio*, p. 275a (valued at £10).

[80] E. Owen, *Arch. Camb.*, 1893, p. 42.

would suggest that the abbey enjoyed in some cases only the advowson and in others merely a portion in the church.[81] Llandeilo Fawr and Llanegwad Fawr were certainly appropriated before 1239.[82]

More evidence is available for Carmarthen. In the thirteenth century Carmarthen was meagrely endowed with spiritual income. Of the fourteen churches and chapels appropriated to the priory at the Dissolution,[83] only four had been appropriated before 1289 and only two of these churches are mentioned in the 1291 valuation: the church of St. Peter's, Carmarthen, valued at £9 6s. 8d., and Newchurch, valued at £6 13s. 4d.[84] The process whereby Carmarthen acquired the rectorial tithes of numerous churches throughout the archdeaconry of Carmarthen was a slow one and had barely begun before the end of the thirteenth century.[85]

III. THE CISTERCIAN ECONOMY

(i) Endowment and Expansion

Before colonies of Cistercian monks had entered *pura Wallia*, the Cistercian fathers had given careful thought as to how monks of their order should earn their livelihood, and as early as 1134 had embodied their ideals in a series of *Instituta* to which theoretically every Cistercian abbey owed obedience.[86] Although the high ideals of the early fathers were never wholly realized even during the twelfth century, this first code of Cistercian law and custom, added to, modified and revised by successive General Chapters, gave to all Cistercian abbeys founded before 1200, an economy which was markedly different from that which obtained on the estates of the Benedictine abbeys and priories.

The main emphasis of the Cistercian economic legislation was on poverty, simplicity and seclusion from the world.

---

[81] See below, p. 171.
[82] E. Owen, *Arch. Camb.*, 1893, pp. 227–8. According to the 1291 valuation, the canons also held portions in the churches of Llangoedmor and Blaenannerch, *Taxatio*, p. 272.
[83] *Valor*, iv, p. 409.
[84] The figures have been arrived at by eliminating from the list of churches in the *Valor* those churches which the *Cartularium* shows were appropriated after 1289.
[85] See Chapter IX, pp. 264–5.
[86] Canivez, *Statuta*, i, pp. 12–33.

Abbeys were to be built in places remote from human settlement, where the monks were to procure their sustenance by the
labour of their own hands in the cultivation of land and the
rearing of flocks. The new abbeys were allowed to exploit
rivers, vineyards, woods, meadows and arable land, but
'unearned income' from rents, milling rights and labour
services was to be abjured. So, too, was spiritual income in the
form of churches, tithes, offerings, altar and burial dues. For
the exploitation of their legitimate resources, granges were to
be established no further than a day's journey from the abbey
and were to be worked by the monks, by lay-brethren and
hired labourers. In the place of the numerous receivers and
dispensers of moneys employed as obedientiaries by the
Benedictine abbeys, the Cistercians substituted a cellarer under
whose individual and centralized control all the material
resources of a Cistercian abbey were to be grouped.

The French Cistercian monks who entered south Wales
and the indigenous monks who replaced them were fully
acquainted with this legislation,[87] and throughout the twelfth
and thirteenth centuries were kept informed of rescissions,
revisions and additions through the attendance of their abbots
at the annual General Chapter. When they entered south
Wales much of the best land had already been settled.
Population had begun to increase and this had led to an
increasing pressure on the land. Even in some well-favoured
areas, such as Glamorgan, land was coming under the plough
for the first time.[88] Partly from choice and partly from
necessity, therefore, the Cistercians settled on land less fertile
and less amenable to immediate exploitation than that enjoyed
by Benedictine foundations such as Brecon, Goldcliff, or
Monmouth.

Many of the lands with which they were initially endowed
would have been considered marginal by twelfth-century
feudal lords and native princes and could be disposed of with
no undue sacrifice of their material resources. The initial

[87] The monks of Strata Florida possessed a *Liber Usuum* which they consulted
when Gerald of Wales tried to pawn his books there in 1202; see *Autobiography of
Giraldus Cambrensis*, ed. H. E. Butler, pp. 250–1.
[88] The present-day Stormy is a typical example. A letter of about the year
1170 describes how years before, Geoffrey Sturmi had built a chapel 'in his vill
which he made in a solitude and on land where no one had ever ploughed before'
(Clark, *Cartae*, i, p. 151).

endowments fall into two main categories. Firstly, there were lands which had probably been exploited as intensively as the native economy would allow before the Cistercian abbeys had been established. Secondly, there were the lands which had either never been previously exploited or had been exploited in the past and gone out of cultivation and reverted to scrub by the twelfth century. In the absence of a Domesday for south Wales, it is obviously impossible to pronounce with any certainty; but into the first category may be placed the initial endowments of Tintern, Margam, Caerleon, Grace Dieu and, perhaps, Whitland. Tintern obtained an endowment which had probably been intensively exploited before its foundation. The founder had granted the abbey *inter alia* the 'hay' or enclosure of Porthcaseg just south of the site of the abbey.[89] Porthcaseg had belonged to the church of Llandaff and being deprived of it was probably one of the many grievances which its bishop, Urban, had against the future founder of Tintern, Walter fitz Richard.[90] Margam's original endowment consisted of 'all the land between the Kenfig and Afan rivers from the brow of the mountains to the sea'.[91] The site was not a rich one, for the slow process of erosion had already begun along the coastal boundary and accumulations of blown sand were being formed in front of the mud flats.[92] Despite this, the heavy concentration of Celtic crosses found in the vicinity of the abbey would suggest that Margam had been the site of an important *clas* church.[93] There are also indications of settlement on the lower slopes of the hills.[94] Caerleon Abbey had been settled by its founder in an area whose tithes had been granted to Glastonbury Abbey and it seems certain that, however marginal the land, the site was not on virgin soil.[95] The abbey of Grace Dieu was originally built on a site from which the Welsh had been ousted.[96]

---

[89] *C.Ch.R.*, iii (1300–1326), p. 88.
[90] *Book of Llan Dâv*, ed. J. G. Evans, pp. 37–8, 93–4, 150.
[91] Clark, *Cartae*, iv, pp. 1219–20.
[92] Leonard S. Higgins, 'An Investigation into the Problem of the Sand Dune Areas of South Wales', *Arch. Camb.*, 1933, pp. 26–7.
[93] V. E. Nash-Williams, *Early Christian Monuments*, pp. 146–54.
[94] See below pp. 79–80.
[95] Dugdale, iv, p. 633.
[96] J. F. O'Sullivan, *Cistercian Settlements*, p. 33.

Into the second category of initial endowments may be placed those of the abbeys of Neath, Strata Florida, and Cwm-hir. The endowment of Neath, a Savigniac abbey until 1147, consisted of 'all the waste which lies between the waters of the Neath, Tawe, Clydach and Pwllcynan'.[97] The buildings of Strata Florida were eventually erected on virgin ground and much of the original endowment consisted of moorland and mountain waste.[98] Cwm-hir was the most remote of all the Welsh Cistercian houses and was described at the beginning of the thirteenth century as situated 'in a mountainous district remote from parish churches'.[99]

The limited nature and extent of the original endowments made the expansion of the Cistercian estates inevitable. Professor E. G. Bowen has shown how Strata Florida's need for low-lying land suitable for grain production and the wintering of sheep determined the abbey's expansion into coastal areas such as Anhuniog, Morfa Mawr and Morfa Bychan, into the Vale of Aeron and the Severn and Wye valleys.[100] A similar trend can be detected in the pattern of estates of other abbeys. Thus, Cwm-hir acquired two parcels of land from Einion Clud and Einion de Port on the upper Wye.[101] Two granges were established there on which the abbey was heavily dependent for its grain supplies. In 1231 Henry III ordered the constable of Hay 'to allow the monks and lay-brethren of Cwm-hir who are staying at their granges of Gubalva and Caernaf to reap and gather in their corn and purchase victuals and necessities without any difficulty'.[102]

The quest of the Cistercian abbeys for lands in the richer lowlands was motivated not merely by a desire to achieve a balanced and integrated economy. Already by the last quarter of the twelfth century, the acquisition of more land was regarded as the only solution to the problems presented by a rapidly growing monastic population and a mounting hospitality bill. By 1190 the expansion of the Cistercian estates had developed into a veritable scramble for land which earned

[97] Birch, *Neath Abbey*, pp. 309–10.
[98] T. Jones Pierce, 'Strata Florida Abbey', *Ceredigion*, i, 1950, p. 28.
[99] *CPL.*, i (1198–1304), p. 131.
[100] E. G. Bowen, 'The Monastic Economy of the Cistercians of Strata Florida', *Ceredigion*, i (1950), pp. 34–7.
[101] W. J. Rees, 'Account of Cwmhir Abbey', *Arch. Camb.*, 1849, p. 257.
[102] *CCR., 1227–31*, p. 547.

for the Cistercians in Wales as elsewhere in western Europe a reputation as 'land-grabbers' and bad neighbours. So widespread was the criticism that the Cistercian General Chapter devoted attention to the problem in 1190. In one of its statutes of that year, it attributed the acquisitiveness of abbots partly to the large volume of recruits which the Cistercian abbeys were attracting. A year or so later, Gerald of Wales, who appears to have been familiar with the legislation of 1190, was perceptive enough to realise that

> this avidity does not proceed from any bad intention. For the monks of this order (though themselves most abstemious) incessantly exercise, more than any others, the acts of charity and beneficence towards the poor and strangers; and because they do not live as others upon fixed incomes, but depend only on their labour and forethought for subsistence, they are anxious to obtain lands, farms and pastures which may enable them to perform these acts of hospitality.[103]

A ban which the General Chapter placed on the purchase of lands and on the reception of new monks and lay-brethren in 1190 seems to have had little effect in curbing the expansion of the Cistercian estates in Wales. The years 1190 to 1215 were to provide both Gerald of Wales and Walter Map with a fund of anecdote and gossip with which they were able to belabour the white monks of Wales and the marches.

Whitland, as we have seen, had already sent out three colonies of monks to relieve the pressure of numbers before the end of the twelfth century.[104] The last of these colonies was established at Cwm-hir in 1176. By the last decade of the twelfth century it would seem that the pressure of numbers and inadequate resources for their maintenance had again landed Whitland in difficulties. Between 1193 and 1202, Peter, a newly-appointed and comparatively young abbot, made a desperate and foolhardy bid to shore up the tottering finances of his house by attempting to convert the recently-founded Premonstratensian abbey of Talley into a Cistercian house.[105] First, he succeeded in winning over the abbot and

---

[103] Canivez, *Statuta*, i, p. 118; Gir. Camb., *Opera*, vi, p. 43. The translation is taken from *Historical Works of Giraldus Cambrensis*, ed. Thomas Wright, p. 361.

[104] See above p. 26.

[105] D. Knowles, 'Some Enemies of Gerald of Wales', *Studia Monastica*, i (1959), pp. 139–40. That the abbey was in financial difficulties at this time appears from

a number of the canons of the house. They were received at Whitland and clothed with the Cistercian habit. He then used all his powers of persuasion to procure the consent of the patron, 'the principal man of the province'. The recalcitrant canons who remained were driven out by an armed band of laymen, and the monks of Whitland took possession. While the new colony from Whitland were chanting their *Salve Regina*, however, the dispossessed canons were already on their way to Canterbury to lay their case before Archbishop Hubert Walter. Peter's plan had misfired. The case went to the Roman *curia* and after lengthy proceedings Talley was restored to the canons. Whitland, however, succeeded in retaining from the spoils the rich grange of Rhuddlan Teifi, 'situated in a fertile and wheat-growing land, with numerous and well-furnished ploughs, and enriched with numberless sheep and cattle in broad pastures'.[106]

Very few abbeys in south Wales escaped attacks on their business morality during this period. Neath Abbey was accused by Walter Map of altering a charter to convert a grant of sixteen acres into one of a hundred acres.[107] The same writer also relates how the monks of Tintern hanged a man at Woolaston (*Wlanstune*) and buried him in the sand; 'the poor wretch had stolen in after their apples, and found eternal rest at the hands of the brethren'.[108] Gerald of Wales attacked Strata Florida for forcing him to sell his books and for its encroachment on the lands of the poor nunnery of Llanllŷr, and devoted a whole chapter of his *Speculum Ecclesiae* to the acquisitiveness of Margam during the abbacy of Gilbert (1203–13)[109]

Both writers had suffered at the hands of the Cistercians, and it seems likely that they exaggerated their grievances and the

---

a chance remark of Gerald that Peter had 'brought his own house to ruin and destruction'; see *Autobiography*, p. 328.

[106] Gir. Camb., *Opera*, iv, pp. 143–5. The translation is from E. Owen, 'A Contribution to the History of the Premonstratensian Abbey of Talley', *Arch. Camb.*, 1893, pp. 123–4.

[107] Walter Map, *De Nugis Curialium*, p. 56.

[108] Ibid. The abbey, unnamed by Map, can be identified from the name of the property. The lordship of Woolaston (*Wllavestune*) was granted to Tintern abbey in the twelfth century but the jurisdictional rights did not include justice of life and limb; see *C.Ch.R., 1300–1326*, pp. 97–98.

[109] Gir. Camb., *Opera*, iv, pp. 129–43; see also below, pp. 123–5.

stories they had heard of Cistercian avarice.[110] When every allowance has been made for partiality and exaggeration, however, it seems clear that Gerald and Map were the mouthpieces of a widespread public opinion; that they were voicing the grievances of a great number of clerics, knights and small freeholders whose livelihood had been affected by Cistercian expansion. They were writing, moreover, at a period when this expansion was almost reaching its limits on a number of abbey estates and when the social implications of Cistercian settlement, the destruction of churches and the removal of tenantry were being fully realized for the first time.

The build-up of the Cistercian estates in south Wales was not a uniform process. Though the pattern of some estates, like that of Margam and Strata Florida, had been firmly drawn by about 1230, other abbeys were making important additions to their estates and were making major alterations in their pattern well after that date. The records available for Neath provide an illuminating illustration of how an abbey, founded in 1130 and still comparatively poor about 1200,[111] managed to become one of the richest abbeys in Wales by the end of the century. Within about sixty years of its foundation, Neath had built up an extensive but widely-scattered estate in Devon and Somerset, and within the lordships of Gower and Glamorgan. The abbey held land at Paviland and Loughor within the lordship of Gower; at Sker, Newton Nottage, Corneli, St. Mary Hill (Gelligarn), and Monknash within the lordship of Glamorgan. In Somerset the abbey had holdings in the former Domesday vill of Exford, at Watchet and at Hornblotton. The abbey estate appears at this time to have been composed of comparatively small units which were too scattered for efficient exploitation, and it seems clear that the abbey administration was at a loss to decide in which areas it should attempt to expand and consolidate its estates. A monk of Neath has recorded that the Gower estates were held to be of little value at this time because, with the change of lords, the area was so frequently laid waste by the Welsh.[112]

---

[110] On this, see the classic chapter in Knowles, *Monastic Order*, pp. 662–78.

[111] Gerald of Wales speaks of Neath Abbey *c.* 1203 as *pauperior*, *Opera*, iv, p. 130.

[112] F. R. Lewis, 'A History of the Lordship of Gower from the Missing Cartulary of Neath Abbey', *BBCS.*, ix (1938), p. 153.

On this score even the site of the abbey must have given the
monks cause for alarm. It occupied an exposed and vulnerable
bridgehead on the west bank of the Neath river between the
lordships of Gower and Glamorgan. The castle of Neath lay
across the river, hardly near enough to afford protection in a
period of unrest such as occurred in the Neath area between
1183–85.[113] Nor did expansion of her estates south-eastwards
offer more promising prospects. Expansion in this direction
would appear to have been blocked by the rich abbey of
Margam. It is small wonder, therefore, that in the 'nineties of
the twelfth century careful thought was given to a plan for
transferring Neath Abbey to the site of its grange of Exford in
Somerset.[114] Here was a promising centre for further expansion
and exploitation. In this part of west Somerset there was no
religious house of any size apart from Ford, which lay to the
south. Neath could lay almost exclusive claim to the patronage
of local landowners in the area. In 1197, however, the abbot of
Revesby took to the General Chapter plans for founding a
daughter house in west Somerset.[115] Despite the protests of the
abbeys of Neath and Ford that such a foundation would be to
their injury, an abbey was founded in 1198 at Cleeve, hardly
more than ten miles from Neath's grange of Exford.[116] There
can be little doubt that the new foundation called a halt to
Neath Abbey's plans for expansion in the area and resulted in
a more concentrated preoccupation with the abbey's estates
nearer home in the lordships of Gower and Glamorgan.

Between 1200 and 1250 the abbey obtained possession of the
fee of Walterston in the lordship of Gower in exchange for its
holding at Hornblotton in Somerset.[117] At the same time the
abbey was extending and consolidating its granges at Monknash and St. Mary Hill, Gelligarn, with lands in Marcross
and lands in the lordship of Ogmore, and was also acquiring
lands in the Welsh lordship of Afan.[118] Neath's expansion into

[113] J. B. Smith, 'The Lordship of Glamorgan', *Morgannwg*, ii (1958), p. 24.
[114] Canivez, *Statuta*, i, pp. 235–6.
[115] Ibid., p. 217.
[116] Knowles and Hadcock, *Medieval Religious Houses, England and Wales* (2nd ed.
1971), pp. 112, 117.
[117] Clark, *Cartae*, ii, 570–72. The date of the deed is doubtful but would seem
to be before 1243, when William de Barry brought a writ of warranty of charter
against the abbot of Neath over lands in Hornblotton; see *Somerset Pleas*, ed.
Charles E. H. Chadwyck-Healey, p. 171.
[118] Clark, *Cartae*, i, pp. 221–2, ii, pp. 315–17, 353, 425.

the latter region triggered off a series of bitterly-fought disputes with the neighbouring abbey of Margam which continued well into the second half of the thirteenth century.[119] The abbey of Neath emerged from these struggles a far richer and better endowed house than it had been at the turn of the previous century.

One important feature of Cistercian estate building deserves to be noted before passing to the question of how their estates were exploited. The expansion of the Cistercian estates coincided with a period when population was increasing and land was at a premium. The lavish and gratuitous benefactions of a former age were long since past. To expand their estates, therefore, the Cistercians had on many occasions to resort either to outright purchases of land for considerable sums or to the more general practice of obtaining land on indefinite lease for a fixed annual payment to the donor or lessor. Grace Dieu, the last Cistercian house founded on Welsh soil, purchased Penyard Regis from the king for the large sum of £120.[120] Neath Abbey paid King John a hundred marks and a palfrey for holding the castlewick which had belonged to Richard de Granville and the land which the latter had held between the rivers Neath and Tawe.[121] More prevalent was the practice of obtaining land on indefinite lease for an annual rent. At the beginning of the thirteenth century Margam Abbey held the greater part of its lands in the Vale and Border Vale by paying annual rents and performing the services attached to such lands. The latter were usually commuted for a money payment. On the Margam estate these annual rents individually never exceeded £2 and were occasionally as low as 3s.[122] Cumulatively, however, the rents due annually for the whole estate must have formed an important item of overhead costs.[123] During the thirteenth and fourteenth centuries most of the rents and services attaching to these lands were quitclaimed by the heirs of the donors and their superior lords. At the

---

[119] F. G. Cowley, 'Neath versus Margam: Some 13th Century Disputes', *Trans. Port Talbot Hist. Soc.*, i, no. 3 (1967), pp. 7–14.

[120] *Pipe Roll, 14 Henry III* (Pipe Roll Society, 1927), p. 218.

[121] Birch, *Neath Abbey*, p. 57.

[122] Clark, *Cartae*, i, pp. 109–10, ii, pp. 269–70, 295–6, 451, 502–3, 572–3.

[123] For some examples on the Tintern estate, see *C.Ch.R., 1300–1326*, pp. 99–100, 103, and for Neath, Birch, *Neath Abbey*, pp. 51, 55–6, 66.

Dissolution they formed only a minor item of Cistercian expenditure.[124]

(ii) *The Grange Economy*

The main unit of exploitation on the Cistercian estates was not the manor, centred around a village with its hall, its church and cluster of peasant cottages, but the grange, a group of buildings which included a granary, stalls and pens for live-stock, living quarters for the lay-brethren and hired labourers, and in some cases a chapel. At the end of the thirteenth century Whitland had seventeen such granges, Strata Florida twenty-three, Margam thirteen, Caerleon thirteen, Tintern eight and Grace Dieu eight.[125] The size of these granges varied from those containing only half a carucate of arable to those with large blocks of arable covering from eight to ten carucates. On average, the granges within the diocese of St. David's had less arable land than those in the diocese of Llandaff. Thus, Whitland's largest arable granges, those of *Oysterlowe*, Hen-llyswen and *Tregrik*, contained only fourteen carucates of arable, an average of four and a half carucates for each grange, whereas most abbeys in the diocese of Llandaff could boast of at least one grange of five carucates. Two abbeys, Margam and Neath, had granges with eight and ten carucates of arable.[126]

A number of these grange sites can still be seen, although the buildings are in many cases completely ruinous. Perhaps the most impressive are the remains of Neath's grange at Monknash near Llanilltud Fawr, where in the thirteenth century ten carucates of land were under the plough. The substantial remains of the vast granary over 200 feet long, the dovecot, and the desolate gable walls of other farm buildings, all confined within a large, embanked enclosure, provide testimony more vivid than the written records of Cistercian farming at its height.[127] Less impressive, but forming the centres of estates almost as large, are the remains of Margam's granges at Stormy and Llangewydd.

---

[124] Glanmor Williams, *Welsh Church*, p. 371. For surviving quit-rents on Welsh Cistercian estates at the Dissolution, see *Valor*, iv, pp. 351, 361, 370, 408.
[125] *Taxatio, passim.*
[126] Ibid., pp. 282, 283b, 284.
[127] Monknash is the *grangia de Asse* mentioned in *Taxatio*, p. 282.

The establishment of the Cistercian grange often resulted in the destruction of earlier settlements and a displacement of population. King John was well aware of this when he confirmed to Neath Abbey the land which Richard de Granville held between the rivers Tawe and Neath. Two saving clauses were added to protect existing tenants in the area:

> saving the tenements of our burgesses of Neath, in such a way that the aforesaid monks may not remove them without judgement but only have their homage and rent. Saving also the tenements of our Welshmen of the aforesaid land, in such a way that the said monks may not remove them without judgement but only have their homage and rent and that we may have the service which they owe us.[128]

On the estates of Margam Abbey a substantial displacement of tenantry took place which can be traced in the scores of deeds and quitclaims which have survived for the late-twelfth and early-thirteenth centuries. When the abbey was founded, the area of the original endowment contained a number of scattered settlements, most of which lay along the river valleys and the lower slopes of the hills. Within a generation of the foundation the abbey had embarked on a policy of clearing the tenantry from the lands within the area of the original endowment. A few examples will serve to illustrate the process. One Herbert, son of Godwinet held land at *Raneth* which can safely be identified as the land near the Arnallt brook, about a mile north of the abbey. Herbert held the land of the abbey for a nominal rent of *2d* per acre annually. His tenancy was only temporary, however, and could be revoked at the pleasure of the abbot. About 1151 the holding was made over to the abbot by Herbert's sons in a deed of surrender so rigid that it precluded any future tenancy:

> Moreover be it known that we have abjured the said land in such a way that never hereafter shall anyone of us or of our kin, hold that land, either from the king, the earl or any lord, French, English or Welsh.[129]

Leuuar, son of Meruit also held land in the vicinity of *Raneth* on terms similar to those enjoyed by Herbert. He held land between the Arnallt brook and the River Ffrwdwyllt and also land to the west of that river. Both tenements were held of

[128] Clark, *Cartae*, ii, p. 309.
[129] Ibid., i, pp. 128–9.

the abbey for a rent of 2*d*. per acre and it was understood that the tenancy was only a temporary one. Probably about the time of the preceding deed, Leuuar surrendered the whole land to the abbey on the same rigid terms as those accepted by the sons of Herbert.[130]

Along the slopes of Mynydd Embroch there are indications of similar temporary tenancies which were either created or confirmed when the abbey was established. Walter, son of Cunnor and his stepson Ifor held land between the Afan river and Embroch and other lands within the abbey bounds. They paid the usual 2*d*. per acre and it was again understood that the tenancy was for a term only. In the second half of the twelfth century they made over the land to the abbey in the usual deed of surrender. The careful wording of the deed gives some weight to the suspicion that the land was not relinquished without some misgivings.

> With good peace and of our own free will we have abjured the land for ever on the altar and relics . . . We have sworn that if anyone, at any time, whether they be of our own kin or of another, presume to claim the land, we shall guarantee the abbey's right whenever it shall be necessary. Be it known also that my wife . . . with her other children have peacefully and freely consented to what we have done.[131]

From these and numerous other deeds,[132] it seems clear that the abbey was clearing the land of tenantry as a preparation for direct and exclusive exploitation by their own lay-brethren and paid servants.

Margam pursued a similar policy on its estates further east in the more thickly populated Vale and Border Vale. In the second half of the twelfth century the abbey acquired from the Scurlage family and their dependants a substantial holding in the knight's fee of Llangewydd.[133] In 1202 the abbey came to an agreement with the holder of the fee, David Scurlage, by which it acquired the remainder of the fee on lease for an annual rent of three marks.[134] The fee possessed a castle and, according to Gerald of Wales, the monks razed this to the ground arguing that a knight's fee without a castle would be

[130] Ibid., pp. 122–3.
[131] Ibid., ii, pp. 417–8.
[132] Ibid., i, pp. 183, 202–3, ii, pp. 233–4, 238–9, 300–1, 581, vi, pp. 2293–4.
[133] Ibid., i, pp. 131–2, ii, pp. 420–1, 431, 436.
[134] Ibid., ii, pp. 269–70.

of less value to a knight, and they might therefore hope to obtain the fee on better terms. The action of the monks caused considerable misgivings in feudal circles and Gerald records that the knight took his case to the secular courts, but without success. One of the objections offered seems to have been that David Scurlage was not of age when he made his agreements with Margam in 1202 and that they were, therefore, void. Margam, however, was able to obtain a number of testimonials certifying that David was of age and that the agreements he had made with the abbey were reasonable. At about the same time as the destruction of the castle, the monks destroyed the church of the fee and expelled the parishioners from their houses.[135]

In the absence of specific evidence for other Welsh houses, it would be unwise to generalize for the whole of Wales. There is enough general evidence, however, to suggest that a similar displacement of tenantry and destruction of settlements were also taking place on the estates of the abbeys of Welsh Wales. Gerald of Wales writes that:

> All the monasteries of Wales are commonly involved in one and the same vice . . . for they are wont to occupy the parishes of mother and baptismal churches and either, in large measure, diminish their extent or obtain complete control over them, expelling the parishioners and leaving the churches empty and deserted or even razing and destroying them completely.[136]

Gerald's testimony is corroborated over sixty years later by a letter which Pecham wrote to Edward I explaining why he had not consecrated the new Cistercian abbey church of Maenan. There was a considerable number of persons, he wrote, who 'have a very great horror of the approach of the aforesaid monks . . . For where they plant their foot, they destroy towns, take away tithes and curtail by their privileges all the power of the prelacy'.[137]

(iii) *Arable Husbandry*

At the end of the thirteenth century when one is able for the first time to obtain some idea of the extent of the Cistercian

---

[135] F. G. Cowley, 'Llangewydd: an Unrecorded Glamorgan Castle', *Arch. Camb.*, 1967, pp. 204–6.
[136] Gir. Camb., *Opera*, iv, p. 177.
[137] See below p. 180.

estates in south Wales, one is immediately impressed by the size of their arable holdings. Margam *circa* 1291 was actively farming nearly 7,000 acres, Neath and Whitland over 5,000 acres, Llantarnam over 4,000 acres, and Tintern well over 3,200 acres. Even the notoriously poor houses of Grace Dieu and Llanllŷr had 1,800 and 1,200 acres respectively under the plough. These figures take no account of the vast tracts of moorland waste and pasture rights of common enjoyed by most of the Cistercian houses.[138] As could be expected from a highland zone, the average size of arable estate of the seven houses cited falls short of the average size of 5,000 acres which has been estimated for Cistercian estates in western Europe as a whole.[139] The discrepancy is not a wide one and is considerably narrowed if the two poor houses are excluded.

The arable holdings of the Cistercian houses in south Wales were sufficiently extensive to supply during normal times grain for the needs of their convents of monks and lay-brethren and for their hired labourers, and in good years, perhaps, to provide a surplus for sale in local markets. As far as grain production was concerned, however, medieval Wales, despite the legendary claims of Anglesey as 'Mam Cymru' (Mother of Wales), was never self-sufficient. The vagaries of weather and an indifferent soil resulted in frequent crop failures which caused distress on a wide scale.[140] Such was the plight of west Glamorgan in 1189 when a local famine, probably caused by a long period of heavy rain, brought crowds of the poor flocking to the gates of Margam Abbey for relief. A ship was despatched to Bristol to buy corn to feed them.[141] In 1234, another year of general scarcity, the abbot of Neath obtained licence to 'buy corn in England for the maintenance of himself and his brethren and his own household and to take it to his house at Neath in Wales'.[142] Freak weather in the years 1257 and 1258 was possibly one of the reasons responsible

---

[138] These figures are based on the carucates recorded in the *Taxatio;* see Appendix II.

[139] L. J. Lekai, *The White Monks*, pp. 222–3.

[140] The Welsh of Welsh Wales, like the Dutch, appear to have been inured to grain shortages. Their diet, drawn mainly from milk, butter, cheese and meat, included 'no great quantity of bread'; Lloyd, *History of Wales*, ii, p. 605.

[141] Gir. Camb., *Opera*, vi, p. 68. For the date, see C. Creighton, *History of Epidemics in Britain.*, i, p. 35.

[142] *CPR., 1232–47*, p. 69.

for the dispersal of the convent of Strata Florida at this period.[143]

Given the limiting factors of climate and terrain, grain production could not be expected to provide the Cistercians of Wales with a profitable substitute for the large and fairly predictable incomes which the Benedictines and regular canons derived from rents and tithes. To finance the ambitious building programmes to which the Welsh Cistercians were committed at the end of the twelfth century and the beginning of the thirteenth, to maintain their well-earned reputation for hospitality and to meet the costs of estate expansion, a steady and substantial flow of ready money was essential. Well before the end of the twelfth century, they had found an answer to their problem by applying themselves to the traditional economy of the land in which they had settled, the rearing of livestock.

(iv) *Livestock*

Livestock formed the mainstay of the Welsh Cistercian economy throughout the period with which we are dealing (1140–1349). At the beginning of the thirteenth century Gerald of Wales records that Strata Florida 'was in process of time enriched far more abundantly with oxen, studs of horses, herds of cattle and flocks of sheep, and the riches they produced, than all the houses of the same order throughout Wales'.[144] By this time most houses were well endowed with livestock. The Annals of Margam record that in 1223 'perverse men' had burned more than a thousand of the abbey's sheep, together with two of its grange buildings. A year later Morgan ab Owain burned one of Neath Abbey's houses with more than four hundred sheep. In 1227 the Welsh again raided three of Margam's granges, destroying oxen, burning sheep, and leading away the cows.[145] The abbeys of Neath and Margam, like Strata Florida, possessed studs where horses were bred, fetching high prices in a society where such animals were essential for war and vital for travel.[146]

---

[143] Canivez, *Statuta*, ii, p. 444; G. Fleming, *Animal Plagues*, p. 78. The effects of the weather were intensified by Llywelyn's campaigns at this time.
[144] Gir. Camb., *Opera*, iv, p. 152.
[145] *Annales Monastici*, i, pp. 34–6.
[146] Gir. Camb., *Opera*, iv, p. 130.

Well into the thirteenth century most abbeys were using their livestock and the by-products of their livestock as a substitute for ready cash to discharge their obligations and pay their debts. Between 1154 and 1189 Margam Abbey, in order to obtain the lease of some dower land belonging to Gunnilda, wife of Geoffrey Sturmi, gave her four marks, lambskins for making a leather garment and twenty sheep. The same abbey gave Ithenard, son of Richard a cow to obtain a quitclaim from him of land in Llangeinor. About 1230 Neath Abbey acquired the lease of thirty acres between Cefn Bryn and Parc le Breos for an annual payment of 24 lambskins.[147] Even as late as 1255 Strata Florida bought a great bell for the abbey church, paying twenty-seven marks, five shillings and two cows.[148]

Livestock, apart from their value as a medium of barter and as producers of milk, butter, cheese and meat, also provided two raw materials of great value: hides and wool. Both were needed to fulfil domestic needs. Hides formed the raw material for leather which was needed for the shoes of the monks and lay-brethren and for the harness of horses and oxen used on the monastic farms. It seems likely, therefore, that most Cistercian abbeys in south Wales had their own tanneries, although only Tintern and Margam are recorded as possessing them in 1291.[149] Wool was also used domestically for making the characteristic white habit worn by Cistercian monks. A number of the south Wales abbeys had fulling mills to process their cloth. Margam had two fulling mills, one at Llanfeuthin and another at Llanfihangel.[150] Grace Dieu had a fulling mill near Monmouth which had been let out to farm by 1291,[151] and Tintern one at *Triket*.[152] Fulling mills are not mentioned in the compressed accounts of the 1291 valuation which are available for the Cistercian houses of the diocese of St. David's. This silence should not, however, be interpreted to

---

[147] Clark, *Cartae*, i, p. 140, ii, pp. 373, 466.
[148] *Brut y Tywysogyon, Peniarth 20*, ed. Thomas Jones, p. 110.
[149] *Taxatio*, pp. 282b, 284.
[150] Ibid., p. 284.
[151] *Taxatio*, p. 172a. There is a record of a dispute over revenues from fulling mills between Grace Dieu and Monmouth Priory in P.R.O., Ancient Deeds E.40, A.14282.
[152] *Taxatio*, p. 282b.

mean that these abbeys did not possess them.[153] The presence
of fulling mills on the abbey estates, as Dr. R. A. Donkin
remarks, provides 'all but absolute proof of weaving'.[154]
Yet there is little to suggest that the Cistercian abbeys were at
any period important centres of cloth manufacture, still less
that the 'monk artisans . . . improved the native art of
weaving',[155] although by their adoption of the fulling mill
they may well have stimulated the growth of the industry in
south Wales. Dr. Donkin has concluded that tanning, like
fulling, 'appears to have been tied to internal needs alone'.[156]

In the twelfth century cattle may well have been as important as sheep on the Cistercian estates. Their grazing
requirements were less demanding than those of sheep and
they were more suited to scrub and coarse, wet herbage,
conditions which prevailed over a large part of Wales. They
could be used for haulage and ploughing and were also
producers of rawhide.[157] Hides formed one of Wales's staple
exports during the middle ages and it seems difficult to believe
that the Cistercian abbeys did not share in the trade. There is,
however, throughout the whole period under discussion only
one reference, as far as is known, to the Cistercians being
engaged in the hide trade. In 1205 a lay-brother of Neath was
ordered to present himself at Cîteaux for punishment because
he cancelled the sale of hides to a lay-brother of Quincy Abbey
and unjustly sold them to another person in order that he
might obtain a higher price.[158]

Whatever had been the position in the twelfth century, it
seems clear that by the first half of the thirteenth century the
Cistercian abbeys of south Wales derived the greater part of
their livestock income from the sale of graded wool. By 1200
most houses seem to have had a surplus available for export.
In 1212 the abbey of Strata Florida obtained a royal licence

[153] For Whitland's three fulling mills at the Dissolution, see Glanmor Williams,
Welsh Church, p. 365.
[154] R. A. Donkin, 'The Disposal of Cistercian Wool in England and Wales
during the Twelfth and Thirteenth Centuries', *Cîteaux in de Nederlanden*, viii
(1957), p. 112.
[155] E. A. Lewis, 'The Development of Industry and Commerce in Wales',
TRHS., xvii (1903), p. 155.
[156] R. A. Donkin, 'Cattle on the Estates of Medieval Cistercian Monasteries
in England and Wales', *Ec.H.R.*, xv (1962), p. 45.
[157] Ibid., pp. 35, 38, 44.
[158] Canivez, *Statuta*, i, p. 310.

'to sell their wool and send it without hindrance beyond sea for three years'.[159] In 1215 Cadwgan, abbot of Whitland, was deposed, according to Gerald of Wales, because he had fraudulently sold wool without the knowledge and consent of his house.[160] In 1250 the abbey of Margam had contracted with merchants of Ghent for 42 sacks of wool and two years later was selling wool to London merchants.[161]

A significant indication of the expansion of Cistercian flocks and the growth of the wool trade at this period is provided by the frequent disputes between abbeys over pasture rights which occurred between 1200 and 1250. Sheep required four to five times as much pasture space as cattle, and there was fierce competition to obtain rights of common of pasture. Many abbeys were attempting to carve out for themselves spheres of influence and, by charter, to exclude neighbouring abbeys from entering those areas. About 1200 Margam Abbey obtained from Morgan ap Caradog a charter which granted common of pasture throughout the whole of his land on the east side of the River Neath, 'in such a way that neither I nor my heirs will ever admit any religious men into that pasture except the aforesaid monks'.[162] In 1226 Strata Marcella obtained a charter from Griffin, son of Llewellyn which granted to the abbey 'the whole land which is between *Corph* and *Euniaun* so that no other monks shall have in it any use, or any common or proprietorship, except the monks of Stratmarchell'.[163] The clause was obviously directed against Cwm-hir, because in the same year both abbeys put their seals to an agreement over disputed pasture rights.[164]

At the end of the thirteenth century, figures are available of the numbers of sheep held by the Cistercian abbeys of Wales.[165] There are reasons for suggesting that they are not typical for the thirteenth century generally and that both herds and flocks had been considerably larger in the first half of the

---

[159] S. W. Williams, *Strata Florida Abbey*, appendix p. xix.
[160] Gir. Camb., *Opera*, iv, p. 166. For the identity of the unnamed abbot, see Lloyd, *History of Wales*, ii, p. 688, n. 201.
[161] CCR., *1247–51*, p. 314; CPR., *1247–58*, p. 166.
[162] Clark, *Cartae*, i, p. 180.
[163] J. Conway Davies, 'Strata Marcella Documents', *Mont. Coll.*, li (1949–50), p. 187.
[164] M. C. Jones, 'The Abbey of Ystrad Marchell', *Mont. Coll.*, iv (1871), pp. 320–22.
[165] See table below.

century. The Welsh wars appear to have seriously reduced the numbers of sheep and cattle on Cistercian estates within the diocese of St. David's, and during the decade or so before the figures were compiled, a serious epidemic of scab had taken a heavy toll of sheep throughout England and Wales.[166] Between 1270 and 1286 the sheep held by the Yorkshire abbey of Meaux had dropped from 11,000 to 1,320.[167] In south Wales the epidemic was at its height during the years 1281 and 1282. A set of local annals, probably compiled in one of the Glamorgan abbeys, records that the scab wiped out nearly the whole sheep population of Glamorgan in 1281. Further west in the diocese of St. David's, the *Annales Cambriae* record a great sheep murrain in 1282.[168]

At about the same time as the valuation of 1291 was made, a list of wool-producing abbeys of England and Wales was compiled.[169] It was incorporated by Pegolotti, a merchant of the Italian house of Bardi, into his book *La Pratica della Mercatura*.[170] In every case the amount of the annual clip available for export is noted, although it is not clear whether these figures represent the total output of the houses listed or only the number of sacks available for export to the merchants of the house of Bardi. For a number of houses the price per sack for the three main grades of wool is also noted. Eleven of the Welsh Cistercian houses are included, but four of the houses cannot be identified with certainty.[171]

Taken in conjunction with one another, the figures of flock size and the figures of annual output can be used to calculate rough but useful minimum figures for the revenues which the abbeys of south Wales received from the sale of wool. In a book on estate management which Robert Grosseteste, bishop of Lincoln, compiled between 1240 and 1241, it was estimated that a thousand sheep in good pasture should yield at least

---

[166] G. Fleming, *Animal Plagues*, pp. 79–89.

[167] R. A. Donkin, 'Cattle on the Estates of Medieval Cistercian Monasteries', *Ec.H.R.*, xv (1962–3), p. 34.

[168] *Arch. Camb.*, 1862, p. 281; *Annales Cambriae*, p. 106.

[169] R. A. Donkin, *Ec.H.R.*, xv (1962–3), p. 35, places the list between the years 1274 and 1296.

[170] F. B. Pegolotti, *La Pratica della Mercatura*, ed. A. Evans (Medieval Academy of America, xxiv, 1936); also W. Cunningham, *Growth of English Trade and Commerce* (5th ed. 1922), pp. 628–41.

[171] Cunningham has identified *Istanforte* as Strata Marcella, but Strata Florida seems a likelier identification. *Chinna* is identified as Cymer but may be Cwm-hir.

fifty marks, in scant pasture at least forty marks, and in coarse and poor pasture thirty marks per year.[172] In the table below the equation of one thousand sheep in scant pasture yielding 40 marks annually has been used to estimate the receipts of the south Wales houses. A similar attempt has been made to estimate net receipts from the number of sacks available for export. A median price has been chosen and this should make full allowance for the transport and other costs involved.

Number of Sheep Held by South Wales Abbeys in c.1291

Abbey	Number	Estimated Revenue £ s. d.		
Margam	5245	139	6	8
Neath	4897	130	13	4
Tintern	3264	86	13	4
Strata Florida	1327	35	6	8
Whitland	1100	29	6	8
Caerleon	588	15	6	8
Cwm-hir	300	8	0	0
Llanllŷr	60	1	6	8
Grace Dieu	22		12	0

Wool Produced for Export by the South Wales Abbeys (Pegolotti, 1274–96)

Abbey	Number of sacks	Median Price	Estimated Revenue £ s. d.		
Morghana (Margam)	25	10 marks	166	13	8
Tanterna (Tintern)	15	15 marks	150	0	8
Biancilanda (Whitland)	15	10 marks	100	0	0
Istanforte (Strata Florida?)	12	8 marks	64	0	0
Nietta (Neath)	10	8 marks	53	6	8
Chinna (Cwm-hir?)	8	10 marks	53	6	8
Lantarname (Llantarnam)	8	10 marks	53	6	8
Lagrziadio (Grace Dieu)	5	10 marks	33	6	8

[172] 'The Rules of Saint Robert, bishop of Lincoln made for the Countess of

There is little correlation between the figures obtained, although Margam and Tintern emerge from both estimates as the richest wool producers in south Wales.[173] From all sources it seems clear that the larger Cistercian abbeys derived a proportionately larger amount of income from wool sales than from any other source. During the wool 'boom' of the thirteenth century, this more than compensated for their lack of substantial sources of fixed income.

The Cistercians had a number of advantages over would-be competitors in the production and marketing of wool. Their extensive estates enabled them to operate on a large scale and the organization of their estates into granges made for more efficient and unified control than was possible on feudal estates with widely scattered manors and vills. Advance contracts with foreign wool-dealers gave them sufficient capital to purchase wool from other producers which went to swell the amount of their own clip. In the lay-brethren they possessed an unpaid labour force which considerably reduced transport costs. These were also reduced by the extensive privileges of immunity from toll enjoyed by the Cistercian abbeys of England and Wales.[174]

(v) *The Compromise with Manorialism and Tribalism*

It has already been shown that the typical unit of exploitation on the Cistercian estates was the grange, an extensive ring-fence farm centred around isolated farm buildings which was worked by lay-brethren and hired labourers. It would give a totally misleading picture of the economy of the south Wales houses, however, if it were assumed that such conditions obtained on every part of the abbey estates. There were varying degrees of 'manorialism' on the estates of every abbey. At an early date, certainly before the end of the twelfth century,

Lincoln to guard and govern her lands' in *Walter of Henley's Husbandry*, ed. Elizabeth Lamond, p. 145.

[173] Cf. the values in pound sterling assigned to wool from Welsh abbeys in another list printed by G. Espinas, *La Vie Urbaine de Douai au Moyen Age*, iii, pp. 232–4. Of the south Wales abbeys which can be identified with certainty, Grace Dieu's wool was valued at £33, Margam's at £50, Neath's at £45, Tintern's at £40 in one entry and £45 in another.

[174] R. A. Donkin, 'The Disposal of Cistercian Wool in England and Wales during the Twelfth and Thirteenth Centuries', *Cîteaux in de Nederlanden*, viii (1957), pp. 126–8.

economic expediency had been allowed to over-rule the ideals and legislation of the early Cistercians. Apart from the leasing of small parcels of land which could not be economically exploited, abbeys had accepted fully developed estates which they had no intention of depopulating and converting into granges. About 1230 Margam had obtained possession of Bonvilston, a vill rated at a half a knight's fee, situated on the main route across the Vale of Glamorgan, the 'Portway' of the thirteenth-century charters.[175] Here was a deeply-rooted, nucleated settlement with a church and fortress, whose lands had been intensively exploited before the Norman conquest.[176] No attempt was made, as at Llangewydd, to destroy the settlement. While the demesne land was probably attached to the land of the neighbouring grange of Llanfeuthin, the abbot took over the feudal rights, privileges and responsibilities of his lay predecessor; held his courts, collected his assised rents and drew heriots and labour services from his tenants.[177] Margam also had a manorial jurisdiction over a small settlement at Horgrove, situated between the granges of Stormy and Llangewydd.[178]

Tintern Abbey had acquired the lordship of Woolaston in the twelfth century, and in a comprehensive charter issued between 1234 and 1241 Gilbert, earl of Pembroke, had granted the abbey the right of holding all its lands 'with soc and sac and tol and team and infangenethef and that they and their men and sergeants shall be quit of shires and hundreds and suits of shires and hundreds'.[179] By the second half of the thirteenth century Tintern appears to have held a central court for all its tenants west of the Wye at Porthcaseg, where fines were levied, heriots paid and manorial justice dispensed.[180]

Obscurity hangs over the estates of the abbeys of west Wales. Although in the compressed accounts of the 1291 valuation the granges appear as the main units accounted

---

[175] Clark, *Cartae*, ii, pp. 572–3, 542.
[176] For the fortress, see Rice Merrick, *A Booke of Glamorganshires Antiquities*, p. 85, and T. Nicholas, *History and Antiquities of Glamorganshire*, p. 115.
[177] For suit of court and heriots, see Clark, *Cartae*, iii, p. 880.
[178] *Taxatio*, p. 284.
[179] *C.Ch.R.,1300–26*, pp. 88, 98.
[180] There is a long run of Porthcaseg court rolls in N.L.W., Badminton Papers 1639–62; see below p. 253.

for by the valuers, there is also mention of rents, mills *cum aliis commoditatibus*.[181] This seems to suggest that the abbeys had taken over some of the fiscal units which had been exploited in earlier times by the native princes of the area. Strata Florida had obtained during the lifetime of the Lord Rhys a number of *trefi* and many of these had been incorporated into the extensive granges which were established in the twelfth and thirteenth centuries. These granges, writes Professor Jones Pierce, 'appear in the main to have been developed hamlets, many of them with servile tenants, transferred by charter from secular to monastic lordship'.[182]

The Cistercian prohibition against the holding of spiritual income had also lost much of its force by 1291. Tintern Abbey had resorted to appropriating churches before the end of the twelfth century and by 1291 possessed two churches and a portion in a third, which were collectively valued at £36 13s. 4d.[183] This is the highest figure recorded for spiritual income held by south Wales Cistercian houses at this time. Further west, Margam had become the farmer of the churches of Kenfig and St. Leonard's, Newcastle, for an annual payment of £23; but since the receipts from tithes sometimes exceeded and sometimes fell below this sum, the over-all profits from the arrangement cannot have been large.[184] In the *Taxatio* of 1291 Margam is only recorded as possessing a portion in the church of Olveston in the deanery of Bristol, valued at 10s. Neath held three appropriated churches, all of them poor: St. Mary Hill, valued at £1; Cilybebyll, valued at 13s. 4d.; and Cadoxton, valued at £3 6s. 8d.[185] Strata Florida had acquired the church of Llangurig, valued at £16, and possibly the church of Pencarreg, valued at £5.[186] No thirteenth-century appropriations are recorded for Whitland, Cwm-hir, Caerleon, Grace Dieu and Llanllŷr. Compared with the Benedictine houses and the houses of regular canons, the spiritual income held by the Cistercian houses in 1291 formed only a modest proportion of total income: at Tintern

---

[181] *Taxatio*, pp. 276–7.
[182] T. Jones Pierce, 'Strata Florida Abbey', *Ceredigion*, i (1950), p. 29.
[183] *Taxatio*, pp. 161b, 196. See also below p. 185.
[184] Clark, *Cartae*, iv, p. 1198.
[185] *Taxatio*, pp. 220, 279b.
[186] *CPL.*, i, pp. 558–9; *Taxatio*, pp. 291, 272b.

about 24 per cent, at Strata Florida about 16 per cent and at Neath only 2 per cent. An average taken for all nine of the south Wales houses would produce a very low percentage.

Already by 1291 there are signs of change and impending change on the estates of the Cistercian abbeys of south Wales. Neath had already made a revolutionary change in her economy as early as 1289 by a mere stroke of the pen. On the estates of other abbeys changes were more gradual and less perceptible. For the sake of clarity, however, it seems best to defer a detailed examination of this difficult question to a later chapter.[187]

IV. THE MONASTIC INCOME

The evidence available for the size of incomes enjoyed by the monasteries of south Wales, and, for that matter, of the rest of Wales before the Dissolution, is disappointingly meagre. With one fortunate exception,[188] no accounts drawn up by monastic obedientiaries, bailiffs or reeves are known to have survived for the Welsh houses. In their absence, three sources of information remain which provide material for comparison and approximate calculation. Firstly, there is the assessment of clerical property made *circa* 1291 known as the *Taxatio Ecclesiastica* of Pope Nicholas IV. The returns for the Welsh dioceses are particularly full, especially those for the diocese of Llandaff. The text of the valuation edited for the Record Commission in 1802 has, however, a number of serious deficiencies. It was based not on the original rolls of the valuation preserved in the Public Record Office but on a fifteenth-century transcript which the editors collated with earlier copies.[189] No attempt was made to identify place-names and the index has to be used with great care. More serious for the historian who is attempting to analyse the sources of monastic income and their relative importance in the monastic economy are the frequent discrepancies between the totals given in the printed edition and the sum

---

[187] See Chapter IX.

[188] Fourteenth century reeve's accounts for Tintern abbey's granges of Porthcaseg and Merthyrgeryn, and early-fifteenth-century cellarer's accounts survive in N. L. W., Badminton Papers, 1571-2, 1574-6.

[189] For the original rolls and manuscript copies, see W. E. Lunt, *Financial Relations of the Papacy with England to 1327*, pp. 666-75.

of the individual items which such totals purport to represent. One example may be quoted. The temporalities of Margam Abbey in the diocese of Llandaff, excluding livestock, are assessed at £100 9s. 2d. The sum of the items which precede this total adds up to only £44 19s. 10d.[190] Everyone who has worked on medieval accounts will be familiar with frequent slips of arithmetic. The discrepancies in the *Taxatio*, are, however, too large to be due to faulty arithmetic alone. One suspects that either the transcripts from which the Record Commission editors worked are faulty or that the editors themselves were careless. These discrepancies deter one from attempting too ambitious a break-down of the figures for the purpose of analysis.

Since the Record Commission text appeared, the figures it contains have been indiscriminately cited by numerous historians as representing net or gross income. But Rose Graham has clearly demonstrated that the assessment of 1291 approximates to the manorial extent rather than to the manorial account roll.[191] Lands were assessed at the lowest figure at which they could be let at farm. Churches, too, were assessed on the same principle. Livestock appear to have been assessed at an arbitrary figure per head which varied slightly from diocese to diocese but was considerably below what it would fetch on the open market.[192] The only items of the assessment which may possibly have been derived from an account roll of an average year are the rents of assise, curial revenue, and income from tanneries. It needs to be stressed again, therefore, that the figures given in the *Taxatio* for the temporalities and spiritualities of religious houses do not represent income either net or gross but approximate roughly to our own concept of rateable value.

Despite the invaluable work done by W. E. Lunt, no reliable equation has been evolved to enable the historian to convert the figures given in the *Taxatio* into figures of either net or gross

[190] *Taxatio*, p. 284. Similar discrepancies have been noted for Caerleon (281b) and Grace Dieu (281). A critical text of the *Taxatio* for the Welsh dioceses is badly needed.
[191] R. Graham, 'The Taxation of Pope Nicholas IV', *EHR*., xxiii, (1908), pp. 434–54.
[192] In Llandaff diocese cows seem to have been valued at 1s. 6d.; in St. David's diocese at 1s. (Whitland) and 1s. 2d. (Cwm-hir). At this period cows were normally sold for 5s.; see Rees, *South Wales and the March*, pp. 80–81.

income. Lunt found marked variations between known figures of net and gross income and the assessed values given in the *Taxatio*.[193] In the majority of cases, however, net and gross income was found to be considerably in excess of the *Taxatio* figures, sometimes by as much as two or three times.

The royal officials who drew up extents of the alien priories in the fourteenth century used methods similar to those employed by the rural deans responsible for the 1291 valuation. Thus, in 1305 it was found that the property of St. Clears was valued at £15 19s. 10d., but that since it had come into the hands of the king 'it has been of no value except £8 10s. 0d'.[194] Over seventy years later, in 1378, the value of the priory was found to be £19 6s. 8d.[195] An extent of Chepstow made in the reign of Edward III gives the value of the priory's temporal and spiritual property as £45 6s. 8d.[196] An extent of Pembroke Priory's property made in 1378 gives its total value as £127 19s. 2½d.[197]

Of greater value than extents are the estimates of income occasionally supplied by letters and reports of monastic and episcopal visitors and by papal bulls. For the south Wales houses these estimates are so few for the whole middle ages that they deserve to be quoted even though most of them, like the extents, fall outside the date limits of the present work. In a visitation made of St. Clears in 1279 it was found that despite alienations, goods to the value of 72 marks remained to the house.[198] In a visitation of Abergavenny Priory in 1320, Adam de Orleton, bishop of Hereford, found that the goods of the priory exceeded the annual value of 200 marks sterling (£133 6s. 8d.). In his final report some days later he stated that the goods of the priory were worth (and had been worth for forty years or more) upwards of 240 marks sterling (£160) annually.[199] Orleton's estimate is obviously based on an examination of the account rolls of the priory and deserves to be compared with the valuation of the house's income given in the *Taxatio* of 1291 (£51 17s. 10½d.)

[193] W. E. Lunt, *Valuation of Norwich*, pp. 573–613.
[194] P.R.O., E 106/4/19. Cf. value given in *Taxatio*, £15 19s. 2d.
[195] P.R.O., E 106/11/1, and British Museum, Add. MS. 6164 pp. 352–3.
[196] P.R.O., SC. 12/12/14. Cf. *Taxatio*, £35 19s. 11d.
[197] Dugdale, iv, p. 321.
[198] G. F. Duckett, *Charters and Records of Cluni*, ii, p. 136.
[199] *Registrum Ade de Orleton*, pp. 151, 191.

In 1383 the abbot and convent of Margam asserted that the fruits, rents and issues of their house 'according to common estimation' did not exceed 400 marks sterling (£266 13s. 4d.). Two years later in letters of Urban VI, it is stated that the fruits, rents and issues of the house from which a hundred persons are maintained 'do not exceed 500 marks (£336 6s. 8d.) by common estimation'.[200]

When Guy de Mone visited Brecon in 1401 he found 'that the possessions and faculties of the said priory of Brecon by common estimation exceed in themselves every year 400 marks sterling (£266 13s. 4d.)'.[201] A similar estimate of income for the priory of Carmarthen can be deduced from the financial regulations which the same bishop drew up in the same year. The temporalities of the house and the fruits of certain churches (St. Peters, Carmarthen, St. David, Abergwili and the chapel of Abernant) were to be allocated to the cellarer for the maintenance of the prior and convent, the entertainment of guests and the payment of servants' wages. From this fund, the prior was enjoined not to spend more than 200 marks (£133 6s. 8d.) without reasonable cause. Guy de Mone also instituted a special fund to pay off the debts of the convent and repair its buildings. This fund was to be derived from the fruits of the churches of Llanfihangel Iorath, Llanllwni, Llanybydder and Llanfihangel Rhos-y-corn. These churches were valued at a total of £41 6s. 8d. in 1535. From these regulations it seems clear that Carmarthen Priory at this time enjoyed an annual income of between £170 and £200, and perhaps more.[202] Carmarthen had, in effect, attained by this date the income it enjoyed at the Dissolution. It is worth emphasizing that much of this income was acquired during the fourteenth century and throws very little light on thirteenth-century conditions.[203]

These references to monastic income are too few and too widely separated in date to provide an adequate basis for generalization. The *Taxatio*, on the other hand, despite its

---

[200] Clark, *Cartae*, iv, pp. 1351, 1361.
[201] *Episc. Reg. St. David's*, i, p. 235.
[202] Ibid., pp. 239–41.
[203] In 1336 the temporalities and spiritualities of Carmarthen were extented at a mere £60 11s. 3d., 'as fully appears by divers certificates sent to Chancery by the king's orders'; *CCR., 1333–37*, pp. 635–6.

limitations, does provide a relative index of monastic prosperity. It shows that the richest houses belonged to the Cistercian order. The property of their nine houses in the two southern dioceses of Wales was valued at £885 6s. 6½d. There are marked variations in the assessed values within the two dioceses. The four houses in the diocese of St. David's accounted for only £185 4s. 1d. of the total. It is possible that this low figure reflects in some measure the recurrent devastation caused in the diocese during the Welsh wars. The richest houses were in the diocese of Llandaff, with Margam (£255 17s. 4½d.), Neath (£236 1s. 5d.) and Tintern (£145 3s. 0d.) heading the list.

There are also marked variations in the assessed values between one house and another. At the bottom of the scale, houses like Llanllŷr (£7 10s. 0d.), Grace Dieu (£18 5s. 8d.) and Cwm-hir (£35 12s. 0d.) were infinitely poorer than the majority of the conventual Benedictine houses and the houses of regular canons. The small nunnery of Llanllŷr had always been overshadowed and occasionally brow-beaten by its richer neighbour at Strata Florida. Grace Dieu never appears to have achieved a stable economy and its changes of site and endowment did little to save it from recurrent trouble. Cwm-hir was perhaps too remote and its patrons insufficiently interested for it to have achieved material prosperity.[204]

Only one Benedictine house and one Augustinian house could vie with the richest of the Cistercians: Goldcliff, assessed at £171 14s. 1d.,[205] and Llanthony Prima, assessed at £233 7s. 0d.[206] Apart from Brecon, with its assessed value of £122 10s. 0d., all the remaining houses were assessed at figures well below the £100 mark. In the highest group were the conventual houses with assessed values ranging from £35 to £85; in the lower group, the seven cells with assessed values from £5 to £20.[207]

---

[204] The patronage had been acquired by the Mortimer family early in the thirteenth century; see S. W. Williams, 'The Cistercian Abbey of Cwmhir', *Trans. Cymm.*, 1894–5, p. 68.

[205] A marginal entry in P.R.O., E 106/4/14 membrane 11, gives Goldcliff's assessment as £175 16s. 4d.

[206] This includes the Irish lands and churches possessed by the priory.

[207] See Appendix III.

V

MONASTIC DISCIPLINE

During the twelfth century and part of the thirteenth, it is possible for the historian of English monasteries to recapture from written lives, letters and chronicles something of the atmosphere of life within the larger Cistercian and Benedictine abbeys. He is able to share the thoughts and feelings of a great Cistercian abbot like Ailred of Rievaulx and form some idea of the highly-charged spiritual atmosphere in which his monks lived. The pages of a chronicler like Jocelin of Brakelond enable him to appreciate, too, some of the daily, material preoccupations of the obedientiaries in the great abbey of Bury under Abbot Samson. For some houses it is even possible to trace for a generation or so the gradual ebb and flow of spiritual fervour in a community.

Such insights are denied to the historian of the Welsh houses. Occasions when the written evidence takes one within the precinct wall, into the monastic cloister and into the choir are rare indeed. When it does the glimpse is brief and fleeting as in the incident recorded by Ralph of Coggeshall in 1202:

> In this year, on the day of Pentecost, a wonderful vision was seen by a certain monk of Strata Florida in Wales, of three angels who censed the altar while Lauds were being sung. One of the angels took the burning charcoal from the thurible and suddenly thrust it into the mouth of the monk as he watched. Wrapped in an ecstasy of mind, he was seized by the angel, raised into the air, so it seemed to him, between his wings and borne by the angel towards the east, remaining there one day and night seeing divers revelations. His body had meanwhile been carried by the monks into the infirmary.[1]

The monk's reverie may well have been induced by high fever, but this brief description of the convent of Strata Florida

[1] *Radulphi de Coggeshall Chronicon Anglicanum* (Rolls Series), p. 141.

engaged in its continual work of corporate prayer provides a useful counterbalance to Gerald of Wales's picture of a grasping, avaricious and insensitive community.[2]

In the absence of more intimate sources, it seems best to approach the whole question of monastic discipline by way of the machinery devised by the church for maintaining standards of observance within monasteries. Even here the records are disappointingly meagre. The earliest episcopal registers for a Welsh diocese (that of St. David's) do not begin until 1397, well outside the limits of the present study. This large gap in the sources can only be partially filled by the facts and impressions recorded by Gerald of Wales and by the injunctions and letters of Archbishop Pecham. For the Cistercian houses the records of the General Chapter provide valuable material for the period 1190 to 1240, but references to Welsh houses become increasingly scarce after this date.

Records of the kind which have survived naturally reflect the pathological side of monastic life. They bring into stark relief the worst features of individual monks and monasteries without indicating whether they were typical of their class and age. One should be on one's guard against allowing them to colour unduly one's impression of Welsh monastic life over a period of two centuries.

I. EPISCOPAL AND METROPOLITAN VISITATION

(i) *Episcopal Visitation*

The right of a bishop to exercise a general surveillance over religious houses within his diocese, of visiting them when he deemed it necessary and of correcting anything which he found amiss, had been recognized in canon law for centuries before the Norman conquest.[3] In the twelfth century such rights were not systematically implemented and little is known of the procedure which bishops adopted in exercising their rights. Even in south Wales, however, where the evidence for almost every class of episcopal act is scarce, one is occasionally

---

[2] Gerald visited Strata Florida in the same year, when he was forced to sell rather than pawn his books (*Autobiography of Giraldus Cambrensis*, ed. H. E. Butler, pp. 250–1). The incident embittered Gerald against the monks of Strata Florida.

[3] C. R. Cheney, *Episcopal Visitation of Monasteries in the Thirteenth Century*, pp. 19–25.

reminded that bishops were sensitive to the state of monastic discipline within their dioceses. Thus, Bernard, bishop of St. David's (1115–48), in a letter to the patron of Brecon Priory, Roger, earl of Hereford, announced that the priory had established its right to Llan-gors Church, and added:

> It should indeed give you pleasure and bring you profit in God's eyes that that house has of late increased to a more than customary degree in religion and charity. Much encouraged by this, we have confirmed the gifts of your ancestors ... by the authority of God and of our ministry.[4]

Gerald of Wales provides three examples of bishops and their officials using coercive power against monks for flagrant breaches of their rule. When Gerald, acting as an envoy of Henry II, visited Rhys ap Gruffydd at Llandovery *circa* 1185, the three or four monks of Great Malvern who occupied a priory cell there had gained such notoriety through the viciousness of their lives that the burgesses of the castle were ready to leave the town and return to England 'for the sake of their wives and daughters whom these monks frequently and openly abused'. Rhys was determined to close the cell, but the good offices of Gerald and a promise of future good behaviour gave the monks a temporary reprieve. Shortly afterwards, however, they were driven out 'by order of the prince and of the bishop of the diocese'.[5] The most notorious of the Llandovery monks later became custodian of another cell of Great Malvern in the Brecon region without the permission of his superior. He was accused of violating a certain nun who was a devotee of the church there, was 'convicted in full chapter, excommunicated by the archdeacon of the same place and driven out from those parts'.[6] Gerald also tells how at Llangenydd a public scandal forced the bishop of St. David's to act. The prior of this alien cell had an adulterous association with a young Gower woman in Gerald's day. He was censured by the ecclesiastical authorities, presumably repented and escaped with a money fine. Shortly afterwards he renewed the association, and the public scandal reached such proportions that the bishop was forced to depose him.[7]

[4] *Brec. Cart.*, pp. 63–4.
[5] *Autobiography of Giraldus Cambrensis*, pp. 85–6; Gir. Camb., *Opera*, iv, pp. 100–1.
[6] Ibid., p. 102.
[7] Gir. Camb., *Opera*, iv, pp. 33–4.

Such exercise of episcopal power was probably exceptional. In all three cases there was little doubt as to the guilt of the parties concerned and the bishop was forced to act to allay public scandal. They do not *per se* constitute evidence for believing that a regular and ordered system of episcopal visitation of monasteries was in existence in the two dioceses of south Wales at the end of the twelfth century or at the beginning of the thirteenth. Systematic episcopal visitation of religious houses did not become normal practice in England until the middle of the thirteenth century. It seems probable that the procedure was being resorted to with growing frequency by the bishops of St. David's and Llandaff at about the same time.

A formulary book of Llandaff letters, now in Cambridge University Library, shows that by the episcopate of John of Monmouth (1297–1323) the procedure of episcopal visitation was fully developed in that diocese and corresponded with current practice in England. It shows, too, that John of Monmouth was accustomed to visit even alien priories within his diocese. In one letter in the collection he notifies the prior and convent of Chepstow that he proposes to visit them and orders them to present themselves before him on a fixed day. In another letter he orders the rural dean of Groneath to approach the abbot and convent of Tewkesbury so that they may make good the defects he had found in their appropriated church of Kenfig. During his visitation he had found that the church possessed insufficient books for singing matins and the canonical hours, no glass in the chancel windows and no canopy over the altar. The church also lacked a suitable building for the reception of visitors. The abbot and convent and vicar were to set matters aright on pain of a fine of 100s.[8]

The exercise of this episcopal jurisdiction was limited in its range. Members of the Cistercian and Premonstratensian orders had their own machinery for maintaining monastic discipline and were exempted from it.[9] Nor does it seem likely that bishops ever systematically visited the very small cells of

---

[8] Cambridge University Library, MS. Dd. 9.38, fols. 93v., 94, 94v.

[9] This exemption was not fully and officially recognized until the thirteenth century: see J.-B. Mahn, *L'Ordre Cistercien et son Gouvernement* (2nd. ed., 1951), pp. 119–55; and H. M. Colvin, *The White Canons in England*, pp. 16–17.

one or two monks. When Bishop Guy de Mone required information on the religious obligations of the prior of Llangenydd in 1400, neither his own memory nor the registers of his predecessors could furnish it; he was forced to appoint a commission of enquiry.[10]

(ii) *Pecham's Metropolitan Visitation in 1284*

Pecham's visitation was the first metropolitan visitation of the Welsh dioceses to be undertaken by an archbishop of Canterbury. Baldwin's tour in 1188 was a recruiting campaign designed to raise troops for the recovery of the Holy Land and was not intrinsically an exercise of metropolitan jurisdiction. Archbishop Boniface had intended to make such a visitation in 1255 but was prevented by war. The visitation undertaken by Pecham followed the collapse of the cause of Welsh independence. He intended it to be at once a formal assertion of the authority of Canterbury over the Welsh dioceses and a means of bringing the church in Wales, which still showed signs of its Celtic past, into line with that of England. These wider implications of his visitation need not detain us here.[11] In the present context, the visitation is primarily of interest because the letters and injunctions which were selected for inclusion in Pecham's register provide the earliest 'official' evidence for the condition of the non-exempt religious houses of south Wales.

Pecham began his visitation of the two southern dioceses of St. David's and Llandaff early in July and completed it on or soon after 7 August. His itinerary enabled him to visit or to enquire into the condition of most of the non-exempt houses of south Wales. Injunctions have survived, however, for only five houses: the two Augustinian houses of Haverfordwest and Llanthony Prima, the two Benedictine priories of Ewenni and Goldcliff, and the Benedictine nunnery of Usk.[12] Common to all the injunctions are the regulations for the establishment in each priory of a central treasury for the

---

[10] *Episc. Reg. St. David's*, i, p. 183.
[11] See especially D. L. Douie, *Archbishop Pecham*, pp. 235–71, and Glanmor Williams, *Welsh Church*, pp. 35–46.
[12] *Registrum Epistolarum*, iii, pp. 782–4 (Haverfordwest), 800–5 (Llanthony Prima), 798–800 (Ewenni and Goldcliff), 805–6 (Usk).

receipt and disbursement of revenue and for a regular system of audit. At Ewenni, for example, Pecham commanded that two brethren should be elected as treasurers. These treasurers should receive into their custody all the moneys of the house whether accruing from granges, appropriated churches or offerings. The prior and obedientiaries were to receive their expenses from the treasurers and from no other source. Only one form of revenue was excepted, namely, that revenue which had been allocated from ancient times to the uses of the almoner. Whenever the prior or one of his subordinates visited a manor, everything received from the custodian should be priced and the treasurers informed of the transaction, either by a written receipt or by tally. The treasurers were to render account before the prior and seniors of the community three times a year: at the beginning of Lent, after Pentecost and at Michaelmas.[13] Here Pecham was applying in a modified form to suit the south Wales houses a system which had already been applied with some success at Christ Church, Canterbury, Reading and Glastonbury.[14]

None of Pecham's injunctions to the south Wales houses refers in detail to the *detecta* of his visitation, to the specific faults of individual canons and monks. Some idea of the short-comings he found, however, may be inferred from the regulations they contain. At Haverfordwest, the prior was urged to show his presence to the community and not to miss being present in the refectory or at the office of compline for the sake of entertaining his guests. Such action could only be condoned when the guests were persons of importance who were able to assist or injure the monastery. The prior and healthy canons were to be content to eat meat 'according to the common custom of the order of St. Augustine' only on three days of the week, namely, Sunday, Tuesday and Wednesday. Lay persons of both sexes were to be prevented from entering the cloister, infirmary, refectory and other internal offices. An exception was made, however, for persons of standing whom it would be impossible to refuse. Anyone who introduced other persons without the special licence of

[13] Ibid., pp. 798–9.
[14] D. Knowles, 'Some Aspects of the Career of Archbishop Pecham', *EHR.*, lvii (1942), pp. 193–5; D. L. Douie, *Archbishop Pecham*, pp. 170–4.

the prior was to sit last at table at the next meal and his pittance for that day was to be withdrawn. When speaking in community the brethren were to take care that they refrained from swearing. Anyone who presumed to take possession of any of the goods of the church was to be punished as a *proprietarius*. At Haverfordwest, as in other south Wales houses, Pecham noted a slackness in the administration of the almonry and made regulations to prevent abuses.[15]

When Pecham visited Ewenni it was ruled by Henry de Wigemore,[16] a successor of the saintly and able John de Gamages. After issuing a warning against the sin of *proprietas*, Pecham reminded the prior personally that it was unlawful to bestow any of the goods of the church on anyone outside without the advice and consent of his brethren. He was greatly surprised that the prior and convent dared to eat meat both secretly and publicly against the rule of St. Benedict and the statute of the legate. He ordered the prior and convent to preserve as far as human frailty would allow the purity of the rule with regard to meat-eating, silence and other observances of monastic discipline. The prior was strictly enjoined to be solicitous for the virtue of his household and to enquire at fixed times both inside and outside the house concerning the virtue of his servants. If he found them guilty of incontinence, he was to remove them either permanently or temporarily. Bailiffs and wardens in charge of the priory's property were to be appointed by the prior in chapter before the brethren and with the advice of the senior monks. The bishop of Llandaff was enjoined to see how the injunctions were observed when he visited the priory and was also to make careful provision that the number of monks was maintained according to ancient custom—and if the goods of the priory would allow, that the number should be increased. Similar injunctions were issued to the priory of Goldcliff.[17]

Pecham found the nunnery of Usk in a most desolate state. To prevent recurrences of trouble in the future he ordered the setting up of a central treasury of receipt, a feature of his visitation which has already been noticed. He also ordered that,

---

[15] *Reg. Epist.*, iii, pp. 782–4.
[16] *Hist. et Cart. Glouc.*, iii, p. 22.
[17] *Reg. Epist.*, iii, pp. 798–800.

with the consent of the diocesan, an experienced priest, circumspect in things temporal and spiritual, should be appointed to act as master of all their goods temporal and spiritual. He was to watch carefully that the discipline of the monastic order was preserved and was not to permit any of the nuns to go beyond the bounds of the monastery without a virtuous and reliable companion. Nuns were not allowed to stay in the houses of secular persons or to remain in their company for longer than three or four days.[18]

The lengthy injunctions which have survived for the Augustinian priory of Llanthony Prima suggest that Pecham found much to investigate and set in order. This impression is confirmed by fragments of information which are available from other sources. In 1274 three of the canons had fled from the priory and were wandering at large.[19] In 1276 the priory was so heavily in debt that it was taken into royal custody.[20] At about the same time it began to be persecuted by powerful magnates in neighbouring lordships. Pecham diagnosed that one of the causes of Llanthony's troubles lay in mismanagement of the priory's resources:

> Mary's role must needs suffer constant interruptions, unless the prudence of Martha . . . makes provision . . . for Mary's sacred ease. For just as nature is the basis of grace, so claustral tranquility is best provided for by a careful administration of things temporal.[21]

He urged that a central treasury should be established and an audit held three times a year. Additional regulations were made for the external administration of the priory's property. A layman was to be appointed as a steward of all the goods of the church and with him was to be associated a canon of the priory as external cellarer. When the prior thought fit or was away on business, both officials were to make provision for the necessities of the house and manage its property jointly, not individually, and always with the advice and consent of the prior. The external cellarer was to have no power of alienating

---

[18] Ibid., pp. 805–6.
[19] *CPR.*, *1272–81*, p. 49.
[20] Ibid., p. 166.
[21] *Reg. Epist.*, iii, p. 800.

the goods of the church and was to receive his expenses either from the treasurers or from the custodians of manors by tally. If he did otherwise he was to be punished as a *proprietarius*. When engaged in business outside the priory, he should be content with the company of one layman or canon and whenever possible should return to the house for meals.

The prior was humbly to discuss all the business of the house with the convent. Business of a more secret nature might be discussed with at least four of the senior canons. Without the latter's advice no obedientiaries or servants were to be appointed or dismissed. Their counsel was also to be taken when any important gift was made in the name of the prior and convent. A general audit of the accounts of the cellarer, the reeves and bailiffs was to be made in October in the presence of the prior, the two treasurers and three or four senior canons.

Pecham drew up a carefully defined scale of punishments for faults committed by the canons. The whole tone of the injunctions here suggests that Pecham was legislating for an autocratic prior and for a dissident and rebellious community rarely at peace with itself or its superior. No one was to be imprisoned unless for an outrageous and manifest crime, such as theft, immodest behaviour, violence, conspiracy and sedition against the prior, disobedience, apostasy or attempted apostasy. These faults were to be punished by imprisonment and the guilty parties could only be absolved by the prior. Those guilty of lesser faults might be absolved by the sub-prior and one other senior canon appointed by the prior as common penitentiary. Those imprisoned could be released after a sufficient show of penitence. The prison cells were to be strong but as airy as security would allow.

Pecham then proceeded to lay down a scale of punishments for the daily faults of omission and commission. These included breaking silence, unbridled talkativeness, unbecoming behaviour, dissolute laughter, lateness, missing a canonical hour, murmuring, abuse, lying, spreading rumours, leaving the cloister without licence, and immoderate drinking. These faults were to be punished by withdrawing the guilty party's pittance, by restricting him to drinking water or making him sit last at table, chapter and choir. In cases of growing insolence, the guilty canon was to be made to sit on the floor during meal times, was to be beaten in chapter and was to lie prostrate on the threshold of the chapter house for the community to walk over him. If he still remained obdurate, he should be separated from the community and remain locked in a room alone until he showed signs of penitence. If even this failed, he was to be imprisoned and chained until the diocesan was consulted as to whether it would be expedient to eject the brother from the order, or incarcerate him for a longer period or for ever.

With an eye to present and possible future discord in the house, Pecham urged the prior to study to be loved by his sons:

> Look with pleasant countenance on those you think less faithful to you, and in choir, chapter and refectory so show them that you are really a prior that your sheep may follow you with joy.

As at Haverfordwest, the prior was enjoined not to leave the community for the sake of entertaining a guest, unless his importance warranted it. No woman, lay or religious, was to spend the night in the monastery except high-born ladies of rank.

In concluding his injunctions, Pecham briefly laid down a procedure for the election of a sub-prior. All the professed canons were to vote and each according to his conscience was to nominate two candidates for the office. The prior was then to nominate as sub-prior that candidate for whom the *pars senior* (the more experienced and elderly section of the community) had cast their votes, unless perhaps the prior had qualms of conscience over the choice. For the prior's special position, as Pecham noted, gave him inside knowledge of the faults of individuals which may have been hidden from the community. Almost as an after-thought, Pecham added that the prior and those responsible should provide such food and medicine for infirm canons as they themselves, in similar circumstances, would wish to receive.[22]

Pecham's injunctions for Llanthony were detailed and thorough and, in the light of subsequent history, almost prophetic in their insight. In the century following his

[22] Ibid., pp. 800–5.

visitation, the reputation of the house was sullied by internal dissension, individual apostasy, theft, violence of a most brutal kind, and even murder.[23]

In the course of his journey through south Wales, Pecham visited a number of houses for which no injunctions have survived.[24] At Pembroke, he deposed Ralph, the prior, and sent him back to his mother abbey. 'Among other enormities and innumerable crimes which we have found R . . . to have committed', wrote Pecham to the abbot of St. Martin, Séez, 'we have learned from reliable reports that he has laboured throughout his whole period of office under the vice of incontinence such that we can in no-wise allow him to continue in the office of prior without scandal and offence to all religion'. The abbot was to prevent his returning to Pembroke for a period of ten years and make provision for a new prior. Pecham meanwhile entrusted the administration of the priory to Andrew, the sub-prior.[25]

At Kidwelly, too, Pecham found it necessary to remove the prior, Ralph de Bemenster, 'because of his manifest faults' and send him back to his abbey of Sherborne. Barely more than a month after he had visited Kidwelly, Pecham learned that the abbot of Sherborne had reappointed Ralph as prior and sent him back to Kidwelly. Pecham wrote to the abbot and strictly enjoined him, under pain of excommunication, to recall Ralph, subject him to monastic discipline and appoint a suitable candidate in his place.[26]

During his stay at Llanthony, Pecham composed two identical sets of injunctions addressed to the bishops of St. David's and Llandaff. The bulk of the injunctions is naturally taken up with the shortcomings he found in the life of the secular clergy and of the people committed to their spiritual care. A brief section, however, was devoted to the religious houses. The bishops were urged to induce all the religious subject to their jurisdiction to an observance of the Rule, to restrain monks especially from the eating of meat 'in accordance

[23] See below p. 134.
[24] Letters dated at St. Dogmaels, Carmarthen and Abergavenny suggest that he may have visited the religious houses there.
[25] *Reg. Epist.*, iii, pp. 786–8.
[26] Ibid., pp. 810–11.

with the Rule of St. Benedict and the statutes of our predecessors', giving no credence to the assertions of those who
claimed dispensations from the pope. They were to prevent
superiors of monasteries from alienating the goods of their
houses on their own authority alone. Pecham reiterated his
regulations for the setting up of treasuries of receipt in the
monasteries.[27]

(iii) *The Condition of Brecon Priory, circa 1276–90*

In 1283 Pecham visited Battle Abbey, and in the course of his
enquiries he caused two monks at the abbey's priory at Brecon
to be recalled and subjected to penance for certain unspecified
faults. We have already had occasion to describe the sequel to
his action on a previous page.[28] There are other indications
that all was not well at the priory at this time. Stitched into
Pecham's register are brief notes which formed the *detecta* of
his visitation at Battle.[29] The two monks recalled by Pecham
are not mentioned, but it was noted that the prior of Brecon
who had previously been removed for incontinence had been
restored to the priorate by the abbot of Battle. During the
visitation the prior had made a fairly obvious attempt to
bribe Pecham himself. A number of his monks had left the
priory and some had laid aside their habit.

Among the manuscripts of Magdalen College, Oxford, is an
imperfect roll containing the written responses of an unnamed
prior of Brecon to a whole catalogue of charges levelled against
him by an episcopal or archiepiscopal visitor.[30] There is no
direct evidence of the date of the document but internal
evidence would suggest that the accused prior was holding
office between 1276 and 1290.[31] Apart from general charges of
managerial ineptitude which the prior freely admitted, the
prior was accused of major infringements of monastic observance and of serious moral lapses. The substance of his replies
seems to indicate that most of the charges were well founded.

---

[27] Ibid., p. 796.
[28] See above p. 41.
[29] *Registrum Johannis Pecham* (Cant. & York Soc., 1910), pp. 198–9.
[30] Magdalen College Muniments, Miscellaneous 297, printed by R. W. Banks
in *Brec. Cart.*, pp. 133–40.
[31] See note at the end of this chapter.

He neglected divine service, rarely lodged in the convent and omitted to observe episcopal statutes or cause them to be recited. He was accused, moreover, of drunkenness, of having revealed the confessions of his brethren, of incontinence (on three counts), of maintaining a kinsman in the schools out of the revenues of the convent, of bribing his colleagues in preparation for an episcopal visitation and of being a liar, a sycophant and an embezzler. The prior reacted strongly to the last charge:

> he replies that he is incapable, as is noted in the first article above concerning his incapacity. For the rest he admits himself blameworthy before God and you and seeks pardon and promises amendment, except on one count, namely, that concerning his embezzlement of goods, because God knows that he was never a thief but was brought up by trustworthy parents and in his youth was well disciplined and on this he calls to witness God and the lord abbot of Battle and brother Robert who was once his schoolmaster.[32]

The prior's replies to the charges against him are alternately naive and ingenious, and frequently amusing. They provide a vignette of life in a dependent priory of south Wales which can be obtained from no other source. Although the monastic life at Brecon Priory had not reached the state of moral decadence and corruption apparent at Abergavenny Priory in 1320, there is clear evidence of laxity, internal dissension and personal immorality on the part of the prior, sufficient grounds for a thorough investigation and an attempt at reformation.

(iv) *Adam de Orleton's Visitation of Abergavenny Priory, 1320*

However frequent or infrequent episcopal visitation may have been, there were occasions when conditions in a religious house had become so bad that a special enquiry was called for. Such appears to have been the state of Abergavenny Priory in 1319. The priory lay in the diocese of Llandaff and was subject, therefore, to visitation by the bishop of the diocese. Early in 1319, however, John de Hastings, the priory's patron, took the unusual step of petitioning Pope John XXII that an

---

[32] *Brec. Cart.*, pp. 139–40.

enquiry should be made into the affairs of the priory. Though
the house was well able to support thirteen monks, only five
resided. They were not visited and lived dissolutely. As a
result of John's petition, a papal mandate of 19 April 1319
ordered the bishop of Hereford 'to examine the matter and
carry out the necessary reform'.[33] There was a long delay
before any decisive action was taken. It was not until 20
September of the following year that Adam de Orleton,
bishop of Hereford, instructed the dean of Abergavenny to
cite the prior and monks to appear before him.[34]

On the day appointed, Orleton, accompanied by the bishop
of Llandaff and numerous monks and laymen, visited the
priory and made a thorough inquisition into its spiritual and
temporal condition. His findings showed that John de Hastings's
petition was amply justified.[35] The goods of the priory, valued
at 240 marks and more, were well able to support thirteen
monks. John de Hastings had even provided an additional
endowment of two carucates of land and £20 from his castle of
Abergavenny. Yet the number of monks professed had for the
past forty years rarely risen above five and occasionally
descended to four. As a result of their negligence in alienating
their temporal and spiritual goods, the priory was in ruins.

Orleton's findings on the spiritual condition of the priory
were more serious. The monks had long since abandoned
observance of their rule and were leading a scandalously
dissolute life. They wandered outside the priory by night and
were sometimes discovered by laymen in the company of
prostitutes. Silence in the cloister and at table was not observed,
and meat was eaten in the refectory on forbidden days. At
times when they should have been reciting the divine office,
monks were to be found playing at dice and other forbidden
games. Some of them were wont to enact parodies of the
Crucifixion for the entertainment of their friends. They came
down from the dormitory, naked, with arms outstretched and
wearing crowns woven from straw on their heads. The monks
were guilty of other scandalous misdeeds about which Orleton
thought it best to remain silent.

[33] *CPL.*, ii, p. 186.
[34] *Reg. Ade de Orleton*, p. 154.
[35] Ibid., pp. 151–3, 190–4.

The prior of the house, Fulk Gastard, had already appeared before Orleton and been convicted of perjury. He had absconded before the bishop's arrival at Abergavenny and managed to remove to remote parts

> two chalices of silver, thirteen silver spoons, five garments of silk, various muniments touching the condition of the priory, certain relics of the saints and other books and goods pertaining to the priory and its church.[36]

During the enquiry it was found that Fulk was guilty of numerous cases of adultery and incontinence and that his presence in the priory could no longer be tolerated without grave scandal.

Orleton's reports show that the monastic life at Abergavenny had reached the nadir of decadence and corruption even by secular standards. That the deterioration had been allowed to reach such an advanced state may have been due to negligence on the part of the diocesan. In the absence of episcopal registers for the diocese of Llandaff, it is impossible to determine how frequently the priory had been visited.[37] A heavy burden of responsibility rested however with the abbots of St. Vincent, Le Mans, who had not visited their dependent priory for forty years.[38]

The speed with which Orleton now acted suggests that much preparatory work had been done before the day of the official visitation. After consultation with John, bishop of Llandaff, Richard, abbot of Dore, and others, he deposed Fulk from the priorate and appointed in his place Richard of Bromwich, a learned monk from Worcester Cathedral Priory.[39] He also decreed that the priory should in future support a convent of twelve monks and a prior and that when a vacancy occurred, the new prior should be elected by the monks themselves, not by the abbot of St. Vincent as hitherto.

---

[36] Ibid., p. 152.

[37] One of Orleton's reports seems to suggest that the priory was visited by no one: see *Reg. Ade de Orleton*, p. 152. It is worth noting that the neighbouring priory of Monmouth, just inside the diocese of Hereford, was visited by the bishop of Hereford in 1275, 1279, 1286, 1292 and 1300: see *Reg. John de Trillek, 1344–61*, pp. 221–2.

[38] *Reg. Ade de Orleton*, p. 191.

[39] Ibid., pp. 154–5.

Orleton added a saving clause to protect the *apport* of 107*s.* which was payable annually to St. Vincent, Le Mans. Five years later the monks of Worcester begged Richard of Bromwich to return to them. So many of the older monks had died that they needed his presence to maintain Worcester's reputation for learning. Richard thereupon returned to Worcester to teach theology to the younger monks.[40]

Meanwhile, the abbot of St. Vincent, Le Mans, was busily prosecuting an appeal against the action of Orleton in deposing Fulk without consulting him. He doubtless considered that the grant of election to the monks of Abergavenny was not only an infringement of his own constitutional rights but a dangerous precedent, a first step perhaps towards the denization of the priory. Orleton was informed of the appeal early in 1321. The parties to the cause were to appear before the pope by their procters.[41] The case dragged on until 1327, when the pope ordered the prior of Monmouth to restore Fulk Gastard to the priorate of Abergavenny. As Rose Graham has shown, it was merely 'a formal assertion of the abbot of St. Vincent's rights, for it was followed immediately by the "free" resignation of Fulk Gastard'. The choice of a new prior was given to a canon of the cathedral church of Le Mans, who was to select a suitable monk from the abbey of St. Vincent.[42]

II. THE MONASTIC MACHINERY FOR MAINTAINING DISCIPLINE

(i) *The Cistercian Constitution*

The leaders of the Cistercian reform devoted much time and thought not only to the problem of transforming their ideals of the monastic life into a concrete institution—the recent history of Molesme had shown that experiments of this kind were rarely of lasting value—but to the more complex task of devising constitutional and administrative machinery for ensuring, as far as was humanly possible, that their own ideals and the fervour which inspired them would be transmitted to

---

[40] R. Graham, 'Four Alien Priories in Monmouthshire', *Jnl. Brit. Arch. Assoc.*, xxxv (1929–30), p. 110.

[41] *CPL.*, ii, p. 211.

[42] R. Graham, op. cit., pp. 110–11. By a slip the author has substituted St. Florent for St. Vincent.

future generations of monks. The evolution of the Cistercian constitution was slower than was at one time thought,[43] but its main features had been firmly established before the entry of Cistercian monks into *pura Wallia*. Uniformity throughout all abbeys of the order was stressed from the first. The Rule of St. Benedict was to be interpreted as it was in the new monastery of Cîteaux. But nothing was left to chance. By about 1150 a detailed code of observance was in existence which regulated almost every aspect of an abbey's internal and external life: liturgy, diet, clothing, church ornaments, architecture, and estate management, with regulations even for the type of animals to be kept. Uniformity and a high level of observance were to be maintained by an annual attendance of abbots at General Chapter and by an annual visitation of daughter houses by their father abbots.

(ii) *General Chapter: Attendance of Welsh Abbots, 1180–1291*

The General Chapter was held at Cîteaux on or about the feast of the Holy Cross (14 September) and lasted for five days.[44] By the end of the twelfth century it had come to exercise a variety of functions. It acted as a forum for the discussion of any question which affected the well-being of the order or its individual members. It was a legislative assembly in which propositions prepared by the *diffinitores* were debated, voted on and passed as *statuta*.[45] It was a judicial court of appeal to which complaints might be brought not only by one abbot against another but by laymen and secular clerics who had grievances against members of the order. Such disputes might either be discussed in open chapter or delegated for investigation and settlement to a commission of three abbots. The General Chapter also acted as a 'chapter of faults' in which one abbot might inform on another for violations of the Rule and statutes of the order. Guilty abbots were given penances which were enrolled in the Chapter proceedings.

Originally, annual attendance of all Cistercian abbots was

---

[43] Knowles, *Monastic Order* (2nd ed., 1963), pp. 752–3. Cf. J. Sayers, 'The Judicial Activities of the General Chapter', *Jnl. Ecc. Hist.*, xv (1964), pp. 18–22.
[44] Jacques Hourlier, *Le Chapitre Général jusqu'au Moment du Grand Schisme*, pp. 65, 166–7.
[45] For the *diffinitores*, see L. J. Lekai, *The White Monks*, pp. 57–8.

expected. With the rapid expansion of the order into distant lands, however, special statutes were passed laying down how frequently abbots in particular countries were expected to attend. No extant statute clearly defines the obligation of the abbots of England and Wales, but in the twelfth century and for a good part of the thirteenth it seems likely that annual attendance was expected of them.[46] In 1305, however, it was reported that the abbots of England and Wales were obliged to attend every second year and the abbots of Ireland and Scotland every third year.[47]

No attendance registers exist to show how frequently abbots discharged their obligations. A rough idea of the attendance record of the Welsh abbots and the part they played in the administrative work of the order may be obtained by inference from the extant records of the Chapter. It may be assumed, for example, that when an abbot was commissioned to investigate and settle a dispute, he was present at the Chapter. It may be assumed, too, that when an abbot was ordered to notify other abbots of a Chapter decision, he was present and those to be notified absent. The presence of at least one abbot may also be presumed if a dispute involving two or more abbeys came up for discussion in a Chapter.

It would be out of place to marshal all the evidence here. Suffice it to say that of the thirteen houses of the Welsh province of the order, Margam, Tintern, Neath and Whitland were the houses most frequently commissioned to investigate and settle disputes.[48] These abbeys were also the ones most frequently asked to notify Chapter decisions to other abbots, while Margam, Neath, Basingwerk and Tintern were the abbeys most frequently involved in disputes. The evidence seems to suggest that the south Wales abbots not only discharged their duties of attendance at General Chapter more diligently than other Welsh abbots, but also bore the heaviest burden of administrative work on behalf of the order in Wales. As far as Margam is concerned, this seems to be borne out by other

---

[46] Hourlier, op. cit., p. 58.
[47] *Rot. Parl.*, i, p. 178.
[48] Since Wales is frequently treated as a distinct province of the order in Chapter records, it has been thought desirable to take account of the north Wales abbeys in what follows.

evidence. In 1218 the abbots of England petitioned the Chapter that abbots from their own land be chosen whose counsel could be taken when grave causes arose which could not wait for the meeting of the annual General Chapter. These might be changed, when it became necessary, with the counsel of the father abbots. The names of the father abbots were given as Fountains, Rievaulx, Waverley, Margam and Beaulieu.[49] Even though Margam at this time had no daughter houses and its abbot was not, technically speaking, a father abbot,[50] the petition leaves little doubt as to the influential position occupied by the abbey at this period.

On no occasion do the records refer to repeated absenteeism on the part of the Welsh abbots. In itself this is of little significance, but in the light of repeated references to the absenteeism of certain Irish abbots,[51] it seems to indicate that the attendance record of the Welsh abbots was not giving cause for serious concern. Individual absences, however, are noted. In 1202 the abbot of Whitland was given a penance because he did not come to the General Chapter 'when he ought to have come'.[52] In 1216 the absence of the abbot of Aberconwy was excused because of his infirmity, but he was ordered to present himself at the next Chapter.[53] In 1277 it was noted that the abbot of Tintern had not attended because of infirmity of long standing. If he did not attend the Chapter in the following year, the father abbot was to receive his resignation.[54]

Recorded, too, are the petitions made by abbots to be excused attendance. For the Welsh houses, they all belong to the second half of the thirteenth century. In 1267 the abbot of Neath petitioned that he might miss his turn for attending the Chapter. In 1271 the abbot of Margam petitioned that he might absent himself for this year. In 1278 the abbot of Whitland petitioned that he might absent himself on one occasion. In 1281 such petitions are recorded for Tintern,

---

[49] Canivez, *Statuta*, i, p. 500.
[50] The Irish abbeys of Maig and Holy Cross were not affiliated to Margam until 1227 and 1228: see Clark, *Cartae*, ii, pp. 446–7, 455–9. These affiliations are a further indication of Margam's influence at this time.
[51] Canivez, *Statuta*, i, p. 457, iii, pp. 86, 94, 156.
[52] Ibid., i. p. 279. The abbot was Peter, then engaged in the St. David's election dispute and subsequently deposed.
[53] Ibid., p. 454.
[54] Ibid., iii, p. 171.

Strata Florida, Caerleon (*Tallion*), and Strata Marcella (*Stranqua*).[55] The years 1278, 1281 and 1282 show a fairly high rate of absenteeism for the order as a whole.[56] Taken in sum, the evidence suggests that the obligation of attendance, however irksome, was acknowledged and generally fulfilled and that a representative number of Welsh abbots attended the Chapter every year at least until the last quarter of the thirteenth century.[57]

(iii) *Visitation*

The *Carta Caritatis* enjoined that the abbot of a mother house should visit all the filiations of his own monastery every year. With the proliferation of daughter houses in the twelfth century, the fulfilment of this obligation became physically impossible for a number of abbots, particularly for the abbot of Clairvaux, whose eighty filiations were scattered throughout every part of Europe. A part of the burden had necessarily to be delegated to co-abbots.[58] References drawn from sources not directly concerned with the visitation process show that houses which were immediate daughters of Clairvaux, L'Aumône and Savigny were regularly visited during the latter half of the twelfth and throughout the greater part of the thirteenth century. Serlo, abbot of L'Aumône, was in the marches of Wales sometime between 1180 and 1183 and doubtless visited Tintern at this time, since no other daughter house of L'Aumône existed in the vicinity.[59] Visitors despatched by the General Chapter came to England in 1188 and received the resignation of three abbots, one of them being William of Tintern.[60] Foreign visitors were at Margam in 1203 when Gilbert was promoted to the abbacy.[61] They probably visited Whitland at about the same time to give effect to the deposition of Peter, abbot of Whitland, on whom Gerald of Wales had

[55] Ibid., pp. 56, 102, 183, 214.
[56] Despite absences, more than 400 abbots appear to have been present at the General Chapter in 1274: see A. A. King, *Cîteaux and her Elder Daughters*, p. 45.
[57] Hourlier, *Le Chapitre Général*, p. 174, reaches a similar conclusion for the whole order.
[58] The latest edition of the *Carta* (second half of the twelfth century?) made provision for this: see L. J. Lekai, *The White Monks*, p. 269.
[59] *Autobiography of Giraldus Cambrensis*, ed. H. E. Butler, pp. 77–8.
[60] *Annales Monastici*, ii, p. 245.
[61] For Gilbert, see below pp. 123–5.

dilated in the previous year.[62] In 1213 visitors sent by the abbot of Clairvaux were again at Margam and secured the resignation of Abbot Gilbert, who retired to Kirkstead Abbey.[63] Between the years 1227 and 1232 visitors were continually passing through south Wales on their way to reform abbeys in Ireland, and they had ample opportunity of noting the observance of the major houses which lay along their route.[64] In 1233 royal protection was given to the abbot of Boxley (a daughter of Clairvaux), 'gone to Wales to make a visitation of the Cistercian houses in those parts'.[65] Since the abbot of Savigny sent visitors to England in 1243, it is possible that Neath was visited at this time.[66] In 1250 visitors from Clairvaux were again passing through Wales *en route* to Ireland.[67] The abbot of Clairvaux was in England in person in 1268, but whether as a visitor or not is uncertain. A visitation of the daughter houses of Clairvaux was certainly made in 1272.[68]

Of the visitations undertaken by Welsh abbots there is less evidence. Gerald of Wales informs us that the abbots of Margam and Neath visited Biddlesden (Bucks.) *circa* 1190 and deposed William Wibert, the cellarer,[69] and that in 1200 Peter, abbot of Whitland, was 'engaged upon a visitation which had been enjoined upon him in the remote parts of Ireland'.[70] In 1196 the General Chapter ordered the abbot of Whitland to visit his daughter house of Strata Florida in person. This seems to suggest that a certain amount of laxity had developed in the visitation of houses of the second generation.[71]

In the absence of the reports of visitors, the records of the General Chapter provide the only official information of the

(iv) *Cistercian Observance and Discipline*

In the absence of the reports of visitors, the records of the General Chapter provide the only official information of the

---

[62] Gerald visited Cîteaux late in 1202, 'where he procured the not unmerited deposition of the abbot of Whitland': *Autobiography*, pp. 265, 335.

[63] *Annales Monastici*, i, p. 32.

[64] *CPR.*, *1225–32*, pp. 176, 505.

[65] *CPR.*, *1232–47*, p. 14.

[66] *CPR.*, *1232–47*, p. 400.

[67] *CPR.*, *1247–58*, p. 61.

[68] *CPR.*, *1266–72*, p. 188, 635.

[69] D. Knowles, 'Some Enemies of Gerald of Wales', *Studia Monastica*, i (1959), p. 138.

[70] *Autobiography of Giraldus Cambrensis*, pp. 77–8. This was a special visitation, since Whitland had no daughter house in Ireland until 1224 when a colony was sent to Tracton.

[71] Canivez, *Statuta*, i, p. 199. Cf. Knowles, *Monastic Order*, p. 655.

standard of discipline and observance in the Welsh houses. This evidence is, by its very nature, extremely limited. The Chapter functioned, as we have seen, as a 'chapter of faults'. One abbot might inform on another for violating the Rule and observances of the order. Accusations of this kind could also reach the Chapter by letter from persons who were not members of the order. It is mainly by virtue of its function as a 'chapter of faults' that the misdeeds of individual abbots are recorded and penances enrolled in the Chapter records. In the General Chapter of 1202, 'it was said' that the abbots of Caerleon, Valle Crucis and Aberconwy rarely celebrated Mass and abstained from the altar. The abbots of Ford and Combermere were commissioned to visit these houses and report their findings to the following Chapter. The three abbots were also to present themselves to answer the charges.[72] In 1217 it was said that the abbot of Tintern spoke after Compline and even drank with the bishop and his monks, and that women lived near the gateway of a grange and worked on grange land. The abbots of Dore and Bordesley were commissioned to investigate and, if the accusations were true, order the abbot to come to the next Chapter to seek pardon. In the same year it was also reported that in the abbeys of Dore and Tintern the office was sung in three-part and four-part voice 'in the manner of seculars'. The abbots of Neath and Flaxley were commissioned to investigate.[73] In 1234 it was noted that the abbot of Valle Crucis had violated the statutes of the order by obtaining letters allowing women to enter the precincts of his house. He was to undergo the penance laid down for a *levis culpa*[74] for six days, two of these on bread and water, and was to remain outside the abbatial stall and abstain from the altar for forty days. He was not to make use of the letters he had obtained.[75]

Throughout the period the lay-brethren were a constant source of anxiety to the order. Though recruited primarily to

---

[72] Canivez, *Statuta*, i, p. 281.
[73] Ibid., p. 472.
[74] A *levis culpa* would seem to have been 'rather a breach of a rule or a statute than a fault against the moral law': see A. A. King, *Cîteaux and Her Elder Daughters*, pp. 114–5.
[75] Canivez, *Statuta*, ii, p. 137. For other infringements of Cistercian observance by Welsh abbots, see ibid., i, pp. 475, 484, ii, pp. 238, 382.

provide a labour force to work the Cistercian estates, it was intended that they should also be 'sharers in the spiritual and temporal blessings of the monastery'.[76] But they were never fully integrated into a regular community life. They did not, and the majority could not, take part in the recitation of the divine office. Their inferior social standing and lack of education set them apart from the literate choir monks; and the provision of a separate church, sleeping quarters and refectory tended to emphasize the gulf between them. It is probable that a number of them conceived of their vocation in no higher terms than did Browning's Fra Lippo Lippi:

> the good bellyful,
> The warm serge and the rope that goes all round.[77]

Less conscious of the sacredness of their vocation, they were more liable to be stirred to anger by petty grievances and unfair treatment by an abbot and his obedientiaries. They spent most of their time working or supervising work at the abbey granges. When an abbey's property was widely scattered the lay-brethren enjoyed a corresponding freedom from control and supervision. Acting collectively, they could intimidate an abbot and his officials and withhold food supplies from the monks.

The discipline of the lay-brethren was not an exclusively Welsh problem,[78] but from about 1190 almost every abbot in south Wales experienced difficulty in controlling them. Initially, at least, trouble appears to have started by allowing beer to be drunk at the abbey granges. In 1190 the abbot of Margam and his community were given a penance because the Chapter's prohibition of beer drinking in their granges was not observed. In the following year, the same abbot was ordered to remain outside the abbatial stall for forty days 'because of the enormities which were committed in his house'. He was to perform the penance laid down for a *levis culpa* for six days, one of them on bread and water. After his return from the General Chapter, two of his lay-brethren, Jordan,

---

[76] Ibid., i, p. 14.
[77] See Map's remarks that the upland Welsh led a more spartan existence than the Cistercians, in *De Nugis Curialium*, ed. E. S. Hartland, p. 53.
[78] See James S. Donnelly, *The Decline of the Medieval Cistercian Laybrotherhood*, pp. 23–4.

hospitalis, and Ralph, were to make their way to Clairvaux and there undergo the penance laid down by the General Chapter.[79] A general prohibition of beer drinking by lay-brethren was issued to the abbots of England in 1192, and no new lay-brother was to be received until it was observed.[80] In 1195 the lay-brothers of Cwm-hir stole their abbot's horses because he had forbidden them to drink beer. They were to make their way to Clairvaux on foot and abide by the decision of the abbot of Clairvaux.[81] The abbots of Wales were ordered to ensure that neither beer nor any liquid other than plain water was drunk on their granges.[82] Meanwhile, trouble had broken out at Strata Florida, and in 1196 the abbot of Whitland was ordered to visit the house, enquire into the excesses of the lay-brothers and compel them to make fitting satisfaction.[83] A really serious revolt of the lay-brothers occurred at Margam in 1206. They formed a conspiracy and rose against the abbot, threw the cellarer from his horse, and in an armed band pursued the abbot for fifteen miles. They then barricaded themselves in their own dormitory and withheld food from the monks. The General Chapter, presumably acting on information provided by their abbot, Gilbert, decreed that the lay-brothers concerned were to be punished as conspirators and the ring-leaders dispersed throughout houses of the order. New lay-brothers were not to be received without the consent of the General Chapter.[84] Gerald of Wales gives a different account of the revolt which is worth quoting:

> The said abbot, being equally hated by his neighbours of the same order through his flagrant injustices against them and by his own house for the internal discord he fomented, strove with all his power to pervert and change for the worse the constitution of his house which had been laid down in the past by religious and holy abbots. Wherefore, when certain monks and brethren, zealous for the reputation of the order, dared to speak out against him, he hired and assembled evil minions of the

[79] Canivez, *Statuta*, i, pp. 123, 138.
[80] Ibid., p. 149.
[81] Ibid., p. 191.
[82] Ibid., p. 193.
[83] Ibid., p. 191.
[84] Ibid., p. 324.

secular power . . . and did not hesitate to drag them violently from their own house as captives . . . with hands tied behind their backs . . . from the cloisters to the prison cells of the castle.[85]

The real reason behind the revolt and the rights and wrongs of the case will probably never be known.

The lay-brothers continued to be a source of trouble to some abbots well into the second half of the thirteenth century. In 1269 the attention of the General Chapter was drawn to the 'frequent and rash audacity of certain lay-brothers of Neath'. They had left their house, taking with them the horses belonging to the father abbot. Unless they returned to the order within a month of a warning being issued, they were to be excommunicated and if possible thrown into prison.[86]

The works of Gerald of Wales provide valuable supplementary evidence on the condition of the Welsh Cistercian houses; much of it has been used in various contexts on previous pages. Some evaluation of the evidence is necessary, however, before attention is directed to the later history of the order. Gerald's mature but embittered work on the religious orders, the *Speculum Ecclesiae*, projected as early as 1191 but not completed until about 1217 or 1218,[87] was the result of over half a century's experience of the religious life of south Wales and of personal acquaintance with numerous abbots. His testimony for the south Wales houses deserves a more serious consideration than his less closely documented accounts of English houses. During his career he made enemies of at least three Cistercian abbots of south Wales: Peter, abbot of Whitland; Cadwgan, successively abbot of Strata Florida and Whitland, and bishop of Bangor; and Gilbert, abbot of Margam. These three abbots furnished him with focal points for his main attack on the order, useful 'pegs' on which charges of a more general kind could be hung.

Peter, abbot of Whitland, before taking the Cistercian habit, had been Gerald's clerk and friend and had shared his board. As Gerald on one occasion admitted, he was a man of talent and learning. During the St. David's election dispute Peter

[85] Gir. Camb., *Opera*, iv, pp. 141–2.
[86] Canivez, *Statuta*, iii, p. 72.
[87] Gir. Camb., *Opera*, i, pp. 409–10, vi, p. 47.

became a candidate for the bishopric and thereby earned Gerald's undying hatred. Gerald accused him of illegitimacy because he was the son of a priest, of incontinence, of over-weening ambition and of having brought his house of Whitland to ruin and destruction. Gerald journeyed to Cîteaux and obtained his deposition in 1202.[88]

Cadwgan was a monk, probably an obedientiary, of Strata Florida when Gerald attempted to pawn his books to the abbey in 1202.[89] At the last moment the monks refused to accept the books on pledge since it was contrary to the institutes of the order, and Gerald was forced to sell his cherished library to the abbey. The monk whom Gerald held chiefly to blame for this was Cadwgan. The sale or, as Gerald would have it, the theft of the books was made the occasion for a vitriolic attack on Cadwgan in which every aspect of his character and achievements was denigrated. He was am-bitious and cunning. Soon after Gerald's visit, he engineered the deposition of his abbot, 'a good and simple man', and procured his own election. Again, not long afterwards, he brought about the deposition of the abbot of Whitland and was himself elected abbot. In 1212, before Cadwgan's promotion to Whitland, the see of Bangor had fallen vacant. During a visit paid by Prince Llywelyn to Cardigan, Cadwgan took steps to cultivate his friendship and secure his support. He invited him to the abbey and entertained him lavishly, claiming between drinks that he was his cousin. It was largely through Llywelyn's influence that Cadwgan was promoted to the see of Bangor in 1215.

Cadwgan was the son of an Irish priest and a Welsh mother. Even when he was abbot, writes Gerald, he disowned his father and refused to compensate him for the money he had expended on his education in the schools. Despite his Irish nationality, Cadwgan's father was a fluent and rousing preacher in Welsh. Cadwgan acquired something of this gift from him and as bishop was accustomed to deliver sermons in the abbeys

---

[88] See the index under Whitland in *Autobiography of Giraldus Cambrensis*, ed. H. E. Butler, and the references given in D. Knowles, 'Some Enemies of Gerald of Wales', *Studia Monastica*, i (1959), pp. 139–40.

[89] For what follows, see Gir. Camb., *Opera*, iv, pp. 161–7.

he visited in England and Wales. They were carefully-composed exercises in plagiarism, writes Gerald, committed to memory word for word and delivered more for show than for the moral edification of his listeners.

Before his promotion to Bangor, Gerald alleges that Cadwgan took to the abbot of Clairvaux letters of Llywelyn, signed with a false seal, which bestowed lands for the foundation of a new abbey which the prince had had no intention of granting. He had also cunningly sold wool without the knowledge or consent of his own house to further his own ambitions. As a result of these charges, he was deposed by visitors a short while before he became bishop of Bangor; but his deposition was not, at that time, known to the archbishop of Canterbury.

Modern historians have been kinder to Cadwgan's reputation. His religious writings and his resignation from Bangor in 1236 to assume the habit of a simple monk in the abbey of Dore have been interpreted as signs of a carefully nourished piety, and have tended to cast an aura of peace over his last years.[90] The records of the General Chapter, however, present a different picture. In 1239 it was reported that Cadwgan, once bishop of Bangor, and Jocelin, ex-bishop of Ardagh, were the cause of grave laxities in the respective houses of Dore and St. Mary's, Dublin, by their neglect of the observances and institutes of the order and of the Chapter, both in the matter of silence and in the manner of their life. They were thereby fomenting dissension and scandal.[91] Cadwgan died two years after his admonition by the General Chapter.

Gerald's animus towards Gilbert, abbot of Margam (1203–13), is more difficult to explain.[92] The vehemence of his attack suggests a personal encounter. On the other hand, Gerald may have acquired both his information and his antipathy from the monks of Neath, whose cause he champions against the richer abbey.[93] He was, says Gerald, a north-

[90] Lloyd, *History of Wales*, ii, pp. 688–9, and the same author's article in *Dictionary of Welsh Biography*, p. 65. For Cadwgan's literary remains, see below pp. 153–4.

[91] Canivez, *Statuta*, ii, p. 206.

[92] Gir. Camb., *Opera*, iv, pp. 129–43. Like Cadwgan, Gilbert is left unnamed by Gerald but the incidents mentioned show clearly that Gilbert is the subject of his attack.

[93] F. G. Cowley, 'Neath versus Margam: Some 13th Century Disputes', *Trans. Port Talbot Hist. Soc.*, i (3) (1967), pp. 10–11.

countryman and appointed to the abbey by foreign visitors. No sooner had he been appointed abbot than he embarked on a policy of aggrandisement against the poorer house of Neath, occupying its lands and pastures and endeavouring by every means to impoverish and even destroy it. In the ensuing feud, even the prize horses of the abbey studs were set to fight each other as champions of their respective houses. The lay-brothers of Margam conceived the cunning device of attaching sharp steel blades to the hoofs of their horse to ensure its victory. One of the Neath monks, Geoffrey, smarting under the injustices inflicted on the abbey by the richer house and seeing no hope of redress at the General Chapter, whither he had so often journeyed with his Abbot Abraham, doffed his monastic habit and buckled on the accoutrements of a knight. He put himself at the head of a band of hired marauders, descended on Margam's granges, and drove all the cattle and horses that could be found to a hide-out in the mountains. The abbot of Margam, vexed and humiliated at his losses, made his way to Neath with five or six of his monks and there protested against an outrage which he felt to be unprecedented in Cistercian annals. He demanded immediate restitution before the incident reached the ears of the General Chapter. Abbot Abraham denied all knowledge of the activities of his monk, but Geoffrey was using the 'lost' livestock as a means of forcing Margam to restore the lands which it had unjustly occupied. By resorting to 'Welsh law', Geoffrey succeeded in gaining for his house a peace which it had failed to acquire by an appeal to canon and monastic law.

While Gilbert, or a man of similar character, was abbot, the monks of Margam obtained the lease of a neighbouring knight's fee. They destroyed the castle of the fee, razed the parish church to the ground and ejected the parishioners from their houses.[94] Gerald claims that 'the outrageous deeds and excesses' of Margam provided ample material for his pen, but he adds only two specific charges to his general indictment of the abbey at this time. One of the monks had in Gerald's time become a convert to Judaism,[95] while Abbot Gilbert, when

---

[94] See above pp. 80–1.
[95] Gir. Camb., *Opera*, iv, p. 139.

opposed by his monks and lay-brothers who had the best interests of the order at heart, called in the assistance of the secular power and had them dragged off to prison.[96] For his misdeeds, continues Gerald, God visited him with a two-fold punishment in his lifetime. He was the victim of epilepsy and on a number of occasions had epileptic fits in the presence of official visitors. He was also deservedly expelled from the house which he had so badly harassed and deposed from the office which he had so shamefully abused.

A bald paraphrase, such as has been attempted above, omitting the digressions, the rhetorical questions and the abusive language, can hardly convey Gerald's undoubted journalistic skill in presenting a case or the vehemence and lack of charity with which he pursued his objective. His main thesis is fairly clear and consistently maintained. The Cistercian houses of Wales, as of England, had lost that pristine spirit which a generation or so earlier had given them a widespread reputation as centres of holiness and boundless charity. Gerald looked back with nostalgic affection to the golden days of Abbot Conan's rule at Margam and contrasted it with the ruthless avarice of later abbots.[97] The facts and incidents which he uses to sustain his thesis, drawn partly from personal observation but mainly from well-informed hearsay, are, when they can be checked, broadly true. The interpretation put upon the facts is Gerald's own, and truth is on more than one occasion sacrificed in the interest of personal prejudice and even of literary effect.[98] There can be no doubt that inter-abbatial disputes were waged with a ferocity unbecoming to an order which had been renowned for its charity.[99] Gerald's account of the conflict between Neath and Margam, however, is over-simplified to the extent of being a travesty of the truth. The charters in the Margam collection show that

[96] See above pp. 120–1.
[97] *Opera*, iv, p. 142.
[98] In his account of the revolt against Gilbert's rule, Gerald could hardly resist the alliterative cadence of *a claustris ad carceres et castra*. Other evidence would suggest that the claustral monks took no part in the revolt and that it was confined to the lay-brothers.
[99] See the letter dated 1235 of Stephen of Lexington (then abbot of Savigny) to the abbot of Margam complaining of the injuries inflicted on Neath Abbey by the cellarer and some of the monks of Margam, in *Registrum Epistolarum Stephani de Lexinton*, pp. 302–3.

legally the abbey of Margam had a strong case against Neath which it would have been foolish not to defend. The abbey of Neath was laying permanent claim to rights of pasture which Morgan ap Caradog had only granted to the abbey for a term of two years and over which Margam had for a long time possessed exclusive rights.[100]

When full allowance has been made for prejudice and partisanship, Gerald's main charges against the Welsh Cistercians may be reduced to two: the emergence of ambitious abbots who were not above using their office merely as a stepping stone for promotion to more exalted posts in the church; and the spread of acquisitiveness and aggressive landlordism which was not only robbing the Cistercians of their earlier reputation for charity but causing real social distress. On both counts, Gerald's charges have a ring of truth. It is indeed possible that both Peter and Cadwgan were not ideally suited to the Cistercian vocation and would have achieved, had they lived at a later date, a more fruitful and happier fulfilment of their undoubted talents in the ranks of the friars.[101] Gerald's charge of acquisitiveness, formulated as early as 1191, is amply borne out by other sources. It needs to be stressed, however, that a corporate society acting in the interest of *esprit de corps* through its chosen officers, can be guilty of acts of injustice completely out of keeping with the characters and ideals of its individual members. On this, Gerald is silent. There are in his works no charges against the Cistercians of widespread depravity and corruption, charges which he levelled with some justice against the inmates of the small cells. In the main, his evidence confirms the impression obtained from official sources that the Cistercian abbeys of Wales, though less fervent in their observance than in previous generations and more ruthless in their policy of agrarian expansion, were still centres untouched by gross scandal where an ordered life of prayer continued to attract men of piety and learning.

---

[100] Clark, *Cartae*, vi, pp. 2284–5. Cf. also ibid., ii, pp. 391, i, p. 180, vi, p. 2283, iii, p. 929.

[101] Knowles (*Religious Orders*, i, p. 6 note 2) has suggested this for Stephen of Lexington, successively monk of Quarr, abbot of Savigny and of Clairvaux. Stephen, despite his ability and reforming zeal, was, like Peter and Cadwgan, deposed from his abbacy and spent his later years under a cloud.

(v) *The Loosening of the Ties with Cîteaux*

For abbots in Wales, and even more so for the Irish abbots, the journey to the General Chapter was long, arduous, expensive, and occasionally fraught with danger. For the abbot of Aberconwy, the most distant of the Welsh houses, the journey could take well over a month and he would have had to leave his house early in August. The abbot of Tintern was nearer Cîteaux by eight days and could afford to delay his departure for at least a week after the abbot of Aberconwy had started out.[102] For a poor house like Cymer the expenses of such a journey could amount to over a third of the house's assessed income.[103] It is small wonder, therefore, that abbots attempted to lessen the incidence of their obligation to attend. In 1209 the Welsh abbots presented a joint petition in which they sought permission that one only of their number should attend General Chapter every year instead of them all coming together. The petition was committed for attention to the abbot of Clairvaux.[104] Subsequent entries in the records show that the petition was not granted. As we have already seen, petitions seeking dispensation from attendance became frequent in the 'seventies and 'eighties of the thirteenth century. Occasionally the king himself wrote letters requesting that certain abbots be excused from attending. In 1293 Edward I requested that the abbot of Aberconwy be excused because he needed him to stay in England.[105] In 1298 the king requested that the abbots of Aberconwy and Valle Crucis be excused attendance; they were 'staying in Wales by the king's command for the king's business and the quiet of the land'. Apart from this, the abbot of Aberconwy was not 'in a fit bodily state to travel'.[106] Powers of dispensing groups of abbots from attending were sometimes granted by the General Chapter to the abbot of Cîteaux when the latter house was heavily in debt. The

---

[102] These estimates of travelling time are based on Gir. Camb., *Opera*, vi, p. 165. The early dates at which letters of protection and travel permits were issued by the royal chancery seem to confirm them.

[103] In 1274 Llywelyn ap Gruffydd gave the abbot of Cymer £10 to enable him to journey to Cîteaux (*Littere Wallie*, ed. J. G. Edwards, p. 33). This was the normal sum allowed for the expenses of Welsh abbots in royal travel permits at the beginning of the fourteenth century.

[104] Canivez, *Statuta*, i, p. 367.

[105] *Cal. Chancery Warrants, 1244–1326*, p. 37.

[106] Ibid., p. 92.

expenses which would normally have been incurred by the dispensed abbots were to be devoted to relieving the financial difficulties of the mother house of the order.[107]

Up until the reign of Edward I, the Cistercians had enjoyed in time of war a degree of freedom in travelling between England and France denied to others. Even with the outbreak of war with France in 1294, Edward left the Cistercians in peace.[108] In June 1298, however, the king forbade all Cistercian abbots to attend the General Chapter or to cause money to be transported to Cîteaux. The ban was reiterated, with some modifications, at intervals throughout the first half of the fourteenth century and later.[109] Edward's prohibition was a significant break with precedent and was motivated to a large extent by the developments which had taken place in the financing of the central organs of the order since the beginning of the thirteenth century. In the *Carta Caritatis* the Cistercian fathers had clearly stated that they had no intention of imposing tallages or apports on the abbeys of the order. But the rapid expansion of the order in the twelfth century brought a corresponding increase in the expenses of the General Chapter. These expenses were too large to be met solely by pious grants and bequests. By 1220 the acquisition of special privileges and their common defence in the courts made it necessary for the order to maintain a small secretariat at Rome.[110] In the face of these growing expenses, the provision made in the *Carta* became unrealistic. Acting on the principle that 'a burden which touches all, should be borne by all', the General Chapter began to levy contributions from the abbeys of the order, a step which received the approval of Innocent III.[111] At the beginning of the fourteenth century it was estimated that an apport of 4,000 marks was being sent every year to Cîteaux from the abbeys of England, Wales, Ireland and Scotland.[112] This was the English kings' main objection to Cistercian abbots attending General Chapter. They were the bearers of

[107] Canivez, *Statuta*, iii, pp. 69, 279.
[108] *Chronicle of Bury St. Edmunds, 1212–1301*, ed. Antonia Gransden, p. 123.
[109] J. F. O'Sullivan, *Cistercian Settlements*, pp. 95–6.
[110] Canivez, *Statuta*, i, p. 527.
[111] J. Hourlier, *Le Chapitre Général*, pp. 224–5.
[112] *Rot., Parl.*, i, p. 178.

moneys raised in England, Wales and Ireland which could, without much difficulty, be diverted to the use of the king's enemies.

The royal prohibition gave a number of abbots a useful pretext for shirking their obligation of attendance. Even in the first decade of the fourteenth century, English and Welsh absenteeism was becoming increasingly common. In 1306 Pope Clement V commanded the archbishop of York and the bishops of London and Winchester to insist that Cistercian abbots attend the Chapter, 'though they say that they are forbidden to do so by the king'.[113] In 1312 some thirty-nine Cistercian abbots, six of them Welsh, attended an assembly in London called by Arnald, a cardinal-legate (and himself a Cistercian). A letter of Pope Clement V was read which again insisted on the attendance of abbots at the Chapter, despite the king's prohibition, and threatened with excommunication those who spurned the decree.[114] In 1328 the General Chapter ordered the abbot of Cîteaux and those of his four elder daughters to send envoys to persuade the king of England to relax the ban and enforce the decree of Clement V (presumably that of 1312).[115] By 1342 the abbots of Waverley, Tintern and Quarr had taken the bold step of convoking their own chapter, passing statutes and imposing penances. The proceedings of this 'provincial' chapter were declared void by the General Chapter.[116]

It would be wrong to imagine that the wars with France caused a complete break in contacts between Cîteaux and the Welsh abbeys. The royal ban was frequently evaded.[117] It was possible, too, to obtain royal permits to attend the Chapter with a fixed money allowance for travelling expenses. Thus, in 1309 a royal licence was granted to the abbots of Margam, Valle Crucis, Strata Marcella and Aberconwy to attend the Chapter with £10 travelling expenses.[118] In 1313 a similar licence was granted to the abbots of Basingwerk, Strata

---

[113] *CPL.*, ii, p. 19.
[114] P.R.O., E 135/1/5. The Welsh abbots present were those of Basingwerk, Aberconwy, Tintern, Caerleon, Neath and Strata Florida.
[115] Canivez, *Statuta*, iii, p. 384.
[116] Ibid., pp. 469–70.
[117] In 1308 seven abbots who had eluded the king's officers along the coast were arrested when they landed at Dover on their return; see *CCR., 1307–13*, p. 79.
[118] Rymer, *Foedera*, ii (1), p. 78.

Marcella and Whitland, allowing each of them 20 marks expenses. The abbots of Whitland and Cwm-hir attended in 1329 with £10 expenses, and the abbot of Tintern in 1331. The abbot of Whitland attended again in 1332.[119] Whitland's attendance during these years was probably prompted by self-interest, for her claim to the filiation of Strata Marcella was being hotly challenged by John Charlton, lord of Powys. The latter wished to subject Strata Marcella to the abbey of Buildwas and put in English monks.[120]

The machinery of visitation also continued to function, though perhaps with less regularity and effectiveness. Visitations of the filiations of Clairvaux are recorded for 1325 (England, Wales and Ireland), 1326, 1335 and 1350 (England and Wales).[121] The abbot of L'Aumône was in England in 1330 'to visit divers houses subject to that order', and Tintern was presumably visited at this time.[122] In 1344 the General Chapter was still sufficiently cognizant of the affairs of the Welsh abbeys to deal with a disputed election at Strata Florida. A report had previously reached the Chapter that a blunder had been made in the election of brother Llywelyn to the abbacy. The abbots of Beaulieu and Thame held an enquiry into the election and declared it to be canonical. The Chapter ratified their decision.[123] In the same year it was noted that the abbot of Whitland, though cited to attend the Chapter, had not put in an appearance nor sent sufficient excuse. He was commanded to explain his absence at the next Chapter.[124] In 1352 the Chapter was again concerning itself with the affairs of Strata Florida. The abbot had translated the abbot of Cwm-hir to the monastery of Strata Marcella without asking or obtaining the licence of the General Chapter. Two Cistercian abbots were commissioned to announce the deposition of both abbots.[125]

---

[119] *CCR.*, *1313–18*, p. 69; *CCR.*, *1327–30*, p. 567; *CCR.*, *1330–33*, pp. 331, 583.
[120] O'Sullivan, *Cistercian Settlements*, pp. 89–91.
[121] *CPR.*, *1324–27*, p. 199; *CCR.*, *1323–27*, pp. 542, 638; *CCR.*, *1333–37*, p. 489; *CPR.*, *1348–50*, p. 497. Other visitations of English and Welsh houses are recorded for 1350 (*CPR.*, *1348–50*, p. 490), 1353, (*CPR.*, *1350–54*, p. 466), 1357 (*CPR.*, *1354–58*, p. 627), 1362 (*CPR.*, *1361–64*, p. 172).
[122] *CCR.*, *1330–33*, p. 145.
[123] Canivez, *Statuta*, iii, p. 494. For other references to this dispute, see *Register of Edward, the Black Prince*, i, pp. 2, 44, 132.
[124] Canivez, *Statuta*, iii, p. 499.
[125] Ibid., p. 525.

(vi) *Other Orders*

During the first half of the twelfth century a number of the new reformed orders developed machinery similar to that adopted by Cîteaux for maintaining monastic discipline. A triennial General Chapter was functioning at Tiron as early as 1120 and the abbot of St. Dogmaels was obliged to attend.[126] Prémontré, as we have seen, also based its institutions closely on the Cistercian model. Like Cîteaux, it held an annual Chapter and also made father abbots responsible for visiting daughter houses. In addition, before the end of the twelfth century, the order had instituted a system of circuits for visitation. Since it was not always possible for a father abbot to visit all his daughter houses every year, two abbots were appointed by the General Chapter to visit the houses of their region. Circuits for visitation were set up and this new machinery supplemented, but did not replace, the older system of visitation by father abbots.[127] The English province was divided into three circuits: the northern, the midland and the southern. The earliest surviving list of abbeys in these circuits (1288) does not include Talley, and Mr. Colvin has inferred that its 'remote situation probably secured its immunity from all but the most determined visitors'.[128] Some time before this date, however, the condition of the abbey was attracting the attention of the authorities. As we shall see, the abbey had suffered badly in the Welsh wars and was in royal custody at least as early as January 1278.[129] Between the latter date and 1291 the abbey was visited, with royal assistance, at least four times.[130] There can be little doubt that the abbey was in urgent need of reform at this time. The king, however, was not a disinterested party. His officials at Carmarthen were usurping the rights of the abbey's Welsh patron, Rhys ap Maredudd,[131] and the king himself was anxious to see the Welsh canons

---

[126] *Cal. Doc. Fr.*, pp. 353–4.
[127] H. M. Colvin, *White Canons*, pp. 19–20.
[128] Ibid., p. 198. Talley first appears in a list of *circariae* drawn up in 1320.
[129] See below p. 214.
[130] In 1278 by the abbot of Halesowen (*CPR., 1272–81*, p. 275), in 1279 by the abbots of Halesowen and Newhouse (*CPR., 1272–81*, p. 299), in 1284 by a former abbot of St. Quiric de Drusa (Colvin, op. cit., p. 202) and in 1291 by the abbots of Halesowen and Newhouse (*Collectanea Anglo-Premonstratensia*, iii, pp. 118–9).
[131] See below p. 220 and n. 126.

removed and English canons set in their place. The political and racial conflict aggravated rather than ameliorated the condition to which the abbey was reduced at this period. Since motives of material self-interest were strong, it is difficult to know what weight to attach to the evidence contained in an undated letter which Edward I addressed to the abbot of Prémontré.[132] A rumour had reached Edward which he felt it his duty to report. The canons were maintaining their mistresses and offspring out of revenues which should have been devoted to the poor and other pious uses. Neglecting 'the apostolic precept, "If you can't be chaste, be careful",' they dared to keep their mistresses openly and gave themselves up to drunkenness. The main point of Edward's letter follows:

> We beg you that . . . without delay you remove those canons from the aforesaid place and put in their place others of the English tongue who are willing and able to observe the rule of religion . . . and lest those put in their place in process of time follow their example, that you command by your letters the abbot of W[elbeck?] to visit those canons as often as shall be necessary and that the paternity of the same place be also assigned to him.

The policy of the English administration appears to have been partially successful, at least for a time. Talley, originally a daughter house of St. Jean, Amiens, was subjected to the English house of Welbeck.[133] In 1347 the abbot of Talley bore the unmistakable English name of Thomas de Pagham. This victory of English policy was achieved at a price, for by this date the abbey had lost most of its lands.[134]

After 1215, in conformity with the decrees of the Lateran Council, the Augustinians and the black monks set up provincial chapters and instituted visitation machinery similar to that employed by the reformed orders. The extant records of the Chapters, however, throw no direct light on the condition of the Augustinian and Benedictine houses of south Wales.

---

[132] *The Liber Epistolaris of Richard de Bury*, ed. N. Denholm-Young, pp. 33–4.

[133] Halesowen may have enjoyed the paternity of Talley for a time; see the documents printed in *Arch. Camb.*, 1893, pp. 233–4, 315–18. Cf. Colvin, op. cit., p. 238.

[134] *Register of Edward, the Black Prince*, i, pp. 117–8.

III. CONCLUSIONS

The foregoing survey of the main body of evidence for monastic discipline has perhaps sufficed to indicate that, although information is rich for certain years and for certain houses, it is never sufficiently comprehensive in depth and range to enable a real comparison of standards to be made from century to century. In most cases it is impossible to get behind vague charges such as 'manifest faults' and 'enormities' to the actual state of affairs in a monastery, while the internal life of several houses, Pill, Cwm-hir, St. Dogmaels, Goldcliff and Monmouth, is wrapped in almost complete obscurity for the greater part of the period. For all that, one obtains an overall impression that standards of observance and monastic morality generally had suffered a marked deterioration between the years 1150 and 1350. A generalization of this kind needs some qualification. The small cells of one, two or three monks presented a constantly recurring problem to the ecclesiastical administrator. In 1400 it was found that the prior and his colleagues at Llangenydd were obliged to 'say the canonical hours every Sunday and on the other solemn and festal days with chant, and they are not bound to other observances'.[135] Far from the house of their profession and rarely disturbed by the diocesan, time must have hung heavily on their hands, providing them with temptations of a kind from which a monk in a larger monastery would have been shielded. In small institutions of this kind, the pattern of life underwent little change during three centuries. Scandals in the fourteenth century can be paralleled by equally serious scandals in the twelfth and thirteenth centuries. In 1279 the prior of St. Clears and his *socius* were at loggerheads with each other and both were leading dissolute lives. The divine office was completely neglected.[136] In 1333 Bishop Grandisson of Exeter was remonstrating with the prior of Saint-Martin des Champs because the latter had appointed the dissolute prior of St. Clears, John Soyer, to Barnstaple Priory.[137] Even in the allegedly conventual house of Pembroke, the scandal dealt with by

[135] *Episc. Reg. St. David's*, i, p. 187–9.
[136] G. F. Duckett, *Charters and Records of Cluni*, ii, p. 136.
[137] Rose Graham, 'The Cluniac Priory of Saint-Martin des Champs, Paris, and its Dependent Priories in England', *Jnl. Brit. Arch. Assoc.*, xi (1948), p. 48.

Pecham in 1284 can be found nearly a century earlier. Gerald of Wales records a deposition of a prior of Pembroke for fornication and tells a story of a Séez monk (presumably from Lancaster Priory) who brought a mistress to Pembroke Priory with him.[138]

More noteworthy, however, is the deterioration in standards at houses which had been noted for their observance at the end of the twelfth and the beginning of the thirteenth century. Gerald of Wales knew Brecon Priory well and singles out for special praise John, the prior of the house at the beginning of the thirteenth century. 'He was a man pleasing to God and the people.'[139] By Pecham's time a dissolute prior was bringing the house to ruin.[140] Llanthony Prima, despite the troubles through which it had passed, still retained at the end of the twelfth century its reputation as an ideal centre of the religious life.[141] In the century following Pecham's visitation this reputation was seriously shaken by a series of scandals. In 1301 Archbishop Winchelsey was complaining to the bishop of St. David's that Thomas of Gloucester, a former prior of Llanthony, was wandering at large with the connivance of the bishop.[142] In 1330 John of Hereford. a canon of Llanthony, was convicted of theft in a civil court and lodged in the bishop of Hereford's prison.[143] At some time before 1376 Nicholas de Trinbey, prior of Llanthony, was attacked by three of his canons while he was saying the office of the dead. He was thrown to the ground and his eyes were torn out. The canons also killed the prior's brother, a layman named John de Trinbey.[144] Some twenty years later, in 1399, one of the ringleaders, John de Wellyncton, obtained a papal pardon for the violence he had committed against 'the late prior Nicholas who had injured him and had wasted the goods of the priory'; he eventually became prior of Llanthony himself.[145]

---

[138] Gir. Camb., *Opera*, iv, pp. 34–55, 51–2.

[139] Ibid., p. 36.

[140] See above, pp. 108–9.

[141] Gir. Camb., *Opera*, vi, pp. 37–47.

[142] *Registrum Roberti Winchelsey*, ii, pp. 732, 744. For an apostate canon of Llanthony Prima reconciled to the order in 1354, see *CPL.*, iii, p. 522.

[143] *Registrum Thome de Charlton*, p. 5.

[144] *CPL.*, iv, p. 223.

[145] Ibid., p. 355; *Episc. Reg. St. David's*, i, p. 285. His enemies suggested that he was an adherent of Glyn Dŵr, see Ralph Griffiths, 'Some Secret Supporters of Owain Glyn Dŵr?', *BIHR.*, xxxvii (1964), p. 88.

In the twelfth century and for part of the thirteenth, the Cistercians formed the *élite* of the monastic orders in Wales. Their austere life, their ability to transform a wilderness into a land of smiling plenty, and the efficiency of their visitation system provoked the grudging admiration of even a hostile critic like Gerald of Wales. By the early-fourteenth century, they had already abandoned many of the characteristic features which had distinguished them from the Benedictines. The early Cistercian statutes regarding the possession of churches and vills, as we have seen, had lost much of their force. The unauthorized eating of meat and the payment to monks of money allowances had also gained ground.

All institutions tend to lose their initial drive once an ordered routine has been long established. The Cistercians firmly believed that an annual assembly of abbots and an effective system of visitation would serve to infuse new life and fervour into institutions which were tending to become lax. In the last resort, however, standards of monastic observance and discipline depend on the quality, moral, spiritual and intellectual, of the aspirants to the religious life. When the monastic vocation is held in high esteem in society, it tends to attract the best that society can offer; hence the strong aristocratic element in the monasteries in the eleventh and twelfth centuries. In the late-thirteenth and early-fourteenth centuries, significant changes were taking place in the climate of social opinion towards the monastic ideal, and these changes were having perceptible effects on monastic recruitment. The ascetic ideal was losing its appeal and the monastic vocation was ceasing to attract the best minds of the age. For many aspirants to the religious life the more active existence of the mendicants was exerting a more potent appeal. In Wales especially, where the opportunities open to the would-be postulant were more restricted than in England, the new friaries were attracting many who in an earlier age would have become Cistercians or regular canons. Even before the end of the thirteenth century, the friars in Wales were approaching, if not surpassing, the Cistercians in numerical strength. In 1285 the Dominican house of Cardiff had thirty friars and that of

Haverfordwest thirty-nine.[146] The declining prestige of the Cistercians probably resulted, in the more provincial monasteries at least, in the reception of monks whose background, upbringing and education rendered them less amenable to the carefully ordered routine of a monastic existence.[147]

These changes in the climate of social opinion were also affecting the lines along which the attempted reform of the Cistercian order proceeded. Pope Benedict XII, himself a Cistercian, issued his reform decree *Fulgens sicut stella* in 1335.[148] The bulk of the provisions are taken up with the administration of the temporalities of a Cistercian monastery and with the question of Cistercian studies. No attempt was made to revive the primitive simplicity of the Cistercian ideal. Benedict's attempted reform 'can be regarded as only a brief halt in the monastic decadence of the fourteenth century'.[149] By 1352, as the General Chapter noted, the Cistercian houses of England, Wales and Scotland were in urgent need of reformation.[150]

---

[146] W. A. Hinnebusch, 'The Personnel of the Early English Dominican Province', *Catholic Historical Review*, xxix (1943–4), p. 340. The same author gives an average membership of 40 for Bangor and 24 for Rhuddlan *circa* 1300 (ibid., pp. 341–2).

[147] See the statutes against the reception as monks of those with a defect of birth or those less qualified for admission, in Canivez, *Statuta*, iii, pp. 318–9, 446–7.

[148] Ibid., pp. 410–36.

[149] J.-B. Mahn, *Le Pape Benoit XII et les Cisterciens*, p. 75.

[150] Canivez, *Statuta*, iii, p. 525.

A Note on Magdalen College Muniments, Miscellaneous 297.

W. D. Macray first drew attention to this roll and printed six of the prior's responses in *Historical Manuscripts Commission, 8th Report,* 1881, p.266b. On palaeographical grounds, Macray considered the roll to belong to the first half of the fourteenth century. Two years later, R. W. Banks printed the roll in its entirety (but without the heading 'Brekonie') as part of an appendix of documents to his edition of the *Cartularium* of Brecon Priory (*Brec. Cart.*, pp. 132–40). He adduced three reasons for believing that the accused prior held office 'from 1260 to 1270, if not until a later period'. Three further reasons are put forward here which support Banks's conclusion that the prior held office in the second half of the thirteenth century, most probably between 1276 and 1290.

1. The prior had dealings with 'Roger Gontyer', whose name occurs twice in the roll. A 'Roger Guntir' appears with Michael, prior of Brecon, as a witness to an agreement dated 1277 (*CCR., 1288–96,* p. 393) and as witness to two deeds of John fitz Reginald fitz Peter, who held the lordship of Blaenllyfni from 1286 to 1310 (*Brec. Cart.*, pp. 21–4).

2. The roll mentions Lord Humphrey de Bohun and Lord Humphrey as patron of the priory. As Banks noted, 'the frequent occurrence of Humphrey as a Christian name in the Bohun family creates confusion'. The mention of 'Gilbert, brother of the earl', and 'John de Scalariis' would seem to indicate that the Humphrey mentioned was Humphrey de Bohun, son of Humphrey de Bohun and Eleanor, who held the earldom of Hereford from 1275 to 1298 (see *Complete Peerage*, vi, pp.463–66). A Gilbert de Bohun and a John de Scalariis were both witnessess to a charter of this Humphrey to Brecon Priory (*Brec. Cart.*, pp. 25–6).

3. The roll mentions the prior's dealings with the Jews and their kindness to him. This suggests that at least some of the charges against the prior referred to activities which occured before the expulsion of the Jews in 1290, but does not preclude the possibility that the prior was holding office after this date.

Both Macray and Banks assumed that the charges against the prior were brought by an abbot of the mother house of Battle. Internal evidence disproves this. The references to the prior's bribing of his colleagues in preparation for the bishop's arrival, to dealings undertaken without episcopal consent or in the teeth of episcopal opposition, suggest an episcopal rather than an abbatial visitation. In this connection one of the charges appears conclusive; 'that he said to his brethren before the visitation of the bishop that if there were any things touching his person which deserved correction, they would be well corrected without the bishop by the abbot who would come in a short time'. The prior's protestation of his desire to obey the bishop in all things, which immediately follows this charge, indicates clearly that the roll forms part of the proceedings of an episcopal or archiepiscopal visitation.

The possibility that the proceedings owed something to the initiative of Archbishop Pecham, who visited Battle Abbey in 1283 and the Welsh dioceses in the following year, cannot be ruled out. The *detecta* of his visitation at Battle in 1283 refer to an incontinent prior and monks who had left the priory. These two charges are echoed in the roll. Apart from the prior's incontinence, it is also noted that the malice of the prior had driven one of the Brecon monks to join the friars. On this question, however, it is impossible to be certain.

VI

LITERARY ACTIVITIES OF THE MONKS

At the end of the eleventh century Wales already had a long and distinguished literary history, unsurpassed as far as vernacular literature was concerned by any of the emerging states of western Europe. Poetry was being composed in the vernacular at least as early as the sixth century. By the eleventh century, the practitioners of this poetic art were trained masters of a complex and highly conventionalized medium, holding positions of prestige and honour in the courts of the princes and in the houses of the powerful. The Welsh people possessed, too, a body of law of native growth, parts of which in the form of *tractates* had possibly been committed to writing before the end of the twelfth century. Despite the ravages of the Norse raids and the lack of intimate contacts with centres of culture in the Latin West, Latin scholarship was still being cultivated at a number of *clas* churches of south Wales.[1]

The successful Norman invasion of south Wales exerted a stimulating effect on this vernacular and Latin literature in a number of ways. The Norman challenge to Welsh independence presented the *Gogynfeirdd* poets with a theme for some of their finest poetry and prompted Welsh clerics to commit to writing, first in Latin, later in Welsh, the lives of their foremost saints.[2] Wales was brought into contact with the vigorous vernacular literature of France.[3] The Normans, Bretons and Flemings, and the institutions which were introduced into south Wales after their coming, became the medium for the transmission to Wales of the new ideas which were stirring opinion and thought in the schools of northern France. The scholarship of the *clas*

---

[1] Notably at Llanbadarn Fawr and Llancarfan. For the former, see N. K. Chadwick, *Studies in the Early British Church*, pp. 121–82.

[2] For a possible propaganda motive behind the writing of the *Life of St. David* by Rhigyfarch, see N. K. Chadwick, op. cit., pp. 174–6.

[3] M. Watkin, 'The French Linguistic Influence in Medieval Wales', *Trans. Cymm.*, 1918–19, pp. 146–222; 'The French Literary Influence in Medieval Wales', ibid., 1919–20, pp. 1–81. Both articles tend to overstate the undoubted case for French influence on the language and literature of Wales.

churches, exemplified at its best by Sulien and his family in west Wales, was 'ingrown'. It was orientated towards, and drew much of its inspiration from Ireland, a land which in the eleventh century had lost the cultural supremacy it had enjoyed in the eighth. The Norman conquest of west Wales brought the area into contact with the fruits of the twelfth-century European renaissance. The old culture coalesced with the new to enrich the literary heritage with the Latin work of Geoffrey of Monmouth, the vernacular prose tales of the *Mabinogion* and the poetry of Dafydd ap Gwilym.

In what follows an attempt will be made to assess in general terms the contributions which the monks of south Wales, both Welsh and Anglo-Norman, made to this literary heritage. A discussion of this kind should seek to answer a number of basic questions. Firstly, how were the monks educated before their reception and what facilities existed for the continuation of their studies after they had become professed? Secondly, what books existed in the monastic libraries of the area during the twelfth, thirteenth and fourteenth centuries to stimulate and mould their thought? Thirdly, to what extent did the monks devote themselves to creative writing in Latin, Welsh and Anglo-Norman? Fourthly, what contacts existed between the monks and writers of secular and religious literature outside the monasteries? Lastly, to what extent did the monks patronize such literature, transcribe or edit it? Unfortunately, not one of these questions can be answered with anything like the completeness or with that degree of certainty which a literary historian would desire. The conclusions reached in what follows will necessarily be tentative, sometimes based on what seems to be the weight of probability, sometimes on meagre information, the implications of which need further study by specialist scholars.

I. MONASTIC EDUCATION

In the twelfth century the only centres in Wales where a higher education of a limited kind could be obtained were at the schools attached to the cathedrals and, where they survived, the *clas* churches. It was at these centres that most postulants at the Cistercian abbeys of Wales received the education necessary for their reception as monks, namely, the ability to read the Latin texts, mainly scriptural, of which the divine office was composed. Before the end of the twelfth century, however, a number of Welsh students, destined for the ranks of the clergy, secular and regular, were pursuing more ambitious studies in abbey and cathedral schools in England and also at the growing university centres of Oxford and Paris.[4] Gerald of Wales, before his appointment as archdeacon of Brecon in 1175, had studied at the cathedral school of St. David's, at the abbey of St. Peter's, Gloucester, and at Paris.[5] Two Welsh Cistercians who gained prominence in the early-thirteenth century may have received a similar education. Peter, abbot of Whitland, as we have seen, had been a secular cleric of some learning and a colleague of Gerald before becoming a Cistercian. Cadwgan, one of Peter's successors, was also educated *in scholis*.[6] It must be emphasized that those Welshmen who proceeded to Oxford and Paris still formed a comparatively small group and that monks like Peter and Cadwgan received their formal education in the schools *before* they became Cistercians.

Within the monasteries themselves opportunities for organized studies were limited and depended a good deal on chance. The continuous presence in a community over a generation or so of one or more monks trained in the schools, whose intellectual attainments raised them above their fellows, could help to build up a tradition of scholarship in a house which succeeding generations of monks might attempt to emulate or maintain. Since scarcely more than a handful of even the richer English houses were able to achieve this distinction in the centuries after the Norman conquest, it is hard to imagine that the small Benedictine priories of south Wales were able to maintain even for a brief period schools of higher studies for their monks, still less for outsiders.[7]

The traditions of the Cistercians were unsympathetic to literary pursuits. They were 'committed by their founders to

---

[4] G. Usher, 'Welsh Students at Oxford in the Middle Ages', *BBCS.*, xvi (1954–6), p. 197.

[5] *Autobiography of Giraldus Cambrensis*, ed. H. E. Butler, pp. 36–7, 79.

[6] See above, p. 122.

[7] This did not prevent subjects discussed in the universities from filtering through even to the small priories. For a monk of Monmouth Priory disputing on the Trinity, see Gir. Camb., *Opera*, ii, p. 148.

being, like St. Benedict, *scienter nescius et sapienter indoctus*.[8] The only instruction allowed for in the early *consuetudines* was training in the chant. The writing of books, without the consent of the General Chapter, was expressly forbidden. Although these restrictions were not rigidly adhered to even in the twelfth century, the Cistercian suspicion of learning for its own sake lingered on into the thirteenth century and later, and lay behind much of the opposition to the inauguration of *studia* for monks of the Cistercian order.[9]

Organized schemes to enable Benedictine and Cistercian monks to pursue their studies at a university did not materialize until the second half of the thirteenth century, when the authorities of both orders began to realize the dangers of remaining isolated from the main stream of the intellectual life of their time.[10] The establishment of common houses of studies was a slow process and met with a good deal of opposition from within the orders themselves. Rewley Abbey, Oxford, was founded as a common house of studies for members of the Cistercian order in 1281.[11] In 1292 the abbot of Cîteaux decreed that every Cistercian abbey in the province of Canterbury which had twenty or more monks was to send one student to Oxford with an allowance of 60s.[12] Gloucester College, Oxford, as it came to be called, was founded as a common house of studies for the Benedictines in 1283.[13] How many monks from Welsh houses resorted to these new *studia* it is impossible to tell. A Master Robert, monk of Margam, appears as a regent master at Oxford in 1315.[14] It is probable that other Welsh abbeys were also sending monk-students up to Oxford well before the middle of the fourteenth century.[15]

[8] C. H. Lawrence, 'Stephen of Lexington and Cistercian University Studies in the Thirteenth Century', *Jnl. Ecc. Hist.*, xi (1960), p. 164.

[9] Ibid., *passim*.

[10] For the beginnings of the movement, see Knowles, *Religious Orders*, i, pp. 25f. Stephen of Lexington, while abbot of Stanley, was urging Irish Cistercian abbots to send their postulants to Oxford and Paris. 'How can a man be a lover of the cloister or of books', he wrote to the abbot of Clairvaux, 'if he knows nothing but Irish?', C. H. Lawrence, op. cit., pp. 168, 173.

[11] R. C. Fowler, 'Cistercian Scholars at Oxford', *EHR.*, xxiii (1908), p. 84.

[12] A. G. Little, 'Cistercian Students at Oxford in the Thirteenth Century', *EHR.*, viii (1893), pp. 83–5.

[13] Knowles, *Religious Orders*, i, p. 26.

[14] *Munimenta Academica*, ed. H. Anstey, i, p. 101.

[15] All the Welsh Cistercian houses appear in a list of contributions for the support of Cistercian scholars at Oxford in 1400: see R. C. Fowler, op. cit., pp. 84–7.

II. MONASTIC LIBRARIES

Monastic libraries were built up haphazardly over the years by purchase, bequest by individual abbots, priors and monks, and by the laborious process of transcribing copies of books borrowed from other libraries. Strata Florida purchased a collection of theological books of unknown number from Gerald of Wales in 1202.[16] In 1248 the abbot and convent of Caerleon gave a late-twelfth-century copy of the Homilies of St. Gregory to the newly-founded abbey of Hailes 'at the urgent request of Lord Richard, earl of Cornwall, the gracious founder of that house'.[17] Sometime in the thirteenth century Walter de Haya, prior of Llanthony Prima, bequeathed to his own house a miscellaneous collection of theological works.[18] Few of the Welsh monasteries could afford the elaborate paraphernalia and staff which a large scriptorium required.[19] The production of manuscripts tended therefore to be limited and their physical quality poor.[20] On general grounds it is unlikely that any of the Welsh houses accumulated collections which could rival the libraries of Lanthony Secunda (500 composite volumes) or even Titchfield (224 composite volumes).[21]

Dr. N. R. Ker, who has carefully examined more than six thousand medieval books for indications of their provenance, has been able to assign only forty-two of them to cathedral and parish churches and monastic and religious houses in Wales. Of these, twenty-seven belonged to Welsh monastic houses and four to Welsh friaries.[22]

With the exception of the two vernacular texts which Dr. Ker has tentatively assigned to Basingwerk Abbey (*Black Book of Basing*) and Carmarthen Priory (*Black Book of Carmarthen*),[23] the authors and works represented by the monastic

[16] *Autobiography of Giraldus Cambrensis*, pp. 250–1.
[17] The volume is still extant (British Museum, Additional MS. 48984). See F. Wormald and C. E. Wright, *The English Library before 1700*, p. 28 and plate 6a.
[18] N. R. Ker, *Medieval Libraries of Great Britain*, p. 276.
[19] See the remarks of N. K. Chadwick on the earlier Welsh scriptoria, in *Studies in the Early British Church*, p. 128, and of Kathleen Hughes, ibid., pp. 271–2.
[20] N. Denholm-Young, *Handwriting in England and Wales*, p. 39.
[21] The largest English monastic libraries c. 1500 possessed over 2,000 composite volumes: see the figures given by Knowles, *Religious Orders*, ii, p. 350.
[22] N. R. Ker, *Medieval Libraries of Great Britain*, *passim*.
[23] Ibid., pp. 7, 48. For some of the vernacular texts and their provenance, see below pp. 156–7.

survivals do not call for special comment. Most, if not all, of them could be found in the larger English monastic libraries. Thus, Llanthony Prima possessed works of Gregory, Jerome, Isidore of Seville, Cicero (the two medieval favourites, *De amicitia* and *De senectute*), the *Polychronicon*, commentaries on the psalms and a miscellaneous collection of theology.[24] Besides its own chronicle, Margam possessed a copy of Domesday Book and a composite volume containing two works of William of Malmesbury, the *Gesta Regum* and the *Novella Historia*, and Geoffrey of Monmouth's *Historia Regum Britanniae*.[25] Another composite work, the bulk of which is taken up with miscellaneous writings of St. Bernard, though tentatively assigned to Tewkesbury's cell of Cardiff, may also have come from Margam.[26] Brecon Priory possessed a Bede, *Pictor in carmine*, and a piece on William the Conqueror.[27] Only two survivals can be traced to the abbey of Caerleon and only one to Tintern. Caerleon possessed St. Gregory's *Homilies* and a late copy of a set of Chester annals; Tintern, a composite volume containing the *Flores Historiarum*.[28] The inevitable interest taken by the monks in canon and civil law is attested by two solitary survivals: St. Dogmaels possessed a copy of glossed Decretals, and Neath a copy of the 'New Digest'.[29]

The composite manuscript volumes which have survived, few though they are, deserve a more intensive treatment and examination than can be given here. Some of them, in addition to the main text, contain minutiae which are of some literary and historical value. St. Dogmaels Abbey, for example, possessed an early-thirteenth-century copy of Eusebius's *Historia Ecclesiastica*, not in itself a rare work. After the text,

[24] Ibid., pp. 119–20. Six of the seven extant survivals are now in Lambeth Palace Library: see M. R. James and C. Jenkins, *A Descriptive Catalogue of the Manuscripts in the Library of Lambeth Palace*, pp. 158–9, 317–8, 478–81, 523–5, 585–7, 595–9.
[25] N. R. Ker, *Medieval Libraries*, p. 129. For the composite volume, see G. F. Warner and J. P. Gilson, *Catalogue of Western Manuscripts in the Old Royal and King's Collection*, ii, p. 109.
[26] N. R. Ker, p. 48, but see below p. 145.
[27] Ibid., p. 12.
[28] For Gregory's homilies, see above, p. 143. The 'Annales Cestrienses' are still in private hands: Ker, p. 23. The manuscript containing Tintern's *Flores* is fully described in G. F. Warner and J. P. Gilson, op. cit., ii, pp. 134–5.
[29] J. K. Floyer and S. G. Hamilton, *Catalogue of Manuscripts Preserved in the Chapter Library of Worcester Cathedral*, pp. 80–1; A. T. Bannister, *A Descriptive Catalogue of the Manuscripts in the Hereford Cathedral Library*, p. 186.

however, a scribe entered in the manuscript some six documents, otherwise unknown, relating to the rights and properties of the abbey.[30] In Margam's twelfth-century copy of Geoffrey of Monmouth, the 'Prophecies of Merlin', an important theme in Welsh literature, are glossed in a late-thirteenth-century hand.[31] The miscellaneous collection of St. Bernard's works already referred to (B.M., Royal 6 B. xi) contains also a set of annals, as yet unpublished, which, though deriving in the main from those of the abbey of Tewkesbury, provides additional details and shows a special interest in the area of Cardiff and Llandaff. This has reasonably led the editors of the printed catalogue to assign the manuscript to one of Tewkesbury's cells, probably Cardiff.[32] Margam Abbey, however, held property in and to the north of Cardiff and can be shown to have had a special interest in the works of St. Bernard. In the seventeenth century, the monk-bibliographer Charles de Visch recorded the presence in his own monastic library of Dunes (now in Belgium) of concordances to St. Bernard's 'Song of Songs', compiled by an abbot of Margam.[33] The monastery of Dunes was transferred to Bruges in 1626 and after the abbey's dissolution a large collection of the abbey manuscripts, together with the abbot of Margam's *Concordantiae*, passed to the municipal library of Bruges, where they are still preserved.[34]

Although it is unlikely that the Welsh monasteries ever housed large collections of books, the survivals clearly represent only a fraction of the books which they contained, say in 1300. A number of monasteries had suffered disastrous losses, mainly of service books, through fires before the Dissolution.[35] The dispersal of books from the monasteries to centres far and near also predates the Dissolution. Loaned books were unreturned

[30] M. R. James, *A Descriptive Catalogue of the Manuscripts in the Library of St. John's College, Cambridge*, p. 5.
[31] G. F. Warner and J. P. Gilson, op. cit., ii, p. 109. Cf. Birch, *Margam Abbey*, p. 278.
[32] B. M., Royal 6 B. xi; G. F. Warner and J. P. Gilson, op. cit., pp. 139–41.
[33] Charles de Visch, *Bibliotheca Scriptorum Sacri Ordinis Cisterciensis* (Dvaci, 1649), p. 117.
[34] A. de Poorter, *Catalogue des Manuscrits de la Bibliothèque de la Ville de Bruges*, ii, p. 117. I am indebted to Gilbert Ouy of the Bibliothèque Nationale, Paris, for his assistance in helping me to locate this manuscript.
[35] *CPL.*, v, pp. 507–8 (Llantarnam); *CPR.*, *1408–13*, p. 306; *CPL.*, viii, p. 51 (Abergavenny); ibid., p. 437 (Beddgelert).

and pawned books unredeemed. Books commanded a high price yet were easily portable. It is small wonder therefore that the superiors of some religious houses used them as security to raise small loans. A prior of Brecon, accused by a visitor in the last quarter of the thirteenth century of allowing books from the library to remain in pawn with the Jews, denied the charge but added that 'a certain burgess of Ludlow has them in safe keeping for the use of the house'.[36] When Bishop Guy de Mone visited Carmarthen priory in 1401 the bible of the monastery was on loan to the vicar of Laugharne, while the decrees, decretals and books of Clement VI and the *casus* of Bernard, 'which deserve to be called the treasures of the house', were at Oxford.[37] It is indeed probable that Carmarthen was depleted of much of its books through continuous financial difficulties during the first half of the fifteenth century. In 1421 the king committed the custody of Carmarthen Priory to the prior of Lanthony Secunda and John Russell for two years.[38] This period of custody may help to explain why numerous manuscripts in the possession of Lanthony Secunda at the Dissolution and still extant are annotated in the fifteenth-century hand of Morgan, canon of Carmarthen.[39]

III. CREATIVE WRITING

By the time that the new Latin monasticism was firmly rooted in south Wales, the 'Benedictine Centuries'—that period when the monasteries of Europe held a virtual monopoly of scholarship and learning—were drawing to a close. The initiative was passing to new centres: the cathedral schools of the larger towns, the royal courts and the nascent universities. The new age was one of movement and intellectual ferment. The growth of centralized monarchies and a centralized church based on the papacy was stimulating the study of civil and canon law at the expense of the traditional studies of the liberal arts. Contacts with the Moslem culture of the Mediterranean,

---

[36] *Brec. Cart.*, p. 135.
[37] *Episc. Reg. St. David's*, i, p. 243.
[38] *CPR., 1416–22*, p. 338.
[39] For the relevant manuscripts, see under 'Morgan' in the index to M. R. James and C. Jenkins, *A Descriptive Catalogue of the Manuscripts in the Library of Lambeth Palace*. Cf. Ker, *Medieval Libraries*, pp. 108–12.

where Arabic scholars had preserved and nurtured the legacy of Greek science and philosophy, were opening up new horizons to the theologian and the student of the new dialectics of the schools.

The monastic order was not ideally fitted either by its rule or by its traditions to be in the intellectual vanguard of this new age. The Rule of St. Benedict, whether interpreted by the traditional Benedictines or the new Cistercians, did not encourage monks to pursue learning or speculation for its own sake, while the monastic vow of stability set an effective check on that freedom of movement from place to place which was in medieval times so essential to a serious pursuit of learning. 'From the accession of Henry II', writes the late Professor Knowles of the English monasteries, 'they gradually became, what they were to remain for at least a century, centres of literary and historical pursuits alone, leaving to the growing universities the direction of the studies of theology, philosophy and law.'[40]

What has survived of the creative writing of the south Wales monasteries may be conveniently divided into two categories. First, there are the corporate works represented by annals and chronicles. These are generally the work of more than one monk, and part of the material incorporated in them derives from centres other than the monastery in which they were compiled and written. Secondly, there are the works composed by, and bearing the names of, individual monks and canons.

By 1200 most monasteries with any pretensions to conventual status kept a set of annals in which were entered year by year the accessions and obits of pontiffs, kings and bishops, details of events of national and local importance, and observations on the weather. The majority of these sets of annals for western Europe as a whole are jejune and lack distinction. Since they were not primarily intended as a medium for fine writing, it would be unwise to regard them as the only index of the cultural potentialities of the houses from which they emanate. Thus, the influential abbey of Clairvaux, with several hundred monks and a rich library, could at the end of the twelfth century produce no more than a diminutive set of annals which

---

[40] Knowles, *Monastic Order*, p. 493.

any provincial house might rival.[41] In certain houses, however, conscious attempts were made to transcend the stilted entries generally found in the annals and to write sustained historical narrative. The best examples of the latter work, the chronicles of monks such as William of Malmesbury and Matthew Paris, are works of great artistry and historical merit. None of the Welsh survivals falls within this class.

Pride of place among the Welsh survivals belongs to the *Brut y Tywysogyon* or *Chronicle of the Princes*. The three authentic versions of this chronicle[42] are independent Welsh translations made from one or more copies of a Latin archetype which has been lost. The anonymous author of the archetype wrote it towards the end of the thirteenth century, probably not long after 1282 (its original terminal date), and there are strong grounds for believing that he was a monk of Strata Florida. He seems consciously to have intended his chronicle to be a continuation of Geoffrey of Monmouth's *History of the Kings of Britain*, for he begins at the point where Geoffrey ends his own work in 681. In a number of manuscripts, too, the *Brut* follows directly after the text of Geoffrey's *History*.

For his final redaction the compiler was able to draw on texts and information from a number of ecclesiastical centres. Up to about the year 1100 the Menevian interest is strong and there can be little doubt that the entries for these years derive from annals written down at St. David's. From 1100 to about 1175 the focus of interest changes and the entries suggest that the material was drawn from annals written by members of the *clas* of Llanbadarn Fawr. After 1175 'the *Brut* is obviously a Strata Florida chronicle and it retains this character to the end'.[43] For this period, however, the compiler did not rely entirely on records kept in his own house. Since all the Cistercian houses of Welsh Wales belonged to the same filiation, it was a relatively simple matter for the annalists of these houses to exchange information. There is evidence that most of these houses, and even Basingwerk, a daughter house of Savigny,

[41] 'Chronicon Clarevallense, 1147–92', in Migne, *Patrologiae*, clxxxv, cols. 1247–51.

[42] Peniarth MS. 20, Red Book of Hergest and Brenhinedd y Saeson versions. For what follows, see J. E. Lloyd, 'The Welsh Chronicles', *Proc. Brit. Acad.*, xiv (1928), pp. 369–91, and Thomas Jones's introduction to his translation of *Brut y Tywysogyon*, *Peniarth 20* (Cardiff, 1952), pp. xi–lxxv.

[43] J. E. Lloyd, op. cit., p. 385.

made individual contributions to the final version of the *Brut*.[44]

The opinion of Welsh scholars would probably be divided were they called to pronounce upon the literary merits of entries in the *Brut* as examples of Welsh prose. Not everyone, for example, would endorse the judgement of Saunders Lewis that the *Brut* is 'one of the masterpieces of our prose'.[45] Thomas Jones noted that it suffers from being a translation of a Latin text rather than a spontaneous and original composition in Welsh.[46] Few would question, however, the value of the *Brut* as a source for Welsh history. Fortunately for the historian, the compiler did not imitate the methods of Geoffrey of Monmouth. He took his role as a recorder of facts seriously and did not tamper with them to achieve literary effect or to suit a theory. 'It is', wrote Sir John Lloyd, 'sober, pedestrian chronicle, occasionally waxing eloquent, but as a rule content to record the simple facts'.[47] Though uneven in its coverage, it remains the greatest single source for the political history of Wales in one of the most crucial periods in her history.

There are only two other surviving monastic chronicles of importance: the *Cronica de Wallia* and the *Annales de Margan*.[48] The *Cronica* is a Latin set of annals which, with some omissions, covers the years from 1190 to 1266.[49] The close correspondence of some of the entries with those in extant versions of the *Brut* led Thomas Jones to suggest that the *Cronica* originated at Strata Florida.[50] More recently Mr. J. Beverley Smith has brought forward a number of convincing arguments in favour of a Whitland provenance.[51]

---

[44] Sir Goronwy Edwards has convincingly argued that the continuation of the *Brut* to 1332, found in the Peniarth version, was probably written in Valle Crucis (*EHR.*, lvii (1942), pp. 372–5).

[45] Saunders Lewis, *Braslun o Hanes Llenyddiaeth Gymraeg*, pp. 46–7.

[46] Thomas Jones, op. cit., pp. lix–lx.

[47] J. E. Lloyd, op. cit., p. 370.

[48] I leave out of account the disappointing chronicle of Aberconwy, for which see R. W. Hays, *History of the Abbey of Aberconway*, pp. 143–53, and also the genealogical annals which survive for Abergavenny (Dugdale, iv, pp. 615–6), Llanthony Prima (ibid., vi, pp. 134–6) and Tintern (ibid., v, pp. 269–72). These latter are unreliable guides even for genealogical information.

[49] 'Cronica de Wallia and Other Documents from Exeter Cathedral Library MS. 3514', ed. Thomas Jones, in *BBCS.*, xii (1946), pp. 27–44.

[50] Ibid., p. 29.

[51] 'The Cronica de Wallia and the Dynasty of Dinefwr', *BBCS.*, xx (1963), pp. 261–82.

The Latin *Annales de Margan* have long been known to historians[52]. They begin with the death of Edward the Confessor and break off abruptly in 1232. For the period before the foundation of Margam in 1147, the annals depend heavily on William of Malmesbury, whose works the abbey possessed. The annals continue to rely heavily on secondary sources until about 1185. After this date they become fuller and are a primary source of great value for Glamorgan history. One unique feature of the annals is the graphic description they give under the year 1204 (*recte* 1203) of the murder of Arthur of Brittany by King John.[53] The details given are found in no other British source.

Extant work written by, and bearing the names of, individual monks and canons is small in quantity and very unevenly distributed. The bulk of the survivals come from the priory of Llanthony Prima and from what was, until the beginning of the thirteenth century, its daughter house of Lanthony Secunda. The priory of Carmarthen is represented by a long poem in Anglo-Norman and the Cistercian abbeys of Welsh Wales by three short works written by Cadwgan, who graduated from the abbacies of Strata Florida and Whitland to the see of Bangor. As yet no work extant has been ascribed with certainty to a monk in any of the Benedictine priories.

The Augustinian priory of Llanthony Prima provided the inspirational background for a number of writers of the twelfth and early-thirteenth centuries. The circumstances of its foundation, the qualities of its early leaders and the favour in which it was held by the highest in the land, made it a centre which, in spite of its remoteness, attracted many men of ability and learning. Within a century of its foundation it had already provided two sees with bishops, Robert de Bethune, the second prior, had studied under Anselm of Laon and William of Champeaux, and had himself been a teacher before entering the religious life. He was elected to the bishopric

---

[52] *Annales Monastici*, i, pp. 3–40; see especially W. Greenway, 'The Annals of Margam', *Trans. Port Talbot Hist. Soc.*, i (1963), pp. 19–31.

[53] *Annales Monastici*, i, pp. 27–8. The monks' source of information was almost certainly William de Breos: see F. M. Powicke, *Ways of Medieval Life and Thought*, pp. 27–37.

of Hereford in 1131.[54] Geoffrey de Henlaw, seventh prior of Llanthony Prima and fifth prior of Lanthony Secunda, though a man of lesser stature than Robert, was famed for his skill in medicine. He was appointed bishop of St. David's in 1203.[55]

Three of Robert de Bethune's immediate successors as prior all left behind them written work of varying importance. Robert de Braci, the third prior (first of Lanthony Secunda), compiled a collection of theology for the use of his house.[56] Though his work is described in the Lanthony Secunda catalogue as *mediocris liber*, Robert drew his material from a wide range of ancient and modern authors.[57] Robert was also the author of another work, 'Expositio Roberti prioris, mediocre volumen', which has not been traced.[58]

William of Wycombe, the fourth prior of Llanthony Prima (1137–50), was more interested in contemporary history. His life of Robert de Bethune, which has survived in at least two manuscripts, has been printed and the greater part translated.[59] Despite the eulogistic platitudes and stock situations common to most saints' lives of the period, the Life is well written and a valuable record of the early fortunes of the priory. William was forced to resign from the priorate in 1150. The canons resented his stern and austere rule. Further pressure was brought to bear on him by Earl Roger. The latter was angered by William's published account of the quarrel which had taken place between his father, Milo, and Robert, bishop of Hereford. It was entitled 'The Whole Tyranny and Malicious Proceedings of the Earl and his Excommunication from the Flock of Christ'.[60]

William was succeeded by Clement, a prolific writer of biblical and theological commentaries. His devotion to learning commanded the immediate respect of canons who had lived under his rule. The anonymous canon who wrote a history of

---

[54] *D.NB.*, xlxiii, pp. 364–5.
[55] J. N. Langston, 'Priors of Lanthony by Gloucester', *Trans. Bristol and Glouc. Arch. Soc.*, lxiii (1942), pp. 29–34.
[56] B.M., Royal 8 D. viii: *Exceptiones Roberti de Bracii*.
[57] For a full description of the manuscript's contents, see G. F. Warner and J. P. Gilson, op. cit., i, pp. 245–7.
[58] J. N. Langston, op. cit., p. 7.
[59] B. M., Cotton Julius D. x, and Lambeth Palace MS. 475 f. 109–80; H. Wharton, *Anglia Sacra*, ii, pp. 293–321. For the translation, see G. Roberts, *Some Account of Llanthony Priory*, pp. 80–116.
[60] Ibid., p. 61. This work has not survived.

Llanthony in the first decade of the thirteenth century had known Clement when he was prior and speaks of him as being extremely learned

> in the study of divinity: his great proficiency therein, his piercing wit, his solid judgement and sound faith, do sufficiently appear in the great volumes which he has writ on that subject, in a plain yet eloquent style.[61]

Seen against the wider background of his age, Clement was not an original thinker nor a brilliant theologian.[62] But there can be no doubt about the popularity of his work. His fame spread beyond the limits of the two priories he ruled and manuscripts of his work were to be found in the libraries of religious houses as far apart as Shrewsbury, Fountains and Canterbury.[63] His works continued to be copied and even translated into English in religious houses all over England well into the fifteenth century.

As far as is known, the last extant work which illustrates the literary activities of the canons of Llanthony is the *History of the Foundation and Translation of the Monastery*.[64] This is a vigorous but nostalgic account of the fortunes of the two monasteries of Llanthony Prima and its daughter house at Gloucester down to 1205, when they were separated and made autonomous houses. The affection with which the anonymous writer speaks of the Welsh house, his constant reminders of how badly it had suffered at the hands of its daughter, and his final reference to the separation of the two houses, make it almost certain that he was a canon of Llanthony Prima and that he was writing soon after 1205.

The surviving works from Llanthony indicate a community of highly literate canons whose thought and expression, as one would expect, were moulded by the study of the Scriptures and the Fathers. The sole surviving piece of creative writing from Carmarthen Priory illustrates another facet of the literary interests of the Augustinian canons in south Wales.[65]

---

[61] Ibid., p. 62.

[62] R. W. Hunt, 'English Learning in the Late Twelfth Century', *TRHS.*, xix (1936), p. 27.

[63] Ker, *Medieval Libraries*, pp. 47, 88, 91, 125, 179, 202.

[64] B.M., Cotton Julius D. x. ff. 31–53b, printed in part by Dugdale, vi, pp. 128–34.

[65] The text with some errors (Kernerthin for Kermerthin) has been printed by H. Stengel, 'Handschriftliches aus Oxford', *Zeitschrift für französische Sprache und Litteratur*, xiv (1892), pp. 147–51. Stengel considered the epilogue of this poem

This is a long, religious poem in Anglo-Norman French written by Simon, a canon of the house some time in the thirteenth century.[66] The poem is a verse sermon on the virtue of penitence. In it the 'straight and narrow way' is compared with the 'broad and easy way', a theme familiar to moralistic literature from biblical times to our own. Simon's poem is not a set piece in the sense of being merely a literary exercise. He had written his *bref sermon* at the request of an unnamed fellow canon, a learned and religious man whose profession was preaching outside the priory. It is clearly inspired by sincere religious feeling and its theme was influenced perhaps by that 'wave of enthusiasm for confession and penance set in motion by the Fourth Lateran'.[67] The whole poem serves as a salutary reminder of the sterling qualities of even the small priories in the first century or so after their foundation.

The Cistercian order in Wales produced throughout the whole of the middle ages only two writers whose works were sufficiently well known to be noticed by the bibliographers of the sixteenth and seventeenth centuries: Walter of Margam and Cadwgan of Bangor. Walter is a shadowy figure whose work has been lost.[68] Much more is known of the background, career and literary work of Cadwgan.[69] He was recognized as a scholar of distinction by his Welsh contemporaries.[70] Three centuries later his work was noticed by Leland, who ascribed to him a volume of *Homilies*, a book entitled *Speculum Christianorum* and other unnamed works.[71] More recently Dr. C. H. Talbot has rescued from oblivion three short works which can be ascribed with certainty to Cadwgan.[72] The first is an

---

to be a separate work and has been followed by Madan and Craster, *A Summary Catalogue of Western Manuscripts in the Bodleian Library at Oxford*, ii, p. 643, and J. C. Russell, *Dictionary of Writers of Thirteenth Century England*, p. 148. See, however, M. D. Legge, *Anglo-Norman in the Cloisters*, pp. 68–9, on which my own account is based.

[66] The poet reveals his identity in the second part of the poem:
   Frere Simun de Kermerthin
   Profes en l'ordre de seint Augstin.

[67] M. D. Legge, op. cit., p. 69.

[68] See below pp. 155–6.

[69] For details of Cadwgan's career, see above pp. 122–3.

[70] 'Cronica de Wallia' in *BBCS.*, xii (1946), p. 35. Cf. *Brut y Tywysogyon*, Peniarth 20, p. 91.

[71] J. Leland, *Commentarii de Scriptoribus Britannicis*, i, p. 251.

[72] C. H. Talbot, 'A List of Cistercian Manuscripts in Great Britain', *Traditio*, viii (1952), p. 408; 'Cadogan of Bangor', *Cîteaux in de Nederlanden*, ix (1958), pp. 18–40.

instructional tract on how to make a confession, entitled
Hic incipit tractatus Caducani Bargorensis episcopi de modo confitendi.[73]
It was probably designed for use in Cadwgan's own diocese of
Bangor and was prompted perhaps by the Lateran decrees on
the sacrament of penance. The second work is a tract on the
verse from the psalms, entitled *Tractatus domini Caducani episcopi
Bangorensis super hunc versum Psalmi, Ostende nobis domine faciem
tuam.* The third work preserved in the same manuscript is a
collection of prayers, entitled *Orationes Domini Caducani episcopi
Bangorensis.*[74]

It seems clear that all three works were written during
Cadwgan's active episcopate at Bangor (1215–36). They are
not of great literary merit, nor of great importance for the
history of Cistercian spirituality. Their main interest lies in
the fact that Cadwgan is the sole identifiable representative of
the culture of the monasteries of Welsh Wales. In his work can
be detected the blending of the older traditions of the Celtic
church with those of the new world of scholasticism. Dr. Talbot
sees his work as 'thoroughly Celtic in spirit and expression'.

> The constant reiteration of the same opening phrases, the piling
> up of attributive adjectives, the pervasive alliteration and the
> marked emotional content are sufficient evidence of this . . .
> The tradition of Welsh poetry keeps breaking through and the
> scholastic veneer is hardly deep enough to keep it concealed
> for long.[75]

Many works written by monks in south Wales monasteries
suffered the same fate as books from the monastic libraries;
they have been lost or destroyed. Among the more important
known losses are the *Register* of Neath, the *Annals* of Strata
Florida and the verse of Walter, abbot of Margam. References
to the *Register* in the work of Rice Merrick, and the fortunate
survival of a copy taken from the *Register* of a 'History of the
Lordship of Gower' show that it was not merely a cartulary
but contained historical narrative and commentary of great

---

[73] London, Dulwich College, MS. xxii, ff. 46–9. The manuscript is described in
G. F. Warner, *Catalogue of the Manuscripts and Muniments of Alleyn's College of God's
Gift at Dulwich*, p. 345. The text may profitably be compared with the Welsh texts
of *Penityas*, for which see Glanmor Williams, *Welsh Church*, pp. 93–4.
[74] Hereford Cathedral MS. O. 6. viii, ff. 59–62v, 63–76. Both texts have been
edited by C. H. Talbot, 'Cadogan of Bangor', *Cîteaux in de Nederlanden*, ix (1958),
pp. 26–29, 30–40.
[75] Ibid., p. 24.

value. *The Register* was available to Dugdale when he was collecting material for his *Monasticon,* but probably disappeared on the extinction of the Stradling line in 1725.[76] The *Annals* of Strata Florida are referred to in both the major versions of the *Brut* under the year 1248.[77] Sir Goronwy Edwards conjectured that this work might be the Latin archetype on which all extant versions of the *Brut* are based.[78] From the context it seems equally possible that the *Annals* were an independent work dealing with the purely domestic history of the abbey in the manner of the celebrated *Chronica de Melsa.*

The poems of Walter, abbot of Margam have also been lost. In spite of official disapproval from the General Chapter,[79] the English Cistercian abbeys produced a small crop of Latin poets at the end of the twelfth and the beginning of the thirteenth century.[80] Even in the Welsh abbeys the annalists were not averse from quoting, if not themselves composing, poetry in their annals.[81] In the light of these facts, the loss of Walter's verse is all the more to be regretted. John Leland, who saw his verses in the *Granarium* of John Whethamstede, abbot of St. Albans, says that he wrote a book of verse on birds and beasts.[82] Bibliographical tradition asserts that Walter flourished about 1219, but there is little to substantiate this.[83] Dr. J. C. Russell failed to trace the verse in the parts of the *Granarium* which survive in the British Museum,[84] and Walter is otherwise unknown as an abbot of Margam. Yet there is little reason to believe that Leland, by a faulty reading, has created yet another bibliographical 'ghost'. Though it is possible that he was mistaken in giving Walter the title of

[76] Rice Merrick, *A Booke of Glamorganshires Antiquities,* pp. 8, 10, 49, 56; F. R. Lewis, 'A History of the Lordship of Gower from the Missing Cartulary of Neath Abbey', *BBCS.,* ix (1939), pp. 149–54.
[77] *Brut y Tywysogyon,* Peniarth 20, p. 108.
[78] *EHR.,* lvii (1942), pp. 371–2.
[79] Canivez, *Statuta,* i, p. 232.
[80] C. J. Holdsworth, 'John of Ford and English Cistercian Writing, 1167–1214', *TRHS.,* xi (1961), pp. 125, 130.
[81] Two Latin poems on the death of Rhys ap Gruffydd (1197) are quoted in the *Brut y Tywysogyon.* The annalist of Aberconwy quotes a Latin couplet on the death of Thomas Becket: see Hays, *Aberconway Abbey,* p. 148. In the Margam annals poetry is quoted under the years 1225, 1226 and 1228.
[82] J. Leland, *De Rebus Britannicis Collectanea,* iv, p. 58.
[83] Because of the similarity of surname (*Morganiensis*), Bale associated Walter with Master Maurice, who is known to have flourished at this time (*Scriptorum Illustrium Brytannie . . . Catalogus,* p. 257.)
[84] J. C. Russell, *Dictionary of Writers of Thirteenth Century England,* p. 179.

abbot, it must be remembered that Leland was able to consult the complete text of the *Granarium* which is no longer available.[85] The subject matter of Walter's verse agrees well with, and indeed supplements, what is known of Cistercian interests at this time. They were interested in the bestiary.[86] This was a zoological encyclopedia, part fact, part fable, but intended as a serious work of reference. There can be little doubt that this interest stemmed from their preoccupation with farming, particularly livestock husbandry. When Cistercian monks got together in conversation, John, abbot of Ford lamented, they were more ready to talk about 'the progeny of bulls and ploughs . . . and the yield of fields' than 'Jesus and the Songs of Sion'.[87]

IV. THE MONKS AS SCRIBES, EDITORS AND COMPILERS

Much of the vernacular poetry and prose which has survived from the middle ages is preserved in the so-called Four Ancient Books of Wales: *The Black Book of Carmarthen*, the *Book of Aneirin*, the *Book of Taliesin* and the *Red Book of Hergest*. Each one of these composite volumes presents the literary historian with a wealth of problems. Only the question of provenance need concern us here. Since the manuscripts themselves give no marks of medieval ownership or date, there has been a good deal of debate on the question where and when they were transcribed. *The Black Book of Carmarthen*, a work which contains the earliest vernacular poetry to be committed to writing, has been ascribed on fairly good authority to the scriptorium of the Augustinian priory of St. John's, Carmarthen,[88] and most scholars would now agree that it was written down sometime between 1170 and 1230.[89] These dates fit in well with what is known of Carmarthen Priory at this time. In 1208 the priory was ruled by a Welsh prior named Cadifor and had clearly been under Welsh control for some time. This period of Welsh influence, however, did not last

[85] Knowles, *Religious Orders*, ii, p. 267.
[86] J. Morson, 'The English Cistercians and the Bestiary', *Bull. John Ryland's Library*, xxxix (1956–7), pp. 146–70.
[87] C. J. Holdsworth, op. cit., p. 136.
[88] D. Huws, 'Gildas Prisei', *NLWJ.*, xvii (1972), p. 319 n.2.
[89] These date limits are given by W. J. Gruffydd and T. Jones in their article in *Encyclopedia Britannica* (1963), vol. 23, p. 505.

long. From 1246 certainly, the priory can be shown to have been predominantly Anglo-Norman in its sympathies and its personnel until well into the fourteenth century.[90]

The *Book of Aneirin*, transcribed in the second half of the thirteenth century, has been ascribed to Basingwerk Abbey,[91] and the *Book of Taliesin*, transcribed about 1275, to Margam Abbey.[92] The *Red Book of Hergest* was transcribed about 1400, and because it contains the Strata Florida version of the *Brut* is said to have been a Strata Florida manuscript or a copy of one.[93] The late Professor G. J. Williams, however, advanced the theory that the *Red Book* may have been copied in a Glamorgan monastery, probably Neath.[94] Some of the poetry which was included in the *Red Book* was available to the monks of Margam, one of whom copied the first *englyn* in the famous *Eiry Mynyd* sequence beneath the flap of an abbey charter. The orthography of this *englyn* is centuries earlier in date than 1400, the date tentatively suggested for the extant *Red Book of Hergest*.[95]

Unfortunately, relations between the bardic order and the monks before the Black Death are obscure. Thomas Stephens suggested that they were sworn enemies.[96] There is surprisingly little evidence to support such a contention. Cynddelw Brydydd Mawr (*fl.* 1155–1200) records in his verse the friction which existed between him and the monks of Strata Marcella. Threatened with excommunication by the abbot and warned that he would not be buried in consecrated ground, he replied:

> Since against me no covenant can be shown
> As the price God well knows,
> More becoming were it for the monks
> To ask than to reject me.[97]

There are also one or two allusions in the vaticinatory verse.

---

[90] See above pp. 44–5.

[91] *The Text of the Book of Aneirin*, ed. J. G. Evans, p. xi.

[92] *Facsimile and Text of the Book of Taliesin*, ed. J. G. Evans, pp. xlii–xliii. The same editor in another context attributes the same book to Neath Abbey: see *The White Book of Mabinogion*, pp. xii–xiii.

[93] N. Denholm-Young, *Handwriting in England and Wales*, p. 40.

[94] Glanmor Williams, *Welsh Church*, p. 25 n.5.

[95] F. G. Cowley and N. Lloyd, 'An Old Welsh *Englyn* in Harley Charter 75 C 38', *BBCS.*, xxv (1974), pp. 407–17.

[96] *Literature of the Kymry* (2nd ed., London, 1876), p. 100.

[97] The translation is from *Mont. Coll.*, ix (1876), p. 154. Cf. Thomas Stephens, op. cit., p. 119.

Like much of the *Gogynfeirdd* verse, this too is intentionally obscure. The following is from the *Afallennau* of the *Black Book*. Although written down before 1230, it may contain material of a much earlier age:

> Sweet apple tree of delicate growth,
> Thy shade is celebrated, profitable and comely,
> Princes will combine upon false pretences,
> With false, luxurious and gluttonous monks,
> And idle talkative youths, to get thy fruit;
> They all prophesy warlike exploits to the Prince.[98]

Another allusion, again brief and obscure, comes from the *Cyfoesi Merddin*, the date of which in its present form cannot be earlier than the twelfth century:[99]

> I will not receive the sacrament
> From excommunicated monks
> With their togas on their knees
> I will commune with God himself.[100]

In the fourteenth century, when the body of extant verse becomes more plentiful and its content less obscure, specific references to the religious begin to appear for the first time. In retrospect, the literary scene is dominated by the genius of Dafydd ap Gwilym, a poet of European importance and certainly the greatest writer of verse in any of the Celtic languages. The tone of much of his verse is irreverent to say the least, and Dafydd can in no way be regarded as sympathetic to, still less a defender of, the monastic ideal. It may be significant, however, that there is not in the work attributed to him any reference to the monks of the Cistercian order. If one excludes some flippant but light-hearted jesting at the expense of the nuns, the shafts of his satire against the religious were reserved for the black and grey friars.[101]

From the middle of the fourteenth century, a large body of laudatory verse addressed to Welsh abbots has survived but is only beginning to be given the attention it deserves.[102]

---

[98] Ibid., p. 213.

[99] There is a reference to Henry II in one of the stanzas: see M. E. Griffiths, *Early Vaticination in Welsh*, pp. 97, 100.

[100] Thomas Stephens, op. cit., p. 119.

[101] *Dafydd ap Gwilym: Fifty Poems*, transl. H. I. Bell and D. Bell, *passim*. The full index appended to *Gwaith Dafydd ap Gwilym*, ed. Thomas Parry, contains no reference to monks, but a number to the friars. The only religious house mentioned by name is the nunnery of Llanllugan.

[102] Glanmor Williams, *Welsh Church*, *passim* and especially pp. 374–411, and

Among the earliest extant poems of this kind is one attributed
to Llywelyn Goch (*fl.* 1360–90) congratulating Llywelyn
Fychan, abbot of Strata Florida, on his recovery from a
'treacherous disease':

> . . . the bulwark of a banqueting country
> A man of marvellous order, the hero
> Of Strata Florida–its sovereign and good protector,
> Llywelyn Fychan, worthy of respect, a well-formed abbot,
> An unblemished man of Garwy sprung,
> Offspring of a well-known leader, a conquering lion,
> Namely, the other Llywelyn, his wise and happy father.[103]

Poetry of this kind poses 'all the problems of satisfactory
interpretation of a highly stylized and rhetorical art form',[104]
and as a source of history has to be used with great caution.
Its existence is nevertheless clear evidence of a close association
between a large number of Welsh poets and the monasteries in
the later middle ages. In the early-fourteenth century, this
association may have been of comparatively recent origin,
the result of changing social and political conditions following
the eclipse of the Welsh princes. Much more work requires to
be done on the chronology and distribution of this type of
verse before one can begin to pronounce with any confidence.

Although no clear picture emerges from the evidence of the
types of contact which existed between the bards and the
monasteries before the middle of the fourteenth century,
there are, nevertheless, a number of general reasons for
assuming that the monks of the Welsh Cistercian monasteries
were responsible, as transcribers, editors and custodians, for
the transmission of a part of what remains of the Welsh literary
heritage of the middle ages. Unlike the cathedral chapters
which always contained a floating population, and the
friaries which were confined to the towns, the Cistercians were
deeply rooted in the soil. The abbeys of Welsh Wales were
closely linked by ties of patronage and affection with the
Welsh princes and with powerful Welsh families whose praises
the bards sang. Some of the monks were younger sons of

more recently C. T. B. Davies, 'Y Cerddi i'r Tai Crefydd fel Ffynhonnell
Hanesyddol', *NLWJ.*, xviii (1974), pp. 268–86, 345–73, which is based on her
unpublished M.A. thesis, 'Cerddi'r Tai Crefydd' (University of Wales, 1973).
    [103] *Myvyrian Archaiology of Wales*, i, p. 516; G. Roberts, 'Strata Florida Abbey',
Arch. Camb., 1848, pp. 129–30.
    [104] Glanmor Williams, *Welsh Church*, p. 374.

princely families. It seems unlikely that their monastic profession made them oblivious of their literary heritage, particularly at a time when its whole basis was being assailed first by the Anglo-Norman barons and in the thirteenth century by the whole weight of the English state.

Many of the bards were themselves men of importance whose rank, by virtue of the art they practised, was recognized by Welsh law. Like many of the princes they praised, they could hope for reception into a religious house before their death and for burial within the precinct walls. The verses of Cynddelw cited on an earlier page seem to indicate that he expected to be buried within the monastic precinct of Strata Marcella. A firm tradition dating from the late-fourteenth century suggests that Dafydd himself was buried within the precinct walls of Strata Florida.[105] Since literature of all kinds stood a better chance of survival in the hands of an undying religious corporation than in the houses of the minor princes and *uchelwyr*, it is possible that the bards, either during their lifetime or immediately before their death, brought their work with them to the monastery of their choice to be transcribed and transmitted by future generations of monks.

Valuable work of another kind was undertaken by the Anglo-Norman monks of Benedictine houses in south-east Wales and the border. In the earlier stages of the colonization of south Wales, the conquerors were as derisive of Welsh culture as they had been in an earlier generation of Anglo-Saxon culture. A number of churches bearing the names of obscure Welsh founders were re-dedicated to saints more widely known by the Anglo-Normans.[106] This movement did not persist. The conquerors had granted a large number of churches dedicated to Welsh saints to priories in south-east Wales and abbeys along the border. Partly as a result of this, the Benedictine monks began to take a genuine interest in the lives of the Welsh saints and began to collect their relics. According to William of Malmesbury, Bernard, the Norman bishop of St. David's, made repeated but vain attempts to find the body of St. David.[107] Sometime before his death (1143?), William,

---

[105] *Dafydd ap Gwilym: Fifty Poems*, pp. 5, 306–9.
[106] Lloyd, *History of Wales*, ii, pp. 458–9.
[107] *Willelmi Malmesbiriensis de Gestis Regum*, i, p. 28.

himself an inveterate relic hunter, journeyed to St. David's and when viewing the body of the hermit Caradog, attempted to steal one of his fingers. He was confounded by the dead saint himself, for Caradog is reported to have clenched his fingers and withdrawn his fist into the sleeve of his gown![108] By the thirteenth century, relics of sixth-century Welsh saints were to be found in the reliquaries of the abbeys of Glastonbury and Tewkesbury.[109] In 1235 H. Tancintune bequeathed relics which had belonged to his father to the abbey of Tewkesbury. Among them were 'three bones of St. Athan which were found at Caerwent'.[110] It was John de Gamages, future abbot of Gloucester, who was responsible for what was probably regarded as the most spectacular relic discovery of the thirteenth century, that of the lost body of St. David. While John was prior of the Gloucester cell of Ewenni, St. David's place of burial outside the south door of the cathedral was revealed to him in a vision. Excavation on the site produced what was believed to be the body of St. David and a new shrine to house it was raised in the cathedral in 1275.[111]

It was interests of this kind, a compound of devotion, self-interest, curiosity and pseudo-historical research which prompted a group of Anglo-Norman monks to compile what is recognized to be one of the best extant texts of the lives of the Welsh saints, that contained in British Museum, Cotton Vespasian A. xiv. Most of the lives themselves were composed and written down in Latin by prominent members of the Welsh *clas* churches between the years 1090 and 1150. About 1200, these lives, with other miscellaneous material, were gathered together and copied into Cotton Vespasian A. xiv. A number of scholars have attempted to ascertain the purpose and provenance of the collection. Dr. Robin Flower suggested that the texts were brought together for a liturgical purpose 'as a supplementary legendary of Welsh saints for use in one

---

[108] 'De sancto Carodoco hermita' in *Nova Legenda Anglie*, ed. C. Horstman, i, p. 176.
[109] G. H. Doble, 'Celtic Saints in the Glastonbury Relic Lists', *Somerset and Dorset Notes and Queries*, xxiv (1944), pp. 86–9.
[110] *Annales Monastici*, i, p. 96.
[111] F. G. Cowley, 'A Note on the Discovery of St. David's Body', *BBCS.*, xix (1960), pp. 47–8.

of the new Benedictine monasteries of Anglo-Norman foundation' and that the manuscript was written in Brecon Priory.[112] Silas Harris convincingly demonstrated, however, that the Calendar which precedes the *Lives* could only have come from Monmouth Priory and concludes that the whole compilation was the work of Monmouth monks.[113] More recently, Dr. Kathleen Hughes has made a thorough examination of the manuscript as a whole and taken the discussion a stage further. She has claimed that a number of influences are apparent in the making of the manuscript: that of Gloucester Abbey, with its early interest in churches in south-east and south-west Wales, and those of the priory of Monmouth and the school of Llandaff, with their own particular hagiographical interests. Dr. Hughes discounts the theory that the collection was meant to serve a liturgical function, but reaches no firm conclusions on the question of the manuscript's provenance. 'Until further evidence is produced', she writes, 'it seems likely that Mr. Harris is right in claiming the Monmouth monks as the actual compilers of the manuscript'.[114]

V. CONCLUSIONS

Future research into manuscript collections in Latin and Welsh will doubtless widen and enrich our knowledge of the literary interests and achievements of the monks and canons of the monasteries in Wales. Yet new discoveries are not likely to alter the basic impression gained from what is already known of the history of the Welsh houses and the writings which can confidently be ascribed to their members. The main bulk of what remains of the Welsh literary heritage, in the vernacular and in Latin, was written outside the monasteries by professional poets and story-tellers, by members of the secular clergy and perhaps, too, by members of the various orders of friars resident in Wales.[115] All three groups were in constant

---

[112] *Vitae Sanctorum Britanniae*, pp. ix–x.

[113] S. M. Harris, 'The Kalendar of the *Vitae Sanctorum Wallensium*', *JHSCW*., iii (1953), pp. 3–53.

[114] *Studies in the Early British Church*, ed. N. K. Chadwick, pp. 185, 197.

[115] It seems probable that the friars of Welsh houses had a hand in the translating and writing of some of the instructional and devotional literature which survives in Welsh: see especially Glanmor Williams, *Welsh Church*, pp. 85–6.

contact with the world. The monks and canons, on the other hand, when they devoted themselves to creative writing, wrote for a more limited audience. This need not mean that their range of interests was narrower. Some of them, as we have seen, were writers of verse on secular as well as religious topics. They were interested in the bestiary and in the writings of contemporary history, as well as in the study of the Scriptures and the Fathers. It remains a fact, however, that none of the Welsh monasteries produced a writer or scholar whose work made an impact outside his own immediate circle.[116] Had they done so, a record of their achievement or copies of their work would surely have survived outside Wales. This line of argument is reinforced by what is known of the activities of a number of Welsh friars. At least six friars of Welsh birth, if not attached to Welsh houses, made their mark in the wider forum of English and European scholarship in the thirteenth and early-fourteenth centuries. There are no known monks of a stature to compare with Thomas Wallensis, John Wallensis, John Gwent, Roger of Conway, Laurence Wallensis or Thomas Waleys.[117] This would have been as St. Benedict and St. Bernard would have wished.

Even after the inauguration of special *studia*, very few monks and canons were university trained. As a body, they were more fitted, by their rule and by their way of life, for the mechanical tasks of transcription than for the production of works of original composition. It is in this field, where they assumed for once the role of Martha, that their contribution was probably of decisive importance for Welsh literature. In the fourteenth century, partly through the loosening of the ties with Cîteaux, the Cistercian abbeys of Wales became less cosmopolitan, more provincial, laxer in discipline and, perhaps as a consequence, more amenable and sympathetic to the secular influences of native culture. There is certainly more evidence in the fourteenth century than hitherto that the monks were actively patronizing the Welsh bards and probably transcribing their work. Without this *rapprochement* it is possible

---

[116] Clement of Llanthony is an exception, but his work was perhaps valued more for its usefulness than for any originality of thought it displayed.
[117] For these, see Glanmor Williams, *Welsh Church*, pp. 26–7, 82–4.

that the questions discussed in the present chapter would never have arisen. The volume of extant Welsh prose and verse would have been too slender to merit serious attention.

VII

THE MONASTERIES AND THE SECULAR CHURCH

I. EARLY DISPUTES

A certain amount of professional rivalry always existed in medieval times between the regular and secular clergy. It found expression in the schools in the familiar debate as to which was the more praiseworthy, the *vita activa* or the *vita contemplativa*, and at the end of the twelfth century it produced a spate of literature of satire and invective written by secular clerics against the monastic order.[1] More practical considerations were responsible for the tension and friction which existed between the episcopate and the new Anglo-Norman foundations in south Wales at the beginning of the twelfth century. The upheavals of invasion and war had resulted in the confiscation of many churches and much church land which had formerly belonged to the bishops or to *clas* churches. A good deal of the confiscated land and many of the churches were devoted to the foundation and endowment of priories dependent on abbeys in England and France. The same period also witnessed a protracted struggle between the bishops of St. David's, Llandaff and Hereford over the extent of their respective dioceses.[2]

Evidence of the disputes which ensued between the episcopate and the new monasteries comes almost exclusively from south-east Wales, where the invasion of the Anglo-Normans was most keenly felt and where their settlements were most intensively concentrated. Here, the conflict appears to have flared up during the troublous episcopate of Urban (1107–34). In 1119 Bishop Urban complained to Pope Calixtus II that his church was 'desolate and despoiled, even its tithes being lost to it . . . both by the lay power and the invasion of the monks'.[3] On 16 October 1119 Calixtus issued general letters

---

[1] Knowles, *Monastic Order*, pp. 662–78.
[2] J. Conway Davies, *Episc. Acts*, i, pp. 147–190.
[3] Ibid., ii, p. 617.

addressed to the secular clergy and also to specifically named barons and knights of the diocese of Llandaff. Among those named, particular mention may be made of Walter fitz Richard, Robert de Chandos, and Bernard Neufmarché. They were ordered to restore 'the lands, tithes, oblations, burials and other goods which they had wickedly withdrawn and detained, either of that church (i.e. Llandaff) or the other churches of that diocese'.[4] A similar mandate was issued by Pope Honorius II on 19 April 1128. This mandate has some new names in its address: Miles of Gloucester, Richard fitz Pons, Robert fitz Martin, and Maurice de Londres.[5] The catalogue of names is significant. Those named were all benefactors to religious houses in England or France and some of them became founders of religious houses in south Wales. When the first mandate was issued, Robert de Chandos and Bernard Neufmarché had already founded the priories of Goldcliff and Brecon. Walter fitz Richard was later to become the founder of Tintern Abbey, the first Cistercian abbey in Wales. Richard fitz Pons was a benefactor to Great Malvern and founded a transitory cell of that priory at Llandovery. Robert fitz Martin was a benefactor to Gloucester Abbey as well as being a founder of the abbey of St. Dogmaels. Maurice de Londres founded Ewenni, a cell of Gloucester Abbey. At the beginning of the twelfth century, the effects of the invasion and the foundation of the Benedictine priories threatened to involve the emergent diocese of Llandaff in financial ruin.

Disputes continued during the episcopate of Uchtryd (1140–48). From the letters of Gilbert Foliot, for example, we learn that Uchtryd was at odds with the monks of Goldcliff in 1143.[6] At about the same time he was disputing the abbot of Tewkesbury's claim to tithes and other rights within the diocese of Llandaff. This dispute was settled in 1146 when Uchtryd granted to Tewkesbury 'all tithes, alms and benefits which are given to them, in the bishopric, or shall be given canonically in the future'.[7] About 1144 a dispute arose between

---

[4] Ibid., p. 616.
[5] Ibid., p. 624.
[6] *Letters and Charters of Gilbert Foliot*, ed. A. Morey and C. N. L. Brooke, pp. 95–6.
[7] Clark, *Cartae*, i, pp. 101–2.

the bishop and John, prior of the newly-founded priory of Ewenni. On the death of Matilda de Londres, sister of the founder, the prior claimed her body for burial at his church in accordance with her last wishes. Uchtryd, however, ordered the body to be removed from Ewenni and conveyed to Llandaff. When the prior showed Uchtryd the papal privileges which supported his claim, Uchtryd retaliated by suspending the prior from communion and interdicting all the abbot of Gloucester's churches within his diocese.[8] The result of the dispute is not known; but the question of burials was still an important issue when Gerald was writing his *Speculum Ecclesiae c.* 1217. The monks, wrote Gerald, snatched the bodies of the dead for burial in their own cemeteries and spurned the rights of the churches whose parishioners they had been. Gerald does not mention mortuary fees, but it seems evident that he was referring to their wrongful diversion from the secular clergy to the monks of the Welsh abbeys and priories.[9]

Similar disputes were arising at a lower level between parish priests and the monks of the newly-founded cells. In 1146, for example, the monks of Basaleg, a cell of Glastonbury, were disputing with Picot, chaplain of *St. Gundleus*, over the bounds of their respective parishes. A settlement was arranged in the presence of Uchtryd himself in 1146.[10]

A stable *modus vivendi* between the Benedictine monks and the bishop of Llandaff was not reached until the episcopate of Nicholas ap Gwrgant (1148–83), 'the first regular to be appointed to a Welsh bishopric'.[11] Before his election as bishop he had spent thirty years as a monk at Gloucester Abbey. In his later years at Gloucester, he had probably been sacristan and had thus gained first-hand experience of the disputes between his abbey and the bishop of Llandaff.[12] The significant fact that Nicholas was a man of two worlds helps to explain the noticeable easing of tension which is apparent when reading his surviving episcopal acts. Bishop Nicholas realistically accepted the new monasticism and came to terms

[8] *Letters and Charters of Gilbert Foliot*, pp. 80–2.
[9] Gir. Camb., *Opera*, iv, p. 177.
[10] *Hist. et Cart. Gloucester*, ii, p. 55.
[11] *Episc. Acts*, ii, p. 542.
[12] Ibid., ii, p. 521.

with it. Throughout his episcopate he showed a benevolent concern for the welfare of the religious houses within his own diocese and particularly of his own house of Gloucester, where he had made his profession as a monk.[13]

No group of documents comparable with the *Book of Llan Dâv* or the Gilbert Foliot letters has survived for the diocese of St. David's by which one can gauge the initial impact of the newly-established religious foundations on the secular church in that area. A number of considerations suggest that the emerging diocese fared better than its neighbour at Llandaff. Even before his consecration, Bishop Bernard received a royal charter confirming his bishopric with all its temporal appurtenances 'as that church or any bishop of it had and held [it] in the time of king Edward and Grifin, or at any other time'.[14] There is a hint here that Bernard perhaps acquired for his church and its possessions something approaching the status of a marcher lordship, that he acknowledged no superior lord save the king.[15] It is significant, too, that the monasteries founded within the diocese of St. David's were more widely distributed than those within Llandaff diocese. Nor had the diocese to contend on its immediate flank with powerful houses such as Tewkesbury and Gloucester, whose patrons had played such a prominent part in the subjugation of Glamorgan. Apart from areas such as Dyfed and Brycheiniog, Norman control over Deheubarth was more tenuous and precarious than in the ancient kingdoms of south-east Wales.

The see of St. David's was fortunate, too, in its first Norman bishop. Bishop Bernard (1115–48) was a *curialis* in high favour with the king, and could speak on equal terms with the highest in the realm. He was also a vigorous protagonist of the rights of his own see. This combination of power and interest saved his diocese from the worst effects of that 'invasion of monks' which threatened almost to engulf the diocese of Llandaff

---

[13] Ibid., pp. 645–67.

[14] Ibid., i, p. 238.

[15] There is no evidence that Llandaff received similar royal support. The first suggestion we have that the latter church was acquiring marcher status and independence from the lordship of Glamorgan is in 1250, when Bishop William admitted that he held nothing of anyone in his diocese of Llandaff save from the lord king *in capite* (Clark, *Cartae*, ii, p. 576). On this question, see also D. Walker, 'The Medieval Bishops of Llandaff', *Morgannwg*, vi (1962), p. 11.

during the same period. It was Bernard who recovered from Battle Abbey the endowment which Henry I had made for the foundation of a cell at Carmarthen.[16] The Battle chronicler states that Bernard was 'charmed by the pleasantness of the place', but one can detect more subtle motives at work. Bernard seems to have been reluctant to abandon a church as important as Llandeulyddog to an English abbey. Not long afterwards, he installed in the church a community of Augustinian canons. Such a community was more amenable to episcopal control and more in keeping with the ancient associations of Llandeulyddog as an important *clas* church.

II. APPROPRIATED CHURCHES

In the eleventh and twelfth centuries the revenues of innumerable churches throughout western Europe went to finance a monastic revival on an unprecedented scale. Apart from the houses of the Cistercian order, to which such income was expressly forbidden, there was hardly an abbey or priory which did not include some form of spiritual income among its possessions. The late Professor Knowles estimated that 'the monasteries and other religious houses of England and Normandy became possessed, by the end of the first century of Norman domination, of perhaps a quarter of the total number of churches in England'.[17] By the end of the thirteenth century, Dr. Moorman considers 'that at least half the parish churches of England had been thus appropriated, by far the majority having gone to religious houses'.[18] The part that appropriated churches played in the economy of individual abbeys and priories in south Wales has already been discussed in a previous chapter. Here some attempt will be made to assess the extent of such appropriations in the dioceses of St. David's and Llandaff and to comment on the conduct of the religious within these dioceses as appropriators of churches.

First, however, something must be said of the churches which served the needs of the Welsh on the eve of the Norman conquest. There were the large *clas* churches like Llanbadarn Fawr, Llanilltud Fawr and Llancarfan. They had originally

[16] See above, pp. 32–3.
[17] Knowles, *Monastic Order*, p. 597.
[18] J. R. H. Moorman, *Church Life in England in the Thirteenth Century*, p. 42.

been monasteries, but by the eleventh century they had become collegiate churches manned by varying numbers of canons or *claswyr*. A number of these appear to have lost or were losing their collegiate character even before the Norman conquest of south Wales.[19] Theoretically dependent on the *clas* churches, but perhaps gradually acquiring an independent life of their own, were the chapels which had been founded as missionary 'out-stations' by monks in the sixth and subsequent centuries. In addition to the *clas* churches and their smaller dependencies, there must also have been a large number of churches erected by important laymen to serve the spiritual needs of themselves and their men. The late Sir John Lloyd inferred that churches of this type were far fewer in Wales than in England 'possibly because building in wood was so much simpler and less costly that there was here no occasion to invoke the aid of wealth when a new sanctuary was raised'.[20] At the end of the eleventh and beginning of the twelfth century, the Normans began to erect churches in large numbers on their newly acquired lands in Wales and they seem to have been emulated by the Welsh.[21]

Apart from the large *clas* churches whose revenues seem to have been derived from a central demesne and from dependent *trefi* in the vicinity, we know little of how the smaller Welsh churches were endowed on the eve of the conquest. Evidence in the *Book of Llan Dâv* suggests that each church had an endowment of land to maintain its minister or ministers. The latter may also have been supported by a contribution similar to tithe, for although tithe as it was understood in the Latin church finds no mention in the pre-conquest evidence for Wales, the ease with which the tithe system was imposed suggests that some system of compulsory contribution to the clergy existed before the Normans came and did not require much modification by ecclesiastical administrators in the twelfth century.[22]

[19] F. G. Cowley, 'The Church in Glamorgan from the Norman Conquest to the Beginning of the Fourteenth Century', *Glamorgan County History*, iii (1971), pp. 115–6.

[20] Lloyd, *History of Wales*, i, pp. 218–19.

[21] *History of Gruffydd ap Cynan*, ed. Arthur Jones, p. 155.

[22] J. Conway Davies, *Episc. Acts*, ii, p. 457; see also, however, the references in G. Constable, *Monastic Tithes*, pp. 17, 26, 36.

A notable feature of many Welsh churches in the twelfth and even in later centuries was their division into moieties and portions. A church of moieties was a church divided into two benefices. A church of portions was a church divided into three or more benefices.[23] Such arrangements originated in one of two ways. The churches were either ancient *clas* churches where two or more clerics possessed and served the church as successors of the original *claswyr*, or churches whose ownership had been divided among co-heirs. The existence of these churches should be borne in mind when one attempts to interpret the early charters in which Norman and Welsh lords grant tithes and churches to monastic foundations. A typical example is the church of Verwick and its chapels in the deanery of Sub-Aeron. This church was confirmed to Chertsey Abbey and its cell of Cardigan Priory by Rhys ap Gruffydd.[24] A little later the same church was confirmed to Talley Abbey by Rhys Fychan, son of Rhys Fychan.[25] The seeming inconsistency is solved by the details which the *Valor* of 1535 gives of the church. The revenues of the church even then were divided into three parts: 'one part of the fruits and emoluments pertains to the prior of Cardigan . . . the second part or portion pertains to the abbot of Talley and the third part or portion pertains to Owain Gruffydd the vicar'.[26] Verwick was clearly a portionary church but the charters give no indication of this.

When a Norman lord granted by charter a Welsh church to a monastic foundation, what in fact was he granting? The evidence from the Brecon Priory cartulary suggests that the priory at first merely acquired the advowson of the church, the right of appointing its priest from whom it received an annual pension in recognition of the priory's rights. The English evidence shows that it generally became possible to strike a hard bargain with the priest and to increase the pension considerably. It then became advantageous to the monastery to seek the bishop's permission to appropriate the rectorial tithes, usually two-thirds of the church's revenues.[27]

---

[23] G. W. O. Addleshaw, *Rectors, Vicars and Patrons in Twelfth and Early Thirteenth Century Canon Law*, p. 11.
[24] E. Pritchard, *Cardigan Priory*, p. 144.
[25] *Arch. Camb.*, 1893, p. 42.
[26] *Valor*, iv, p. 393.
[27] Knowles, *Monastic Order*, pp. 592–606.

The process whereby a church was formally appropriated to a monastery by the bishop was generally a slow one. The churches of Talgarth and Llan-gors, for example, although they had been granted to Brecon Priory by its founder early in the twelfth century, were not formally appropriated to the priory by the bishop of St. David's until a century later.[28] Many churches granted to religious houses were never appropriated and continued to pay only a pension to the religious houses which held their advowson.

By the end of the thirteenth century it becomes possible to make a rough tally of the churches in the dioceses of St. David's and Llandaff which were appropriated to religious houses. A convenient check-list of churches is provided by the *Taxatio* of Pope Nicholas IV drawn up in 1291. This record, however, does not record appropriations with any consistency, and its evidence has to be supplemented by twelfth- and thirteenth-century charters and by a cautious use of the later evidence provided by the episcopal registers of St. David's and the *Valor* of 1535.

The *Taxatio* records details of 131 churches in the diocese of Llandaff, of which 40 are known to have been appropriated to religious houses when the assessment was made.[29] Most of these appropriations were in the eastern deaneries of the diocese. There were ten in the deanery of Abergavenny, six in the deanery of Usk, and eight in the deanery of Lower Gwent. Further west there were two appropriated churches in the deanery of Newport, three in the deanery of Llandaff, seven in the deanery of Groneath, and four in the deanery of Kenfig.

The assessment for St. David's is far less complete than that for Llandaff, and far more reliance has to be placed on charter evidence, which is sometimes difficult to evaluate, and on the evidence of the later episcopal registers and the *Valor*. Of the 223 churches listed, it seems clear that at least 46 were appropriated to religious houses when the assessment was made. Although the diocese of St. David's was nearly four times as large as the diocese of Llandaff, the appropriated churches were

[28] See below p. 175.
[29] See Appendix IV.

not more evenly spread. Again, the significance of the distribution can best be appreciated from the table in Appendix IV showing the appropriations in each deanery. From this it can be seen that the appropriated churches were more thickly spread in the lowland areas and in areas where Anglo-Norman settlement was most intensive.

The figures obtained from the *Taxatio* and other relevant evidence reveal that in the diocese of Llandaff between a quarter and a third of the churches had been appropriated to religious houses before the end of the thirteenth century. In the diocese of St. David's the proportion was a good deal less, more in the region of a fifth of the total number of churches. Had the cartularies of all the religious houses in the diocese survived, the percentage obtained would probably have been higher, but hardly higher than that for the diocese of Llandaff. The diocese of St. David's was a large one. The religious houses within it were more evenly spread and Anglo-Norman influence was less extensive than within the diocese of Llandaff. It would be in keeping with the evidence to suggest that the diocese of St. David's had proportionately fewer churches appropriated to religious houses than the diocese of Llandaff.

III. THE ORDINATION OF VICARAGES

When a bishop appropriated a church to a religious corporation, it was incumbent upon him to ensure that the church services continued to be adequately performed and that the spiritual needs of the parishioners were not neglected. The religious corporation was in the position of a rector or parson who could not reside and provision had therefore to be made for the appointment of a chaplain or vicar to perform the services in its place. As early as the seventh century, church councils had been at pains to make provision for churches whose rector was unable to reside and exercise the cure of souls in person. These early rudimentary measures were refined and developed into a clear, coherent system by the legislation of the reforming papacy, particularly that of Urban II (1088–99), Alexander III (1159–81) and Innocent III (1198–1216). The main principle behind the legislation on vicarages was that where a rector could not reside, a perpetual vicar should be appointed in his place by the rector, but should be presented to, and instituted by, the diocesan. He was to have security of tenure and an income sufficient to maintain himself, and this usually, though not invariably, comprised a third of the total revenue of the church appropriated.[30] The appropriation of churches in large numbers to religious houses during the twelfth and thirteenth centuries, though it did not initiate the vicarage system, certainly accelerated its adoption. The earliest known vicarage in England is that of Leeds, which came into existence as a result of Archbishop Thomas of York's confirmation of the appropriation of the church to the priory of Holy Trinity, Micklegate, York, sometime between 1109 and 1114.[31] This is an extremely early example, for it is not until after 1150 that the ordination of vicarages becomes commonplace in the records of the English dioceses.

R. A. R. Hartridge, arguing from the solitary nine vicarages recorded for the whole of Wales in the *Taxatio* of 1291, inferred that vicarages had not been properly ordained in Wales.[32] There is sufficient evidence to show, however, that the bishops of Llandaff and St. David's were as anxious as English diocesans to apply the vicarage system to appropriated churches within their own dioceses. When Nicholas ap Gwrgant, bishop of Llandaff (1148–83), confirmed to Tewkesbury Abbey a number of churches within his diocese, he stipulated that when the rectors of these churches died 'the monks should institute in them suitable vicars, namely, priests who were to answer to the bishop *de spiritualibus* and that an honest maintenance be assigned to them'.[33] Between 1186 and 1191 William, bishop of Llandaff, gave episcopal authority to the monks of Gloucester to convert the churches of Newport to their own use, 'saving in all things the dignity of the church of Landav and the honest maintenance of the vicars ministering in those churches'.[34] By 1254, when the valuation of Norwich was made, there were at least thirty-three vicarages within the diocese of Llandaff, though not all of them were valued.[35]

[30] G. W. O. Addleshaw, *Rectors, Vicars and Patrons*, pp. 12–17.
[31] C. T. Clay, 'A Worcester Charter of Thomas II, Archibishop of York; and its Bearing on the Early History of the Church of Leeds', *Yorks. Arch. Jnl.*, xxxvi (1944–7), pp. 132–6.
[32] *History of Vicarages*, p. 87.
[33] Clark, *Cartae*, i, pp. 133–5.
[34] *Episc. Acts*, ii, pp. 671–2. For other examples, see ibid., pp. 677–8, 725.
[35] W. E. Lunt, *Valuation of Norwich*, pp. 314–25.

Though no figures exist for the diocese of St. David's, the gradual growth of the vicarage system in the area can be studied in the charters relating to the churches of Talgarth, Llan-gors, Llanigon and Hay, all of which were appropriated to Brecon Priory. The churches of Talgarth and Llan-gors had been granted to Brecon by its founder, Bernard Neufmarché, early in the twelfth century.[36] The churches of Llanigon and Hay were granted to the priory by Henry of Hereford sometime before 1175. This grant stipulated that the prior and convent were to maintain the first vicar to serve these churches 'as long as he lived and was faithful to them, such that every year he render therein to the monks of St. John of Brecon five marks of silver'.[37] All four churches were confirmed to the priory *in proprios usus* by William de Breos and Matilda his wife in the presence of Geoffrey, bishop of St. David's, in 1207–8.[38] The prior and convent were to find suitable chaplains to serve the four churches, two at Hay, one at Llanigon, two at Talgarth and one at Llan-gors, and retain them at their own table. It was Geoffrey, bishop of St. David's (1203–14), who was responsible for the formal appropriation of these churches to Brecon Priory and the ordination of vicarages in them. He granted and confirmed the four churches to the priory *in proprios usus*, 'for the sustenance of the brethren and the maintenance of hospitality and alms . . . saving in all things the customs pertaining to the bishop and his own, and saving also the benefices canonically occupied by Thomas, clerk in the church of Hay, Hugh, chaplain in the church of Llanigon, Walter, clerk in the church of Talgarth, and William, chaplain in the church of Llan-gors, as long as they live, saving also the honest sustenance of the vicars in the aforesaid churches canonically assigned to them'.[39]

Separate deeds regulated the details of the individual vicarages. On the death of William, priest of Llan-gors, 'a vicarage of 100s. was to be assigned and received by the vicar of the same church'. The vicar was to minister in his own person and answer fully to the bishop and his officials.[40] After the

---

[36] *Brec. Cart.*, pp. 69–70.
[37] Ibid., pp. 79–80.
[38] Ibid., pp. 83–4. For the dating, see *Episc. Acts*, i, pp. 332–3.
[39] *Brec. Cart.*, pp. 56–7; *Episc. Acts*, i, pp. 333–4.
[40] *Brec. Cart.*, p. 67.

death of Thomas of Hay, a vicarage of ten marks was to be established in the church of Hay.[41] Similar charters ordaining vicarages in the churches of Llanigon and Talgarth were drawn up; but unfortunately their texts have not survived in the Carte transcript of the Brecon cartulary.[42]

IV. THE RELIGIOUS AS APPROPRIATORS

The subject of appropriations has always been a controversial one and still lacks a definitive study. Historians since the Reformation have questioned the justice of a system whereby the larger part of a church's income was diverted to a religious foundation which rendered little if anything in return, and they have emphasized the disastrous effects which such appropriations had on parochial finance. More recently attempts have been made to justify, if not defend, monastic appropriations. It has been pointed out that tithes were not paid solely for the support of the clergy. 'They constituted a general fund applicable to such objects as the repair of the church fabric, the relief of destitution, hospitality to travellers and indeed any recognized church purpose'.[43] This fund was technically at the disposal of the bishop, who could, if he saw fit, allocate part of it to work outside the bounds of the parish. Many bishops in the late-eleventh and early-twelfth century favoured the transfer of a church from the seigneurial *dominium* of a layman to the patronage of a monastery, since the latter, imbued with the reforming ideals of the papacy, was more likely to provide suitably qualified and celibate parsons to its churches than a layman. Such hopes, however, were rarely realized and by the thirteenth century appropriations had come to be regarded as something in the nature of a necessary evil, sanctioned and even indulged in by the bishops themselves.

Bishops in the poorer dioceses of Wales and Ireland were particularly aware of the inherent injustice of the system and of the negligence of monastic appropriators. The appropriations most difficult to defend were those of churches at a great distance from the monastery. Llanthony Prima had obtained in

[41] Ibid., pp. 67–8.
[42] Their texts were noted by Tanner; see ibid., p. 68.
[43] H. P. R. Finberg, *Tavistock Abbey*, p. 20. Cf. also G. W. O. Addleshaw, *Rectors, Vicars and Patrons*, pp. 5–6.

the second half of the twelfth century a group of churches in Ireland which contributed more than £70 to the priory's treasury. In 1233 Richard, bishop of Meath, in an outspoken protest, complained that the priory unjustly held these churches 'to the grave prejudice and no small injury of the church of Meath'. Their fruits were transported to Wales, when by justice and right they should have been devoted to the needs of the poor parishioners of the diocese of Meath.[44]

The religious often regarded an appropriated church exclusively as a financial asset and tended to forget that they also had responsibilities to the church as a cure of souls. English canon law allowed a patron six months to fill a vacancy in a church whose rector or vicar had died.[45] There is some evidence to suggest that the monks made full use of the letter of the law and occasionally failed to present a vicar within the canonical time. Sometime between 1200 and 1215 Giles, bishop of Hereford, collated a chaplain to the vicarage of Humber because Brecon Priory had failed to present a vicar within the time laid down by the Lateran Council.[46] Between 1240 and 1253, Peter, bishop of Hereford, collated William de Agathe to the vicarage of Woolaston because Tintern Abbey had similarly failed to present a vicar within the canonical period.[47] In 1318, Bishop Adam de Orleton ordered an enquiry into Llanthony Prima's alleged neglect of the parish of Orcop, where parishioners were dying without the sacraments. It was alleged that the priory neglected the cure of souls and failed to cause the church to be served by a suitable vicar or competent priest.[48]

It became a matter of policy, too, for the religious to economize on the main 'overhead' of an appropriated church, the salary of the vicar. When a parish prospered and the tithe increased, the vicar did not invariably share in the prosperity. In 1242 Llanthony Prima, by a deed of Albert, archbishop of Armagh, imposed a 'wage-freeze' on its Irish vicars which prevented the value of vicarages from being augmented.[49]

[44] *Irish Cartularies of Llanthony Prima et Secunda*, pp. 41–2, 146.
[45] G. W. O. Addleshaw, *Rectors, Vicars and Patrons*, p. 20.
[46] *Brec. Cart.*, pp. 38–9.
[47] *CPL.*, i, p. 288.
[48] *Registrum Ade de Orleton*, p. 62.
[49] *Irish Cartularies*, pp. 26–7. In fairness to Llanthony Prima, it should be pointed out that their vicars in Ireland were not too badly off.

Disputes between vicar and appropriator were frequent even when they were in continuous and close contact. At Brecon, the priory church was divided into a parochial church and a monastic church. The parochial church was appropriated to the priory from early times. In 1248 Master Benedict, the vicar, was at odds with the priory over his share of the church's revenues. They submitted the dispute to the arbitration of Thomas le Waleys, bishop of St. David's, who ordained that:

> the said Master Benedict and all vicars after him for ever, should receive ten marks annually from the said prior and convent . . . The prior and convent were to receive all the revenues both of the mother church and of its chapels, besides the second legacy (*secundum legatum*) and single Mass pence on the four main festivals . . . and besides single Mass pence at a burial (*pro corpore presenti*).

The prior and convent were to bear all charges, ordinary and extraordinary.[50]

A similar dispute between vicar and appropriator had arisen at Carmarthen in 1278. The vicar of St. Peter's, which was appropriated to the Augustinian priory of Carmarthen, claimed that his vicarage had been meagrely endowed and that his portion was insufficient to pay for food, clothing and other expenses, 'the prior and convent constantly affirming the contrary'. The dispute was settled by Bishop Richard de Carew, who ordained that the vicar and his successors should receive for ever ten marks annually. The vicar was to have the mortuaries in the parish, together with the Mass pence. If the offerings from mortuaries or purifications on any day exceeded the Mass pence, he should be content with the Mass pence only. As at Brecon, the prior and convent were to defray all ordinary and extraordinary expenses.[51]

Information on the incomes enjoyed by Welsh vicars before 1349 is meagre. Later evidence would suggest, however, that the 10-mark vicarages of Brecon and Carmarthen were exceptional before the Black Death. The vicar of Chepstow had 40s. with board and other services in 1398 and the vicar

---

[50] *Brec. Cart.*, pp. 14–5.
[51] F. T. Brigstocke, 'The Settlement of a Medieval Dispute at Carmarthen', *Carmarthen Antiquary*, ii (1957), pp. 212–3.

of Cardigan a vicarage of 100s.[52] Both were comparatively rich churches. By contrast, the majority of Welsh livings were miserably poor and provincial councils made allowance for this when they attempted to define a suitable value for a vicarage. In 1222 the Council of Oxford ruled that 'there be assigned to a perpetual vicar at least five marks of the returns . . . unless, perhaps, it be in those parts of Wales, where on account of the slenderness of the churches vicars are content with a smaller stipend'.[53]

The information on the values of vicarages provided by the assessments of 1254 and 1291 is tabulated in Appendix V. It relates solely to the diocese of Llandaff. It is worth emphasizing again that the figures do not represent income. The rural deans, who appear to have been responsible for the valuation of spiritualities, returned their *verus valor* 'at the lowest amount at which benefices could be farmed'. 'Although', writes Rose Graham, 'it was unusual in the thirteenth century to farm vicarages, they were assessed on the same principle.'[54] For this reason the evidence does not easily lend itself to valid generalization. A few points, however, deserve notice. In the 1254 valuation only 18 of at least 33 vicarages which are known to have existed within the diocese were considered of sufficient value to come within the terms of the valuation. Only two of these, Llanilltud Fawr and Kenfig, were valued at or above 5 marks. The remainder were valued at figures ranging from the lowest, Matharn at 13s. 4d., to the highest, Grosmont at £2 6s. 8d.

A more significant fact is that only three of the eighteen vicarages were in churches appropriated to the bishop or chapter. The church of Matharn had been appropriated to the chapter of Llandaff well before the 1254 valuation. The church of Langstone was also a chapter church in the thirteenth century.[55] Basaleg with its chapels had been granted to the bishop and chapter between 1230 and 1240 by the abbot of Glastonbury to hold by a perpetual farm of 35 marks, and by virtue of this the bishop appointed the vicar.[56] Yet in all three

---

[52] *CPL.*, v, p. 258, vi, pp. 248, 439.
[53] Hartridge, *Vicarages in the Middle Ages*, p. 21.
[54] R. Graham, *EHR.*, xxiii (1908), p. 446.
[55] C. A. H. Green, *Notes on Churches in the Diocese of Llandaff*, pp. 30–1.
[56] *Episc. Acts*, ii, pp. 719, 721.

churches the vicarages were valued at a low figure—Matharn, an ancient Llandaff church, at the lowest figure of all eighteen vicarages. It would seem that in the diocese of Llandaff the vicar of a church appropriated to the bishop or chapter fared as badly as, if not worse than, the vicar of a church appropriated to a monastery. This inference seems to be borne out by the evidence of the 1291 assessment. Of the nine vicarages listed, all are monastic vicarages. The values of both church and vicarage, as one would expect from a more stringent valuation, had risen considerably. All the vicarages were valued above the five-mark level, with Christchurch at the exceptionally high figure of £8. It is worth remembering, however, that these nine vicarages represented a fraction of the total number of vicarages which had been ordained within the diocese when the assessment was made. The majority of the vicarages were either too poor to be assessed or their values were included in that of the church.

V. THE CISTERCIAN ORDER

The attitude of the secular clergy to the monks of the Cistercian order is admirably summed up by a letter which Archbishop Pecham wrote to Edward I in 1284, when the latter was forwarding his plans for the transfer of the Cistercian monks of Aberconwy to a new site at Maenan:

> Although I am ready, as far as is in me, to dedicate the place for the Cistercian monks at Maenan, yet I could not do it without full assent of the bishop and of his chapter and of the parson of the place, who, with plenty of other people, have a very great horror of the approach of the foresaid monks. For though they may be good men, if God please, still they are the hardest neighbours that prelates and parsons could have. For where they plant their foot, they destroy towns, take away tithes and curtail by their privileges all the power of the prelacy.[57]

When the Cistercians first entered England and Wales the social and ecclesiastical implications of their settlement were hardly realized. They were welcomed as a monastic *élite*, but few could predict what effect their particular form of economy, so different from that of the black monks, would have on rural life within the framework of the parish.

[57] *Registrum Epistolarum*, ii, p. 769.

The early Cistercian fathers, when they ruled that their members should earn their livelihood from the labours of their own hands, eschewing feudal forms of revenue and spiritual income from churches, tithes and burial fees, presupposed that their abbeys would be far removed from centres of population. In practice, most abbeys held lands which were not far from, and often adjacent to, lands which were intensively settled.

When a Cistercian abbey obtained land within such a parish, it was the practice, whenever feasible, to dispense with the services of the tenantry who were settled there and to make provision for their settlement elsewhere. The land was then attached to the nearest monastic grange and worked by the abbey lay-brethren and hired labourers. Although the process was usually a long one, extending perhaps over a generation before the tenantry were removed, the final result was that the parish church was deprived of a substantial portion of its revenue, since from 1132 the Cistercian order had obtained exemption from payment of tithes.[58] Occasionally, the area of a whole parish or chapelry fell to the control of a Cistercian abbey and when the tenantry had been removed, the church, left without any income, became virtually redundant. The next step was to come to some arrangement with the parson and make satisfaction to the diocesan over the rights involved. The redundant church could then be destroyed or incorporated into grange buildings.

The evidence for this aspect of Cistercian settlement has been fully explored for England.[59] That the same process was also being extensively applied on the estates of the Welsh abbeys is attested by the remarks of Gerald of Wales in his *Speculum Ecclesiae*:

> It is wonderful how all the houses of this order almost throughout the whole of Wales are contaminated by the infectious vice of avarice. For they recklessly take possession of churches by occupying parts of parishes; many, too, they presume to ruin and utterly destroy by a wholesale purchase of their lands and by expelling the very cultivators from whose tithes and oblations the priests of Levi are accustomed to be maintained.[60]

[58] L. J. Lekai, *The White Monks*, p. 212.
[59] R. A. Donkin, 'Settlement and Depopulation on Cistercian Estates during the Twelfth and Thirteenth Centuries', *BIHR.*, xxxiii (1960), pp. 141–65.
[60] Gir. Camb., *Opera*, iv, pp. 136–7. Cf. also ibid., p. 177.

Specific examples of the process at work in Wales come from Margam, the best documented of the Welsh Cistercian houses. In the last quarter of the twelfth century, the monks of Margam acquired, parcel by parcel, control over the knight's fee of Llangewydd, which in the following generation they were to convert into a large grange of eight carucates. During the slow process of acquisition, they obtained the patronage of the ancient church of Llangewydd from the holder of the fee, Herbert Scurlage.[61] Probably as a result of Herbert's grant the monks in 1188 came to an agreement with William, clerk of Llangewydd, by which the latter handed over all his land and revenues to the monks for his lifetime for an annual payment of 20s. and a premium of a horse and 4½ marks.[62] Some time between 1191 and 1196 the whole question of the monks' rights over the church came before papal judges-delegate. In the presence of Roger, abbot of Evesham, and Peter, archdeacon of Worcester, Rivanus, a priest who alleged that he was parson, abjured the church for ever and promised that he would not vex the monks thereafter. The monks *pro bono pacis* and for his labours and expenses gave Rivanus two marks of silver.[63] It was probably not long after this that the church was destroyed. The abbey records are silent, but a brief entry in a list of Llandaff synodals shows that by the middle of the thirteenth century the church had ceased to exist.

The church was probably destroyed well before 1217, for Gerald of Wales in his *Speculum Ecclesiae* gives a graphic account of the whole operation, omitting as was his practice the names of persons and places. According to Gerald, the monks took the church at farm from the parson and then proceeded to eject the parishioners from their ancient home-steads. At night time the lay-brothers and servants, acting on the instructions of their superiors, razed the church to the ground. With admirable foresight, continues Gerald, they carted all the building material, both wood and stone, away from the site so that no trace might remain of the ancient church. A few days later, the parson, passing through the area, found to his astonishment that his church had disappeared.

---

[61] Clark, *Cartae*, ii, p. 431.
[62] Ibid., i, pp. 200–1.
[63] Ibid., pp. 206–7.

Acting on information obtained from the inhabitants of neighbouring vills, he began the laborious process of defending his rights in the secular and ecclesiastical courts but to little or no avail. The riches of the abbey, writes Gerald, blinded the eyes of the judges and prevented a just judgement.[64]

The fate of Llangewydd was shared by a number of other churches and chapels on the estates of Margam Abbey. In 1234 Elias, bishop of Llandaff, confirmed to the abbey the chapels of Resolven, Penhydd, Hafodheulog, Stormy and Llangeinor, 'free and quit of all service, exaction and custom both ecclesiastical and secular'.[65] This was not a deed of appropriation. All the chapels were withdrawn from parochial use. They were either destroyed, allowed to stand as private grange chapels or converted into farm buildings. As Gerald remarked, the Cistercians had no qualms about disturbing the bones of the dead when they stood in the way of efficient farming.[66]

Bishops were as strict in maintaining their rights to grant or withold permission to build private chapels at abbey granges as they were at the private residences of laymen. Such chapels, it was justly argued, might acquire a standing in the locality to the financial detriment of neighbouring parish churches. Between 1219 and 1229, William, bishop of Llandaff, allowed the Margam monks to have a chapel and to celebrate mass at their new grange at Resolven, but he was careful to stipulate that this should be for the monks only. They were only allowed to celebrate mass in the ancient chapel (on the site of the old grange which they had abandoned) on the anniversary of its dedication.[67] In 1239 Elias, bishop of Llandaff, gave them permission to celebrate mass at their grange of Melis, which lay within the lordship of Afan and not far from the abbey.[68]

The grange chapel, where it existed, formed part of the complex of grange buildings situated within an enclosure wall. Bishop Elias dedicated such a chapel within the grange court of Llangewydd between 1230 and 1240. When the monks

[64] Gir. Camb., *Opera*, iv, pp. 135–6. See also F. G. Cowley, 'Llangewydd: an Unrecorded Glamorgan Castle', *Arch. Camb.*, 1967, pp. 204–6.

[65] Clark, *Cartae*, ii, p. 492.

[66] Gir. Camb., *Opera*, iv, p. 137.

[67] Clark, *Cartae*, ii, p. 383.

[68] Ibid., p. 512.

constructed a chapel outside the court of the grange, the bishop gave strict orders that it should be destroyed and mass celebrated in the chapel he had dedicated.[69]

Laymen were not allowed to receive the sacraments at a Cistercian church nor at the grange chapels. This restriction was meant to prevent offerings from being diverted from their lawful recipient, the local parish church. An interesting example of the stringency with which this regulation was applied can be seen in a papal licence issued to Cwm-hir in 1232. It gave licence 'to the Cistercian abbot and convent of Cwm-hir, who are in a mountainous district remote from parish churches, to hear the confessions of, and administer the sacraments to their servants and household'.[70]

Well before the end of the twelfth century the restrictions which the Cistercian authorities had placed on receiving revenues from churches, tithes, altar and burial dues were being ignored and nowhere more blatantly than in England.[71] In south Wales the practice of appropriating churches to Cistercian abbeys gained ground more slowly than in England and was resorted to more frequently by abbeys under Anglo-Norman patronage than by the abbeys of Welsh Wales. Neath, as one might expect from a former Savigniac abbey, held varying forms of spiritual income from its foundation and did not relinquish them on becoming a member of the Cistercian order in 1147.[72] Before 1206 Margam Abbey had become the farmer of Tewkesbury's church of Kenfig for an annual payment of ten marks, but had taken the precaution of obtaining the consent and confirmation of the Cistercian General Chapter.[73] As far as Tewkesbury was concerned, the agreement appears to have provided a satsifactory solution to a difficult problem, for not only was Kenfig far distant from the appropriating abbey and its tithe difficult to collect, but Margam Abbey itself was already drawing tithe from certain of its own estates situated within the parochial boundaries.[74] After a

[69] Ibid., p. 473.
[70] CPL., i, p. 131.
[71] Knowles, Monastic Order, p. 355.
[72] Birch, Neath Abbey, pp. 58–9.
[73] Clark, Cartae, ii, pp. 276–7, 277–8, 304.
[74] This appears from a charter of Henry, bishop of Llandaff, by which he granted to the monks of Margam inter alia 'all their own tithes in the parish of Kenfig' (Clark, Cartae, ii, pp. 226–7).

long-drawn-out dispute, a similar agreement was reached over the church of St. Leonard's, Newcastle in 1265.[75] Apart from the tithe it acquired as farmer of the churches of Kenfig and Newcastle, and a single advowson (that of Bonvilston),[76] the abbey remained singularly free from spiritual sources of revenue until the fourteenth century.

The earliest real appropriation of a church by a Cistercian abbey in south Wales was Tintern's appropriation of the church of Woolaston and the chapel of Alvington between 1186 and 1199. The deed of appropriation is an interesting one because it shows that William de Vere, bishop of Hereford, was fully aware that his action in licensing the appropriation was contrary to Cistercian law and custom:

> Although by the custom of the English church it is not permitted for monks of the Cistercian order to convert parish churches to their own uses; yet, since we love and are bound to love the church of St. Mary, Tintern, which our ancestors founded, with some special degree of favour, we ought, for the maintenance of the brethren serving God there, to add somewhat to their means by the favour of a more extended dispensation, so that they may be able more readily to attend upon the poor in the showing forth of their charity . . .[77]

In the abbeys of Welsh Wales within the diocese of St. David's, such appropriations were extremely rare. Before the fourteenth century there is record of only one church being appropriated to a Cistercian abbey in the area. Cadwgan, bishop of Bangor, between 1215 and 1236 granted the church of Llangurig to the abbey of Strata Florida, the house where he first made his profession as a monk.[78]

In the last quarter of the thirteenth century and the first half of the fourteenth, there are signs in south Wales that the traditional Cistercian economy was breaking down. Tenants were returning to the extensive grange lands which had previously

---

[75] Ibid., pp. 673–77, 677–81, 696–7.
[76] Ibid., p. 492.
[77] B.M., Arundel MS. 19, f. 31. This is a small Tintern cartulary which was transcribed in the sixteenth century. There is a transcript of this deed and of other Tintern material in a valuable collection of transcripts made by the late J. G. Wood, now preserved in the Newport Public Library. I am indebted to Mr. W. J. Collett for drawing my attention to this valuable collection.
[78] CPL., i, pp. 558–9.

been cultivated by lay-brethren and hired labourers. This frequently fomented disputes between the rectors of churches and the monks, for the latter often held lands within the boundaries of intensively settled parishes. Who was to receive the tithe of the newly-settled abbey tenants: the rector of the parish within whose boundaries the tenants worked, or the Cistercian abbot as landlord? The problem was a difficult one, for the Cistercians, although they claimed exemption from payment of tithes themselves, were not slow to exact them from their tenants.[79] The problem was aggravated by the existence of grange chapels for, as thirteenth-century bishops had wisely foreseen, such chapels, if not carefully supervised, were liable to syphon off revenues which rightly belonged to a neighbouring parish church. Trouble seems to have flared up on the estates of Whitland and Strata Florida during the episcopate of Henry Gower (1328–47), perhaps as a result of an attempt on the part of these abbeys to implement a bull which Boniface VIII issued to the Cistercian order in 1302. This bull enabled Cistercian abbeys to lease their noval land[80] 'without subjecting it to the claims of rectors or other parish tithe-owners'.[81] Both Whitland and Strata Florida held lands in parishes whose churches were either appropriated to the collegiate churches of Abergwili and Llanddewibrefi or under the direct patronage of the bishop. Agreements between the bishop and the two abbeys over the rival claims to tithe were reached in 1338 and 1339.[82] The method finally agreed on for dividing the tithe was that the prebendaries, rectors and vicars of the churches involved were to receive from the abbey tenants two-thirds of the great and predial tithes and the whole of the small tithes. The abbeys were to receive a third of the great and predial tithes. All the tenants' oblations were to go to the prebendaries, rectors and vicars, except free will offerings made by tenants when they visited the monasteries and their chapels.

[79] See the deed of Bishop John de Eaglescliff in 1339 by which he admitted Margam's claim to tithe of corn and hay at Resolven, Hafod-y-Porth and Penhydd: Clark, *Cartae*, iv, pp. 1236–7.

[80] Noval land was land which the monks had been the first to bring under cultivation.

[81] J. S. Donnelly, 'Changes in the Grange Economy of English and Welsh Cistercian Abbeys', *Traditio*, x (1954), p. 421.

[82] J. F. O'Sullivan, *Cistercian Settlements in Wales and Monmouthshire*, pp. 50–1; S. W. Williams, *Cistercian Abbey of Strata Florida*, appendix, pp. l-lii.

Already by the middle of the fourteenth century, therefore, the Cistercian abbeys of south Wales were becoming substantial tithe owners. Their holdings of tithe increased as leasing of parcels of the abbey estates became more frequent in the second half of the fourteenth and during the fifteenth century. Distress during the fourteenth century also prompted Cistercian abbeys to attempt to appropriate churches in a desperate bid to increase their sources of fixed income. Such attempts, however, were not always successful.[83] This dual process—tithe agreements with the secular clergy and appropriations licensed by the bishop—continued throughout the later middle ages and explains why an order which had originally eschewed all forms of spiritual income was in some cases so heavily dependent on it at the Dissolution.

VI. THE MONKS AND PAROCHIAL WORK

The monastic order played little part in the pastoral work of the parishes of south Wales. The work of administering the sacraments to the laity, of preaching to them and of providing them with a rudimentary education, was performed with few exceptions by the secular clergy.[84] In this respect, the area differed little from England. 'To the end', writes Egerton Beck, 'it was always regarded as an anomaly for monks to be engaged in parochial work.'[85] The numerous churches appropriated to priories and abbeys were served either by perpetual vicars or by stipendiary chaplains appointed by the monks, and it was only in exceptional circumstances that parochial duties were performed by the monks themselves. In 1279, for example, the priory of St. Clears was so impoverished that its prior was forced to find work as a chaplain to maintain himself.[86] Occasionally a bishop would make provision for a church or its chapels to be served by monks,

---

[83] On this, see below pp. 265–7.

[84] A school was granted to Brecon Priory in the twelfth century (*Brec. Cart.*, pp. 12–13), but there is no evidence that the monks taught there or indeed if the school continued in existence. An entry in a St. Dogmael's book now in St. John's College, Cambridge, refers to boys in the choir and it is possible that there was a song school there in the thirteenth century; see M. R. James, *Descriptive Catalogue of Manuscripts in the Library of St. John's College, Cambridge*, p. 5.

[85] E. Beck, 'Regulars and the Parochial System in Mediaeval England', *Dublin Review*, clxxii (1923), p. 237.

[86] G. F. Duckett, *Charters and Records of Cluni*, vol. 2, p. 136.

but only if there was a shortage of available chaplains. In 1248 Thomas le Waleys, bishop of St. David's, ruled that three chaplains should be appointed to help the vicar of Brecon to serve the dependent chapels, adding that 'since these three chaplains cannot suffice for the celebration of divine services in all the chapels, the prior and convent shall cause the said chapels to be adequately served by approved monks'. The bishop was careful to stipulate that 'the cure of souls should remain wholly with the vicar and the secular chaplains'.[87] It is doubtful if the monks of Brecon took advantage of the privilege.

There is only one incontestable case of Benedictine monks in south Wales serving parochial churches as a matter of course during this period. The monks of the priory cell of Cardigan had, in their own persons, served their appropriated churches in and around Cardigan from the thirteenth century until 1428, when they successfully petitioned the pope that they should in future be served by secular priests.[88]

Private chapels and chantries were a different matter. At Chepstow, the prior, presumably as a condition of his tenure, was obliged to 'find one of his monks to celebrate divine service in the castle of Strugull three times a week', and in 1227 arrangements were made for three Cistercian monks of Grace Dieu to serve a royal chantry at St. Briavels.[89]

The Augustinians were a semi-monastic order and their canons had from the first been deemed capable of occupying and serving parish churches. In this they were encouraged by the reforming movement in the church which saw them as 'a leavening element in the clerical life of the country'.[90] In England, many of their communities were established in large churches in public use.

In the twelfth century it seems possible that houses such as Carmarthen and Llanthony served some of their churches with their own canons. The Welsh evidence is silent on the question; but Llanthony Prima was obliged to send some of its canons to

---

[87] *Brec. Cart.*, p. 14.

[88] *CPL.*, viii, p. 51, cited by E. Beck, *Dublin Review*, clxxii (1923), p. 237.

[89] *Cal. Inq. Post Mortem*, iv, p. 299; *C.Ch.R.*, i, p. 4; *Rotuli Litterarum Clausarum*, ii (1224–27), p. 132.

[90] Knowles, *Religious Orders*, ii, p. 289.

Ireland to reside and serve their church of St. Peter's, Drogheda, as late as the beginning of the thirteenth century. Between 1257 and 1260, Abraham, archbishop of Armagh, absolved them from their obligation because 'prevented by various reasons they cannot make residence'.[91] It is possible that the arrangement had become a dead letter much earlier. In 1256, for example, the canons of the Augustinian house of Haverford obtained a papal indulgence to quash the vicarage ordained in their church of St. Martin, Haverford, not in order that the church might be served by their own canons but 'by chaplains, as hitherto'.[92] One of the reasons which may have caused the abandonment of early practice among the regular canons of south Wales was the smallness of their communities. When a canon served a church he was obliged to take a fellow-canon with him as a *socius*. By the thirteenth century, perhaps only Llanthony Prima could afford to send canons to serve some of its churches without seriously affecting the liturgical functions of the monastery.

The Premonstratensian order had enjoyed the privilege of presenting canons to the vicarages of their appropriated churches since 1188. In England the canons do not appear to have made use of the privilege until late in the reign of Henry III.[93] Talley Abbey, the only member of the order in Wales, had a number of churches in the Towy valley appropriated to it but does not appear to have presented its own canons to vicarages until the fifteenth century, when it was clearly regarded as exceptional.[94]

Cases of monks preaching to the laity are also rare. Between 1113 and 1115 Wilfrid, bishop of St. David's, is alleged to have granted to the monks of Gloucester Abbey who were residing in west Wales 'licence to preach to the people and to excommunicate in the manner of priests and to direct the Flemings, from the pasture of real sheep to which they devote their time, to the pastures of life'.[95] The form and tenor of this

[91] *Irish Cartularies of Llanthony Prima and Secunda*, pp. 19–20, 29.
[92] *CPL.*, i, p. 329.
[93] H. M. Colvin, *White Canons in England*, pp. 277–8.
[94] The three recorded cases involve only one church, that of Cynwyl Gaeo: *Episc. Reg. St. David's*, i, p. 277, ii, pp. 565, 833.
[95] *Hist. et Cart. Gloucester*, i, pp. 265–6.

document, however, lead one to suspect that it belongs to a group of later forgeries, concocted by Gloucester monks to bolster their claims against the monks of Chertsey who, some time at the end of the twelfth century, had managed to secure for themselves the church of Cardigan and its dependent chapels.[96]

It seems clear that monks preached to the laity only in exceptional circumstances. One such occasion was the preaching of the crusade in 1188. The Cistercians, thanks to the initial example of St. Bernard, held an honourable place in the crusading tradition. It was but natural, therefore, that, when Archbishop Baldwin entered Wales in 1188 to preach the crusade, he should have been assisted by Welsh Cistercian abbots. Both John, abbot of Whitland, and Seissil, abbot of Strata Florida, preached sermons to the people at Lampeter. Seissil preached at least a second time in Anglesey.[97] Strata Florida produced a more famous preacher in the person of Cadwgan, who became successively abbot of Strata Florida, abbot of Whitland and, in 1215, bishop of Bangor. Cadwgan probably owed his gift to his father, an Irish cleric who preached in Welsh throughout Ceredigion and Powys. Cadwgan's eloquence, however, appears to have been reserved for the cloistered monks in the abbeys he visited in England and Wales.[98]

The Augustinian canons with their more flexible rule had, as we have seen, greater opportunities for pastoral work than the monks proper. One devout canon of Carmarthen in the middle of the thirteenth century devoted much of his time to preaching outside the priory and asked one of his colleagues to write a sermon in verse for him. The poem which gives these details is the only evidence we have of normal preaching activities undertaken by members of the monastic order in south Wales.[99]

---

[96] H. E. Malden, 'The Possession of Cardigan Priory by Chertsey Abbey; a Study in Some Mediaeval Forgeries', *TRHS.*, v (1911), pp. 141–56.
[97] Gir. Camb., *Opera*, vi, pp. 119, 126.
[98] Ibid, iv, pp. 161–7; Lloyd, *History of Wales*, ii, p. 688 note 201.
[99] M. D. Legge, *Anglo-Norman in the Cloisters*, pp. 68–9, and above pp. 152–3.

VII. THE MONKS AS ADMINISTRATORS

In an age when the monastic order was in high favour, it was natural that the monasteries should provide recruits for the episcopate.[100] Of the fifteen bishops who occupied the see of Llandaff between 1056 and 1361, five belonged to the monastic or canonical orders. Nicholas ap Gwrgant (1148–83) had been a monk of Gloucester abbey; William of Saltmarsh (1186–91) had been prior of the Augustinian priory of St. Augustine's, Bristol. Both these religious houses held extensive properties within the diocese and both were patronized by the earls of Gloucester, who were also lords of Glamorgan. The remaining three all came from religious houses within the diocese. Henry de Abergavenny (1193–1218) had been prior of the Benedictine priory of Abergavenny; William de Goldcliff (1219–29) had been prior of the Benedictine priory of Goldcliff, a dependency of the celebrated abbey of Bec which had produced Lanfranc and Anselm. John de Ware (1254–56), the only Cistercian to become bishop of Llandaff, had been abbot of Margam and had come out of retirement to become bishop.

Of the sixteen bishops who occupied the see of St. David's between 1064 and 1349, only three belonged to the monastic or canonical orders. Peter de Leia (1176–98) had been prior of the Cluniac house of Much Wenlock. Geoffrey de Henlaw (1203–14) had been prior of the Augustinian house of Llanthony. Iorwerth or Gervase (1215–29) had been abbot of the Premonstratensian house of Talley.

In addition to those who became bishops of St. David's and Llandaff, two religious houses provided bishops for other sees. The saintly Robert de Bethune, bishop of Hereford (1131–48), had been prior of Llanthony at a time when it was celebrated throughout the land for the austerity of its régime and the stark beauty of its surroundings. Cadwgan, bishop of Bangor (1215–36), had graduated to his see from the abbacies of Strata Florida and Whitland.

This monastic group of bishops was neither large nor particularly distinguished. The majority of them, however,

---

[100] For much of what follows, see J. Conway Davies, 'The Welsh Bishops, 1066 to 1272', in *Episc. Acts*, ii, pp. 537–69, especially pp. 542–5, and D. Walker, 'The Medieval Bishops of Llandaff', *Morgannwg*, vi (1962), pp. 5–32.

were hardworking and a number of them made contributions of permanent value to the sees they ruled. Peter de Leia, despite his long absences from his see, was responsible for the building of the Norman nave of his cathedral church.[101] Gervase, though regarded by Gerald of Wales as somewhat of a mediocrity, reformed the constitution of the cathedral chapter and rebuilt portions of the cathedral church.[102] Henry de Abergavenny took in hand the re-organization of the Llandaff chapter and it was during his episcopate that canonries and prebends first made their appearance in the cathedral church.[103] Cadwgan of Bangor also acquired a fame of sorts, though not as an administrator. He is the only Welsh monk to find a place in the pioneering bibliographies of Leland and Bale. Some of his literary work has survived and it shows that Cadwgan was trying to apply the legislation of the Fourth Lateran Council within his own diocese of Bangor.[104]

Equally important to the life of the church was the work of abbots and priors as part-time ecclesiastical administrators. At the beginning of the twelfth century, the bishops of the emerging dioceses of Llandaff and St. David's were faced with the formidable task of reshaping and re-organizing their dioceses more in accordance with the practice of the Latin church and with the reforming decrees of the papacy. With an increasing volume of ecclesiastical business to be transacted and with constant friction arising from the contact of new ideas with older and deeply-ingrained modes of thought and practice, some process of delegation was inevitable. For assistance in this work, the popes and the bishops could not rely on the time-honoured, native communities of *claswyr*. In south Wales, at least, the *clas* organization had been discredited and the greater part of the wealth of their communities confiscated by the invaders. The new monastic foundations in south Wales, however, possessed a fund of administrative ability which could not fail to be of assistance to the papacy and the bishops in running the new and more complex machinery of church government.

---

[101] *Dictionary of Welsh Biography*, p. 750.
[102] *Episc. Acts*, i, pp. 355–6; *Dictionary of Welsh Biography*, p. 416.
[103] *Episc. Acts*, ii, pp. 691, 699.
[104] See above pp. 153–4.

In the twelfth and, increasingly, in the thirteenth century when the records become fuller, one finds abbots and priors taking a constructive part in the administrative and legal life of the church, acting as judges-delegate, proctors and commissioners, applying the canon law to local cases and keeping the central authorities at Rome and Canterbury, and, at a lower level, at St. David's and Llandaff, informed of their findings and decisions. The monastic chapter house frequently became a court house where the legal business of the secular church was transacted.[105]

This was exacting, time-consuming and, as far as the monks were concerned, unrewarding work. Apart from its value to the bishops, it was of vital importance to the church in Wales in this formative period. Together with the bishops and those clergy who were fortunate enough to have been educated in the schools of England or northern France, the monasteries of south Wales formed an important channel by which the thought, law and practice of the Latin church found their way into an area which had been impervious to their influence for so long. This combined influence of bishop, educated cleric and cosmopolitan monk was responsible for converting what had approximated to a disorganized Uniate church into a recognizable territorial, and, for a time, national member of the Latin church.

[105] For examples, see *Episc. Acts*, i, pp. 369–70, 411–12, ii, pp. 672, 714, 718, 730, 743, 748–9, and also *CPL.*, i, pp. 85, 131.

VIII

THE MONASTERIES AND LAY SOCIETY

I. MONASTIC PATRONS

Medieval people believed profoundly in the efficacy of corporate prayer as a means of promoting both material and spiritual well-being. This was one reason why barons and knights in the eleventh and twelfth centuries had allocated lands and revenues for the foundation of religious houses and why many of their dependants followed their example, as far as their resources would allow, by becoming benefactors.

A man acquired the patronage of a religious house in a number of ways: by inheritance as heir of the founder, by right of marriage into the founder's family, by right of conquest, or by gift. Morgan ab Owain acquired the patronage of the Norman foundation of Goldcliff by force of arms during the troubled years which followed Henry I's death. The victories of the Lord Rhys in the years 1165 and 1166 acquired for him the patronage of the Cistercian abbeys of Whitland and Strata Florida and the Benedictine cells of Cardigan and Llandovery. The Mortimer family acquired the patronage of Cwm-hir Abbey in the thirteenth century by conquest and by marriage into the founder's family.[1] Less frequently the patronage of a monastery was acquired by gift. In 1322, for example, Edward II granted to Hugh Despenser, the younger, the 'advowsons' of Caerleon Abbey and Usk Priory.[2]

By whatever means he might acquire the patronage, a patron could expect to enjoy the fruits of his predecessors' investment and share fully in the spiritual and material benefits which attached to such patronage. It was tacitly understood that the monks would pray for the souls of himself and his family during their lifetime and after their death, that they would not harbour his enemies and that they would

---

[1] Lloyd, *History of Wales*, ii, pp. 477–8 and n. 63, pp. 596–8; S. W. Williams, 'The Cistercian Abbey of Cwmhir', *Trans. Cymm.*, 1894–5, pp. 67–8.
[2] *C.Ch.R.*, iii, p. 449.

entertain him with his entourage when he visited the house. A patron could also expect his wishes on matters of external policy which concerned him to be respected. Even in Cistercian houses where the patron had no formal rights in elections, there is evidence that the patron's wishes carried weight in the abbey counsels on questions such as monastic hospitality.[3] In return, the monks could hope for a certain measure of protection and goodwill, the promotion of their interests and, perhaps, further endowment.

In this way there grew up a natural bond of self-interest between the monasteries and their patrons. The bond was strongest when the patron resided or had important interests in the neighbourhood of the monastery; weakest, when the patron was a great lord with country-wide interests. Professor T. Jones Pierce has noted the dynastic and provincial loyalty which bound the abbey of Strata Florida to the house of Dinefwr. Successive generations of the founder's family were buried there and 'the interest and affection felt by them for the abbey . . . was amply reciprocated in the attitude of the brethren there as expressed in their *chronicle* which has so clear a bias in favour of the house of Dinefwr'. It is only when the interests of the princes of Aberffraw coincided with those of the abbey's patron 'that a newer and more expansive patriotism can be discerned' in the *Brut*.[4]

A close attachment of a similar kind could exist between patrons and smaller conventual priories like Ewenni, Brecon and Abergavenny. The de Londres, with but a limited field in which to nourish their family pride, devoted much attention to their small foundation at Ewenni, where many of their family were buried.[5] The de Breos lords had a similar affection for Brecon Priory. William de Breos (d. 1211) bequeathed his body to the priory church of St. John wherever he died, whether in England or Wales, 'because this is the church which I love before all others and because after God and St. Mary I have greater confidence in St. John'.[6] Even with the succession

---

[3] See Gilbert de Clare's writ to Margam Abbey cited below p. 205.
[4] T. Jones Pierce, 'Strata Florida Abbey', *Ceredigion*, i (1950), p. 23.
[5] Three elegantly carved family tombs and a fragment of another survive; see C. A. Ralegh Radford, *Ewenny Priory, Glamorgan*, pp. 5–6, 17–18.
[6] *Brec. Cart.*, pp. 84–5; for the Brecon tombs, see G. E. F. Morgan, 'The Vanished Tombs of Brecon Cathedral', *Arch. Camb.*, 1925, pp. 257–74.

of more distant patrons—the Bohun earls of Hereford—an amicable, though perhaps more one-sided, relationship could exist. In the second half of the thirteenth century a prior of Brecon got into trouble with an episcopal visitor because of his indiscriminate gifts from the goods of the priory. His defence was that

> the lord Humphrey very often complained to him of his poverty and lack of goods and wishing to relieve him, as was becoming, since he was his patron, he gave him two mares and afterwards one horse valued at five marks; likewise to Amian, his counsellor, he gave one mare . . . Likewise, he gave to the lord Gilbert, brother of the earl, one ox for starting his new manor.[7]

The tombs and effigies surviving in the priory church of Abergavenny, perhaps the finest collection in Wales, show that here, too, a close connection existed between patron and priory.[8] The monks of Abergavenny kept a set of annals and genealogical notes relating to their patrons' families.[9] One of the priory's patrons, John de Hastings, took more than a conventional interest in the foundation of his ancestors. Appalled by the viciousness of the monks' lives and their depleted numbers, he successfully petitioned the pope for the priory's reformation in 1319 and granted two carucates of land and twenty pounds sterling annually from his castle to bring the number of monks up to strength.[10]

Not all monasteries could hope for as zealous and as attentive a patron as John de Hastings. The monks of Neath and Margam, for example, could hardly expect their powerful patrons, the earls of Gloucester, to take an exclusive interest in their own abbeys. In the Margam annals one cannot help detecting the absence of a close and intimate association between abbey and patron. For the earls of Gloucester it was Tewkesbury that enshrined their family traditions; it was the abbey which most frequently witnessed their nuptials and christenings and received their bodies when they died.[11]

---

[7] *Brec. Cart.*, p. 139.

[8] Octavius Morgan, *Ancient Monuments in the Priory Church, Abergavenny;* W. Kemp, 'St. Mary's Church, Abergavenny', *Arch. Camb.*, 1936, pp. 350–7.

[9] Dugdale, iv, pp. 615–6. Similar genealogies were kept by Tintern and Llanthony Prima; see ibid., v, pp. 269–72, vi pp. 134–6.

[10] *CPL.*, ii, pp. 186, 211; *Registrum Ade de Orleton*, p. 151.

[11] 'Annales de Theokesberia' in *Annales Monastici*, i, pp. 43–180; *Complete Peerage*, v, pp. 694–715.

This absence of a strong patron near at hand was unfortunate for Neath and Margam, for both abbeys lay in a buffer zone between the Welsh and the Anglo-Norman settlements in the Vale of Glamorgan and fell an easy prey to marauders not only from the Welsh of the hill lordships but from 'the men of Brecon'. At the end of the twelfth century Margam Abbey found it necessary to create a rudimentary police force from local Welsh landowners to help to defend the abbey estates.[12] Oaths sworn on relics of the Cross, which Margam Abbey had acquired by the mid-thirteenth century, provided additional insurance against broken agreements and sacrilegious attack.[13] Before the middle of the thirteenth century, there was a real danger that the patronage of the abbey would fall to the Welsh lords of Afan by right of conquest.[14] Though an independent Welsh lordship embracing the abbey of Margam never emerged, it seems probable that by the second half of the century the local power and proximity of the Afan lords gave them many of the privileges and influence which attached to *de iure* patronage.

Though the extent of a patron's interests and commitments were important factors in determining his relationship to his foundation, much depended on personal predilection. This could vary from generation to generation even in one family; much more so when lordships changed hands. Tintern, for example, owes much of its present fame to the interest taken by its patron, Roger Bigod, earl of Norfolk (1270–1306), in the rebuilding of the abbey church on a more lavish scale. The decision to rebuild had been taken before he succeeded to the earldom and work had begun in 1269.[15] It was his generous benefactions, however, which made possible the continuance and completion of the work during a period fraught with difficulties for many religious houses.[16] His arms were emblazoned in the rose window above the high altar

---

[12] Clark, *Cartae*, vi, pp. 2271, 2277.
[13] Ibid., iii, pp. 916–7.
[14] See especially the charter by which Morgan Gam (d. 1241) confirms to Margam the grants of his overlord, Gilbert de Clare: ibid., iii, p. 927.
[15] 'Chronicle of the Thirteenth Century', *Arch. Camb.*, 1862, p. 282.
[16] *C.Ch.R.*, iii, p. 31, 99–100, 105–6. The new church was completed in 1301; see William Worcestre, *Itineraries*, p. 61.

and it is with some justice that the fifteenth-century anti-quarian, William of Worcester, names him as the builder of the church of Tintern.[17]

The English kings had taken but a small part in the direct work of founding religious houses in south Wales. For the greater part of the twelfth century they were distant suzerains and their contacts with Welsh monasteries were limited. Their preoccupation with Welsh affairs during the thirteenth century brought them into closer touch with the monasteries. They acquired direct patronage over a number of religious houses by right of conquest or escheat and began to exercise a more effective control over monasteries within the privileged marcher lordships.[18]

II. ELECTION AND CUSTODY

In theory the religious houses of south Wales enjoyed in the twelfth and thirteenth centuries a considerable freedom from the formal rights which patrons exercised during vacancies. It is unnecessary to attribute such freedom to a favourable environment fostered by native Welsh law. The largest of the south Wales houses belonged to the Cistercian order and it was understood that their patrons could not claim custody during vacancies nor licence and assent in elections to the abbacy.[19] All the Benedictine priories were dependent on houses in England or France and elections to the priorate were conducted at their mother abbeys. The question of licence to elect did not therefore arise. Rights during vacancies in non-Cistercian houses, however, were not taken for granted and were frequently committed to writing.

Robert fitz Martin, the founder of the Tironian abbey of St. Dogmaels, for example, decreed that 'in the said abbey nothing can be instituted by any secular power contrary to canonical authority, neither by the king himself nor by any prince of his soever, nor by any of their successors'.[20] In the early years of the abbey's history the appointment of the abbot appears to have rested with the abbot and the convent of

---

[17] Ibid.
[18] See below, pp. 216–28.
[19] S. Wood, *English Monasteries and their Patrons*, pp. 3–4, 84.
[20] Dugdale, iv, p. 130. Cf. E. M. Pritchard, *St. Dogmaels Abbey*, p. 46.

Tiron.[21] Such a practice, however, fell into abeyance long before the end of the thirteenth century. In 1329, when the lordship of Cemais was in the hands of the crown because of the minority of James, son of Nicholas Audeley, the abbot, John le Rede, died and an inquisition was ordered into the rights which the patrons exercised during a vacancy. It was established that the 'founders of the abbey were wont from the time of its first foundation to take no issues of its temporalities . . . they were wont to place a keeper there over the temporalities . . . so that he might see that the issues . . . were not impaired, but were expended for the uses of the abbey, and that the keeper should leave without taking any issues for the use of the founders when the abbot was elected and confirmed and his fealty had been taken'.[22] From later evidence it would seem that the convent also had the right of free election 'without asking or obtaining the licence and authority of the superior or founder of the same monastery'.[23]

The Benedictine houses of south Wales were all dependencies and as such the priors in charge of them were 'momentary' or 'dative', that is, their priors were chosen not by their convents (where they existed) for life, but by the abbot and convent of the mother house. Such a prior was also removable by the abbot of the mother house at the latter's own discretion, without needing the consent of the bishop or patron.[24] The rights enjoyed by patrons when vacancies arose in these houses varied considerably. Since the evidence is fragmentary and incomplete, it would be unwise to make any broad generalization for all the south Wales houses. According to a statement of rights drawn up by the priory of Brecon in 1529, the monks themselves had the custody and free administration of all the goods of the priory during a vacancy.[25] Though an attempt was made in the fourteenth century to break away from the mother abbey of Battle,[26] the latter house maintained its right

[21] Ibid., pp. 43–4.
[22] CCR., 1327–1330, p. 455; Cal. Inq. Misc., ii, p. 273.
[23] Episc. Reg. St. David's, ii, p. 495.
[24] S. Wood, English Monasteries and their Patrons, p. 53.
[25] Brec. Cart., p. 129.
[26] M. A. Lower, Chronicle of Battel Abbey, p. 204.

to appoint and remove priors of Brecon up to the time of the Dissolution.[27]

In 1250 the custody of Abergavenny Priory, a dependency of St. Vincent, Le Mans, was acquired by the bishop of Llandaff, who committed the 'cure' of that house to Adam of Llandeilo Porth Halog, dean of Upper Gwent. The latter does not appear to have taken any of the issues of the priory during the vacancy.[28]

Sometime in the reign of Henry III, Edmund, earl of Lancaster, made an enquiry into his rights in the small cell of Llangua, a dependency of Lire. He found that the prior or *custos manerii* was removable by the abbot of Lire and that he himself could not reasonably exact anything under the pretext of such removal. This had not always been the custom under Edmund's predecessors.[29]

The evidence available for practice at Goldcliff Priory, the richest of the Benedictine houses in south Wales, is confusing and contradictory. This is probably due to the fact that questions relating to the patronage of the priory became at the end of the thirteenth century one of the many points at issue between its patron, Gilbert de Clare, and the crown. The heat generated by this conflict was probably responsible for exaggerated claims being made by both sides, particularly by the crown.[30]

Founded by Robert de Chandos, the patronage of the priory passed at the end of the twelfth century to the Welsh lords of Caerleon, thence to William Marshall, and then to the house of Clare.[31] By this time, if not earlier, the priors elected to Goldcliff at Bec Abbey had to be presented to the Clares and it is probable that the Clare family also had the guardianship of the temporalities during a vacancy.[32] During the course of a long-drawn-out suit between the prior and Gilbert de Clare

[27] See the deed of obedience sworn by the priors at their election in the early-fifteenth century in *Brec. Cart.*, pp. 141–2.

[28] P.R.O., *Ancient Deeds, Court of Augment.*, B.8493, paraphrased in *Episc. Acts*, ii, p. 730.

[29] Dugdale, iv, pp. 1015–6.

[30] Glanmor Williams, *Welsh Church*, pp. 46–8; W. Greenway, 'The Election of John of Monmouth, Bishop of Llandaff', *Morgannwg*, v (1961), pp. 3–22.

[31] M. M. Morgan, 'The Abbey of Bec-Hellouin and its English Priories', *Jnl. Brit. Arch. Assoc.*, v (1940), p. 34.

[32] Ibid., p. 51.

which began in 1291, the latter produced letters of the abbot of Bec presenting priors of Goldcliff to him and 'added that the present prior had been removed once and later, at Gloucester's intercession, sent back to Goldcliff *tanquam prior amobilis*'.[33] All this is contradicted by a statement written down in the Register of Tewkesbury Abbey in the fifteenth century:

> from Henry I's time to Henry VI, that is for three hundred and eighteen years, no prior was admitted to the priory of Goldcliff, except previously he had presented himself to the king and had been licensed by the king and admitted, inducted and instituted by the bishop of Llandaff and his archdeacon.[34]

This statement was written long after the break-up of the Clare estates (1317) and reflects partial royal opinion. While the statement is no doubt true for the fourteenth and fifteenth centuries, it cannot be taken as valid evidence for practice in the twelfth and thirteenth centuries.

By the beginning of the thirteenth century, it was already an 'ancient custom' at the Augustinian priory of Llanthony Prima for the canons to elect their prior during a vacancy without their patron's consent and to present him to the bishop for confirmation of the election. Walter de Lacy, patron of the priory, confirmed this custom sometime between 1186 and 1205, adding that neither he nor his successors would attempt to molest or trouble the canons in their possessions during such a vacancy.[35] The custom was put to the test during a vacancy in 1322 when the patronage was in the hands of the king. It was found on inquisition that the canons had always elected their priors without asking licence from the founders. They presented elected priors to the diocesan alone and the canons themselves had custody of the temporalities. The priory had enjoyed this liberty from its foundation 'by virtue of a deed of Walter de Lacy, founder thereof'.[36]

Conditions were far different at Carmarthen Priory, a house under royal patronage and situated close to a centre of royal power. Here, after 1241, election practice is illustrated fairly fully by the chancery enrolments. On the death or resignation of a prior, the temporalities of the priory were taken into the

[33] Ibid., p. 53.
[34] *Episc. Acts*, ii, pp. 618–9.
[35] Dugdale, vi, p. 138, no. vi.
[36] *CCR., 1318–1323*, p. 590.

hands of one of the king's representatives, usually the bailiff of Carmarthen or the justice of west Wales. The sub-prior and canons then sent one or two of their number to the king, with a letter asking for licence to elect. Such a letter has survived for the year 1277, when the lordships of Cardigan and Carmarthen were held by Edmund, earl of Lancaster. The sub-prior and canons stated that their house had been without a prior through the resignation of brother Th[omas] and that they were therefore sending brother Richard, son of Cogan, and Richard of Hereford to ask for a free licence to elect a suitable man in his stead.[37] Personal attendance on the king was insisted upon even if it meant a journey overseas.[38] Only occasionally was the obligation waived, as in 1265 when Richard, bishop of St. David's, pleaded that assent to the election be given by the king's bailiff of Carmarthen on his behalf. 'It is unsafe for them to make the journey *propter hostilitatem*', he wrote, 'and owing to the destruction of their house they cannot well afford the expense of the journey.'[39] Henry III consented and granted licence to elect in the following year, but ordered his bailiff that before restoring the temporalities he should first receive from the prior and convent letters patent that 'this grace will not be drawn into a precedent in other voidances to the king's prejudice'.[40] When the royal order to restore the temporalities had been made, it was customary for a further writ to be despatched to the bishop to institute the newly-elected prior.

What the king gained from vacancies at Carmarthen it is difficult to say. Edward II promised that 'because we take no revenues from the aforesaid priory during a vacancy of the same, neither will we present to the churches pertaining to the said priory during a vacancy of the same'.[41] Probably only a fee was demanded for licence to elect and for the issue of writs to the custodian and the bishop of St. David's.[42]

[37] P.R.O., Ancient Deeds, DL 25/L 974.
[38] All abbots and priors of non-exempt houses worth over 50 marks per annum were required, when necessary, to journey to the king abroad; see S. Wood, *English Monasteries and their Patrons*, p. 70.
[39] *Calendar of Ancient Correspondence Concerning Wales*, ed. J. G. Edwards, p. 15.
[40] *CPR., 1258–66*, pp. 561, 563.
[41] *Carm. Cart.*, p. 15; *CPR., 1327–1330*, p. 321.
[42] Later in the century, however, Richard II was presenting to the priory churches during vacancies: see *CPR., 1381–1385*, p. 206; *CPR., 1388–1392*, pp. 21, 119.

Although the evidence is meagre, a similar procedure seems to have operated at Haverford. In 1331 when Haverford was in the hands of the king, the canons obtained royal licence to elect on the death of their prior, Richard de Honyburgh. The new prior, John de Honyburgh, was admitted by Henry, bishop of St. David's, on 11 December of the same year and the temporalities were ordered to be restored on 20 January of the following year.[43]

III. MONASTIC HOSPITALITY AND ALMSGIVING

The Rule of St. Benedict enjoined that guests should be received 'as Christ himself', and throughout the middle ages the reception of guests remained an acknowledged obligation and a regular, if unpredictable, item of monastic expenditure. Unlike the present-day monastery, whose guests are either relatives of monks or priests and laymen on retreat or curious tourists, the medieval monastery was called upon to cater for a more assorted cross-section of society: members of the royal family and nobles; the clergy, secular and monastic, on visitation or other ecclesiastical business; merchants, officials and a host of less respectable persons whose credentials it was difficult to challenge. Apart from the inconvenience and expense, there was always, too, the need for diplomacy 'for friends are multiplied by agreeable words'.[44] The guest-house might harbour a potential benefactor or an enemy.

In Wales these difficulties were aggravated by special circumstances. In a sparsely populated country, where urban settlements were small and few, the monasteries were called upon to bear a burden of hospitality which was perhaps incommensurate with their material resources. Even those houses which one would consider today to be remote from the main lines of communication—a house like Cwm-hir—were in medieval times frequently situated near important trackways in constant use.

There were, too, the racial differences in temperament and manners, more apparent in medieval times, which distinguished

---

[43] *CPR., 1330–1334*, p. 168; *Calendar of Ancient Correspondence Concerning Wales*, ed. J. G. Edwards, pp. 191–2; *CPR., 1330–1334*, p. 231.
[44] *Barnwell Observances*, cited by J. R. H. Moorman, *Church Life in England in the Thirteenth Century*, p. 353.

the Welsh from the Anglo-Norman monks and canons who were
obliged to entertain them. The Welsh frequently descended on
an Anglo-Norman house along the border or in south Wales
with all the high-spiritedness of American cattlemen reaching
a small town. They were received with mixed and often
justifiable feelings of fear and patronizing condescension.
Uproar and violence in the monastic guesthouse were not
infrequent in the twelfth century. In 1135 a Welshman of
some standing sought refuge from his enemies at Llanthony
Prima and brought his whole household with him. They
commandeered the monastic refectory and the shocked
chronicler records that their womenfolk 'were not ashamed to
sing, and prophane the place with their light and effeminate
behaviour'.[45] At the end of the century Gerald of Wales refers
to an affray in the guest-house at Margam in which one of the
guests lost his life.[46] In the last quarter of the thirteenth
century a prior of Brecon, accused of drunkenness by an
official visitor, replied that it was customary, particularly
when entertaining Welsh guests, to make a pretence of getting
drunk.[47] However lame the excuse, it provides an illuminating
insight into the attitude of the Anglo-Norman monks towards
their Welsh guests.

By the beginning of the fourteenth century, the entertainment of Welsh guests was straining the nerves and the purse-
strings of the priors of a number of the border houses of south-
east Wales.[48] In sanctioning an appropriation to the
impoverished priory of Clifford in 1331, the bishop referred
to the priory as 'situated in the lower parts of Wales where
daily a multitude of Welshmen come together to whom
hospitality cannot be denied without grave risk'.[49]

A particularly heavy burden of hospitality was borne by
those houses which lay along the main south Wales coastal
road. It was the road taken by armies *en route* to Ireland and
the road most frequently used by Irish travellers who had
business in England or on the Continent. Margam Abbey
especially paid heavily for the important information which its

[45] G. Roberts, *Some Account of Llanthony Priory*, p. 57.
[46] Gir. Camb., *Opera*, vi, p. 68.
[47] *Brec. Cart.*, p. 134.
[48] A. T. Bannister, *History of Ewias Harold*, pp. 64–5.
[49] *Registrum Thome de Charlton*, p. 9.

chronicler was able to pick up from noblemen staying in the monastic guest-house.[50] King John and his army were entertained by the abbey on two occasions in 1210: on his way to Ireland at the end of May and on his return three months later. In compensation the abbey was exempted from the general extortion to which John was subjecting the abbeys of the Cistercian Order.[51] So onerous did this dispensing of hospitality become that sometime between 1218 and 1230 the abbey's patron, Gilbert de Clare, issued a firm directive to the abbot. The abbot was not to permit 'those coming to an assembly or the army to be entertained and fed contrary to the ancient customs and assises which your house had in the time of our predecessors. The ancient custom which existed in their time with regard to neighbouring Welshmen whose frequent arrival burdens the house to excess, was to be maintained.'[52] In 1220 Whitland appears to have complained to the General Chapter of the demands which were being made on its hospitality by Irish and English abbots of the order. The Chapter decreed that the Irish and English abbots who stayed at the abbey for longer than fifteen days were to make their own provision for fodder and be content with what was given them.[53]

In the thirteenth century it was customary for Cistercian abbeys in financial difficulties to apply to the General Chapter for a licence to dispense them from their obligations of hospitality. In 1258, for example, the monks of Strata Florida were forced to disperse. On condition that the abbot was able to maintain his convent in his own house, he was to be dispensed from the reception of guests for three years. Margam Abbey was similarly dispensed for five years in 1268.[54]

Guests were occasionally entertained at 'hospices' at a distance from the monastery. Between 1155 and 1159, Walter the Constable granted Brecon Priory 'a guest-house at Ilay with his man staying in the same'.[55] The monks of Strata Florida appear to have entertained the lords of Cydewain at

---

[50] F. M. Powicke, *Ways of Medieval Life and Thought*, pp. 27–37.
[51] 'Annales de Margan' in *Annales Monastici*, i, pp. 29–30.
[52] Clark, *Cartae*, ii, pp. 360–61.
[53] Canivez, *Statuta*, i, p. 521.
[54] Ibid., ii, p. 444, iii, p. 61.
[55] *Brec. Cart.*, pp. 80–81.

their grange of *Aberunhull* (Aber-miwl?).[56] They may also
have kept hostels for travellers and pilgrims at Ysbyty Ystwyth
and Ysbyty Ystradmeurig.[57] Tavernspite was certainly situated
on monastic land belonging to Whitland Abbey and served as
a hospice for travellers.[58] Hospices of this kind were the
forerunners of many a sixteenth-century inn.

It is extremely difficult to establish whether the numerous
ysbytai scattered throughout Wales were hostels or small
hospitals. It is equally difficult to establish their affiliation,
though their presence on monastic or episcopal land sometimes
gives a clue to their origin.[59] A number of them clearly belonged
to the Knights Hospitallers. Of the twenty-five Welsh
'hospitals' which appear in the list compiled by Professor
Knowles and Mr. R. N. Hadcock, many are doubtful and
only two can be said with certainty to have been affiliated to
a monastic house: the hospitals of Holy Trinity and St. Mary's,
Monmouth, both of which were dependent on Monmouth
Priory.[60] Despite this, it seems clear from the twelfth and
thirteenth-century evidence that Welsh monasteries opened
the doors of their infirmaries to laymen in need of medical
attention. Most monasteries contained at least one monk
with medical knowledge to act as infirmarer and during the
twelfth century a few monks and canons acquired more than a
local reputation as consultant physicians.[61] Geoffrey de Henlaw,
prior of Llanthony (1178–1203) and later bishop of St. David's
(1203–1214), probably acquired his fame as a physcian before
he became an Augustinian. He is first found at Bristol in the
service of one Robert Hardynge. His services were obtained
by Roger of Norwich, the sixth prior of Llanthony, who
'enriched him with very large gifts, and keeping him near his
person till the day of his death . . . treated him with singular
affection, and upon his deathbed nominated him his successor'.

[56] For the claims made by Edmund Mortimer for similar treatment, see
CPR., 1281–92, p. 459.
[57] Knowles and Hadcock, *Medieval Religious Houses, England and Wales*, (2nd.
ed. 1971), p. 132; S. Lewis, *Topographical Dictionary of Wales*, ii, p. 444.
[58] W. Thomas, *Antiquities of Whitland*, pp. 52–3; *AMC. Pembs.*, p. 152.
[59] *Clafdy* (house of the sick) is found as an element in Welsh place-names and
occasionally has monastic associations, e.g. Cwrt y Clafdy Farm situated on
monastic land about a mile from Neath Abbey: see Birch, *Neath Abbey*, p. 121.
[60] *Medieval Religious Houses*, pp. 312–38; Dugdale, iv, pp. 597–8.
[61] Knowles, *Monastic Order*, pp. 516–18.

Geoffrey subsequently became physician to Hubert Walter, archibishop of Canterbury, and it is to this circumstance that Gerald of Wales attributed his success in obtaining the bishopric of St. David's in 1203.[62]

The *Brut y Tywysogyon* shows that many of the Welsh princes when aged and infirm, or when they had been severely wounded in battle, spent their last days in the monastic infirmary.[63] Nor were such facilities restricted to those of noble birth. The monks of Margam undertook to receive Geoffrey Sturmi into their fraternity when he became infirm and a later document shows that he had been clothed with the habit of lay-brother.[64] A blinded hostage, Canaythen, son of Robert ab Einion, gave his land in Resolven to Margam Abbey, became a lay-brother and 'lived most securely all the days of his life'.[65] Such arrangements, however, approximated more to a corrody than gratuitous relief.

It has already been shown that all the conventual houses had almonries, presided over in Benedictine and Augustinian houses by an almoner to whom specific revenues were assigned for the relief of the poor.[66] Even for the better documented English houses it is difficult to estimate what proportion of monastic income was devoted to such relief and how effectively and consistently it was applied from century to century.[67] For the south Wales houses the evidence is meagre indeed. For the period before the Black Death all that remains are two general tributes to the relief work done by the monks and canons, the records of a number of benefactions made specifically for the maintenance and relief of the poor, and some brief but significant regulations relating to the almonry in Pecham's injunctions to a number of south Wales houses. Gerald of Wales, who was familiar with most of the religious houses of south Wales, refers more than once to the lavishness of

[62] G. Roberts, *Some Account of Llanthony Priory*, p. 28; *Autobiography of Giraldus Cambrensis*, pp. 147–8.
[63] *Brut y Tywysogyon, Peniarth 20 Version*, ed. T. Jones, pp. 73, 79, 99; S. W. Williams, *Strata Florida Abbey*, appendix pp. i–ii. Cf. also the letter of Gruffydd ap Gwenwynwyn to Henry III in *Calendar of Ancient Correspondence Concerning Wales*, pp. 19–20: Gruffydd was 'very ill in a certain abbey'.
[64] Birch, *Margam Abbey*, pp. 51, 77.
[65] Clark, *Cartae*, ii, pp. 347–8.
[66] See above pp. 61–2.
[67] For the later middle ages, see Glanmor Williams, *Welsh Church*, pp. 380–82.

Cistercian hospitality and their acts of charity and beneficence towards the poor and strangers.[68] Although he was inclined to believe that the agrarian policy of the Cistercians created many of the poor they fed, he ungrudgingly singles out for special mention the abbey of Margam during the abbacy of Conan. 'It was at this time', he writes, 'more celebrated for its charitable deeds than any other of that order in Wales.'[69] In 1242, Albert of Cologne, archbishop of Armagh, paid a tribute to the reputation enjoyed by Llanthony Prima. 'Situated in the midst of two warring nations . . .', he wrote, 'you extend the hands of charity to both, being liberal to guests, merciful to the poor and compassionate towards the weak and infirm.' The priory had, moreover, been a refuge and retreat for the archbishops of Armagh in difficult times.[70]

In the second half of the thirteenth century there are indications of a slackening of effort and even a lowering of standards with regard to almsgiving in a number of houses in south Wales. As with most social services, the efficient discharge of obligations tended to create a growing clientele for which many monasteries had insufficient funds to cater. A visitor at Brecon Priory seems to have shown concern that the cellarer held the offices of chamberlain and almoner in his own person *contra statutum episcopi*.[71] There was a danger here that revenues specifically assigned for poor relief would be diverted to other purposes. Pecham was fully aware of this when he visited the south Wales houses. In his regulations for the setting up of central treasuries of receipt at Haverfordwest, Ewenni and Goldcliff, he was careful to except 'those moneys, if there are any, which have been set aside from ancient times for the almonry', which 'should freely remain in the office of him who supervises the keeping of the almonry'.[72] More significant are his injunctions regarding the remains from meals. These had been traditionally assigned by monastic legislators to the almoner for distribution to the poor. The custom, however, was being ignored, and such food and drink was frequently being diverted to relatives and friends of the monks and even to

[68] Gir. Camb., *Opera*, iv, p. 142; vi, p. 43.
[69] Ibid., p. 67.
[70] *Irish Cartularies of Llanthony Prima and Secunda*, ed. E. St. John Brooks, p. 25.
[71] *Brec. Cart.*, p. 138.
[72] *Registrum Epistolarum*, iii, pp. 783, 798.

dogs.[73] In his injunctions for Haverfordwest, Ewenni, Goldcliff and Llanthony Prima, Pecham ordered that the remains of meals in food and drink should be carefully collected for distribution to the poor. No monk or canon was to divert the food remaining from meals to other uses. In his injunctions to Ewenni, Pecham decreed that there be distributed every day, in addition to the remains of the meals, 'a measure of grain which is commonly called a bushel and this measure is to be doubled on Sunday so that every week a greater measure of grain commonly called a *summa* be distributed with the remains of the tables to the poor and needy'. At Llanthony he found it necessary to emphasize that a canon, 'pious and merciful to the poor', should be appointed to the office of almoner.[74] These references to the almonry, scanty though they be, are symptomatic of a general slackening in monastic discipline which is apparent in a number of houses at this period.

IV. THE WELSH WARS

No account of the relations between the monasteries of south Wales and society can afford to ignore the special conditions and circumstances which obtained in Wales during the period under review. From the time of the Conqueror, Norman and Anglo-Norman lords had, with the assent or connivance of the crown, carved out for themselves patrimonies from lands won from the Welsh. Within the marcher lordships thus created, the new lords assumed all the 'high privileges and immunities, which historically were a survival of the royal powers formerly enjoyed under Welsh law by the Welsh princes who had ruled in these districts before the Normans came'.[75] Among these privileges was the right to wage private war. The English kings had normally very little effective power within the marcher lordships; 'their writ did not run'. Marcher lords, however, owed fealty and homage to the English crown and their lands were subject to royal wardship during minorities and to escheat on failure of heirs.

[73] Moorman, *Church Life in England in the Thirteenth Century*, p. 357.
[74] *Registrum Epistolarum*, ii, pp. 783, 799, 804.
[75] J. G. Edwards in *Littere Wallie*, p. xlvii. See also the same author's 'The Normans and the Welsh March', *Proc. Brit. Acad.*, xlii (1957), pp. 155–77.

In *pura Wallia,* those Welsh princes who had not been drawn into the ambit of the new marcher lordships enjoyed an even greater measure of regal independence. Theoretically they too owed fealty and homage to the English kings, but their lands were not liable to royal custody during a minority or to escheat through failure of heirs. Their lands were subject neither to the law of England nor to the law and custom of the march, but to that body of native Welsh law which tradition associated with the name of Hywel Dda. It was a vigorous, organically developing body of laws which, in response to new needs, was receiving revisions and additions as late as the thirteenth century.

Most of the monasteries of south Wales were situated within marcher lordships. The pattern of territorial power as between Welsh and Anglo-Norman, however, was constantly changing as the tide of invasion advanced or receded, and it would serve no useful purpose to draw a careful line of demarcation. Strata Florida, Whitland and Cwm-hir, for example, were certainly in *pura Wallia* in the last quarter of the twelfth century. By 1250, both Whitland and Cwm-hir had acquired Anglo-Norman patrons.

The monks of the conventual houses, wherever they were situated, were primarily concerned with the maintenance of an ordered life of prayer made possible by the exploitation of the lands with which they had been endowed; but they were drawn inevitably into the political and military conflict which was being waged between the Welsh and the Anglo-Normans. The superior of every house in Wales by 1200 owed ultimate allegiance to the English king. They also owed fealty and homage to their patrons who were the immediate guarantors of their lands and liberties.[76] A further complicating factor was added when the patronage of a religious house whose inmates were not only Welsh but related to powerful Welsh princes was acquired by an Anglo-Norman lord by right of conquest.

During the twelfth and thirteenth centuries, Whitland, Strata Florida and Cwm-hir were faced with this dilemma of conflicting loyalties in its worst form. They had to choose

---

[76] Rhys ap Maredudd claimed as patron of Talley that he had always received the homage of the abbot of Talley. In the following century Rees ap David, abbot of Talley, did homage to the Black Prince at Cardigan for his Cardiganshire lands and at Carmarthen for his Carmarthenshire lands, see E. Owen, *Arch. Camb.,* 1893, p. 236.

between their allegiance to an often distant English king, the fealty and homage they owed to their patron, and the natural loyalty they owed their kinsmen whose language they spoke and whose cultural heritage they shared. At this period it is perhaps incongruous to speak of a national consciousness or of national aspirations, but one can sympathize with the superiors of houses who were prepared, at grave personal risk both to themselves and their convents, to align themselves with the interests of their own people against an alien invader fortified by all the powers which a centralized church and state could muster against them.

The extent and nature of the ecclesiastical pressure brought to bear on houses with Welsh sympathies will probably never be known. There are, however, one or two pieces of evidence which seem to suggest that the English crown was using its influence in the Cistercian General Chapter to discredit the abbots of some of the Welsh houses who were supporting Llywelyn ab Iorwerth. In 1217 the abbot of Strata Florida was deposed by the General Chapter because he 'had written to a cardinal, without the knowledge of other abbots but in their name'. The priors who were party to the act were to be removed from office and sent to other houses. The father abbot (i.e., Whitland), who was ordered by the legate [Guala] to punish the abbot of Strata Florida 'according to the form of the order' but did not do so, was similarly deposed.[77] The Welsh chroniclers are silent about the whole incident, but the chronicle of the Scottish house of Melrose provides some additional details. The chronicler records that two abbots and five priors from Wales were deprived of office and removed from their houses in the General Chapter of that year 'on account of their excesses against the aforesaid cardinal'. The abbots involved, wrote the chronicler, were from Whitland and Strata Florida.[78] It is obvious that something more than a breach of monastic discipline was involved here. Bearing in mind that the legate Guala had laid an interdict on Wales towards the end of 1216 because the Welsh had supported the invasion of Louis,[79] it is possible that the abbot of Strata Florida had written to one in

---

[77] Canivez, *Statuta*, i, p. 484.
[78] *Chronicle of Melrose*, p. 68.
[79] Lloyd, *History of Wales*, ii, p. 651.

authority to protest against the unfair use by the English crown of ecclesiastical sanctions against his nation and to defend the conduct of the Welsh. It would not have been the last time that Welsh Cistercian abbots were to write in defence of their country and native princes. In 1274 the abbots of Whitland, Strata Florida, Cwm-hir, Strata Marcella, Aberconwy, Cymer and Valle Crucis wrote to the pope defending the reputation and integrity of Llywelyn ap Gruffydd against the charges laid against him by Anian, bishop of St. Asaph.[80]

Abbeys such as Strata Florida, Cwm-hir and Whitland paid heavily for their loyalty to their Welsh patrons and to the wider cause of Welsh independence. In 1212 King John ordered his henchman, Falkes de Breauté, to destroy the abbey of Strata Florida 'which harbours our enemies'.[81] The abbot appears to have prevented the destruction of his house by the payment of a massive fine of 700 marks.[82] In 1228 the monks of Cwm-hir had their grange of Gwern y Gof burnt to the ground because of the assistance they gave to the Welsh.[83] In 1231 a monk or lay-brother of the same abbey succeeded by a trick in leading the English army into an ambush. In revenge Henry III burned one of the abbey granges and levied a fine of 300 marks on the abbot.[84] In 1257 Stephen Bauzan, Nicholas, lord of Cemais, Patrick de Chaworth, lord of Kidwelly and the lord of Carew, accompanied by a band of armed knights, battered in the door of Whitland Abbey, belaboured the monks, stripped the lay-brethren, took the abbey servants into the monastic cemetery and slew them. When they left, the raiders took with them all the horses and all the abbey valuables except those in the church.[85]

Similar attacks were being made by the Welsh on Anglo-Norman houses. In 1223 Gruffydd ap Llywelyn burned the priory church of Kidwelly to the ground.[86] Grace Dieu was

---

[80] Haddan and Stubbs, *Councils*, i, pp. 498–9. Cf. J. F. O'Sullivan, *Cistercian Settlements*, pp. 67–8, and Lloyd, ii, pp. 745–6.

[81] Williams, *Strata Florida*, appendix p. xx.

[82] The fine was not paid off until 1253: see *CCR., 1251–1253*, p. 398. There is some evidence that the fine had an earlier origin and was even more crippling: see *Pipe Roll, 13 John*, p. 235.

[83] Lloyd, *History of Wales*, ii, p. 668.

[84] Ibid., p. 676.

[85] *Annales Cambriae*, p. 92.

[86] Lloyd, *History of Carmarthenshire*, i, p. 334.

burned by the Welsh in 1233.[87] Carmarthen Priory, which lay outside the walled town, was destroyed sometime between 1257 and 1265.[88] Even Margam, situated in a lordship firmly held by the Clare lords, suffered heavy damage to its lands, crops and stock from raids by local Welshmen. The damage caused by Morgan ab Owain was assessed in 1246 at £153, and that by the sons of Alaythur in the same year at £324.[89]

The Edwardian conquest, though it gave Wales a measure of stability which it had not enjoyed for many a year, did not put an end to private war between marcher lords or to the inherent restlessness of a conquered people. Within three years of the statute of Rhuddlan, Rhys ap Maredudd, a former loyalist, had revolted and the subsequent war caused devastation throughout Cantref Gwarthaf. 'You are aware', wrote the master of Slebech to the prior of Barnstaple in 1288, 'that there has been war in Wales for a year and the whole countryside of St. Clears has been destroyed.' The prior of St. Clears had absconded, leaving a debt to the bishop of St. David's unpaid.[90] The private war between Bohun and Clare was followed in 1294 by 'Madoc's War'. This triggered off separate revolts in south Wales which added to the difficulties of the religious in the area. Strata Florida, which had barely recovered from the disastrous fire caused by lightning in 1286,[91] was put to the flames again in 1295, this time by a royalist force but apparently against the king's wishes.[92] The houses of south-east Wales suffered further damage during the rising of Llywelyn Bren in 1316 and during the Despenser wars of the 1320s. Rebellion broke out in Glamorgan soon after the death of Gilbert de Clare in 1314.[93] The monks of Neath were 'plundered of their goods by reason of rebellion of certain Welshmen . . . and their house devastated and ruined'.[94] Llywelyn Bren put pressure on the abbot of Caerleon to grant him various lands

[87] *Annales Monastici*, ii, p. 312.
[88] *Calendar of Ancient Correspondence Concerning Wales*, p. 15.
[89] Clark, *Cartae*, ii, pp. 532–4.
[90] Bibliothèque Nationale MS. L. 875, cited by R. Graham, 'The Cluniac Priory of Saint-Martin des Champs, Paris, and its Dependent Priories in England and Wales', *Jnl. Brit. Arch. Assoc.*, xi (1948), p. 48.
[91] Clark, *Cartae*, iii, p. 858.
[92] *CPR., 1292–1301*, p. 499.
[93] A. Leslie Evans, *Margam Abbey*, p. 77.
[94] *CPR., 1316–17*, p. 263.

on lease for life and for terms of years. After the rebellion had been put down, these lands were taken into the hands of the crown, together with lands and chattels belonging to abbey tenants who had joined the rebels.[95] The Despenser wars ranged over a wider area, and houses as far apart as Brecon and Margam were affected.[96]

It had been customary for compensation to be paid to the church for war damage at least from the beginning of the thirteenth century. King John appointed two Glamorgan knights in 1213 'to make inquisition in the bishopric of Llandaff, on the damages done to the church and clergy in the time of the discord between the king and the clergy of England'.[97] Henry III made a few gifts to south Wales houses which were certainly intended as compensation for war damage.[98] For the last war of Edward I against Llywelyn, figures are available for the compensation paid to the church in Wales.[99] Of the total of about £1,700 paid, £897 16s. 8d. was paid to fourteen religious houses. Twelve of these houses were in the two northern dioceses and the amount of compensation paid to them confirms the impression obtained from other sources that in the last war against Llywelyn the north Wales houses suffered more heavily than those of south Wales. Even so, there are some curious omissions. In the south only two religious houses received compensation. Strata Florida received £78 and the abbey of Llanllŷr 40 marks—small sums when compared with the £160 paid to Valle Crucis and the £100 apiece to the abbeys of Aberconwy and Basingwerk and the Dominicans of Rhuddlan. Conspicuously absent from the list of those compensated are the abbeys of Whitland and Talley. Both are known to have suffered heavy damage during the war. Talley was taken into the king's hands as early as 1278 'by reason of its impoverishment through the Welsh war and by divers inconveniences it has sustained because of that war'.[100] As for Whitland, it is known that a royal inquest during the

[95] P.R.O., SC. 8/119/5948. Bradney, *History of Monmouthshire*, vol. iii, part ii, p. 225, gives an English paraphrase.
[96] *Rot. Parl.*, i, p. 408; *Cal. Chancery Warrants*, i, p. 517.
[97] *Episc. Acts*, ii, p. 688.
[98] See below pp. 217–8.
[99] For what follows, see Glanmor Williams, *Welsh Church*, pp. 43–4, and *Littere Wallie*, ed. J. G. Edwards, *passim*.
[100] *CPR., 1272–81*, p. 251.

reign of Edward I had confirmed as correct a claim of £260 made by the abbey for war damage. The abbot was still suing for payment during the reign of Edward II.[101] It is possible that both abbeys had forfeited the right of compensation by their overt assistance to the Welsh.[102]

In the absence of detailed evidence for the whole period, the cumulative effect of the wars on the monasteries can only be assessed in general terms. There can be little doubt that recurrent war and local unrest had an adverse effect on monastic discipline. Apart from the distractions caused by the passage of armies and the reception of refugees, a frontier area between two warring nations is scarcely conducive to a high standard of monastic observance. In Wales, as in Ireland, the conflict was not merely a political one, but one between two cultures, two ways of life. The tensions produced by this conflict were often projected into the cloister with disastrous results for monastic discipline. The conclusion reached by a Cistercian historian after a study of the racial conflict in Ireland, probably holds true for a number of abbeys in Wales. 'Had the Cistercian order in Ireland', writes Dom Colmcille, 'been allowed to develop normally without undue interference from outside it is unlikely that the abuses which caused such scandal in the second and third decades of the thirteenth century would ever have attained such serious dimensions.'[103]

Materially the effects of the wars are more difficult to assess. Campaigns, however violent, were generally of short duration. It is possible, too, that the religious in their petitions to pope and king tended to magnify the havoc wrought on their property in order to evade taxation or to gain new sources of revenue. For all that, the extent of the destruction at certain times and places cannot be gainsaid.[104] Many houses were left ill-equipped to face the economic recession which lay ahead. The diocese of St. David's throughout the period suffered heavily, far more heavily than the diocese of Llandaff. Geographical factors were responsible for this. The main lines of

[101] P.R.O., SC 8/34/1681, cited in J. F. O'Sullivan, *Cistercian Settlements*, pp. 75, 81.
[102] For the strict conditions laid down by Edward I in the matter of compensation, see the writ printed by J. G. Edwards in *Littere Wallie*, pp. 107–8.
[103] Colmcille, *Story of Mellifont*, p. 1.
[104] See especially Bishop Richard de Carew's report on the diocese of St. David's in 1259, in *Episc. Acts*, i, p. 395.

communication into and from the hinterland of Wales radiated from Carmarthen and Cardigan. Houses situated along these routes were particularly vulnerable to passing armies in search of provisions, horses and loot. By contrast, the diocese of Llandaff, cushioned by the Black Mountains, remained relatively free from raids by large hostile armies. The raids of the two Llywelyns into Glamorgan were hit-and-run affairs and largely confined to the hill regions.[105] Nevertheless, they had important consequences for the monasteries of the area. They stimulated the Clare lords to devote increasing attention to securing the ill-defined mountain frontier against attack. Between 1289 and 1295, Gilbert de Clare took over large tracts of land in the *Blaenau* belonging to the abbeys of Neath, Margam and Caerleon. The abbeys of Margam and Caerleon received little if any compensation and their pleas for a redress of grievances were being heard long after the break-up of the Clare estates after 1314.[106]

V. THE GROWTH OF ROYAL POWER

The period from the Norman conquest to the reign of Edward III witnessed a gradual but steadily increasing growth in the power exercised by the crown over the Welsh church. Even in the twelfth century, when English kings rarely entered Wales except to quell some of the more troublesome of the Welsh princes with a brief and often ineffectual display of force, a vigilant eye was kept on appointments to Welsh sees. By the beginning of the fourteenth century the crown had an important, often decisive, though not always exclusive, voice in the election of bishops to all four of the Welsh sees. Royal contacts with the monasteries were, at first, more limited. Though Henry I had taken an interest in the foundation and endowment of Llanthony Prima,[107] the crown was the immediate patron of only one religious house in south Wales: the Augustinian house which adjoined the royal borough of Carmarthen. Even here the bond was somewhat tenuous in the twelfth century. At least from the reign of Henry I, however, a

---

[105] Lloyd, *History of Wales*, ii, p. 674 (1231). Llywelyn extorted 60 marks from Margam Abbey on this occasion. Cf. also ibid., pp. 721, 752–3.
[106] See Chapter IX, pp. 249, 252.
[107] G. Roberts, *Some Account of Llanthony Priory*, pp. 54–5, 119–20.

number of monastic houses situated within the marcher lordships of south Wales had begun to look beyond their immediate patrons to the English king as the ultimate protector of their lands and liberties. Henry I issued a writ of protection to Pembroke Priory, and charters to Llanthony Prima, Carmarthen, Tintern and St. Dogmaels.[108] During the reign of Henry II newly-founded abbeys situated in *pura Wallia* began to approach the crown for confirmation of their charters. Strata Florida acquired such confirmations from both Henry II and John.[109] Formal contacts of this kind increased as the thirteenth century advanced. The new preoccupation of the English crown with Welsh affairs was largely responsible for this. In north Wales, Llywelyn ab Iorwerth's determination to carve out for himself a large feudal state beyond the confines of Gwynedd convinced the crown that the traditional royal policy of periodic displays of force was inadequate to the new situation. The emergence at the same time of a baronial opposition to the crown which could, and did, enlist Welsh support, gave to the Welsh question a more vital importance. During the reigns of John and Henry III a number of monasteries in *pura Wallia* and in the marcher lordships began to feel the heavy hand of the English kings. Strata Florida, which Gerald of Wales could describe at the beginning of the thirteenth century as 'far from the power of the English' and a 'sanctuary and quiet place of refuge',[110] was to become before the end of John's reign only too aware of the ruthlessness of royal power. Margam Abbey, despite its situation in the exclusive domain of the Clares, had in 1242 to obtain the remission of the king's anger for having received William de Mariscis and his men.[111]

There was, however, a more constructive side to this new assertion of royal power. An enthusiastic builder like Henry III could make small but disinterested gifts of money, materials and livestock to monasteries in south Wales with which he had no intimate ties. In 1220 Talley Abbey received a grant of 20*s*. from the king 'probably towards the completion or

[108] *Episc. Acts*, i, pp. 247, 254, 255; J. F. O'Sullivan, *Cistercian Settlements*, p. 39; E. Pritchard, *St. Dogmaels Abbey*, pp. 42–3.
[109] S. W. Williams, *Strata Florida Abbey*, appendix pp. xiii–xiv, xvii–xix.
[110] *Autobiography of Giraldus Cambrensis*, ed. H. E. Butler, p. 250.
[111] *CPR.*, *1232–47*, p. 302.

enlargement of the house'.[112] In 1234 the abbot of Tintern was granted forty mares with their foals of three years in the king's forest of Dean 'for the losses he has sustained in the time of the war between the king and Richard Marshall'. The prior of Monmouth in the same year received a gift of thirteen oaks from the forest of Dean 'to repair the church of St. Thomas the Martyr which was burnt in the war'. Grace Dieu received gifts of twenty *fusta ad operacionem domus sue* in 1235, four oaks in 1240 and two oaks in 1253. In 1246 the king ordered the keeper of the lands of the late earl of Pembroke 'to cause the abbot and convent of St. Dogmaels to have 20 marks of the king's gift . . . for the fabric of their church'. Such acts are typical of a king who spent a tenth of his income on building.[113]

It was probably during the reign of Henry III that the crown first began to utilize the services of the abbots and priors of south Wales as administrators, envoys and commissioners.[114] In 1223 the abbots of Talley and St. Dogmaels and the prior of Cardigan were members of a commission appointed to make an inquisition into the lands held by certain Welshmen. In 1236 John, a former abbot of Grace Dieu, was sent by Henry III on a mission to Gascony 'to further some business for him there'.[115] The abbot of Tintern was given a variety of tasks to perform by both Henry III and Edward I. In 1266 he was ordered to make an inquisition of the lands and castles of the late Richard de Clare. In 1267 he was included among those who were assigned to hear the plaints of the disinherited. In the same year he helped in the negotiations and judicial proceedings which followed the peace with Llywelyn, while in 1271 he was appointed to assess the tallage of the town of Bristol.[116]

When the counties or honours of Carmarthen and Cardigan were definitively acquired by the crown in 1241, it is probable that the duties of the priors of Carmarthen and Cardigan as

[112] E. Owen, 'A Contribution to the History of the Premonstratensian Abbey of Talley', *Arch. Camb.*, 1893, p. 229.

[113] *CCR., 1231–34*, p. 538; *CPR., 1232–47*, p. 74; *CCR., 1231–34*, p. 445; *CCR., 1234–37*, p. 44; *CCR., 1237–42*, p. 185; *CCR., 1253–54*, p. 11; *Calendar of Liberate Rolls*, iii, p. 44.

[114] Although few records of the marcher lordships or of the Welsh patrimonies have survived, it seems probable that marcher lords and Welsh princes were using the religious as administrators and envoys at a much earlier date.

[115] *CPR., 1216–25*, pp. 413, 481; *CPR., 1232–47*, pp. 169, 192, 201.

[116] *CPR., 1258–66*, pp. 662–3; cf. also ibid., pp. 676, 586; *CCR., 1264–68*, p. 361; *CPR., 1266–72*, pp. 254, 592; *CCR., 1272–79*, pp. 392–3.

part-time royal administrators increased. Early references to their activities, however, are few.[117] In 1272 the prior of Carmarthen served on a commission of oyer and terminer.[118] In 1278 and 1279 Robert de Henley, prior of Cardigan, is found as viewer and auditor for the work being done on the new royal castle at Llanbadarn.[119] It was not until the later years of Edward I's reign that the prior of Carmarthen took an important part in what had, by then, become the principality of west Wales. In 1299 the prior of Carmarthen was appointed to the important office of treasurer of west and south Wales'.[120] As such he was 'the chief fiscal officer and head of the exchequer at Carmarthen'.[121] It was an office which he and his successors were to hold for considerable terms throughout the first half of the fourteenth century.[122]

It is extremely difficult to detect any general trend in royal policy towards the Welsh monasteries during the reigns of the first three Edwards. The Edwardian conquest and settlement, and the acquisition by the crown of extensive lands within Wales, produced a growing volume of records relating to Welsh affairs. References to the monasteries naturally become more frequent in all classes of central government records. Such references, however, are still fragmentary and incidental to the work of government. They cannot be related to records of other kinds, such as the records of marcher lordships, the records of the chancery at Carmarthen and the diocesan registers which have either been lost or destroyed. Often it is difficult to know what weight to attach to such isolated and unrelated pieces of evidence. For all that, one gains from the records two somewhat contradictory impressions. Firstly, there are indications of increasingly frequent contacts between monasteries in Wales and the English crown in the royal courts of chancery and exchequer and in the more specialized royal

---

[117] Perhaps because both areas were administered as a marcher lordship between 1254 and 1279, first by the Lord Edward and from 1265 by his brother Edmund: see A. H. Williams, *An Introduction to the History of Wales*, ii, p. 135.

[118] *CPR., 1266–72*, p. 709.

[119] *Littere Wallie*, p. 131.

[120] *CFR., 1272–1307*, p. 411.

[121] D. L. Evans in *History of Carmarthenshire*, ed. J. E. Lloyd, i, p. 209. The offices of treasurer, chamberlain and receiver were synonymous: see A. H. Williams, op. cit., p. 144.

[122] See especially the references given in R. A. Griffiths, *The Principality of Wales in the Later Middle Ages: The Structure and Personnel of Government*, pp. 168–73.

courts of justice, and an extension to Wales of the kind of surveillance which the English kings were exercising over monasteries in England. Secondly, there is a good deal of evidence to suggest that the monasteries were being subjected to increasing local pressure from marcher lords, crown officials and even from their own patrons. Overall it seems certain that throughout the period secular society was exercising a greater control over, and intervening more frequently in, the affairs of the religious than ever before.

The growing power and prestige of the crown *vis à vis* the monasteries are exemplified by a number of developments during the reigns of the first three Edwards. In 1276 a royal clerk was appointed to the custody of the priory of Llanthony Prima 'in debt'. In 1277 or 1278 Edward I took the Premonstratensian abbey of Talley into royal custody because of its impoverishment through the Welsh wars.[123] The practice of taking impoverished English houses into royal custody gained ground during the reign of Henry III and owed as much to the initiative of the religious themselves as to royal aggrandizement.[124] In Wales the practice was, as far as the records indicate, unprecedented and would have been unthinkable a half-century earlier. Neither Llanthony Prima nor Talley was under royal patronage, normally a pre-condition of royal intervention.[125] Talley's patron at this time was the ill-starred Rhys ap Maredudd and it is perhaps significant that he was at odds with the royal officials of Carmarthen in 1277, either immediately before or soon after the abbey was taken into royal custody.[126] The precedents established during the reign of Edward I were strengthened during the reigns of his weaker successors. In 1321 Edward II, at the prior's request, granted the custody of Goldcliff to Thomas, earl of Norfolk, 'with the usual clauses touching the debts and maintenance of the house'.[127] In 1322 the priory cell of Cardigan, 'which has fallen into debt through wars, dearths and other tribulations',

---

[123] *CPR., 1272–81*, pp. 166, 251.
[124] K. L. Wood-Legh, *Studies in Church Life in England under Edward III*, pp. 1–37.
[125] Ibid., p. 5.
[126] J. E. Morris, *Welsh Wars*, p. 151. Cf. also the petition in which he claimed that the homage of the abbey of Talley due to him was being diverted to the crown, in *Arch. Camb.*, 1893, p. 236.
[127] *CPR., 1317–21*, p. 576. This occurred during a period of peace with France and had nothing to do with the alien status of Goldcliff.

was taken into royal custody, and in 1348 the temporalities of Llanthony Prima were again in the king's hands 'for some causes'.[128]

By this time, however, royal custody had been experienced by a number of religious houses of south Wales. With the outbreak of the war with France in 1294, Edward I had taken into his own hands the property belonging to the alien priories. Of the hundred or so houses involved, seven were in south Wales: the conventual houses of Goldcliff, Monmouth, Abergavenny, Chepstow and Pembroke, and the two cells of Llangenydd and St. Clears. Although the earliest writs for the seizure of these houses are not to be found in the chancery enrolments, the Alien Priory Bundles in the Public Record Office show that there was no delay in dealing with even the smallest of the south Wales houses. The small cell of St. Clears was entrusted to Hugh de Cressingham, who acted as custodian from 22 August 1294 to 29 September 1297, when he was relieved by Walter Hackelut. The latter acted as custodian until 20 March 1303.[129] Both men were trusted royal officials with wide experience. Goldcliff was also seized immediately and a number of its monks removed 'for lack of sustenance'.[130] Despite the absence of early evidence for the other south Wales houses, it is probable that they were treated in a similar manner. This first confiscation lasted until 1303. The priories were again under royal control between 1324 and 1327 and again from 1337 to 1360.[131] Such breaks in the continuity of administration had serious effects for conventual priories. Continuous financial pressure during these periods was probably one reason for the reduction in the number of monks in the priories during the fourteenth century. The seizures also rendered a number of priories more vulnerable to intrigue and local persecution.[132]

During the reigns of Edward II and Edward III it became customary for alien priors to petition the king to secure the

[128] CPR., 1321–24, p. 211; CPR., 1348–50, p. 217.
[129] P.R.O., E 106/4/19.
[130] R. Graham, 'Four Alien Priories in Monmouthshire', Jnl. Brit. Arch. Assoc., xxxv (1929), p. 111.
[131] M. M. Morgan, 'The Suppression of the Alien Priories', History, xxvi (1941), pp. 205–6.
[132] For an affray at Pembroke Priory in 1339, see CCR., 1339–41, p. 111.

custody of their houses in return for an annual payment or 'farm' to the royal exchequer. Thus, in 1339 Poncius, prior of St. Clears, petitioned that he might be given the custody of his priory. He was to pay £4 from the time when the alien priories were seized (1337) and 40s. per annum after the custody had been formally committed to him.[133] Even when the custody had been granted to the prior or an outsider for an annual rent, the king was careful to retain the right of appointing to vacant livings in the gift of the priories. This proviso, so frequently included in grants of custody, considerably enlarged the fund of patronage at the disposal of the crown in south Wales.

The alien priories were not the only monasteries to feel financial pressure from the crown. It was during the reign of Edward I that the clergy of Wales began to be systematically taxed by the king for the first time.[134] A heavy burden of this taxation fell upon the monastic order. In the *Taxatio* of 1291, on which royal levies were subsequently based, the property of the clergy, both secular and regular, within the dioceses of St. David's and Llandaff was assessed at £4,756 14s. 5d.[135] The assessment of the temporal and spiritual income of the monks accounted for between a third and a half of this total.[136] The thankless task of collecting the tenths fell with regularity throughout the fourteenth century on a select number of monastic superiors within the two dioceses. In Llandaff diocese the abbot of Margam or Tintern usually acted as deputy-collector; in the larger diocese of St. David's, the office was generally shared by the priors of Carmarthen and Llanthony Prima.[137]

The financial needs of the crown and preoccupation with Welsh affairs following the Edwardian conquest were probably the main factors responsible for the summoning to Parliament

---

[133] *CFR.*, *1337–47*, p. 136.

[134] Glanmor Williams, *Welsh Church*, pp. 58–61.

[135] The total figure of £2,679 2s. 1d. for St. David's diocese, not given in the text of the *Taxatio*, is provided by W. L. Bevan, *St. David's*, p. 114. The *Taxatio* gives the assessments of spiritual and temporal income of Llandaff diocese as £1,154 14s. 8d. and £922 17s. 8d. respectively, giving a total of £2,077 12s. 4d.

[136] An exact figure for monastic property cannot be given because appropriated churches are rarely noted in the text for St. David's diocese.

[137] See the list printed in W. E. Lunt, *Financial Relations of the Papacy with England to 1327*, pp. 625–38.

of a number of Welsh abbots during the reigns of Edward I and Edward II. The writs of summons for the early part of Edward I's reign have not survived but a regular series begins in 1295. The abbots of only four houses, all of them Cistercian, were summoned: Whitland, Strata Florida, Tintern and Basingwerk. Whitland (*Blanca Landa*) was summoned on but two occasions during the reign, Strata Florida seven times, Tintern five times, and Basingwerk six times.[138] The criteria which determined the choice of abbots summoned have not been, and probably never will be, satisfactorily explained.[139] The two largest wool-producing abbeys, Margam and Neath, never appear to have received a summons. Equally puzzling is the absence from the extant writs of the abbot of Aberconwy, who held extensive lands in Edward's newly constituted principality. In the reign of Edward II only Basingwerk received writs of summons to Parliament. No Welsh abbots were summoned during the reign of Edward III.

By the end of the thirteenth century one detects a subtle change in the climate of opinion towards the monasteries. It is a change easier to illustrate than define. There was no violent reaction against the *raison d'être* of the monastic life such as occurred in certain groups and at certain centres in the early-sixteenth century. On the contrary, many patrons were genuinely concerned that their foundations were not performing the spiritual and social obligations for which they had been founded. There was, however, an attempt, perhaps unconscious, to reappraise the role of the monasteries in a changing society. Symptomatic of the new social climate are the passing in 1279 of the Mortmain statute which set a curb on the granting of lands to religious corporations, the growing popularity of chantries in parish and monastic churches where funds were set aside for spiritual services more specific and more readily controlled than those provided by the monks acting as a corporate body, and, lastly, the understandable, though occasionally misguided, body of opinion which attributed the *malaise* of the monks to the contributions being paid to monasteries in France.

[138] F. Palgrave, *Parliamentary Writs*, i, pp. 448, 475, 850, 866.
[139] For a recent statement of the problem, see R. A. Donkin, 'Localisation, Situation Economique et Role Parliamentaire des Abbés Cisterciens Anglais (1295–1341)', *Revue d'Histoire Ecclesiastique*, lii (1957), pp. 832–41.

Added edge was given to such opinion in south Wales by the developments which accompanied and followed the Welsh wars. Many marcher lords, some of them fighting on their own account and not in the royal pay, emerged from the campaigns financially exhausted. In their attempts to increase the revenues of their lordships, they viewed with resentment the liberties and immunities enjoyed by the monasteries and were not loath to resort to high-handed and even violent action to defend or further their own interests. A few of them were little better than gangsters, prepared to dispense summary justice on behalf of those prepared to pay. On several occasions in 1277, the servants of Reginald fitz Peter, lord of Blaenllynfi and a notorious persecutor of the church, descended on the manor of *Olrewas* (Alrewas?) which belonged to Llanthony Prima and distrained its cattle:

> the reason for these seizures was that a woman, by name Agnes Aubrey of Brech' demanded of the prior 25 sacks of wool, and when he did not acknowledge the debt, came to Sir Reynold and offered him a third of the wool provided that he would distrain for the whole.[140]

In 1279 Theobald de Verdun, lord of Ewyas, seized beasts belonging to the prior in his manors of Oldcastle and Red-castle. The prior was not allowed to replevy them 'until some had perished of hunger and until he had agreed with the said Theobald as to certain undue exactions'. Other unnamed persons had come by night to the prior's manor of Newenton,

> broke his houses there, beat and wounded the prior and his men and certain of his fraternity and canons, and killing two of the said canons.[141]

In 1299 Gilbert de Bohun and men from Crickhowell invaded the prior's lands 'and led away a large number of beasts and other goods and detained them in the parts of Cruchowell'.[142]

Similar pressures were being exerted on monasteries in the Clare lordships to the south. In 1285 Robert le Veal, sheriff of Glamorgan, seized two of Margam's granges, Terrys and New Grange, on behalf of Gilbert de Clare.[143] In 1291 the abbey was forced into a one-sided agreement with the earl by which it lost

[140] *Cal. Inq. Misc. (Chancery)*, i, pp. 337–8.
[141] *CPR.*, *1272–81*, p. 350.
[142] *CPR.*, *1292–1301*, pp. 465–6.
[143] 'Chronicle of the 13th Century', *Arch. Camb.*, 1862, p. 281.

a good part of its lands in the mountains.[144] A year later the abbot of Cîteaux was complaining to the king on Margam's behalf that Gilbert de Clare was troubling the abbey without reasonable cause.[145] Goldcliff was another house which suffered at Gilbert's hands. In 1289 he took the liberties of the priory into his own hands, 'asserting that the prior and monks of the place abused their liberties to his detriment'. Two years later he was attempting to implead the prior in his court of Caerleon over the advowson of Undy Church.[146]

In the diocese of St. David's pressure on the monasteries from marcher lords is less in evidence than encroachment on monastic liberties by the royal officials who were administering the southern principality and holding royal castles. As early as 1252 an inquisition found that the monks of Strata Florida, 'after that the lord king constructed his castle of Montgomery. . . did not use their liberties and articles contained in their charters'.[147] At Carmarthen in 1276 the bailiffs of Edmund, the king's brother, had ejected the prior of Carmarthen from certain of his lands and tenements and forced the prior and his men to come to Edmund's court. A later record shows that the prior's trading privileges in Old Carmarthen had also been usurped by royal officials at this time.[148] In 1290 the prior of Brecon was complaining of the conduct of John Giffard, keeper of the royal castle of Builth, who was challenging his right to tithes, a free court and trading privileges at the town of Builth.[149]

In the reign of Edward II 'Wales fell more or less completely under the control of the marcher lords',[150] and one would naturally expect an increase both in the number and in the seriousness of complaints from monasteries in south Wales. One obtains from the available evidence, however, the contrary impression that pressure from marcher lords was being eased. It was during Edward II's reign and in the earlier years of that of his successor, that the abbeys of Caerleon and Margam

---

[144] See Chapter IX, pp. 248–9.
[145] *Cal. Chancery Warrants*, i, p. 31.
[146] M. Morgan, *English Lands of the Abbey of Bec*, pp. 29–30; 'The Abbey of Bec-Hellouin and its English Priories', *Jnl. Brit. Arch. Assoc.*, v (1940), pp. 52–3.
[147] Williams, *Strata Florida Abbey*, appendix, p. xxx.
[148] *CPR., 1272–81*, p. 182; *C.Ch.R.*, iii, p. 397.
[149] *CPR., 1281–92*, p. 402.
[150] Glanmor Williams, *Welsh Church*, p. 51.

obtained some sort of redress for the encroachments made on
their propetry during the last years of Gilbert de Clare (d.
1295).[151] The volume of complaints from south Wales monasteries, too, appears to have been smaller than in the last
decades of the thirteenth century. This impression, however,
may well be deceptive. The machinery of government had
increased in scale and complexity and the chancery enrolments
can no longer be expected to give even a rough conspectus of
the range of government business, still less a survey of local
conditions.

One important result of the growing local pressure on the
monasteries was that abbots and priors began with increasing
frequency to take their grievances to the king in council and in
parliament, and to make greater use of the royal courts of
common law. It will not be possible to see this comparatively
new activity in its proper perspective until the petitions of the
religious and the legal records of the crown have been published
and studied more intensively. From the sources already
published, however, the general trend is clear. In the *Curia
Regis* rolls of the first half of the thirteenth century, the abbots
and priors of south Wales rarely make an appearance unless
they were involved in pleas relating to land within English
shires.[152] By the end of the century pleas of priors and abbots
of south Wales were being tried by the king and council in
parliament, and in the courts *Coram Rege* and of King's Bench.[153]
It was a development welcomed by the crown apart from
financial considerations, for it provided a useful lever against
marcher privilege. Edward I, in his contest with the powerful
marcher Gilbert de Clare, had found the grievances of the
prior of Goldcliff a useful addition to his legal armoury.[154] By
the fourteenth century the religious were fully aware that their
grievances against an overbearing marcher patron would be
given a sympathetic hearing by the king. In the reign of
Edward III the prior of Pill petitioned the king that David,

---

[151] *CCR.*, *1313–18*, p. 406; Clark, *Cartae*, iii, pp. 1153–8.
[152] Cf. *Curia Regis Rolls*, xi (1223–24), p. 151.
[153] An interesting indication of the increasing use made of the royal courts by
south Wales houses is the occasional appearance of Welsh cases in the professional
Year Books: see *Year Book, 33–35 Ed. I*, pp. 330–3 (Grace Dieu), *Year Book,
20–21 Ed. I*, p. 44, and *Year Book, 11–12 Ed. III*, p. 387 (Llanthony Prima).
[154] Glanmor Williams, *Welsh Church*, pp. 46–8.

son of Thomas de la Roche, had laid waste the goods of the priory and seized his monks,

> whereupon he begs the favour that he will cause him to come before the justices of the King's bench to answer for the trespass *since our lord the king has cognizance of all trespasses which his tenants in chief commit.*[155]

It is difficult to draw up a balance sheet of what the monasteries lost and gained from the growth of royal power and prestige in Wales. On both sides the relationship was essentially one of self interest. There were no traditional bonds of mutual affection such as existed between the royal family and royal foundations like Westminster, Battle and Beaulieu. The king certainly gained a welcome addition to his revenue from the fees and fines received from the issue of letters of protection, confirmation charters, and from pleas before the royal courts. By the beginning of the fourteenth century the king had also begun the practice of rewarding his aged servants and retainers with corrodies in the border houses of Tintern and Goldcliff.[156]

For the monasteries the story is one of loss and gain. They gained a greater measure of security for their lands and liberties, at least in the long run, but forfeited the greater freedom and many of the immunities they had enjoyed in earlier ages. On the other hand royal justice was slow, expensive and occasionally ineffectual even under a strong ruler like Edward I. The plea of Llanthony Prima against Theobald de Verdun, already cited, began in 1279 before the Hopton commission. After spending a number of years *Coram Rege*, it was finally settled thirteen years later at the Parliament of Abergavenny. The result of the case was impressive and in keeping with Edward's policy of making inroads on marcher privilege. Theobald forfeited his liberty of Ewias.[157] Within seven years, however, the prior was again complaining to the king that Theobald and his subjects were continuing to harass him.[158] It would be unrealistic to blame Edward I or his successors for failing to tackle and solve the problem of lawlessness within the complicated mosaic of marcher lordships which stretched in an

---

[155] Pritchard, *St. Dogmaels Abbey*, pp. 132–3; the italics are mine.
[156] *CCR., 1302–07*, p. 208; *CCR., 1313–18*, p. 192 (Tintern); *CCR., 1302–07*, p. 313; *CCR., 1313–18*, p. 436; *CCR., 1343–46*, pp. 229, 644 (Goldcliff).
[157] J. Conway Davies, *Welsh Assize Roll*, p. 184 and notes.
[158] *CPR., 1292–1301*, pp. 465–6.

arc from Chester to Pembroke. The problem of maintaining law and order was difficult enough in the more settled and easily policed areas of lowland England. By the time the English government had sufficient power and adequate machinery to approach the problem with anything like a promise of success, the monasteries had disappeared.

IX

CRISIS AND CHANGE

I. FINANCIAL DIFFICULTIES

For Wales, as for western Europe generally, the thirteenth century had been one of economic expansion and, in spite of the wars, of comparative prosperity. There are many indications of this. The large sums of money which the English kings were able to demand and receive from the Welsh princes of north Wales,[1] the ambitious building programmes initiated by churchmen and laymen and completed in the thirteenth century, and the large arable farms consolidated by the Cistercians—all argue a period of general agrarian prosperity. This prosperity was not evenly shared by the landowning community. The largest profits were reaped by the greater landowners, ecclesiastical and lay, while many knights and freeholders with more modest holdings experienced periods of real hardship. Well before the end of the thirteenth century there are signs that this period of prosperity was coming to an end.

Between the last quarter of the thirteenth century and the Black Death, most monasteries in south Wales passed through a series of crises which appear to have become progressively worse as the fourteenth century advanced. Monasteries, great and small, of all orders were affected, but it is in the smaller houses that financial difficulties are apparent earliest. The conventual priory of Monmouth was in desperate straits as early as 1264.[2] The appointment to the priorate of Geoffrey Moreteau, a capable administrator from the mother abbey, brought no long-term relief, for in 1279 Thomas de Cantilupe, bishop of Hereford, found it necessary to come to the assistance of the priory by issuing an indulgence to those who visited the priory church and recited certain prayers there.[3] By 1315 the

---

[1] See J. G. Edwards in *Littere Wallie*, p. li, note 1.
[2] R. Graham, 'Four Alien Priories in Monmouthshire', *Jnl. Brit. Arch. Assoc.*, xxxv (1929–30), p. 108.
[3] P.R.O., Ancient Deeds, E 210/D4610.

priory was so impoverished that the abbot of St. Florent could
not find a monk willing to take on the task of administering the
priory and restoring it to its former state. It was becoming
increasingly difficult to maintain a convent of monks.[4] The
small priory of St. Clears was in difficulties in 1279; the goods
of the church had been alienated and the prior forced to work
as a chaplain to maintain himself.[5] In 1288 the bishop of St.
David's had sequestrated the priory because its prior, William
of Airaines, had absconded leaving a debt unpaid to the
bishop.[6] In 1305 royal officials reported that 'the said priory
from the time it was taken into the hands of the king has been
of no value except £8 10s.', despite the fact that the goods of
the priory had been extented at over £16.[7] In 1276 plans were
made to move the abbey of Grace Dieu to a more suitable site.
It is not known whether the move was made; but four years
later the abbots of Tintern and Thame were commissioned by
the General Chapter to visit 'and diligently to enquire into the
causes of the ruin of the said house'.[8] The monks of Goldcliff,
the richest and best endowed of the Benedictine houses in
south Wales, had begun to complain of their poverty in 1290.
In that year Edward I granted the priory a yearly fair at
Goldcliff, and to save the monks unnecessary expense, sealed
the grant himself 'because they are poor and are not sufficient
for making fine'.[9]

With the exception of those houses in the diocese of St.
David's which had been severely affected by the Welsh
wars,[10] the larger Cistercian houses seem to have fared better in
the last quarter of the thirteenth century. The abbots of Neath
and Tintern, for example, felt sufficiently confident of the
future to embark on large-scale building programmes during
the period.[11] In the second and third decades of the fourteenth
century, however, Margam Abbey, the richest Cistercian
house in south Wales, was finding it difficult to pay the rents

[4] Paul Marchegay, Les Prieurés Anglais de Saint-Florent Près Saumur, p. 23.
[5] G. F. Duckett, Charters and Records of Cluni, ii, p. 136.
[6] See above p. 213.
[7] P.R.O., E 106/4/19.
[8] Canivez, Statuta, iii, pp. 161, 200–1.
[9] C.Ch.R., ii, p. 356.
[10] See above pp. 209–16.
[11] Glanmor Williams, 'Neath Abbey', in Neath and District: a Symposium,
ed. Elis Jenkins, pp. 80–1; for the rebuilding of Tintern, see below pp. 255–6.

and services due for certain properties.[12] By the 'thirties almost all the Cistercian houses and Benedictine priories were in severe difficulties. In 1335 the abbot of Grace Dieu was excommunicated for not paying the tenth.[13] In 1336 the abbot of Margam was complaining of the burden of royal and papal taxation and in the following year forfeited the land of Llangeinor because he was not able to pay the rent for it due to the lord of Ogmore.[14] In 1338 the abbot of Strata Florida was excommunicated for his refusal to pay the tenth,[15] and a year later a document refers to the house as 'manifestly oppressed with the burden of poverty'.[16]

Debts of South Wales Monasteries, 1280–1341

House	Date	Amount £ s. d.			Creditor
Brecon	1288	10	0	0	Ralph le Boteller
Goldcliff	1320	63	13	4	Philip de Columbariis
	1332	600	0	0	Michael Minyot
	1334	200	0	0	Walter Turk
Llanthony Prima	1280	46	13	0	Agnes Aubrey
	1281	6	0	0	Henry le Tyeis
	1290	24	0	0	William le Brun
	1325	48	0	0	Thomas Evenefeld
	1341	50	0	0	Baldo Orlandini
Strata Florida and Whitland	1295	560	0	0	William of Estavayer
Tintern	1340	174	0	0	Michael Simonetti

The evidence for monastic indebtedness during the period, though meagre, is occasionally revealing. The above table has been constructed entirely from entries in the published *Calendars* of Close Rolls between 1280 and 1341. In all the cases the creditors of the monks had taken the trouble to have their

[12] For payments by Margam of arrears of rents, etc., for lands at Hafodheulog and Bonvilston, see Clark, *Cartae*, iii, pp. 1040–1, 1135–6.
[13] *Registrum Thome de Charlton*, p. 57.
[14] Clark, *Cartae*, iv, pp. 1199, 1573–79.
[15] Glanmor Williams, *Welsh Church*, p. 141.
[16] Williams, *Strata Florida Abbey*, appendix, p. liii. For similar difficulties experienced by Goldcliff sometime before 1332, see *Register of Ralph of Shrewsbury, Bishop of Bath and Wells*, p. 105; and for Monmouth in 1334, see *Registrum Thome de Charlton*, p. 55.

claims acknowledged by the monks and officially enrolled by
the chancery clerks. The entries do not, therefore, reveal the
total indebtedness of each house. Nor do the enrolments
indicate whether the debts were incurred by outright borrowing
or by failure to meet obligations.

Debt, a familiar phenomenon to the monastic historian, need
not be a sign of financial instability.[17] When money borrowed
is invested in land, in the capitalization of agriculture or even in
plate, jewels and relics, such debts may give every indication of
a healthy and expanding economy. The combined evidence
for the south Wales houses would suggest that their indebtedness was not due to borrowings for investment. The debts
represent either accumulated arrears through failure to meet
obligations as they arose, or money borrowed for immediate
consumption. Loans of the latter kind, to use Pirenne's words,
'were contracted as a result of some urgent necessity; the money
received would be spent at once, so that each sum borrowed
represented a dead loss'.[18] The table shows that in the 'thirties
Goldcliff was in debt for an amount at least three times that of
its annual income. Bearing in mind the fairly substantial income
which Llanthony Prima enjoyed at the end of the thirteenth
century, the debts recorded in the table are large but not un-
manageable. It will be remembered, however, that the priory
was taken into the king's hands for debt in 1276 and was again
in royal custody in 1348 'for some causes'.[19] Brecon Priory, too,
was probably more indebted than the table reveals. In a
visitation made in the last quarter of the thirteenth century, it
was suggested that the priory was 'much more bound by debts
than the prior says'.[20]

When one attempts to isolate the primary causes of this
distress, one encounters immediate difficulties. Detailed
evidence in the form of accounts from year to year are not
available for any Welsh house during the period. The histories
of the richer English abbeys, so frequently cited to illustrate the
continuance of high farming well into the fourteenth century,[21]
provide no guiding light for the historian of the Welsh houses,

[17] E. Power, 'Medieval Monastic Finance', *Ec.H.R.*, vii (1936), pp. 90–1.
[18] H. Pirenne, *Economic and Social History of Medieval Europe*, p. 121.
[19] See above pp. 220–1.
[20] *Brec. Cart.*, p. 137.
[21] Cf. M. McKisack, *The Fourteenth Century*, pp. 320–2, 328.

whose economies always tended to be precariously balanced. Nor do we know the extent of the financial pressures (over and above the apport) which mother houses were exerting on their dependent priories.[22]

At first sight, war damage, the crippling effects of royal taxation, the consequences following the seizure of the alien priories and chronic mismanagement readily suggest themselves as explanations of the widespread distress among the Welsh monasteries. A closer examination of the evidence would indicate that even this substantial catalogue of causes does not satisfactorily explain the condition of every house. The effects of the Welsh wars, as we have seen,[23] were unevenly felt. Few of the houses of south-east Wales were seriously affected and it seems unlikely that the effects of warfare lay behind the distress of houses such as Goldcliff and Monmouth. It is a little surprising, too, that a house like Strata Florida, badly affected by the wars and, perhaps because of this, lightly assessed in the *Taxatio* of 1291, should not have shown any recovery in the early decades of the fourteenth century. Royal taxation and the seizure of the alien priories came in the last decade of the thirteenth century and both would seem to be aggravating factors rather than primary causes of the distress of the monasteries. Here again it is worth noting that both Monmouth and Goldcliff were in difficulties before they were taxed by the king and before they were seized as alien priories.

As far as mismanagement is concerned, every house at one time or another had its share of bad administrators. In the last quarter of the thirteenth century, one prior of Brecon was, on his own admission, an incompetent administrator.[24] In 1314 the subprior of Montacute was forced to admit to visitors that the prior of Malpas (a dependency of Montacute) was not a very good administrator.[25] Yet it would be wrong to assume from such cases that the south Wales priories were convenient

[22] A list of receipts printed by A. A. Porée, *Histoire de l'Abbaye du Bec*, ii, p. 3 note 3, shows that between 1284 and 1303 Bec was receiving large sums from its English priories and Goldcliff to finance the rebuilding of the abbey choir.
[23] See above pp. 209–16.
[24] *Brec. Cart.*, p. 133. In his defence he added that the outbreak and continuance of war had rendered his task impossible.
[25] G. F. Duckett, *Visitations and Chapters-General of the Order of Cluni*, p. 303.

dumping grounds for monks with little talent or experience. The prior of Brecon already mentioned had served at the mother abbey of Battle 'in many offices, namely the sacristry, the hostelry, the refectory and cellar for five years and in the office of steward for three years'.[26] One of his fellow monks, brother Robert, sent by the abbot of Battle as a companion for the prior, had been the latter's master in the schools.[27] Many of the south Wales priors were men of proven ability who were subsequently promoted to higher office. Reginald, prior of Brecon, was elected to the abbacy of Battle in 1260.[28] Geoffrey Moreteau, prior of Monmouth, was elected to the abbacy of St. Florent près Saumur in 1270.[29] William de Wycomb, prior of Carmarthen, was elected to the abbacy of Hartland in 1281.[30] Most famous of all was John de Gamages, successively prior of Ewenni and of St. Guthlac's, Hereford. In 1284 he was elected to the abbacy of Gloucester, a house which had been in financial difficulties for nearly half a century.[31] He restored the finances and left the abbey 'free of debt and rich in flocks'.[32]

Royal charges of maladministration against native Welsh abbots need to be treated with caution. The charge made by Edward III in 1330 that Whitland was 'ruined by the levity of the Welsh' was prompted by John Charlton's desire to introduce English monks into Whitland's daughter house of Strata Marcella.[33] Similar propaganda of a more unsavoury kind was being circulated in official quarters against the Welsh canons of Talley.[34] The standards of administrative efficiency in the Welsh houses were probably no better and no worse than in houses of comparable size in England. The size of the Welsh houses and their environment had an important bearing on the question of mismanagement. Mismanagement was more likely to occur in the smaller monasteries. Its effects would tend, too, to be more serious in a country such as Wales, where the margin of economic prosperity was a narrow one.

[26] *Brec. Cart.*, p. 140.
[27] Ibid., p. 138.
[28] *CPR., 1258–66*, p. 130.
[29] P. Marchegay, *Les Prieurés Anglais de Saint-Florent Près Saumur*, p. 41 note 2.
[30] *CPR., 1272–81*, p. 430. Cf. also *CCR., 1272–79*, p. 427.
[31] *VCH., Gloucester*, ii, p. 55.
[32] Knowles, *Religious Orders*, i, pp. 290, 314–5, ii, p. 35.
[33] J. F. O'Sullivan, *Cistercian Settlements*, pp. 89–91.
[34] See above p. 132.

Wales, because of its comparative poverty, had always been treated as a 'special area' by ecclesiastical legislators. The Council of Oxford, as we have seen,[35] specifically exempted 'those parts of Wales' from its regulations for a minimum wage for vicars. The contributions demanded for the administrative expenses of the Cistercian General Chapter were also scaled down for the Welsh houses because of the poverty of their environment.[36] The Welsh economy was determined by a damp climate and a highland terrain which limited profitable arable farming to favourable areas mainly along the coastal plains and river valleys. The balance of such an economy, as Vinogradov pointed out, was particularly sensitive to disturbances caused by murrain, bad seasons, fire, war and the like,[37] and may well have been more vulnerable to changing economic conditions. It is, indeed, possible that the effects of the fourteenth-century slump, which was to affect most countries of western Europe with varying degrees of severity, was felt earlier and lasted longer in Wales than in richer countries with more diversified economies. This at least would help to explain the distress of most of the south Wales houses in the last quarter of the thirteenth century. By the 'twenties and 'thirties of the fourteenth century the abbots and priors of these houses were fighting against economic forces over which they had little control. Their plight is symptomatic of a *malaise* not confined to the monasteries alone.[38]

Meanwhile, developments in the wool trade, locally and nationally, were tending to aggravate the distress experienced by the Welsh Cistercian abbeys. Although the larger abbeys continued to maintain large herds and flocks throughout the

---

[35] See above p. 179.

[36] This appears from an entry in the General Chapter records for 1281 in which the abbot of Dore successfully petitions that, because of poverty, he may be considered among the Welsh abbeys for taxation purposes; see Canivez, *Statuta*, iii, p. 210.

[37] Cited by W. Rees, *South Wales and the March*, p. 20.

[38] In 1322 the abbot of Tintern was finding it impossible to obtain payment of the debts owed to him in the Forest Deanery: see *Registrum Ade de Orleton*, pp. 256–7. For defaulting tenants on the Brecon and Kidwelly Priory estates, see *C. Inq. Misc.*, ii, p. 327; *CCR., 1333–37*, p. 583, and D. Daven Jones, *History of Kidwelly*, p. 52.

fourteenth century,[39] there are grounds for believing that the profits from wool sales were dwindling and ceasing to constitute a satisfactory substitute for the fixed rents and tithes enjoyed by the Benedictine and Augustinian houses. Towards the end of the thirteenth century, the lords of a number of marcher manors, particularly in south-east Wales, had begun to engage in sheep rearing on an extensive scale for the first time, and their activities assumed increased importance during the fourteenth century.[40] Such lords were providing formidable competition for wool-growers like Margam, Tintern and Grace Dieu. Of more serious consequence, however, were the changes which were taking place in the organization of the wool trade on a national level. Royal taxation, the setting up of the Staple and the emergence of middlemen were reducing the large profits enjoyed by the Cistercian wool-growers in the previous century.[41]

II. LEASING ON THE BENEDICTINE ESTATES

However debatable the initial causes of the financial difficulties of the monasteries, their response to them is fairly clear. One of the recognized methods of stabilizing income in times of distress was to substitute a policy of leasing in place of one of direct exploitation. In this way a landowner could be sure of receiving a fixed and fairly predictable amount of cash at the end of each financial year instead of a wildly fluctuating return depending on the vagaries of weather, the price of grain and the availability and cost of labour. The leasing out and the letting to farm of temporal and spiritual sources of income seem to have begun on the Benedictine estates of south Wales before the end of the thirteenth century and gathered speed as the fourteenth century advanced. Frequently the lease was used as a convenient means of anticipating income to pay pressing debts.[42]

---

[39] There is a dearth of figures for the period. See, however, the grant by Richard de Turberville of Coety in 1360 of free pasture on Cefn Cribwr for specified numbers of livestock from Margam's granges at Llangewydd and Stormy, in Clark, *Cartae*, vi, pp. 2380–1. As late as 1428 John, abbot of Strata Florida, set a value of 2,000 marks on livestock rustled from the abbey's estates by John, abbot of Aberconwy: see R. W. Hays, *History of the Abbey of Aberconway*, pp. 132–3.
[40] W. Rees, *South Wales and the March*, pp. 195–7, 256–7.
[41] E. Power, *The Wool Trade in English Medieval History*, pp. 94–5; Knowles, *Religious Orders*, i, p. 77.
[42] R. H. Snape, *English Monastic Finances*, p. 138.

A piece of land or a church was leased or let to farm for a substantial down-payment at a comparatively small annual rental.

A particularly valuable insight into the tendencies at work on the estates of Brecon Priory is provided by a roll of charges made against a prior in the last quarter of the thirteenth century.[43] Despite the prior's protestations to the contrary, it would seem that the priory at this time was labouring under a fairly heavy burden of debt, consisting, as far as one can determine, not of large amounts but of numerous modest sums to many individuals. To meet his commitments, the prior had resorted to a number of expedients. Among them, the farming out of spiritual income takes a prominent place. He had handed over to farm his portion in the church of Defynnog to a married man named John Vaughan 'against the prohibition of the bishop'. He had also farmed out the church of Talgarth for seventy marks, which he immediately paid to usurers. Books from the monastic library and silver had already been pawned to burgesses in Ludlow and Hereford. To raise further cash, the prior had sold a corrody without the bishop's consent ('because he was in remote parts and the great necessity of the house was increasing and the harvest was bad'), mortgaged land, and manumitted serfs on the priory estates.[44] Since the priory's most distant possessions at Berrington and Bodenham were apparently still being exploited directly by a bailiff,[45] it would seem likely that the prior was, by sheer necessity, the initiator of a policy which was in the fourteenth century to result in the abandonment of direct exploitation in favour of an economy based on rents received from farmers of the priory's property, both temporal and spiritual. Later evidence would certainly suggest that the policy of farming out and leasing temporal and spiritual income, far from being checked during the fourteenth century, gathered strength and became more customary than hitherto.[46]

Parts of Kidwelly Priory's comparatively small demesne of a

---

[43] For the date of this roll, see above pp. 137–8.
[44] *Brec. Cart.*, pp. 135–8.
[45] See above p. 62.
[46] For the later evidence for Brecon and Kidwelly priories, see Glanmor Williams, *Welsh Church*, pp. 169–70.

hundred acres or so were also being leased at about the same time. Hugh, abbot of Sherborne (1286–1310), leased to Llywelyn Drimwas and his wife, Gwenllian, 'Seinte Marie lond' for life, in return for their rendering annually to the priory of Kidwelly 12*d*. at Michaelmas. They were not allowed to sell, mortgage or alienate the land and it was to revert to the prior on their death.[47] Later court rolls show that the practice of leasing continued during the fourteenth century.[48]

In 1315 the abbot of St. Florent noted with regret that the priors in charge of the dependent priories of Sele and Monmouth 'have alienated many of the immobile goods of the priory' and farmed them out, 'sometimes for three, sometimes for eight years and in other cases for no small term'.[49]

A similar trend towards leasing can be discerned on the estates of Goldcliff, the richest of the Benedictine priories in south Wales. In 1331 the prior, Philip Gopillariis, leased out the Devon manor of Membury for seven years at an annual rental of £20.[50] In 1332 William Martel leased the priory's Somerset manors of Preston and Selver to Sir John Inge for life at an annual rental of a red rose for the first ten years and £20 annually thereafter.[51] By 1337 only the manors of Goldcliff and Coldra remained to the priory; 'all other manors and lands belonging thereto were demised to divers persons for life by William Martel, late prior'.[52] As early as 1317, Goldcliff's spiritual income in the diocese of Bath and Wells—the churches of Nether Stowey, Puriton and Wullavington—had been uncanonically farmed out to laymen.[53]

III. LEASING ON THE CISTERCIAN ESTATES

The trend towards a policy of leasing and letting lands to farm is also apparent on the estates of the Cistercian abbeys of

[47] P.R.O., Ancient Deed E 210/D3375. The name seems to indicate the glebe attached to the priory church.
[48] D. Daven Jones, *History of Kidwelly*, pp. 52–3.
[49] P. Marchegay, *Les Prieurés Anglais de Saint-Florent Près Saumur*, p. 23.
[50] *CPR., 1330–34*, p. 320. The manor was assessed at £7 in 1291: see *Taxatio*, p. 152.
[51] *Descriptive Catalogue of Ancient Deeds*, ii, p. 271. Sir John Inge was sheriff of Glamorgan for a period. For his dealings with Neath Abbey, see below p. 247.
[52] *CFR., 1327–37*, p. 49; *CCR., 1337–39*, p. 175.
[53] *Register of Bishop John de Drokensford* (Somerset Record Soc., i, 1887), p. 130. For similar conditions in the 'thirties, see *Register of Ralph of Shrewsbury*, pp. 253–4.

south Wales. The Cistercians had from the first been committed
by their statutes to a policy of direct exploitation. But the ideal
economy envisaged by the early legislators was rarely realized
in practice. By the thirteenth century most abbeys were, in
fact, operating a dual economy. On the one hand, there were
the extensive granges being worked by a labour force which
consisted in the main of lay-brothers and hired labourers. In the
twelfth and thirteenth centuries these were the typical units of
exploitation on Cistercian estates. On the other hand, and
generally of subsidiary importance, there were the manorialized
vills and hamlets acquired by gift, purchase and on lease,
which the new Cistercian landlords exploited in the same way
as their lay predecessors.

Such vills and hamlets were particularly valuable when they
existed near grange centres. The labour services of the
customary tenants there could be used to assist the lay-brothers
and hired labourers in working the granges. Tintern Abbey, for
example, used the customary services of tenants in the nearby
dependent hamlets of Howick, St. Wormets and St. Arvans on
their large grange of Rogerstone (4 carucates of arable in
1291).[54] Margam was utilizing the services of villeins on the
grange of Llanfeuthin.[55] The demesne lands of the small
manorial centres possessed by Cistercian abbeys could sometimes be consolidated with nearby grange lands. On the
Margam estate, the small demesne at Bonvilston, as we have
suggested earlier, was probably integrated with the grange
lands of Llanfeuthin.[56] In some cases, however, these demesnes
were too isolated to be consolidated with the grange lands.
Cophill on the Tintern estates is a typical example of an
isolated parcel of demesne land. It was over a mile to the south
of Rogerstone grange.[57]

For abbeys in the diocese of Llandaff, a rough idea of the
relative importance of grange lands and manorial sources of
income, and also of the extent to which leasing had proceeded,

---

[54] N.L.W., Badminton 1640 (Porthcaseg Court Roll, dated 1269): 'Walter . . .
makes two bedrips at Rogerstone'. The court rolls provide numerous examples of
this practice. Colin Platt, *The Monastic Grange in Medieval England*, pp. 83–86,
has stressed how important assistance of this kind was on Cistercian granges.
[55] *Taxatio*, p. 284.
[56] See above p. 90.
[57] W. Rees, *South Wales and the Border*, SE sheet.

may be obtained from the fairly full accounts available in the valuation of 1291. In the valuation of the properties of Margam, Tintern, Caerleon and Grace Dieu, assised rents are a significant, though far from major, item of overall income.[58] Margam drew a total of £13 0s. 9d. from ten centres: from tenants at Llanfeuthin grange (£2), from Bonvilston (£3 4s. 2d.), from Horgrove (15s. 6½d.), from Winterbourne, Gloucestershire (£2 3s.), from Dinas Powis (£1 4s.), and from burgage tenements in Cardiff (5s. 4½d.), Kidwelly (6s.), Neath (8s.), Kenfig (1s.), *Niger Burgus* (1s. 8d.) and Bristol (£2 8s.). Tintern Abbey was drawing £3 13s. 3d. from assised rents:[59] from the grange of Assart (£1 2s.), from St. Brides (5s.) from various places near Magor (18s.), from Undy (13s. 4d.), from Chepstow (4s. 5d.), from Triket (12s.), from Usk (1s. 4d.) and from tenants on two unnamed granges (2s. 4d.). On the estates of the abbey of Caerleon assised rents totalled £5 10s. and on those of Grace Dieu £2 5s. The rents drawn from urban property are not of great importance in the present context, but the entry of assised rents under certain granges shows clearly that parcels of land belonging to granges had been leased out to tenants. In addition to assised rents, the valuation of 1291 also took note of curial revenue for Margam (£2) and Tintern (£1), and boon works at Margam's grange of Llanfeuthin (5s. 10d.) and labour services at Bonvilston (½d.).

Although the *Taxatio* suggests that some granges had acquired or were acquiring manorial features, it would be wrong to regard even Margam and Tintern as 'thoroughly feudalized by 1291'.[60] The valuation of manorial types of income from these houses formed a comparatively small item of the total valuation figures. The high figure for Margam (£13 0s. 9d. for assised rents and £2 for curial income) represented only about 6 per cent of its total assessed value of £255 17s. 4½d. and may profitably be compared with the

---

[58] There is reason to believe that the figures for assised rents and perquisites of court were based on account rolls for average years and therefore approximate more to real income figures than the values given to lands. The assised rents collected by Neath Abbey at this date are exceptional and are reserved for detailed treatment below.

[59] The valuation of 1291 is curiously silent about Tintern's lands east of the Wye and the figure must therefore be regarded as a minimum one.

[60] J. F. O'Sullivan, *Cistercian Settlements*, p. 58.

figures available for the poorer though substantial Benedictine house of Goldcliff. In 1291 assised rents on Goldcliff's
south Wales estates were valued at £23 13s. 4d. and curial
income at £13 16s. 8d. These two items represented over 25
per cent of the assessed value of the priory's estates in this area.

The valuation of 1291 also provides some evidence for the
letting to farm of granges and other sources of revenue. Strata
Florida, for example, had already farmed out its distant grange
of Dolfeithin in Meirionydd.[61] Grace Dieu, it is noted, had been
accustomed to farm out its fulling mill at Monmouth.[62]

The process by which the grange lands and isolated pieces of
demesne were broken up into parcels for leasing or leased as
whole units was a slow and complex one. Much depended on
the location of the lands, their fertility and the population
density of the surrounding area. These factors also tended to
influence the type of lease adopted. In sparsely populated
areas with little urban development, one would expect tenancies
on a share-cropping basis to predominate and, in more densely
populated areas, tenancies at will and for periods of years
at money rents.

The manner of the change-over from direct exploitation, and
the pace at which it occurred, varied from abbey to abbey and
from grange to grange. It should be remembered, too, that
individual abbots were not entirely free agents able to pursue
without restriction what they considered to be the best interests
of their own houses. Even at the end of the thirteenth century,
the General Chapter at Cîteaux could still command a certain
amount of respect and obedience on questions of estate management, however ineffectual its real coercive power might be.
By this time, however, the rigour of the early statutes against
leasing land had been considerably modified. After a certain
amount of wavering in the first two decades of the thirteenth
century, the early legislation against leasing was rescinded
in 1220 and the General Chapter allowed the leasing of granges
and of 'less useful' lands to *coloni* for a term of years, provided

---

[61] *Taxatio*, p. 293b. The grange is not named, but the *quandam terram in
Archid. de Merônyth* is certainly the grange later referred to as *Doverchen* and
identified by J. Conway Davies as the present Dolfeithin: *Province*, xiv (1963),
p. 79.
[62] *Taxatio*, p. 172.

this was done with the counsel of the senior monks, father abbots or visitors.[63] This legislation does not appear to have resulted in a spate of leases on the estates of the abbeys in England and Wales, though it doubtless salved the consciences of numerous German abbots, the management of whose vast estates necessitated a large-scale policy of leasing.[64]

Apart from the fact that grange farming was profitable for most abbeys well into the thirteenth century, there were more compelling local factors urging restraint. A Cistercian abbot who wished to lease grange lands situated within the clearly defined bounds of a parish would be certain to provoke a claim from the rector of the parish for tithe from the land leased. A limited creation of tenancies on Margam's grange of Llanfeuthin may well have been the reason which provoked the dispute with Gloucester Abbey (the rector of Llancarfan) over 'tithes issuing from the lands of the same abbot and convent of Margam in the parish of the church of Llankarvan' in 1262.[65] The potential legal obstacle to leasing, presented by the question of tithe, was removed by a bull which Boniface VIII issued to the Cistercian order in 1302. It 'stipulated that Cistercian lands, either under domestic cultivation or leased to *coloni*, were not to be subject thenceforth to tithe, if no one had been collecting tithes from the possessions up to that time'.[66]

It is difficult to know what advantages the bull conferred in practice on the abbeys of England and Wales. J. S. Donnelly has argued that Margam Abbey made use of the bull, since John de Eaglescliff, bishop of Llandaff inspected it in a charter to the abbey in 1339.[67] On the same day, by virtue of this bull, John also exempted the abbey from payment of tithe for their holdings at Resolven, Penhydd, higher and lower, and Hafod-y-Porth.[68] The latter document is strong evidence

---

[63] J. S. Donnelly, 'Changes in the Grange Economy of English and Welsh Cistercian Abbeys', *Traditio*, x (1954), pp. 420–21 and note 141.

[64] Pressure from the German abbeys between the Elbe and Oder may indeed have been responsible for the 1220 legislation: see J. S. Donnelly, *Decline of the Medieval Cistercian Laybrotherhood*, pp. 40–1.

[65] Clark, *Cartae*, ii, pp. 666–8. Cf. A. Leslie Evans, *Margam Abbey*, p. 74 and Birch, *Margam Abbey*, p. 275. Margam won the case. It seems likely that Llanfeuthin acquired its status as an 'extra-parochial' area as a result of this case, a status it retained until comparatively recent times.

[66] J. S. Donnelly, *Traditio*, x (1954), p. 421 and n. 145.

[67] Ibid., p. 422 and Clark, *Cartae*, iv, pp. 1234–5.

[68] Ibid., pp. 1236–7.

that tenancies were being, or had been, created in substantial numbers on these former grange lands.[69] There is some later evidence that the abbey of Caerleon, alias Llantarnam, also derived some benefit from the bull during the episcopate of the same bishop. In a case which came before the Court of Augmentations in the sixteenth century, the complainant stated that

> the abbey of Llantarnam . . . and the late abbot and his predecessors by force of a composition made about 200 years ago between David, sometime abbot . . . and John, bishop of Llandaff . . . were seized of all tithes of corn and grain in said parishes (of *Henllyse, Bassalecke, Mynethystlan and Bedwelly*)[70]

In the diocese of St. David's, the abbeys of Whitland and Strata Florida appear to have made little or no use of the bull, for in 1338 and 1339 both abbeys made compromise agreements with the bishop of St. David's on the question of tithes owed by their tenants.[71]

Towards the end of the thirteenth century and increasingly throughout the fourteenth century, two main factors were prompting Cistercian abbots to lease out grange lands either wholly or in part: a decline in the number of lay-brothers and a decline in the profitability of demesne and grange farming.

In the twelfth and early-thirteenth century the lay-brethren had formed a class indispensable to the management and working of the granges. Social conditions in western Europe generally were such that recruits to the profession were far more numerous than those who entered the novitiate to become choir monks. The available evidence would suggest that the lay-brothers outnumbered the choir monks of an abbey by two and sometimes three to one.[72] By the last quarter of the thirteenth century this ratio was being considerably reduced in most abbeys.[73] This reduction in numbers was partly due to the

---

[69] See also the evidence for these lands below pp. 248–9.

[70] E. A. Lewis and J. Conway Davies, *Records of the Court of Augmentations*, pp. 134–5. Henllys was a grange of Caerleon Abbey; see C. J. O. Evans, *Monmouthshire*, p. 301. Mynyddislwyn appears as a Caerleon possession in the *Taxatio*.

[71] See above p. 186.

[72] Rievaulx, for example, had 140 monks and 500 lay-brethren under Abbot Ailred; see C. Platt, *The Monastic Grange in Medieval England*, pp. 80–1.

[73] J. S. Donnelly, *Traditio*, x (1954), p. 452–4. The lack of recruits to the lay-brotherhood was felt as early as 1274; see Canivez, *Statuta*, iii, p. 128.

reluctance of abbots to encourage recruitment to a class which was notoriously difficult to manage, but mainly to a general fall in population which occurred in the fourteenth century. The resultant fall in land values and increase in wage rates began to provide landless younger sons with more lucrative opportunities as estate labourers and tenant farmers.[74]

While the prospects of the peasant farmer were beginning to become brighter, the large landowners, even before the Black Death, had entered a period of economic recession which necessitated in the long run a radical transformation in the traditional methods of estate management. Throughout the fourteenth century the price of cereals was falling, gradually at first but markedly after 1379. During the same period the wages of hired labourers were steadily increasing.[75] Both factors were tending to make the intensive cultivation of large demesnes unprofitable and urging large landowners to lease and let to farm for money and food rents lands which they had hitherto directly exploited.

How potent these general forces were in transforming the economy of the Cistercian houses of south Wales it is difficult to say. Margam's ratio of forty lay-brothers to thirty-eight monks in 1336 appears exceptionally high when compared with the figures available for some comparable English houses,[76] but may have appeared less so had figures survived for the houses in west and central Wales. Even on the Margam estate there are signs of a growing labour shortage between the years 1291 and 1349.[77] Throughout the fourteenth century the wages of skilled and unskilled labourers in south Wales seem to have been increasing at the same pace as in England. The prices of cereals, however, seem to have retained a greater stability and may even have shown an overall increase during the same period.[78]

---

[74] It is significant that in areas of great land scarcity, such as the Netherlands, lay-brothers continued to be very numerous well into the later middle ages: Bloemhof had 1,000 in 1300 and Aduard had 3,000 as late as 1417; see B. H. Slicher van Bath, *Agrarian History of Western Europe*, p. 155.

[75] Ibid., pp. 138–9.

[76] Clark, *Cartae*, iv, p. 1199. For numbers in English Cistercian houses, see the examples cited in J. S. Donnelly, *Traditio*, x (1954), pp. 452–3.

[77] See below pp. 249–52.

[78] W. Rees, *South Wales and the March*, pp. 263–5.

The evidence for the break-up of the grange lands and monastic demesnes of the south Wales abbeys is meagre, scattered and never sufficiently abundant to illustrate the process over the whole estate of one abbey. Most of the evidence, too, is indirect and incidental, suggestive rather than conclusive. A closer examination of the evidence for a select number of houses may help to shed some light on the pace of the changes, the manner in which they were accomplished, and some of the local factors which assisted them.

IV. SOME CASE HISTORIES

(i). *Neath Abbey*

Between the years 1289 and 1295 the fortunes of the abbeys of Neath, Margam and Caerleon were closely bound up with the politics of their patron, Gilbert de Clare, the 'Red Earl'. Both Gilbert and his father Richard de Clare had done much to consolidate their lordship of Glamorgan by obtaining direct control over the Welsh hill lordships of Glynrhondda, Meisgyn and Senghennydd.[79] The northern perimeter of the lordship still remained vague and ill-defined, vulnerable to a powerful Welsh prince or a marcher lord intent on aggrandizement. Such fears had prompted the building of the castles of Caerphilly (begun in 1268) and Morlais (1288–9). While the latter castle was being built there was still a number of weak links in the chain of mountain lands directly controlled by the earl of Gloucester. The land between the rivers Tawe and Neath had been in the hands of Neath Abbey as early as the reign of John.[80] Margam Abbey had acquired Resolven in the uplands of the Welsh lordship of Afan and a large tract of land to the west and south-west of the earl's castle at Llangynwyd. Caerleon Abbey held extensive mountain land in Senghennydd, Meisgyn and Gwynllŵg.

Either with the intention of more effectively containing the Welsh lordship of Afan, or in anticipation of the coming conflict with Humphrey de Bohun, lord of Brecon,[81] Earl Gilbert

---

[79] J. Beverley Smith, 'The Lordship of Glamorgan', *Morgannwg*, ii (1958), pp. 31–37.

[80] See above p. 79.

[81] For the latter, see J. E. Morris, *Welsh Wars of Edward I*, pp. 220–39.

entered into an exchange agreement with the abbey of Neath in April 1289.[82] By the terms of the agreement Adam of Carmarthen, abbot of Neath, granted to Gilbert all his lands and tenements in Briton Ferry (*La Brittone*), a part of the lands of *Assart*, an extensive tract of mountain land between the rivers Tawe and Neath, and land lying between Kilvey hill and the river Neath, with the exception of the fisheries and weirs between the abbey and the sea and rights of access to them. Gilbert granted the abbot and convent in exchange a hundred pounds of annual dry rent from certain specified tenements in the boroughs of Neath, Cowbridge, Cardiff and Caerleon and in the manors of Llanblethian and Llanilltud Fawr, with the exception of wards, homages, reliefs, escheats and other services arising therefrom. If payments of these rents were in arrears, the abbot was permitted to distrain in the tenements whence they were derived until full payment was made.[83]

A number of reasons may have prompted Adam of Carmarthen to take such a momentous step. Difficulties in the management of the lay-brethren may have been one. As late as 1269 a number of them had abandoned their order, taking with them the horses of the father abbot, and this does not appear to have been an isolated incident.[84] The local tenantry, too, were frequently troublesome. Merrick, the sixteenth-century antiquarian who had access to the Register of Neath, stated that this was the main reason for the exchange agreement.[85] His claim is supported by an interesting entry in the General Chapter records of a much earlier date. In 1247 the abbot petitioned the General Chapter 'that permission be granted for the celebration of the feast of St. Margaret in his own house which was frequently disturbed by a profusion of wars, so that he might the more easily obtain the favour of his persecutors who for some reason or other held that virgin in great devotion and veneration and had a chapel dedicated to her'.[86] A further reason which probably carried considerable

---

[82] The agreement is noted in the south Wales chronicle printed in *Arch. Camb.*, 1862, p. 281.
[83] Clark, *Cartae*, v, pp. 1677–9; D. Lewis, 'Notes on the Charters of Neath Abbey', *Arch. Camb.*, 1887, pp. 113–5.
[84] Canivez, *Statuta*, iii, p. 72.
[85] Rice Merrick, *A Booke of Glamorganshires Antiquities*, p. 56.
[86] Canivez, *Statuta*, ii, p. 318. The chapel is mentioned in the exchange agreement and was located above Crumlyn bog.

weight with the abbot was the extensive building activity which was in progress at this time at the abbey and a nearby grange, and the need for ready money which such operations entailed.[87]

The abbey had handed over the whole of the land which less than a century earlier had been purchased from King John for 100 marks. By a stroke of the pen, the abbey was henceforward to derive a considerable portion of its income (in 1291 perhaps a third) from a tenantry over which it had no effective jurisdictional control. Neither the abbot nor the earl could have predicted, when the agreement was made, the economic recession which lay ahead. The power of distraint was of little use when tenements and burgages fell vacant and were not reoccupied, or were reoccupied at lower rents. This appears to have happened during the fourteenth and fifteenth centuries. At the Dissolution the abbey was drawing less than half of the £100 rent which it had acquired by the exchange agreement of 1289.[88]

A further step in abandoning direct control over the abbey estates was taken in 1322. In that year, David, abbot of Neath, and his convent leased to Sir John Inge for life at an annual rental of £13 6s. 8d.

> the manor of Exeforde and all the lands and tenements, mills, meadows, pastures, marshes, liberties and free customs and services both of free tenants and villeins with all their issue which we have in Chubbizete, Scharpecote Niewelonde, Lauercoumbe, Blakelonde and Alschave and elsewhere in all places of the county of Somerset.[89]

The description of Exford as a manor and the careful inclusion of the services owed by free and unfree tenants are a significant indication of the changes which had overtaken the former grange to which the convent of Neath had once considered moving their abbey.[90] In the case of the medium and larger sized granges, 'manorialization' was an essential prerequisite to

---

[87] On the same day as the exchange agreement the earl granted to Neath wood for the building of the monastery and the grange and sheepfold of Tetteberne: see Clark, *Cartae*, v, pp. 1684–5.
[88] *Valor*, iv, p. 351.
[89] Birch, *Neath Abbey*, pp. 123–4.
[90] See above p. 76.

leasing granges as whole units. Few landowners, however wealthy, would be prepared to obtain the lease of a large estate for which there was no labour force bound to the soil and its lord by tenurial ties.

(ii) *Margam Abbey.*

In 1291 the abbot of Margam, perhaps reassured by the generous terms obtained by the abbot of Neath, also entered into an exchange agreement with the earl. The main terms seem to have been drawn up before September, for in that month the General Chapter at Cîteaux gave its consent to the exchange on condition that three Cistercian abbots were present when it was ratified.[91] The abbey had already been roughly treated by the earl and his servants. In 1285 Robert le Veal, sheriff of Glamorgan, had seized the abbey lands at Terrys Grange and New Grange, and sometime later More Grange was also seized into the earl's hands.[92] Though the text of the 1291 agreement is not extant, it would seem from other evidence that the abbot handed over to Gilbert de Clare the grange of Resolven and a good deal of the mountain land around Penhydd and Hafod-y-Porth, receiving in return Terrys Grange and More Grange, common of pasture in Cefn Cribwr and a lease of Kenfig mill, the latter for an annual rent of 8 marks.[93] Despite the earl's pretext that he wished to afforest the lands he had obtained from the abbey, one cannot help detecting more practical motives at work. The possession of Resolven gave the earl a base within the Welsh lordship of Afan, and the mountain lands around Penhydd and Hafod-y-Porth enlarged the extent of Tir Iarll and provided the earl with a more extensive control of the south-eastern frontier of the Afan lordship. It is significant that during the rebellion of Morgan in 1294, the lands involved in the exchange agreements with Neath and Margam were among the targets singled out for devastation by the rebels.[94]

[91] Canivez, *Statuta*, iii, p. 254.
[92] *Arch. Camb.*, 1862, p. 281. Terrys grange is identical with Theodoric's Grange; see F. G. Cowley, 'The Besanding of Theodoric's Grange, Margam', *Arch. Camb.*, 1963, pp. 188–90. For the seizure of More grange; see Clark, *Cartae*, v, p. 1156.
[93] Ibid., pp. 1155–6; *C. Inq. Post Mortem*, iv, p. 323; ibid., v, p. 334.
[94] Ibid., iii, p. 245.

As far as Margam was concerned, the exchange agreement was not a success. On the showing of the available evidence it was patently unjust. As early as 1292 difficulties had arisen between the abbey and the earl. In February the abbot of Cîteaux wrote to Edward I complaining that Gilbert de Clare 'troubles the abbey of Margam without reasonable cause'.[95] Little appears to have been done, however, either to annul the agreement or to enforce a more just settlement.

By 1329 the abbey was in serious straits. In a petition to William la Zouche, lord of Glamorgan, the abbot and convent complained that since the seizure of the mountain lands by Gilbert de Clare, they had been forced to reduce their convent by ten monks. They begged for

> grace and redress of these aforesaid hardships and wilful acts, for it would be a greater act of charity to make redress for these serious wrongs and privations, to restore the alms that have thus been taken away and to bring up to strength the service of God by so many monks than to found over again a new house for a like number.

Perhaps because of the implied hint of a possible dispersal of the remaining monks, the petition was given a sympathetic hearing and a jury empanelled to examine the grievances. They declared that, although there was an agreement with the earl, it was forced upon the abbot and made without the consent of the convent. On the strength of their findings, the so-called agreement of 1291 was annulled and the mountain lands of Resolven, Penhydd and Hafod-y-Porth restored to the abbey.[96] These lands had been in secular hands for nearly thirty years and it seems likely that the grange economy previously operated there had been considerably modified. It is certainly significant that the bishop of Llandaff admitted Margam's claim to tithes of corn and hay from these lands in 1339.[97]

When the exchange agreement of 1291 was drawn up, the abbey was probably already beginning to feel the effects of a

---

[95] *C. Ch. Warrants*, i (1244–1326), p. 31.
[96] Clark, *Cartae*, v, pp. 1155–9. I am indebted to the late Professor Knowles and Mr. W. A. Sullivan, University College, Cardiff, for their comments on the Old French of this passage. Birch's paraphrase (*Margam Abbey*, p. 300) is incorrect.
[97] See above p.

labour shortage on its estates. This at least would help to explain the elaborate arrangements which the abbey made in that year to secure the recruitment as lay-brother of Madoc Vydir, a middle-aged man (possibly a widower) with at least three sons. In a written deed his sons bound themselves to indemnify the abbot for all debts and things touching their father, Madoc Vydir of Llandyfodwg, lay-brother of Margam, against the claims of Gilbert de Clare, his heirs, assigns, executors, bailiffs and servants.[98] In 1325 John, son of John Nichol bequeathed his land to Margam in return for being made a 'free serjeant' of the abbey with a fixed allowance of food and drink.[99]

The impression gained from these mere fragments of information is reinforced by a comparison of the acreages given in the valuation of 1291 with those given in an extent drawn up in 1336.[100] Between these dates there is a noticeable decline in the arable acreage recorded for five of the abbey granges. The location of the granges concerned is of some importance. The arable acreage of Stormy, situated within walking distance of Horgrove (a manorialized hamlet belonging to the abbey), dropped from seven to six carucates. At the grange of *Gardino* (not identified but certainly in the region of Newcastle, Bridgend), the arable acreage had dropped from eight to seven carucates. At Llanfeuthin, where the presence of labour services and assised rents has already been noted, the arable acreage dropped from six to five carucates.[101] Llangeinor, which had one caracute of arable in 1291, had dropped out of cultivation altogether by 1336, and it comes as little surprise that in the following year the abbey forfeited the property to the lord of Ogmore through non-payment of rent.[102] At Horgrove the one carucate of arable demesne recorded in 1291 had dropped to half a carucate.

One looks in vain in the 1336 extent for a corresponding rise in assised rents to account for the fall in the amount of arable demesne, but the conclusion is difficult to resist that in certain

[98] Clark, *Cartae*, vi, pp. 2356–7.
[99] Ibid., iii, pp. 1131–2.
[100] Ibid., iv, pp. 1196–9.
[101] Llanfeuthin is styled a 'manor' as early as 1347: see Clark, *Cartae*, iv, pp. 1264–6.
[102] Ibid., p. 1574. Cf. Birch, *Margam Abbey*, p. 342.

marginal lands direct exploitation of the arable was becoming increasingly unprofitable and that even on grange lands situated in the more fertile grain-producing areas, a labour shortage or increased labour costs was prompting the monks to lease small parcels of grange lands to tenants for rents or services or both, which for some reason or other were not included in the extent drawn up in 1336.

Direct evidence of leasing on the abbey estates during the fourteenth century, is rare. While there are records of fourteen leases for the period 1188 to 1300,[103] only four have survived for the first half of the fourteenth century and the records of the second half of the century add only one to this total.[104] There is little reason to suppose that the extant deeds are a complete collection of the abbey muniments, but one should perhaps expect in a period of falling land values that leases were committed to writing less frequently than during a period of land hunger.[105]

With one exception all the extant leases are either of burgages or of lands situated within the patchwork of strips surrounding manorial centres such as Kenfig, Corneli, Bonvilston and Newcastle, where in the thirteenth century the abbey was attempting to consolidate small demesnes. They fell within the class of 'less useful' lands which the abbey could not profitably exploit from main grange centres. The General Chapter, as we have seen, had allowed the leasing of such lands in 1220. The extant lease for 1349, however, differs significantly from the earlier leases in that the land leased, though small in acreage, lay within a consolidated grange within the bounds of the original endowment of the abbey. The abbot and convent leased to John Lange and Ieuan ap Phelipot 'eight acres of arable land from the demesne of their grange of Terrys'.[106] The words used seem to suggest that Terrys grange was already assuming manorial features and that this was not the first tenement established within its bounds. The land was to be held for life on condition that the tenants performed specified

[103] Clark, *Cartae*, i, pp. 193–4, ii, pp. 355, 471, 517, 531, 539–40, 576–8, 613, 623, 687–8, iii, pp. 737, 880–1, 1006–7.
[104] Ibid., pp. 988–9, 1005–6, iv, pp. 1227–8, 1267–8.
[105] I owe this suggestion to Professor Glanmor Williams.
[106] Clark, *Cartae*, iv, pp. 1267–8.

works in repairing the sea walls. It seems probable that the effects of the Black Death had intensified the labour shortage on the abbey estates and was making a policy of leasing no longer one of expediency but of harsh necessity.

(iii) *Caerleon Abbey*

Caerleon, alias Llantarnam, like Margam, had also entered into some form of exchange agreement with Gilbert de Clare, though even less is known of the details. In 1317 the abbot and convent petitioned the king that whereas they had once been the richest and most enfeoffed abbey of all Morgannwg, Earl Gilbert had taken from them the greater part of their possessions, promising them lands and rents elsewhere. This promise was not fulfilled. His son, Gilbert, had undertaken to honour the agreement on his return from Scotland, but was killed at Bannockburn in 1314. As a result, wrote the abbot,

> our abbey is so poor that it cannot there sustain except barely twenty monks where there were wont to be, before their possessions were taken away, sixty monks serving God, and more.[107]

The abbey had also been seriously affected by the revolt of Llywelyn Bren in 1316. Llywelyn had, either before or during the rebellion, desired part of the abbey's lands, and because of the local power and influence he wielded, the abbot was forced to grant lands to him, some for life, and some for term of years. After the defeat of Llywelyn these lands had escheated to the Crown and were being administered by royal bailiffs. The abbey's tenants in the mountains were put to ransom. In a petition to the king the abbot and convent pleaded that the lands leased to Llywelyn should be restored to them, that they should be permitted to ransom their tenants ('their people will not engage in war except they are surrounded on all sides by men of war') and that the keeper of the lands of Glamorgan should pay them the ten marks which the king had granted them from the issues. Only the latter part of the petition seems to have been granted.[108]

---

[107] P.R.O., Ancient Petition 8368, paraphrased by Bradney, *History of Monmouthshire*, vol. iii, part ii, pp. 224–5.

[108] P.R.O., SC 8/119/5948. The date of the petition must have been between 14 March and 15 May 1317: see *CCR.*, 1313–18, pp. 406. Cf. also Bradney, op. cit., p. 225.

(iv) *Tintern Abbey*

On the Tintern Abbey estates, the dual economy of large demesne granges interspersed with manorial vills and hamlets, which has already been noted as a feature of Cistercian estates at this period, is particularly in evidence. The largest of Tintern's granges devoted to arable husbandry—Trelleck (6 carucates in 1291), Rogerstone (4 carucates), Assart (3 carucates), Pellenni (3 carucates)—lay in a compact group west of the Wye river within a radius of three miles of the abbey. Even by 1291 it is probable that the monastic demesnes of these granges had been considerably curtailed by leasing or by the reversion of land to waste.[109] At the hub of this group of estates lay Porthcaseg, which served as a central court for the abbey tenants west of the Wye. The court was held at irregular intervals but generally not less than three times a year.

The extant records of this court for the last part of the thirteenth century and the first half of the fourteenth are unevenly distributed.[110] Their limitations in other respects should also be appreciated. The court of Porthcaseg, like other manorial courts, was mainly concerned with day-to-day business: levying amercements for breaches of manorial custom and for disturbing the 'peace' of the abbot, recording entry fines and heriots paid by incoming tenants and appointing juries to arbitrate disputes. The minutiae of such records, particularly from such a small and unevenly distributed sample, can hardly be expected to reflect major changes in the abbey economy.

The court rolls are valuable, nevertheless, in showing on every part of the abbey estates west of the Wye, a numerous tenantry not of recent creation but deeply rooted in the soil. As one would expect from an abbey situated in the Welshry, the Welsh element in this tenantry was strong if not predominant.

---

[109] Between 1148 and 1176 Richard, earl of Pembroke had confirmed to Tintern 'twelve carucates of arable land in the "lawn" (*landa*) of Trillec': *C.Ch.R., 1300–26*, p. 98. In 1291, however, the grange of Trelleck contained only six carucates of arable.

[110] The records of the number of court days for which extant rolls exist are as follows: one court day for 1262, two for 1263 (N.L.W., Badminton MS. 1639), four for 1269 (1640), two for 1302–3 (1641), one for 1312 (1642), one for 1315 (1643), one for 1331 (1644), three for 1340, five for 1341, one for 1342 (1645), one for 1349 (1646) and one for 1357 (1647). For the purposes of this study, I have not examined the rolls beyond this date.

They lived in vills and hamlets on the fringes or in the vicinity of the granges of Trelleck, Rogerstone, Merthyrgeryn and More. To such tenants the grange and its buildings were as familiar as the abbot's demesne and his manorial hall on the estates of Benedictine houses. It was there that many of their labour services were performed and it was the centre on many occasions where disputes with neighbouring tenants were thrashed out and settled.[111]

The more enterprising of these tenants were increasing their holdings by entering into profitable marriages, by assarting land with or without the licence of the abbot, and by obtaining leases of small parcels of monastic demesne. Thus, in 1302 Nicholas Hathol paid 2s. entry fine for a tenement which belonged to Alice Derneford, whose daughter he had married, for an annual rent of 6d., suit of court, heriot and relief.[112] The Dernefords belonged to a knightly family whose members figure occasionally as parties and witnesses to abbey charters.[113] In 1312 Nicholas le Wyte paid an entry fine of two *lagenae* of wine for a certain plot of waste land between his house and Gatehull for an annual rent of 12d.[114] In 1331 Roger Crolle paid 6s. 8d. entry fine for one acre of land lying 'in campo de Wondy', rendering for life 3d. annually for all services.[115] The pressures exerted by such tenants, intent on enlarging their holdings and improving their livelihood, were to assist in the gradual disintegration of the abbey granges, large and small.

The amount of entry fines and amercements recorded for individual courts fluctuated considerably during the first half of the fourteenth century. In the absence of a more evenly distributed run of court rolls, it would be unwise to attempt to assess their significance. The format of the rolls, however, would seem to suggest that the abbey was paying more attention

[111] Badminton 1639 (court for April 1263): 'John ab Ithel, complainant, and John textor, Blethin ab Ythel, defendants, have taken a love day at the grange of Trellek . . .'. Cf. Badminton 1639 (court held in August 1263): John balle 'given a day at the grange of More'.
[112] Badminton 1641.
[113] *C.Ch.R., 1300–26*, pp. 98, 99, 104, 105. See also E. Owen, *Catalogue of Manuscripts Relating to Wales*, part iii, p. 623.
[114] Badminton 1642. For an unlicensed assart, see Badminton 1639.
[115] Badminton 1644. Tintern had only a small extent of demesne at Undy. In 1291 it consisted of only 19 acres of arable and 14 acres of meadow. For an earlier lease (1269) of 12 acres of arable and 2 acres of meadow, see Badminton 1640.

to curial revenue during this period than it had been in the thirteenth century. In the extant rolls for 1262–3 and 1269 only the value of entry fines was noted in the margins of the rolls and no attempt was made to total the perquisites received. The roll for 1302 is the first one extant where amercements are noted in the margin. By 1312 it was becoming customary for the total perquisites received to be entered at the foot of the roll. In the rolls for the early 'forties one gains the impression that the manorial rights of the abbot were being more vigorously exploited. Fines for unlicensed marriages and for *leyrewite* are particularly prominent in these years. There is evidence, too, of active, personal resentment against the abbot and monks. In May 1340 Phillip Riband was brought before the court 'for the divers transgressions he had committed and for the contemptuous and arrogant words he had spoken against the abbot and monks'.[116] One should be on one's guard against lifting the more colourful entries in the rolls to suit a theory. Yet there is evidence from another source which shows that in the first half of the fourteenth century the abbey was exerting a more than ordinary pressure on its tenantry, especially with regard to carriage duties, *merchet* and *heriot*. Acle manor in Norfolk was admittedly a comparatively recent acquisition.[117] However, the attempt of the abbot, Hugh le Wyke, to fine his villeins there £1,000 for not rendering their manorial obligations, and the remarkable response of the villeins in taking their grievances before the court of King's Bench in 1306, indicates that the abbot was anxious to exploit to the limit his rights to labour services and fines of a kind which had in earlier centuries been a recognized feature of servile tenure.[118] The abbot won his case, but as late as 1346 one of his successors found it necessary or desirable to obtain an attested copy of the findings and have it enrolled on the patent roll.[119] The reason for this anxiety is not too difficult to explain. The building of the new, enlarged abbey church, begun as early as 1269 and completed in 1301,[120]

---

[116] Badminton 1645, sheet 9.
[117] See below p. 266.
[118] *Year Books, 34–35 Edward I* (Rolls Series), pp. 309–11. I am indebted to the Rev. D. H. Williams for this reference to the case.
[119] *CPR., 1345–8*, pp. 162–3.
[120] William Worcestre, *Itineraries*, p. 61 n. 2.

was followed by new buildings in the domestic range, notably the abbot's hall.[121] Such prolonged building operations put a heavy strain on the abbey finances. Indeed, Illtyd Gardiner, in his study of the abbey architecture was probably correct in inferring that the new buildings 'crippled the finances of the abbey'.[122]

Of the effects of the Black Death on the abbey estates, there is little evidence. There is no mention of the pestilence in the extant court roll for May 1349, when it was already taking a heavy toll of lives in neighbouring manors.[123] A more than usual number of deaths is recorded, however, and a new reeve was elected. All the tenements vacated were taken up by close or distant relatives of their previous holders.

At the end of the fourteenth and the beginning of the fifteenth century, the fortunate survival of a short run of bailiff's accounts for Merthyrgeryn,[124] of reeve's accounts for Porthcaseg,[125] and of two cellarer's accounts[126] throws valuable retrospective light on developments at some of the abbey granges and on the abbey administration generally.

Merthyrgeryn was in the late-thirteenth century one of Tintern's smaller granges with a demesne of two and a half carucates and nineteen acres of arable. There were also detached parcels of demesne lying in the vicinity of the grange: at *Hardstrete* (one carucate), in St. Bride's parish (thirty acres), near Magor (fifty-two acres) and at Undy (nineteen acres).[127] By 1387 most of this demesne had been leased out and a predominantly *rentier* economy was being operated.[128] Of the total of £15 6s. 10d. received by the bailiff, only £1 9s. 4d. was received from the exploitation of the much-reduced demesne. The remaining receipts were drawn from rents (78s. 11d.), sale of pasture (11s. 4d.), pleas and perquisites of four courts

---

[121] O. E. Craster, *Tintern Abbey, Monmouthshire*, p. 19.
[122] *Jnl. Brit. Arch. Assoc.*, xxxv (1929), p. 5.
[123] Badminton 1646; W. Rees, *South Wales and the March*, pp. 241–3.
[124] Badminton 1571 for the years 1387–8, 1388–9.
[125] Badminton 1572 for the years 1392–3 (sheet 4), 1393–4 (sheet 2), 1394–5 (sheet 3), 1396–7 (sheet 1), and Badminton 1574 for the year 1411–2.
[126] Badminton 1575 (1411–2) and 1576 (1434–5).
[127] *Taxatio*, p. 282b.
[128] Badminton 1571. The mill of Merthyrgeryn, not mentioned in the *Taxatio* of 1291, had been farmed out to one of the abbey tenants as early as 1302; see Badminton 1641.

(19*s*. 1*d*.), and 'foreign' receipts (£8 2*s*. 2*d*.). This latter item is misleading. It consisted in large measure of rents derived from leases of former demesne land.[129]

It has been suggested on earlier pages that in the 1291 valuation, figures for rents of assise may have been taken from account rolls of an average year. At that date assised rents on the whole of the abbey estate were valued at £3 13*s*. 3*d*. At the end of the fourteenth century, the Porthcaseg reeve's accounts show that even in the very limited area under his jurisdiction, receipts from assised rents were more than double this figure. The earliest of the rolls shows how this increase was being achieved.[130] In the year 1392–3 receipts from assised rents amounted to £6 0*s*. 4½*d*. The roll also records separately under 'new rents' £2 16*s*. 2¾*d*. received from seventeen fairly recently created tenancies.[131] Of the lands leased only two parcels were carved out of the waste. The remaining fifteen leases were of demesne land either at the grange of Rogerstone or at isolated demesnes situated at such places as Cophull and Pencrek. Ten of the leases were for life, two at farm, one for three years and one for thirty years. In the following year a new rental was drawn up, and in the account for 1393–4 and subsequent accounts the 'new rents', with one exception, were merged with the assised rents.[132]

The extant cellarer's accounts are chiefly of value in demonstrating how radically the traditional methods of Cistercian administration and estate management had been altered between 1200 and 1400. In the twelfth century, the Cistercian cellarer exercised a direct control over the farming of the abbey estates and was the central receiving officer for all revenues.[133] His wide experience often made him an obvious choice for succession on the death or resignation of the abbot. The cellarer's account for 1411–12 shows that much of this power had

---

[129] Badminton 1571.

[130] Badminton 1572, sheet 4.

[131] Some of the tenancies were created within the previous ten years: *Et de Vs. rec. de Moris ap Hopkyn pro terra dominicali apud pencrek sibi dimissa ad terminum xxx annorum, hoc anno vii. Et de xxs rec. de terra dominicali de Cophull dimissa Eeuan ap Howell . . . ad terminum iij annorum, hoc anno primo.*

[132] The demesne land of Cophull in the accounts after 1393 is recorded as let to farm for 20*s*.

[133] Gerald of Wales's remarks (*Opera*, vi, p. 45) show that this central control still obtained at the end of the twelfth century.

been lost in the intervening centuries. By this date the cellarer accounted for barely a tenth of the abbey's income.[134] He was still an important and ubiquitous official but his power was nominal rather than real.[135] The reins of financial control had passed to two treasurers or bursars,[136] who acted as central receivers for the bulk of the abbey's revenue and made payments from the receipts to other officials, including the cellarer. When this development took place it is difficult to say. It may have occurred before 1240 since bursars were well established at Tintern's daughter house of Kingswood by this date.[137]

By the beginning of the fifteenth century, the cellarer of Tintern had become an administrative 'odd job man'. He was frequently on the road, journeying from estate to estate. He made small purchases of stock, hired and paid for the services of shepherds, harvest-workers and labourers, carpenters and tilers engaged in repair work at the abbey or the manors.[138] Much of the power he still wielded as the abbot's deputy came from his presiding at the manorial courts with the steward, an official who was acquiring a position of growing authority and prestige on the estates of most abbeys. Stewards were at first drawn from landowners of modest rank who lived in the vicinity of the abbey. Thus, John Lovel, who held land around Corneli and was perhaps lord of that small vill, was steward of Margam and represented the abbey in a plea concerning wreck in 1333.[139] In the later middle ages there was a growing tendency for the monks to select their stewards from the ranks of the nobility or the wealthier gentry, men who wielded great political as well as local power.[140] The prominent position occupied by the steward in the administration of the abbey estates is sympto-

[134] Total receipts for the year came to £27 2s. 11d. and some of this was received from the treasurers.
[135] His name still continued to appear with that of the abbot at the head of the Porthcaseg court rolls.
[136] They are called 'treasurers' in the cellarer's account but 'bursars' in the Porthcaseg reeve's account of the same date (Badminton 1574).
[137] V. R. Perkins and P. H. Jeayes, 'Documents relating to the Cistercian Monastery of St. Mary, Kingswood', *Trans. Brist. Glouc. Arch. Soc.*, xxii (1899), pp. 179–256. Cf. Knowles, *Religious Orders*, i, p. 76.
[138] Badminton 1575.
[139] Clark, *Cartae*, iv, pp. 1186–7.
[140] Glanmor Williams, *Welsh Church*, pp. 367–8. Cf. also A. E. Levett, *Studies in Manorial History*, pp. 104–5.

matic of the withdrawal of the monks from the direct exploitation of their lands. This is also apparent at a lower level. The *grangiarius* or *magister grangiae* makes no appearance in the cellarer's accounts of 1411–12 and 1434–35. When a property is mentioned it is invariably found to be in the hands of a bailiff. Even Tintern's home farm, Riding (called in 1291 the grange of Assart), was managed by a bailiff.[141] The spiritual property would appear to have been farmed out by this date.[142]

(v) *Strata Florida Abbey*

The pall of obscurity which hangs over developments on the estates of the abbeys of west and central Wales during the fourteenth century is rarely relieved. Attention has already been directed to the agreements drawn up between the bishop of St. David's and the abbeys of Whitland and Strata Florida in 1338 and 1339.[143] The agreements provide valuable testimony that tenements were being carved out of the grange lands of these abbeys and farmed by dependent tenants. Of equal interest are the terms used to describe the tenants involved. They are described in the agreements as *coloni partiarii* and *tenentes censuales*.[144] The *colonus partiarius* was equivalent to the French *métayer*, who paid his rents with a part of the produce of the land he farmed.[145] The censory tenants were rent-paying tenants who held their land on a customary basis and, unlike the *coloni*, usually held their land only for life. It seems likely that many of both classes of tenant were originally of villein stock 'whom the favourable hand of time hath much enfranchised'.[146] In Pembrokeshire, at least, the *coloni* and censory tenants continued to owe labour services and incidents such as heriots as well as rents in cash and kind.

---

[141] Badminton 1575.
[142] Ibid.: *Et de* [damaged] *s.iiijd. receptis de firmario ecclesie de Lyde.*
[143] See above p. 186.
[144] S. W. Williams, *Strata Florida Abbey*, appendix p. li. The translation of the terms is faulty.
[145] Lewis and Short, *Latin Dictionary*, p. 1308, and *Mediae Latinitatis Lexicon Minus*, ed. J. F. Niermeyer, fasc. 8 (1960), p. 768.
[146] See the details given of the Pembrokeshire *coloni* and censory tenants in B. E. Howells, 'Pembrokeshire Farming', *NLWJ.*, ix (1956), pp. 414–6. A number of former villeins were being received on the grange lands of Aberconwy at the beginning of the fourteenth century: see R. W. Hays, *Aberconway Abbey*, p. 90.

The evidence from the tithe agreements is supplemented by two brief lists of the possessions of the abbey of Strata Florida which are entered in the Register and Chronicle of Aberconwy.[147] The first list records the main temporal and spiritual possessions of the abbey and a money value is given to each item. Twelve temporal possessions whose value add up to £102 1s. 8d. are noted, and two churches: Llangurig valued at £20 and Pencarreg valued at £10. In the second list nine properties are recorded, for seven of which are given varying numbers of truggs, presumably of oats. Two of the properties are given a money value: '*Y dewarchen*' (Dolfeithen?) is given a money value of five nobles, which corresponds exactly with the value given to *Dywarthen* in the first list.[148] Cwmteuddwr is also given a money value of £6, which corresponds exactly with that given it in the previous list. Three places included in the first list do not occur in the second (Cwmystwyth, Nantbey and Aber-miwl) and one place is mentioned in the second list which does not occur in the first (Morfa Mawr). The names of the properties and the money values given them correspond more closely to those given in the Dissolution accounts than to those in the *Taxatio* of 1291. There is little reason to believe, however, that the lists were drawn up later than 1400 and they may well belong, like the list of Aberconwy's possessions which precedes them in the manuscript, to the years 1356 or 1357.[149]

In the absence of even a brief, descriptive rubric, the lists are difficult to interpret. The list of the number of truggs due from possessions named in the second list shows that the *coloni partiarii* of the agreement of 1339 were widely distributed over the abbey estates and were particularly numerous on the granges of Hafodwen (232 truggs) and Morfa Mawr (192 truggs).[150] The lists provide a valuable but tenuous link in the chain of evidence connecting the *coloni partiarii* of 1339 with the abbey tenants who owed substantial rents in kind at the Dissolution.[151]

[147] 'Register and Chronicle of the Abbey of Aberconway', *Camden Miscellany*, 1847, p. 9.
[148] The noble, first minted by Edward III, was worth 6s. 8d.
[149] R. W. Hays, *Aberconway Abbey*, pp. 105f.
[150] The other figures given are Pennardd (28), Mefenydd (92), Blaenaeron (88), Anhuniog (48) and Morfa Bychan (12).
[151] G. D. Owen, 'Agrarian Conditions and Changes in West Wales during the Sixteenth Century', (University of Wales Ph.D. thesis, 1935), pp. 190–5.

(vi) *Cwm-hir Abbey*

For the poor moorland abbey of Cwm-hir, the evidence is even scarcer than that for Strata Florida. The entry in the *Taxatio* of 1291 for the abbey's distant grange of Nantyrarian, *duas carucatas terrae inculte cum uno molendino et parte alterius molendini*,[152] suggests that here, as on the granges of Margam Abbey, the frontiers of cultivation were receding. The earliest evidence for leasing comes from an illuminating entry in an inquisition made of the lands of Thomas, earl of Warwick in 1397:

> On and after the day of his forfeiture the said earl held in his possession to himself and his heirs the two granges of Kybalva and Carnayth in Elvell, worth . . . *s.* net yearly, belonging to the abbey of Combehire, at a yearly rent of 26 quarters of wheat, but by what title or on what condition the jurors in no wise know.[153]

Other details provided by the inquisition show that parcels of these granges had already been leased out to under-tenants. The presence of a flock of 251 sheep at the grange of Gabalfa suggests that the abbey was making use of a stock-and-land lease, but this is not certain.[154]

The case histories examined would seem to indicate a general movement away from the traditional Cistercian economy of direct exploitation to one based on rents. If one excepts Neath Abbey, which had adopted a predominantly *rentier* economy well before the Black Death, the movement was a slow one, having its origins in the thirteenth century but gradually gathering momentum in response to financial difficulties and the economic changes of the fourteenth century. Leasing of granges as whole units would appear to have been rare before the Black Death. Strata Florida had let to farm its grange of Dolfeithin before 1291 and Neath Abbey had leased its grange

---

[152] *Taxatio*, p. 276b.
[153] *Cal. Inq. Misc. (Chancery)*, vi (1392–99), no. 228, p. 107.
[154] The expedient of letting out the demesne with the stock in return for every third sheaf harvested had become prevalent in the Radnor area by this time; see W. Rees, *South Wales and the March*, pp. 182–3.

of Exford in 1322. Both granges were situated at a distance from their abbeys and were consequently more difficult to exploit directly. A richer documentation would doubtless have furnished more examples.

A number of the Cistercian granges in south Wales were too large and too undeveloped in the manorial sense to be leased as whole units at this time and continued, as far as one can tell, under immediate abbatial control. Within granges of this kind the most significant change which can be detected from the evidence is the diminution in the extent of the demesne. On some granges this was due to land being allowed to revert to waste.[155] On other granges there is sufficient evidence to suggest that the demesne was diminishing in extent through the creation of new tenancies. The creation of comparatively recent tenancies can be inferred on the estates of Strata Florida and on the upland granges of Margam before the middle of the fourteenth century. A number of the lowland granges of Margam and Tintern were acquiring distinct 'manorial' features at about the same time.

Suggestive as the evidence is, one would like to know more about developments on some of the larger granges in south-east Wales. Margam's grange of Llangewydd was a grange in the true Cistercian sense in the early-thirteenth century,[156] and still comprised a fairly large arable demesne in 1336. After this date the available evidence throws no light on its history until the Dissolution. The same is true of the neighbouring grange of Stormy. By the early-sixteenth century, this grange had been divided into a 'Greater' and a 'Lesser' and the latter of these had been further divided into moieties.[157] The pre-Dissolution evidence, however, gives no indication of the date at which these changes took place. Perhaps more light will be thrown on these problems when scholars have examined in greater detail the sixteenth-century evidence for the monastic estates of south-east Wales.

[155] One example of this was Tintern's land at *Platelanda*. The abbey had three carucates here in 1291. In 1302 the abbey exchanged the 'manor' of *Platelanda* for Roger, earl of Norfolk's manor of *Aluredeston* (*C.Ch.R., 1300–26*, p. 31). In 1306 *Plattelond* consisted of 130 acres of arable, 100 acres of waste and 7 acres of pasture (*Cal. Inq. Post. Mortem*, iv, p. 296).

[156] See above pp. 80–1, 182–3.

[157] Birch, *Margam Abbey*, pp. 354, 365.

V. THE QUEST FOR NEW ENDOWMENTS.

A policy of leasing, however well planned and carefully regulated, usually resulted, initially at least, in a fall in the income which in more favourable times would have been received when temporal and spiritual assets were directly exploited. In an attempt to recoup some of their losses and to bolster their finances in the face of a growing economic recession, most houses tried to obtain additional endowments. In spite of the statute of Mortmain, land was not too difficult to obtain. Llanthony Prima, though heavily in debt, was acquiring fairly large grants of land in the last two decades of the thirteenth century.[158] As the fourteenth century advanced and land values fell, landowners were only too glad to lease or sell waste and marginal land to those who were anxious or enterprising enough to farm it. The abbey of Grace Dieu, a meanly-endowed house, which had been forced by financial difficulties to alienate the richest of its possessions in 1267,[159] acquired in 1334 two messuages, four carucates of land, twelve acres of meadow, twenty acres of pasture and twelve acres of wood at Colrugge and Aston.[160] In 1338 the abbot paid the king 40s. for '36 acres of waste of the king's soil of Wyget and Langeford within the metes of the forest of Dene' near the abbey grange of Stowe.[161]

By this period, however, most of the religious houses were less interested in land per se than in fixed rents and in assets which could be readily farmed out for a fixed cash return. In the early part of the century the abbot and convent of St. Dogmaels petitioned the king and his council that 'they may have help from a lady who wishes to advance them by a rent of eleven shillings in the town of Cardigan',[162] and in 1320 the abbot obtained the king's pardon for appropriating without licence

---

[158] CPR., 1281-92, p. 477; E. Owen, Catalogue of Manuscripts Relating to Wales in the British Museum, part iii, pp. 682-3.
[159] The abbey leased the manor of Penyard Regis to Joan de Knovile in 1267 for an annual rent of 1 lb. of cumin and a down-payment of £200; see C.Ch.R., 1257-1300, p. 304. The arrangement was virtually a sale as royal officials were later to recognize; see Rotuli Hundredorum, i, p. 176b.
[160] CPR., 1330-34, p. 523.
[161] CFR., 1337-47, p. 65.
[162] P.R.O., Ancient Petition 6880, transl. in E. Pritchard, St. Dogmael's Abbey, p. 52.

the church of Maenclochog and two annexed chapels.[163]
Pembroke Priory acquired in 1299 the church of St. Michael,
Castlemartin, and in 1301 a perch of land and the advowson of
Manorbier.[164] Haverfordwest Priory acquired the church of St.
Ismael in Lambston in 1331.[165] In 1348 Brecon Priory received
a royal licence to appropriate the church of Agmondesham in
the diocese of Lincoln but does not appear to have secured
permanent possession.[166] The most spectacular gains during
the period were made by Carmarthen Priory. For a house
extended at a mere £60, 'manifest poverty', the canonical
prerequisite of appropriation, was much in evidence.[167] The
history of the priory's appropriations during the fourteenth
century illustrates more clearly than for any other Welsh house
the difficulties involved. The complex negotiations which
resulted in the appropriation of the church of Llanllwni
extended from 1291 to 1333. In 1291 over a score of Welshmen
granted to the priory one messuage, which constituted the glebe,
and all their share in the advowson of the church. In 1309
another large body of Welshmen, who also claimed rights of
patronage, granted land and their interest in the advowson to
Walter Winter, son of Thomas Winter of Carmarthen. In the
same year Edward II gave the priory licence to appropriate
half of the church which was said to be valued at five marks. In
1329 Walter Winter granted the priory two acres and the
advowson of half the church with licence to appropriate. By
1333 the church had been sufficiently 'consolidated' for
complete appropriation. It was formally appropriated to the
priory in the same year by Henry, bishop of St. David's.[168]

During the Black Prince's tenure of the principality, Carmarthen priory acquired two other valuable churches:
Llanfihangel Iorath and Llanybydder.[169] According to the
prior, William Symons, writing in 1367, they were worth 'in
common years' 100 marks.[170] The priory owed much of its

---

[163] Ibid., pp. 82–3.
[164] CPR., 1330–34, pp. 67–8.
[165] CPR., 1324–27, p. 50.
[166] CPR., 1348–50, p. 39.
[167] CCR., 1333–37, pp. 635–6.
[168] Carm. Cart., nos. 46–50.
[169] Ibid., nos. 65–7, 69–72.
[170] Ibid., no. 74.

comparative prosperity at the Dissolution to the efforts of indefatigable fourteenth-century priors like William Symons. In 1360, when William was still in office, his convent voted him an anniversary obit in recognition of the 'service, sweat and labours which he still expends to the advantage of our house'. It is an unfortunate comment on the rigour with which the Augustinian rule was maintained at this time that the obit was also to be made the occasion for the distribution of 20s. among the canons.[171]

The gains made by the Cistercians during the fourteenth century, even taken as a whole, were not impressive. As with the Benedictines and Augustinians, they were unevenly distributed between one house and another and widely separated in time. The houses of west and central Wales, Whitland, Strata Florida and Cwm-hir, gained little if anything during the period. After the statute of Mortmain, would-be donors to religious houses were obliged to secure royal licences before alienating their lands and these licences were enrolled. It seems unlikely that major grants were made which escaped the vigilance of the royal officials. Apart from a grant by David de Rupe of common of pasture in Presely to the abbey of Whitland in 1303, and a royal confirmation to the same abbey of a number of grants, one of which may have been recent, there is little to record for these houses.[172] In the unsettled conditions of the fourteenth century, even the record of a grant to a religious house is no guarantee that the house gained possession. In his desperate flight westward in 1326, Edward II had nothing to lose by being generous. He granted to Margam Abbey his manor of Kentone, and, if the grant did not materialize, lands and rents to the value of £50 elsewhere.[173] There is no evidence that the monks acquired either seisin of the manor or the compensation. In 1325 royal licence was given to Caerleon Abbey to appropriate the church of Llangathen, but the monks never gained permanent possession.[174]

[171] Ibid., no. 75.
[172] E. J. L. Scott, 'Some Original Documents relating to the South Part of Pembrokeshire', *Jnl. Brit. Arch. Assoc.*, xli (1885), p. 168; *CPR., 1313–17*, p. 348.
[173] *CPR., 1324–27*, p. 336.
[174] *CPR., 1324–27*, p. 94. The same church was granted to the nuns of Chester in 1362: see Glanmor Williams, *Welsh Church*, p. 165.

Tintern was among the more fortunate of the south Wales abbeys. Under the beneficent patronage of Roger Bigod, earl of Norfolk, the abbey made permanent acquisitions of considerable value. The Norfolk manor of Acle, granted to the abbey by the earl in 1302, must have added between £20 and £50 to the abbey's income.[175] Later in the same year the earl granted the abbey his manor of Alvington (*Aluredeston*) in Gloucestershire in exchange for the manor of *Platelanda*.[176] In 1307 the king allowed the abbey to retain the church of Halvergate (Norwich diocese) which had been 'wrongfuly appropriated',[177] and sometime between 1291 and 1351 the abbey also acquired the valuable church of Lydd in Kent.[178]

It was unfortunate for the Cistercians that by the time they had completely abandoned the restraint they had exercised in former centuries in acquiring spiritual income, such income was becoming increasingly difficult to obtain. In 1311 the abbey of Neath succeeded in securing a more equitable share of the tithe from its appropriated church of Cadoxton-juxta-Neath,[179] and before 1344 it had secured the appropriation of the church of Neath itself and of the church of St. Donat's.[180] Somewhat earlier, the poor house of Grace Dieu had acquired the church of Skenfrith.[181] Margam Abbey was comparatively late in the field. It acquired the advowson of the church of Llangynwyd and one acre of land in 1331,[182] and before 1349 had appropriated the church without first obtaining a royal licence.[183] On Hugh Despenser's death in 1349, the advowson was recovered by the king and a royal licence allowing the abbey to appropriate was not issued until 1353.[184] Margam retained this church until the Dissolution.

---

[175] *C.Ch.R., 1300–26*, p. 31. Acle had an 'extented' value of £14 13s. 4d. at the time of Domesday; see *VCH, Norfolk*, ii, pp. 56–7. In 1535 it was the richest of all the abbey's possessions and valued at £50: *Valor*, iv, p. 370.

[176] *C.Ch.R., 1300–26*, p. 31.

[177] *CPR., 1301–1307*, p. 531.

[178] *Registrum Simonis de Langham Cantuariensis Arch.*, p. 394.

[179] *Taxatio*, p. 279b; Glamorgan County Record Office, Tyrwhitt Drake Collection, D/D TD 18.

[180] *C.P.Pets.*, i, pp. 40, 62.

[181] The advowson was acquired in 1291 (*CPR., 1281–92*, p. 451), and it seems probable that it was appropriated soon afterwards.

[182] Clark, *Cartae*, iii, pp. 1172–3.

[183] A. Leslie Evans, *Margam Abbey*, pp. 81–2.

[184] Clark, *Cartae*, iv, pp. 1290–1.

Most of Margam's appropriations belong to the last quarter of the fourteenth century and were made to alleviate the distress caused by recurrent outbreaks of the pestilence. Again, however, it should be emphasized that the record of a licence to appropriate is not necessarily proof that the appropriation became effective. Two royal licences were issued in 1377 for the appropriation of St. Fagans Church to Margam Abbey, but the abbey never appears to have obtained permanent possession.[185] In the 'eighties the abbey incurred considerable expense in obtaining the churches of Aberafan and Pen-llin.[186] The former church was an asset of doubtful value. At the Dissolution the vicarage was worth £10 10s. 8d., but the abbey, as rector, could only claim tithes to the value of £1 13s. 4d.[187]

It is not difficult to find reasons for the relative failure of monasteries to acquire additional endowments in the four-teenth century. A period of falling land values and general economic dislocation created intense competition among landowners for sources of fixed income. In such an age, when the monastic ideal had lost much of its social prestige, the monasteries could hardly hope to make spectacular gains. Well into the fifteenth century, many of them were fully preoccupied in defending their existing possessions against secular encroachment. With the exception perhaps of Tintern and Carmarthen, the south Wales houses had no powerful patrons near at hand or sufficiently interested to give them substantial assistance. The emerging families of local stock were busy establishing their own fortunes. For many of them, the monasteries were possible sources for exploitation rather than outlets for their material acts of piety and benefaction.

---

[185] CPR., 1377–8, p. 8. St. Fagans was not an appropriated church in 1535; see Valor, iv, p. 348.

[186] Birch, Margam Abbey, pp. 319–23.

[187] C. A. H. Green, Notes on Churches in the Diocese of Llandaff, p. 83, but see also the document cited by A. Leslie Evans, Margam Abbey, p. 144.

X

CONCLUSION

In the early spring of 1349 the Black Death, which had already taken a heavy toll of life in England, was transmitted to Wales. It is reasonable to infer that Wales was as violently and as unevenly affected as England, but there is hardly a scrap of direct evidence to show how heavily the pestilence fell either on individual monastic communities or on the tenants and workers on the monastic estates. The onset of the plague has been chosen as the *terminus ad quem* of the present study, therefore, not because of any cataclysmic effect it may have had on the monasteries but rather for reasons of convenience. It has provided a convenient means of demonstrating, if indeed there is still need, how many developments and tendencies which have in the past been attributed to the pestilence, were in fact under way more than a generation before it reached Wales.

The number of monks in the monasteries of south Wales was decreasing well before the middle of the fourteenth century, most markedly perhaps in the Cistercian houses. In 1317 the abbot of Caerleon, with a convent of twenty monks, could point to happier times when there were sixty or more. But even in the very much smaller Benedictine priories, such as Abergavenny and Brecon, numbers were falling well below what was regarded as the minimum number for the satisfactory performance of the divine office. The decline cannot be attributed solely to failing material resources. By the early-fourteenth century the religious climate had changed. The monastic ideal was no longer the attractive force it had been a century and a half earlier, and the would-be monk was finding an alternative vocation in the ranks of the friars or an alternative career in administration and law.

Financial difficulties were, nevertheless, a potent force in setting a curb on recruitment. In the last quarter of the thirteenth century the monasteries of south Wales experienced what were to be the first warning signals of the coming recession, and their financial difficulties became more serious as the fourteenth century advanced. In the face of these difficulties most monasteries began to lease out their lands and attempted to acquire fixed sources of income which would not fluctuate too greatly over the years. For the Benedictines and Augustinians the process was not a revolutionary one since they had always relied heavily on rent and tithe. But for the Cistercians the change-over was novel. It conflicted directly with the early ideals of the order embodied in legislation promulgated by the General Chapter and eventually resulted in making Cistercian abbeys very much like those of other orders.

In about 1250 a Cistercian abbey like Margam could be readily distinguished from a Benedictine or Augustinian house by the way its estates were organized, managed and run. By the early-fourteenth century these differences were becoming blurred. The lay-brethren were disappearing as a class and the former granges which they had supervised and worked were becoming more like manors with a substantial body of small tenants. A century and a half later there was little save the austere architecture of the abbey church and the white habits of its handful of monks to distinguish Margam from a Benedictine house of comparable size and income. Even before the Black Death the shades of the long monastic twilight of the later middle ages could already be discerned.

APPENDIX I

MONASTIC FOUNDATIONS IN SOUTH WALES
FROM *c.* 1066 TO 1271

1. *Benedictine Priories*

Name	Founder	Mother House	Date
Abergavenny	Hamelin of Ballon	St. Vincent, Le Mans	1087–1100
Basaleg	Robert of Hay	Glastonbury	1116
Brecon	Bernard of Neufmarché	Battle	*c.* 1110
Cardiff	Robert fitz Hamon	Tewkesbury	–1106
Cardigan	?	Gloucester	1110–15
		Chertsey	1165–
Carmarthen	Henry I	Battle	*c.* 1110
Chepstow	William fitz Osbern	Cormeilles	–1071
Ewenni	Maurice de Londres	Gloucester	1141
Goldcliff	Robert de Chandos	Bec	1113
Kidwelly	Bishop Roger of Salisbury	Sherborne	1114
Llanbadarn Fawr	Gilbert fitz Richard	Gloucester	1116–17
Llandovery	Richard fitz Pons	Great Malvern	*c.* 1110
Llangenydd	Henry, earl of Warwick	St. Taurin, Evreux	1106–15
Llangua	?	Lire	–1074
Llansbyddid	?	Great Malvern	–1127
Monmouth	Wihenoc	St. Florent près Saumur	1074–86
Pembroke	Arnulf of Montgomery	St. Martin, Séez	*c.* 1098

2. *Cluniac Priories*

Name	Founder	Mother House	Date
Malpas	Winibald of Caerleon	Montacute	–1122
St. Clears	?	St. Martin des Champs, Paris	1147–84

3. *Tironian Houses*

Name	Founder	Mother House	Date
St. Dogmaels Abbey	Robert fitz Martin	Tiron	priory 1113–15 abbey 1120
Pill Priory	Adam de Roche	St. Dogmaels	*c.* 1200
Caldy Priory	Geva, mother of Robert fitz Martin	St. Dogmaels	1113–15

4. Cistercian Abbeys

Name	Founder	Mother House	Date
Caerleon alias Llantarnam	Hywel ab Iorwerth	Strata Florida	1179
Cwm-hir	Cadwallon ap Madog?	Whitland	1176
Grace Dieu	John of Monmouth	Dore	1226
Margam	Robert, earl of Gloucester	Clairvaux	1147
Neath	Richard de Granville	Savigny	1130
Strata Florida	Robert fitz Stephen	Whitland	1164 new site 1184–
Tintern	Walter fitz Richard	L'Aumône	1131
Whitland	John of Torrington	Clairvaux	1140 new site c. 1151

5. Regular Canons

AUGUSTINIAN

Carmarthen	Bernard, bishop of St. David's		–1127
Haverfordwest	Robert fitz Richard		–1200
Llanthony Prima	Hugh de Lacy		c. 1118
St. Kynemark	?		1254–71

PREMONSTRATENSIAN

Talley	Rhys ap Gruffydd	St. Jean, Amien	1184–89

6. Nunneries

Usk (Benedictine priory)	Richard de Clare and Gilbert de Clare		–1236
Llanllŷr (Cistercian abbey)	Rhys ap Gruffydd	Strata Florida	–1197

APPENDIX II

THE SIZE OF ESTATES OF SOUTH WALES MONASTERIES, c. 1291

Until a more critical text of the *Taxatio* based on the original rolls appears, the figures given in this and the following appendices are to be treated as tentative. They are intended to provide only a rough basis for comparison. Appropriated churches are rarely noted in the valuation of St. David's diocese and there are notable omissions even in the valuation of Llandaff diocese. Appropriations of certain churches have therefore been inferred from other evidence and their values supplied by the *Taxatio* are enclosed in square brackets in Appendix III. Although great care has been taken to take account of all the evidence in the *Taxatio*, while at the same time avoiding the ever-present dangers of double-counting, the total valuation figures for the Monmouthshire houses do not agree with those given by Rose Graham. Attention is drawn to these and other discrepancies in the notes.

(i) *The Cistercians*[1]

	Arable (acres)	Meadow (acres)	Total (acres)
Caerleon[2]	4260+	20	4280+
Cwm-hir[3]	[3000]		[3000]
Grace Dieu[4]	1800		1800
Llanllŷr	1200		1200
Margam	6420	517	6937
Neath[5]	4883+	325	5208+
Strata Florida[3]	[6360]		[6360]
Tintern[6]	3048+	165	3213+
Whitland	5040		5040
Total	36011+	1027	37038+

[1] These figures refer to land actively farmed and take no account of rough mountain pasture or waste nor, possibly, of land leased. Recent work by Dr. R. W. Hays would suggest that the actively farmed area formed less than a fifth of the total area of a Cistercian abbey's property (*History of Abbey of Aberconway*, p. 104).

[2] The extent of land at *Crip*, *Gaynet* and *Enesnacrinet* is not given. From the valuation figures, it would seem that each of these properties was under one carucate in extent.

[3] The valuations of Cwm-hir and Strata Florida are not sufficiently detailed to provide reliable figures. The figures given in square brackets are rough estimates based on the valuation figures.

[4] Appurtenant meadow land is noted but its extent is not given.

[5] The figures for Neath do not include Exford grange in Somerset, whose size is not given in the *Taxatio*.

[6] Two granges appear to have been omitted from the valuation: Woolaston and Modesgat, both in Hereford diocese.

(ii) *Benedictines and Tironians*[1]

	Arable (acres)	Meadow (acres)	Total (acres)
Abergavenny	240		240
Cardigan	240		240
Chepstow	201	110½	311½
Ewenni	300		300
Goldcliff[2]	1221+	125+	1346+
Kidwelly	121		121
Llangenydd	120		120
Llangua	480		480
Malpas	20	33	53
Monmouth	480		480
St. Clears	12		12
St. Dogmaels	720		720
Usk	24		24
Total	4179+	268½+	4447½+

[1] No figures are given for Pembroke, Brecon, Cardiff or Pill.
[2] The size of Goldcliff's Somerset manors is not given.

(iii) *The Regular Canons*

	Arable (acres)	Meadow (acres)	Total (acres)
Carmarthen	960		960
Haverfordwest[1]			
Llanthony Prima[2]	1080+	14	1094+
St. Kynemark	136	6	142
Talley[3]	480+		480+
Total	2656+	20	2676+ acres

[1] No acreage figures are given in the *Taxatio.*

[2] The figures are for Llanthony's estates in Hereford diocese only. The extent of the priory's estate in St. David's diocese is not given. The priory also held a small landed estate in the diocese of Meath, Ireland.

[3] Much of Talley's lands had been leased and let to farm by 1291 and their extent is not noted.

APPENDIX III

ASSESSED VALUES OF SOUTH WALES MONASTERIES *c.* 1291

(i) *Cistercians*

	Temporalities £	s.	d.	Spiritualities £	s.	d.	Total £	s.	d.
Caerleon	44	15	0				44	15	0
Cwm-hir	35	12	0				35	12	0
Grace Dieu	18	5	8				18	5	8[1]
Llanllŷr	7	10	0				7	10	0
Margam	255	7	4½		10	0	255	17	4½[2]
Neath	231	1	5	5	0	0	236	1	5
Strata Florida	82	6	9	16	0	0	98	6	9
Tintern	108	9	8	36	13	4	145	3	0
Whitland	43	15	4				43	15	4[3]
Total	827	3	2½	58	3	4	885	6	6½

[1] J. F. O'Sullivan, *Cistercian Settlements*, p. 34, has £18 5s. 10d.
[2] J. F. O'Sullivan, op. cit., p. 29, has £255 7s. 4½d. but seems to have omitted from his calculations the 10s. from Olveston.
[3] J. F. O'Sullivan, op. cit., p. 9, has £44 5s. 4d. but seems to have double-counted the 10s. rent from Haverford.

(ii) *Benedictines and Tironians*

	Temporalities £	s.	d.	Spiritualities £	s.	d.	Total £	s.	d.
Abergavenny	13	17	10½	38	0	0	51	17	10½[1]
Brecon	36	3	4	[86	6	8]	[122	10	0]
Cardiff		10	0	[20	0	0]	[20	10	0]
Cardigan	2	13	4	[13	6	8]	[16	0	0]
Chepstow	15	13	3	20	6	8	35	19	11[2]
Ewenni	14	3	0	42	0	0	56	3	0
Goldcliff	98	18	1	72	16	0	171	14	1[3]
Kidwelly	2	15	0	[13	6	8]	[16	1	8]
Llangenydd	4	16	0		?		4	16	0+
Llangua	10	2	0		10	0	10	12	0
Malpas	4	19	8	1	0	0	5	19	8
Monmouth	22	19	6	62	19	2	85	18	8[4]
Pembroke	19	6	3½		?		19	6	3½+
Pill	21	4	10		?		21	4	10+
St. Clears	2	12	6	[13	6	8]	[15	19	2]
St. Dogmaels	52	11	4	6	0	0	58	11	4
Usk	1	12	8	40	13	4	42	6	0
Total	324	18	8	430	11	10+	755	10	6+

[1] Rose Graham (*Jnl. Brit. Arch. Assoc.*, xxxv, 1929–30, p. 109) gives £61 8s. 2½d.
[2] £22 6s. 7d. according to Rose Graham.
[3] The true figure for Goldcliff's assessment is probably provided by the marginal entry in P.R.O., E 106/4/14 membrane 11: £175 16s. 4d. Rose Graham, op. cit., p. 108, gives the much larger figure of £195 19s. 5d. and appears to have double-counted some items. Figures for the same item are occasionally repeated in the printed edition of the *Taxatio*.
[4] £78 5s. 8d. according to Rose Graham.

(iii) *The Regular Canons*

	Temporalities			Spiritualities			Total		
	£	s.	d.	£	s.	d.	£	s.	d.
Carmarthen	13	16	2	[16	0	0¹]	[29	16	2]
Haverford	17	6	8		?	²	17	6	8+
Llanthony Prima	64	5	4	[169	1	8³]	[233	7	0]
St. Kynemark	7	7	4	4	0	0	11	7	4
Talley	5	9	10	[56	13	4⁴]	[62	3	2]
Total	108	5	4	245	15	0	354	0	4+

¹ The *Taxatio* does not mention the priory's spiritual income but see above p. 69.
² Too little is known of Haverford to hazard precise figures for spiritual income.
³ The Irish spiritualities valued at £71 have been supplied from *The Irish Cartularies of Llanthony Prima and Secunda*, ed. Eric St. John Brooks, p. 146.
⁴ The *Taxatio* notes only a portion in Llangoedmor (£2) and a portion in Blaenannerch (£1 6s. 8d.). Edward Owen (*Arch. Camb.*, 1893, p. 235) assumed that Llandeilo Fawr (£13 6s. 8d.), Llanegwad Fawr (£6 13s. 8d.), Berwick (£4), Penbryn (£16) and Cynwyl Gaeo (£13 6s. 8d.) were appropriated to the abbey by the beginning of the fourteenth century.

APPENDIX IV

APPROPRIATED CHURCHES IN LLANDAFF AND ST. DAVID'S DIOCESES *c.* 1291

(i) *Llandaff Diocese*

Church	Appropriator	Value in 1291		
		£	s.	d.
ABERGAVENNY DEANERY				
Abergavenny	Abergavenny Priory	15	0	0
Llanfihangel Crucornau	Abergavenny Priory	5	6	8
Grosmont	Abergavenny Priory	10	0	0
Llangatwg Feibion Afel	Monmouth Priory	5	18	0
Llangatwg Lingoed	Abergavenny Priory	4	0	0
Llanddewi Ysgyryd	Abergavenny Priory	2	13	4
Llanelen	Abergavenny Priory	1	0	0
Rockfield	Monmouth Priory	2	10	0
Wonastow	Monmouth Priory	2	0	0
Llangua	Lire Abbey		10	0
USK DEANERY				
Raglan	Usk Priory	10	0	0
Mykenny (Mathenni?)	Usk Priory	6	6	8
Usk	Usk Priory	13	6	8
Langrinon (Llangyfiw?)	Usk Priory	2	0	0
Llanbadog	Usk Priory	3	0	0
Kylgoygan (Llanfihangel Pont-y-moel)	Usk Priory	2	0	0
LOWER GWENT DEANERY				
Goldcliff	Goldcliff Priory	26	13	4
Christchurch	Goldcliff Priory ⎫			
Peterstone-Wentlloog	Goldcliff Priory ⎬	26	13	4
Caldicot	Llanthony Prima Priory	16	0	0
Chepstow	Chepstow Priory	12	0	0
St. Arvans	St. Kynemark's Priory ⎫			
St. Kynemark	St. Kynemark's Priory ⎬	4	0	0
Porthcaseg	St. Kynemark's Priory ⎭			
NEWPORT DEANERY				
Basaleg	Basaleg Priory	13	6	8
Malpas	Malpas Priory	1	0	0
LLANDAFF DEANERY				
Llancarfan	Gloucester Abbey	10	0	0
Cardiff	Tewkesbury Abbey	20	0	0
Cogan	Tewkesbury Abbey	2	13	4

Church	Appropriator	Value in 1291		
		£	s.	d.

GRONEATH DEANERY

Ewenni	Ewenni Priory ⎫			
St. Brides Major	Ewenni Priory ⎬	40	0	0
Colwinston	Ewenni Priory ⎭			
Llanblethian	Tewkesbury Abbey ⎱	60	0	0
Llanilltud Fawr	Tewkesbury Abbey ⎰			
St. Mary Hill	Neath Abbey	1	0	0
Llandyfodwg	Ewenni Priory	2	0	0

KENFIG DEANERY

Kenfig	Tewkesbury Abbey	10	0	0
Newcastle	Tewkesbury Abbey	16	0	0
Cilybebyll	Neath Abbey		13	4
Cadoxton-juxta-Neath	Neath Abbey	3	6	8

(ii) *St. David's Diocese*

ULTRA AERON DEANERY

None

SUB AERON DEANERY

Cardigan	Cardigan Priory	13	6	8
Verwick	Cardigan Priory ⎱	4	0	0
	Talley Abbey ⎰			
Penbryn	Talley Abbey	16	0	0
Llangoedmor	Talley Abbey	2	0	0

EMLYN DEANERY

Castell-llan	Slebech Commandery		10	0

CEMAIS DEANERY

New Castle	Pill Priory	8	0	0
Llantood	St. Dogmaels Abbey	4	0	0
Mynachlog-ddu	St. Dogmaels Abbey	2	13	4
Eglwyswrw	St. Dogmaels Abbey	4	0	0

CARMARTHEN DEANERY

Carmarthen	Carmarthen Priory	9	6	8
Eglwys Gymyn	St. Clears Priory	5	0	0
Abernant	Carmarthen Priory	9	6	8
St. Clears	St. Clears Priory	13	6	8

YSTRAD TYWI DEANERY

Cynwyl Gaeo	Talley Abbey	13	6	8
Llandeilo Fawr	Talley Abbey	13	6	8
Llanegwad	Talley Abbey	6	13	4
Llandyfeisant	Talley Abbey	1	6	8
Llanfihangel Aberbythych	Talley Abbey	3	6	8

IN LLANDAFF AND ST. DAVID'S DIOCESES *c.* 1291

Church	*Appropriator*	*Value in 1291*		
		£	s.	d.
GOWER DEANERY				
Oystermouth	Ewenni Priory	5	0	0
KIDWELLY DEANERY				
Kidwelly	Kidwelly Priory	13	6	8
Pembrey	Ewenni Priory	6	13	4
St. Ishmael	Ewenni Priory	6	13	4
BRECON DEANERY				
Hay	Brecon Priory	14	0	0
Llanigon	Brecon Priory	10	0	0
Talgarth	Brecon Priory	18	0	0
Llan-gors	Brecon Priory	8	0	0
Brecon	Brecon Priory	20	0	0
Llansbyddyd	Great Malvern Priory	6	0	0
EWYAS DEANERY				
Cwmyoy	Llanthony Prima Priory	2	0	0
PEBIDIOG DEANERY				
Granston	St. Dogmaels Abbey	5	6	8
Fishguard	St. Dogmaels Abbey	8	0	0
RHOS DEANERY				
Steynton	Pill Priory	18	0	0
Roch	Pill Priory	13	6	8
New Moat	Pill Priory	4	13	4
Haverfordwest	Haverfordwest Priory	10	0	0
Camros	Haverfordwest Priory	12	0	0
Llanstadwel	Haverfordwest Priory	6	13	4
St. Ishmaels	Haverfordwest Priory	8	0	0
Dale	Haverfordwest Priory	5	6	8
Haroldston	Haverfordwest Priory	2	0	0
PEMBROKE DEANERY				
Castlemartin	Pembroke Priory	26	13	4
Martletwy	Slebech Commandery	9	6	8
Newton North (Llys Prawst)	St. Dogmaels Abbey	2	0	0
Caldy	Caldy Priory	3	6	8
Monkton	Pembroke Priory	26	13	4
Pembroke, St. Michael's	Pembroke Priory	10	0	0

APPENDIX V

VICARAGES IN THE DIOCESE OF LLANDAFF
VALUED IN THE ASSESSMENTS OF 1254 AND 1291

| | 1254 | | 1291 | |
	Church £ s.d.	Vicarage £ s.d.	Church £ s.d.	Vicarage £ s.d.
1. Abergavenny (Abergavenny Priory)	6 13 4	1 10 0	15 0 0	4 6 8
2. Llanfihangel Crucornau (Abergavenny Priory)	2 13 4	1 10 0		
3. Grosmont (Abergavenny Priory)	6 13 4	2 6 0	10 0 0	5 0 0
4. Llangatwg Feibion Afel (Monmouth Priory)	5 8 0	1 10 0		
5. Rockfield (Monmouth Priory)	3 0 0	1 10 0		
6. Wonastow (Monmouth Priory)	2 0 0	1 4 0		
7. Llangatwg Dyffryn Wysg (?)	1 6 8	1 0 0		
8. Magor (St. Mary's de Gloria, Anagni)	10 0 0		26 13 4	5 6 8
9. Langstone (Llandaff)		1 0 0		
10. Christchurch (Goldcliff Priory)			26 13 4	8 0 0
11. Matharn (Llandaff)	12 0 0	13 4		
12. St. Mellons (St. Augustine's Abbey, Bristol)	9 0 0	1 0 0		
13. Basaleg (Llandaff)	18 0 0	2 0 0		
14. Newport (St. Peter's Abbey, Gloucester)	8 0 0	2 0 0		
15. Rhymni (St. Augustine's Abbey, Bristol)	18 0 0	2 0 0		
16. Llanilltud Fawr (Tewkesbury Abbey)	26 13 4	5 0 0	60 0 0	6 0 0
17. Llanblethian (Tewkesbury Abbey)	12 0 0	2 0 0		5 0 0
18. Llantrisant	8 0 0	1 0 0		

APPENDIX V
VICARAGES IN THE DIOCESE OF LLANDAFF
VALUED IN THE ASSESSMENTS OF 1254 AND 1291

	1254		*1291*	
	Church £ s. d.	*Vicarage* £ s. d.	*Church* £ s. d.	*Vicarage* £ s. d.
19. Kenfig (Tewkesbury Abbey)	6 14 4	3 6 8	10 0 0	5 0 0
20. Cadoxton-juxta-Neath (Neath Abbey)		2 0 0	3 6 8	5 0 0
21. Newcastle (Tewkesbury Abbey)			16 0 0	5 0 0

BIBLIOGRAPHY

I. CONTEMPORARY SOURCES

(a) MANUSCRIPTS

Aberystwyth, National Library of Wales:
Badminton MSS. 1571, 1572, 1574, 1575, 1576, 1639, 1640, 1641, 1642, 1643, 1644, 1645, 1646, 1647.

Cambridge University Library:
MS.Dd.9.38, folios 93–94.

Cardiff, Glamorgan County Record Office:
D|D TD18.

London, British Museum:
Additional MS.6164.
Arundel MS.19.

London, Public Record Office:
DL 25|L974 (Ancient Deeds, Duchy of Lancaster).
E 40|A14282 (Ancient Deeds).
E 106|4|14 (Alien Priory Bundles).
E 106|4|19 (Alien Priory Bundles).
E 106|11|1 (Alien Priory Bundles).
E 135|1|5 (Exchequer Ecclesiastical Documents).
E 210|D3375 (Ancient Deeds).
E 210|D4610 (Ancient Deeds).
E 210|D7221 (Ancient Deeds).
SC. 8|119|5948 (Ancient Petitions).
SC. 12|12|14 (Rentals and Surveys).

Newport (Gwent), Public Library:
J. G. Wood MSS.

(b) PRINTED WORKS

Ancient Charters, ed. J. H. Round (London, Pipe Roll Soc., x, 1888).
Annales Cambriae, ed. J. Williams 'Ab Ithel' (London, R.S., 1860).
'Annales Dorenses' in G. H. Pertz, *Monumenta Germaniae Historica, Scriptores*, vol. xxvii (Hanover, 1885), pp. 514–31.
Annales Monastici, ed. H. R. Luard (5 vols., London, R.S., 1864–9).
The Black Book of Carmarthen, reproduced and edited by J. Gwenogvryn Evans (Pwllheli, 1906).
Brut y Tywysogyon or The Chronicle of the Princes, Peniarth MS.20 Version, transl. and ed. Thomas Jones (Cardiff, 1952).

Calendar of Ancient Correspondence Concerning Wales, ed. J. G. Edwards (Cardiff, 1935)
Calendar of Chancery Rolls, Various (London, 1912).
Calendar of Chancery Warrants, 1244–1326 (London, 1927).
Calendar of Charter Rolls (London, 1903–).
Calendar of Close Rolls (London, 1892–).
Calendar of Documents Preserved in France, ed. J. H. Round (London, 1899).
Calendar of Fine Rolls (London, 1911–).
Calendar of Inquisitions, Miscellaneous (London, 1916–).
Calendar of Inquisitions Post Mortem (London, 1904–).
Calendar of Liberate Rolls (London, 1917–).
Calendar of Papal Letters (London, 1894–).
Calendar of Papal Petitions, 1342–1419 (London, 1897).
Calendar of Patent Rolls (London, 1891–).
Cartae et Alia Munimenta quae ad Dominium de Glamorgan Pertinent, ed. G. T. Clark (2nd. ed., 6 vols., Cardiff, 1910).
Cartulaire de l'Abbaye de Saint-Vincent du Mans, ed. R. Charles and M. D'Elbenne (Le Mans, 1886–1913).
Cartularium Prioratus S. Johannis Evangelistae de Brecon, ed. R. W. Banks (London, Cambrian Archaeological Association, 1884).
Cartularium S. Johannis Baptistae de Carmarthen, ed. Thomas Philipps (Cheltenham 1865).
A Catalogue of Manuscripts Relating to Wales in the British Museum, ed. Edward Owen (1 vol. in 4, Cymm. Rec. Ser., 1900–22).
Chapters of the Augustinian Canons, ed. H. E. Salter (Oxford Hist. Soc., lxxiv, 1922).
Chapters of the English Black Monks, ed. W. A. Pantin (Camden Soc., 3rd Ser., 3 vols., 1931–7).
Charters and Records of Cluni, ed. G. F. Duckett (2 vols., Lewes, 1888).
Chronicle of Bury St. Edmunds, 1212–1301, ed. Antonia Gransden (London, 1964).
Chronicle of Melrose (Facsimile edition, London, 1936).
'Chronicle of the 13th Century, 1066–1298', *Arch. Camb.*, 1862, pp. 272–83.
Chronicon Monasterii de Bello, ed. J. S. Brewer (London, Anglia Christiana Soc., 1846).
Collectanea Anglo-Premonstratensia, ed. F. A. Gasquet (3 vols., London, Camden Soc., 1904–1906).
Councils and Ecclesiastical Documents Relating to Great Britain and Ireland, ed. A. W. Haddan and W. Stubbs (3 vols., Oxford, 1869–78).
Cronica de Wallia and Other Documents from Exeter Cathedral Library MS. 3514, ed. Thomas Jones in *BBCS.*, xii (1946), pp. 27–44.
Curia Regis Rolls (London, 1923–).
Dafydd ap Gwilym: Fifty Poems, transl. by H. I. Bell and D. Bell (London, Cymmrotdorion Soc., 1942).
Deputy Keeper's Reports, vii (London, 1846).
Descriptive Catalogue of Ancient Deeds (6 vols. London, 1890–1915).
A Descriptive Catalogue of Penrice and Margam MSS., Series I–IV, ed. W. de Gray Birch (London, 1893–5).
Documents Relating to the Cistercian Monastery of St. Mary, Kingswood, ed. V. R. Perkins and P. H. Jeayes in *Trans. Bristol and Glouc. Arch. Soc.*, xxii (1899), pp. 179–256.
DUGDALE, William. *Monasticon Anglicanum*, eds. John Caley, Sir Henry Ellis and Rev. Bulkeley Bandinel (6 vols. in 8, London, 1846).
The Episcopal Registers of St. David's, 1397–1518, ed. R. F. Isaacson (3 vols. Cymm. Rec. Ser., 1917–20).

Facsimile and Text of the Book of Taliesin, reproduced and edited by J. Gwenogvryn Evans (Llanbedrog, 1910).

Foedera, Conventiones, Litterae, etc., ed. Thomas Rymer (4 vols. in 7, London, Record Commission, 1816–69).

GIRALDUS CAMBRENSIS. *Opera* (8 vols., R.S., 1861–91).

GIRALDUS CAMBRENSIS, *The Autobiography of*, edited and translated by H. E. Butler (London, 1937).

Great Roll of the Pipe for the Thirteenth Year of the Reign of King John, ed. Doris M. Stenton (London, Pipe Roll Soc., 1953).

Great Roll of the Pipe for the Fourteenth Year of the Reign of Henry III (London, Pipe Roll Soc., 1927).

Historia et Cartularium Monasterii S. Petri, Gloucestrie, ed. W. Hart (3 vols. London, R.S., 1863–7).

History of Gruffydd ap Cynan (1054–1137), ed. Arthur Jones (Manchester, 1910).

Irish Cartularies of Llanthony Prima and Secunda, ed. Eric St. John Brooks (Dublin, 1953).

LELAND, John. *Itinerary in Wales*, ed. L. Toulmin Smith (London, 1906).

Letters and Charters of Gilbert Foliot, ed. Adrian Morey and C. N. L. Brooke (Cambridge, 1967).

Liber Epistolaris of Richard de Bury, ed. N. Denholm-Young (Oxford, Roxburghe Club, 1950).

Littere Wallie, ed. J. G. Edwards (Cardiff, 1940).

MAP, Walter. *De Nugis Curialium*, transl. M. R. James, ed. E. Sidney Hartland (London, Cymm. Record Series, ix, 1923).

MERRICK, Rice. *A Booke of Glamorganshires Antiquities*, ed. J. A. Corbett (London, 1887).

Munimenta Academica, or Documents Illustrative of Academic Life at Oxford, ed. H. Anstey (2 vols., London, R.S., 1868).

The Myvyrian Archaiology of Wales . . ., eds. O. Jones, E. Williams and W. O. Pughe (2nd ed., Denbigh, 1870).

Nova Legenda Anglie, ed. C. Horstman (2 vols., Oxford, 1901).

Papsturkunden in England, ed. Walther Holtzmann (3 vols., Berlin and Göttingen, 1930–52).

Parliamentary Writs and Writs of Military Summons, ed. F. Palgrave (London, 2 vols., 1827–34).

Patrologiae cursus completus, series Latina, ed. J. P. Migne (Paris, 1844–64).

Radulphi de Coggeshall Chronicon Anglicanum, ed. J. Stevenson (London, R.S., 1875).

Records of the Court of Augmentations Relating to Wales and Monmouthshire, eds. E. A. Lewis and J. Conway Davies (Cardiff, 1954).

Regesta Regum Anglo-Normannorum: 2. Regesta Henrici Primi, 1100–1135; eds. C. Johnson and H. A. Cronne (Oxford, 1956).

Register and Chronicle of the Abbey of Aberconway, ed. H. Ellis (London, Camden Soc., Miscellany, i, 1843).

Register of Edward, the Black Prince (4 parts, London, 1930–3).

Register of John de Drokensford, Bishop of Bath and Wells, A.D. 1309–1329, ed. E. Hobhouse (Somerset Rec. Soc., i, 1887).

Register of Ralph of Shrewsbury, Bishop of Bath and Wells, A.D. 1329–63, ed. T. S. Holmes (Somerset Rec. Soc., 1896).

Registrum Ade de Orleton, Episcopi Herefordensis, A.D. MCCCXVII–MCCCXXVII, ed. A. T. Bannister (Cant. and York Soc., 1908).

Registrum Edmvndi Lacy, Episcopi Herefordensis, A.D. MCCCCXVII–MCCCCXIX, ed. J. H. Parry (Cant. and York Soc., 1918).

Registrum Epistolarum Fratris Johannis Peckham, ed. C. T. Martin (3 vols., R.S. 1882–5).

Registrum Epistolarum Stephani de Lexinton, ed. P. Bruno Griesser (Analecta Sacri Ordinis Cisterciensis, viii, 1952).

Registrum Johannis Pecham (Cant. and York Soc., 1910).

Registrum Johannis de Trillek, Episcopi Herefordensis, A.D. MCCCXLIV–MCCCLXI, ed. J. H. Parry (Cant. and York Soc., 1912).

Registrum Roberti Winchelsey, Cantuariensis Archiepiscopi, 1294–1313, ed. R. Graham, (2 vols., Cant. and York Soc., 1952–6).

Registrum Simonis de Langham Cantuariensis Archiepiscopi, ed. A. C. Wood (Cant. and York. Soc., 1956).

Registrum Thome de Cantilupe, ed. R. G. Griffiths (Cant. and York Soc., 1907).

Registrum Thome de Charlton, A.D. MCCCXXVII–MCCCXLIV, ed. W. W. Capes (Cant. and York Soc., 1913).

Rotuli Hundredorum, eds. W. Illingworth and J. Caley (2 vols., London, 1812–18).

Rotuli Litterarum Clausarum in Turri Londinensi Asservati (2 vols., London, 1833–44).

Rotuli Parliamentorum (7 vols., London, Record Commission, 1783–1832).

Saint Dunstan's Classbook from Glastonbury; introd. by R. W. Hunt (Amsterdam, 1961).

'Some Original Documents relating to the South Part of Pembrokeshire', ed. E. J. L. Scott, *Jnl. Brit. Arch. Assoc.*, xli (1885), pp. 153–75.

Somerset Pleas, ed. Charles E. H. Chadwyck-Healey (Somerset Rec. Soc., ii, 1897).

Statuta Capitulorum Generalium Ordinis Cisterciensis, ed. J. M. Canivez (7 vols., Louvain, 1933–39).

Taxatio Ecclesiastica Angliae et Walliae . . . P. Nicholai IV (London, Record Commission, 1802).

The Text of the Book of Aneirin, reproduced and edited by J. G. Evans (Pwllheli, 1908).

The Text of the Book of Llan Dâv, ed. J. G. Evans (Oxford, 1893).

The Text of the Mabinogion and Other Welsh Tales from the Red Book of Hergest, eds. J. Rhys and J. G. Evans (Oxford, 1887).

Valor Ecclesiasticus, eds. J. Caley and J. Hunter (6 vols., London, Record Commission, 1810–34).

Visitations and Chapters-General of the Order of Cluni, ed. G. F. Duckett (London. 1893).

Vitae Sanctorum Britanniae et Genealogiae, ed. A. W. Wade-Evans (Cardiff, 1944).

Walter of Henley's Husbandry, ed. E. Lamond (London, 1890).

The Welsh Assise Roll, 1277–1284, ed. J. Conway Davies (Cardiff, 1940).

WHARTON, Henry. *Anglia Sacra, sive collectio historiarum, partim antiquitus, partim recenter scriptarum de archiepiscopis & episcopis Angliae . . .* (2 vols., London, 1691).

WORCESTRE, William. *Itineraries*, ed. J. H. Harvey (Oxford, 1969).

Year Books, Edward I, ed. A. V. Horwood (5 vols., London, 1866–79).

Year Books, Edward III, eds. A. V. Horwood and L. O. Pike (15 vols., London, 1883–1911).

II. MODERN WORKS

(a) PRINTED WORKS

ADDLESHAW, G. W. O. 'The Church between the Conway and the Dee, 400–1100', *Province*, xvi, 1965, pp. 14–21.

ADDLESHAW, G. W. O. *Rectors, Vicars and Patrons in Twelfth and Early Thirteenth Century Canon Law* (York, 1956).

BALE, John. *Scriptorum Illustrium Brytannie . . . Catalogus* (Basle, 1557–9).

BANNISTER, A. T. *A Descriptive Catalogue of the Manuscripts in the Hereford Cathedral Library* (Hereford, 1927).
BARING-GOULD, S. and FISHER, J. *Lives of the British Saints* (4 vols., London, 1907–13).
BECK, Egerton. 'Regulars and the Parochial System in Mediaeval England', *Dublin Review*, clxxii (1923), pp. 235–51.
BEVAN, W. L. *St David's* (London, S.P.C.K. Diocesan Histories, 1888).
BIRCH, Walter de Gray. *A History of Margam Abbey* (London, 1897).
BIRCH, Walter de Gray. *A History of Neath Abbey* (London, 1902).
BOWEN, E. G. 'Carmarthen Town Plan', *Trans. Carm. Antiq. Soc.*, xxv (1934), pp. 1–7.
BOWEN, E. G. 'The Monastic Economy of the Cistercians of Strata Florida', *Ceredigion*, i (1950), pp. 34–7.
BOWEN, E. G. *The Settlements of the Celtic Saints in Wales* (2nd ed., Cardiff, 1956).
BRADNEY, J. A. *History of Monmouthshire* (4 vols., London, 1904–33).
BRIGSTOKE, F. T. 'The Settlement of a Medieval Dispute at Carmarthen', *Carmarthen Antiquary*, ii (1957), pp. 212–3.
BROOKE, C. 'The Church and the Welsh Border in the Tenth and Eleventh Centuries', *Flintshire Historical Society Journal*, xxi (1964), pp. 32–45.
BUTLER, L. A. S. 'The Augustinian Priory of St. Kinmark near Chepstow', *JHSCW.*, xv (1965), pp. 9–19.
BUTLER, L. A. S. 'St. Kynemark's Priory, Chepstow', *Monmouthshire Antiquary*, ii (1965), pp. 33–41.
CHADWICK, N. K. ed. *Studies in the Early British Church* (Cambridge, 1958).
CHADWICK, O. *John Cassian* (Cambridge, 1950).
CHARLES, B. G. *Old Norse Relations with Wales* (Cardiff, 1934).
CHENEY, C. R. *Episcopal Visitation of Monasteries in the Thirteenth Century* (Manchester, 1931).
CLAY, C. T. 'A Worcester Charter of Thomas II, Archbishop of York; and its Bearing on the Early History of the Church of Leeds', *York. Arch. Jnl.*, xxxvi (1944–7), pp. 132–6.
COLMCILLE, Father. *The Story of Mellifont* (Dublin, 1958).
COLVIN, H. M. *The White Canons in England* (Oxford, 1951).
THE COMPLETE PEERAGE, ed. G. E. Cokayne (13 vols., London, 1910–59).
CONSTABLE, G. *Monastic Tithes from their Origins to the Twelfth Century* (Cambridge, 1964).
CORBETT, J. S. *Glamorgan: Papers and Notes on the Lordship and its Members* (Cardiff, 1925).
COULTON, G. G. *Five Centuries of Religion* (4 vols., Cambridge, 1927–50).
COWLEY, F. G. 'The Besanding of Theodoric's Grange, Margam: Some New Evidence', *Arch. Camb.*, 1963, pp. 188–90.
COWLEY, F. G. 'The Church in Glamorgan from the Norman Conquest to the Beginning of the Fourteenth Century', *Glamorgan County History*, iii (1971), pp. 87–135.
COWLEY, F. G. 'The Cistercian Economy in Glamorgan, 1130–1349', *Morgannwg*, xi (1967), pp. 5–26.
COWLEY, F. G. 'Llangenydd and its Priory', *Glamorgan Historian*, v (1968), pp. 220–8.
COWLEY, F. G. 'Llangewydd: an Unrecorded Glamorgan Castle', *Arch. Camb.*, 1967, pp. 204–6.
COWLEY, F. G. 'Neath versus Margam: Some 13th Century Disputes', *Trans. Port Talbot Hist. Soc.*, i (1967), pp. 7–14.

COWLEY, F. G. 'A Note on the Discovery of St. David's Body', *BBCS.*, xix (1960), pp. 47–8.

COWLEY, F. G. and LLOYD, Nesta. 'An Old Welsh *Englyn* in Harley Charter 75 C 38', *BBCS.*, xxv (1974), pp. 407–17.

CRASTER, O. E. *Tintern Abbey* (London, 1956).

CREIGHTON, C. *A History of Epidemics in Britain* (2 vols., Cambridge, 1891).

CUNNINGHAM, W. *The Growth of English Industry and Commerce during the Early and Middle Ages* (5th ed., Cambridge, 1922).

DAVID, C. M. *Some Notes on the Church of St. David and the Village of Laleston* (Bridgend, 1958).

DAVIES, E. T. *An Ecclesiastical History of Monmouthshire* (Risca, 1953).

DAVIES, J. Conway. 'The Despenser War in Glamorgan', *TRHS.*, ix (1914), pp. 21–64.

DAVIES, J. Conway. *Episcopal Acts Relating to the Welsh Dioceses, 1066–1272* (2 vols., Hist. Soc. of Ch. in Wales, Cardiff, 1946–8).

DAVIES, J. Conway. 'Ewenny Priory: Some Recently-Found Deeds', *NLWJ.*, iii (1943–44), pp. 107–37.

DAVIES, J. Conway. 'Giraldus Cambrensis, 1146–1946', *Arch. Camb.*, 1947, pp. 85–108, 256–80.

DAVIES, J. Conway. 'Strata Marcella Documents', *Montgomeryshire Collections*, li (1949–50), pp. 164–87.

DENHOLM-YOUNG, N. *Handwriting in England and Wales* (Cardiff, 1954).

DICKINSON, J. C. *Monastic Life in Medieval England* (London, 1961).

DICKINSON, J. C. *The Origins of the Austin Canons and their Introduction into England* (London, 1950).

Dictionary of Welsh Biography down to 1940 (London, Cymm. Soc., 1959).

DONKIN, R. A. 'Cattle on the Estates of Medieval Cistercian Monasteries in England and Wales', *Ec.H.R.*, xv (1962), pp. 31–53.

DONKIN, R. A. 'Cistercian Sheep Farming and Wool Sales in the Thirteenth Century', *Agricultural History Review*, vi (1958), pp. 1–8.

DONKIN, R. A. 'The Disposal of Cistercian Wool in England and Wales during the Twelfth and Thirteenth Centuries', *Cîteaux in de Nederlanden*, viii (1957), pp. 109–31, 181–202.

DONKIN, R. A. 'Localisation, Situation Economique et Role Parliamentaire des Abbés Cisterciens Anglais (1295–1341)', *Revue d'Histoire Ecclesiastique*, lii (1957), pp. 832–41.

DONKIN, R. A. 'Settlement and Depopulation on Cistercian Estates during the Twelfth and Thirteenth Centuries', *BIHR.*, xxxiii (1960), pp. 141–65.

DONNELLY, J. S. 'Changes in the Grange Economy of English and Welsh Cistercian Abbeys', *Traditio*, x (1954), pp. 399–458.

DONNELLY, J. S. *The Decline of the Medieval Cistercian Laybrotherhood* (New York, 1949).

DOUIE, D. L. *Archbishop Pecham* (Oxford, 1952).

DU CANGE, C. Du F. *Glossarium Mediae et Infimae Latinitatis* . . . (10 vols., Niort, 1883–87).

EASSON, D. E. *Medieval Religious Houses, Scotland* (London, 1957).

EDWARDS, J. G. 'The Normans and the Welsh March', *Proc. Brit. Acad.*, xlii (1957), pp. 155–77.

EMERY, F. V. 'Cwrt-y-Carne Grange', *South Wales Evening Post*, 16 Nov. 1956.

ESPINAS, G. *La Vie Urbaine de Douai au Moyen Age* (4 vols., Paris, 1913).

EVANS, A. L. *Margam Abbey* (Port Talbot, 1958).

EVANS, C. J. O. *Monmouthshire; its History and Topography* (Cardiff, 1954).

FINBERG, H. P. R. *Tavistock Abbey* (Cambridge, 1951).

FLEMING, G. *Animal Plagues: their History, Nature and Prevention* (London, 1871).
FLOYER, J. K. and HAMILTON, S. G. *Catalogue of Manuscripts Preserved in the Chapter Library of Worcester Cathedral* (Oxford, Worcs. Hist. Soc., 1906).
FOSTER, I. 'The Book of the Anchorite', *Proc. Brit. Acad.*, xxxvi (1950), pp. 197–226.
FOWLER, R. C. 'Cistercian Scholars at Oxford', *EHR.*, xxiii (1908), pp. 84–5.
GALBRAITH, V. H. *An Introduction to the Use of the Public Records* (Oxford, 1934).
GOUGAUD, L. *Christianity in Celtic Lands* (London, 1932).
GRAHAM, R. 'The Cluniac Priory of Saint-Martin des Champs, Paris, and its Dependent Priories in England and Wales', *Jnl. Brit. Arch. Assoc.*, xi (1948), pp. 35–59.
GRAHAM, R. *English Ecclesiastical Studies* (London, 1929).
GRAHAM, R. 'Four Alien Priories in Monmouthshire', *Jnl. Brit. Arch. Assoc.*, xxxv (1929–30), pp. 102–21.
GRAHAM, R. 'The Taxation of Pope Nicholas IV', *EHR.*, xxiii (1908), pp. 434–54.
GREEN, C. A. H. *Notes on Churches in the Diocese of Llandaff* (Aberdare, 1906–7).
GREENWAY, W. 'The Annals of Margam', *Trans. Port Talbot Hist. Soc.*, i (1963), pp. 19–31.
GREENWAY, W. 'The Election of John of Monmouth, Bishop of Llandaff', *Morgannwg*, v (1961), pp. 3 22.
GRIFFITHS, R. A. *The Principality of Wales in the Later Middle Ages: The Structure and Personnel of Government, I. South Wales, 1277–1536* (Cardiff, 1972).
GWYNN, A. and HADCOCK, R. N. *Medieval Religious Houses, Ireland* (London, 1970).
HAGUE, D. B. 'Some Welsh Evidence [for Buildings of Ecclesiastical and Related Type]', *Scot. Archaeol. Forum*, v (1973), pp. 17–35.
HARRIS, S. M. 'The Kalendar of the *Vitae Sanctorum Wallensium*', *JHSCW.*, iii (1953), pp. 3–53.
HARTRIDGE, R. A. R. *A History of Vicarages in the Middle Ages* (Cambridge, 1930).
HASKINS, C. H. *Norman Institutions* (New York, 1960).
HAYS, R. W. *The History of the Abbey of Aberconway, 1186–1537* (Cardiff, 1963).
HEMP, W. J. 'St. Mary's Church, Abergavenny', *Arch. Camb.*, 1936, pp. 350–7.
HIGGINS, L. S. 'An Investigation into the Problem of the Sand Dune Areas on the South Wales Coast', *Arch. Camb.*, 1933, pp. 26–67.
HILL, B. D. *English Cistercian Monasteries and their Patrons in the Twelfth Century* (Urbana, 1968).
HINNEBUSCH, W. A. 'The Personnel of the Early English Dominican Province', *Catholic Historical Review*, xxix (1943–4), pp. 326–46.
HOLDSWORTH, C. J. 'John of Ford and English Cistercian Writing, 1167–1214', *TRHS.*, xi (1961), pp. 117–36.
HOURLIER, J. *Le Chapitre Général jusqu'au Moment du Grand Schisme* (Paris, 1936).
HUNT, R. W. 'English Learning in the Late Twelfth Century', *TRHS.*, xix (1936), pp. 19–42.
HUWS, D. 'Gildas Prisei', *NLWJ.*, xvii (1972), pp. 314–20.
JAMES, M. R. *A Descriptive Catalogue of the Manuscripts in the Library of St. John's College, Cambridge* (Cambridge, 1913).
JAMES, M. R. and JENKINS, C. *A Descriptive Catalogue of the Manuscripts in the Library of Lambeth Palace* (5 parts, Cambridge, 1930–2).
JANAUSCHEK, L. *Originum Cisterciensium* (Vienna, 1877).
JOHNS, C. N. 'The Celtic Monasteries of North Wales', *Trans. Caern. Hist. Soc.*, xxi (1960), pp. 14–43; xxiii (1962), pp. 129–31.

JONES, A. 'The Estates of the Welsh Abbeys at the Dissolution', *Arch. Camb.*, 1937, pp. 269–86.

JONES, D. D. *A History of Kidwelly* (Carmarthen, 1908).

JONES, T. *Brut y Tywysogion* (Cardiff, 1953).

KER, N. R. *Medieval Libraries of Great Britain: A List of Surviving Books* (2nd ed., London, Roy. Hist. Soc., 1964).

KING, A. A. *Cîteaux and Her Elder Daughters* (London, 1954).

KNOWLES, D. *The Monastic Order in England* (2nd ed., Cambridge, 1963).

KNOWLES, D. *The Religious Orders in England* (3 vols., Cambridge, 1948–59).

KNOWLES, D. 'Some Aspects of the Career of Archbishop Pecham', *EHR.*, lvii (1942), pp. 1–18, 178–201.

KNOWLES, D. 'Some Enemies of Gerald of Wales', *Studia Monastica*, i (1959), pp. 137–41.

KNOWLES, D. and HADCOCK, R. N. *Medieval Religious Houses, England and Wales* (2nd ed., London, 1971).

LANGSTON, J. N. 'Priors of Lanthony by Gloucester', *Trans. Bristol and Glouc. Arch. Soc.*, lxiii (1942), pp. 1–143.

LAPIDGE, M. 'The Welsh-Latin Poetry of Sulien's Family', *Studia Celtica*, viii/ix (1973–4), pp. 68–106.

LAWRENCE, C. H. 'Stephen of Lexington and Cistercian University Studies in the Thirteenth Century', *Jnl. Ecc. Hist.*, xi (1960), pp. 164–78.

LEGGE, M. D. *Anglo-Norman in the Cloisters* (Edinburgh, 1950).

LEKAI, L. J. *The White Monks* (Okauchee, Wisc., 1953).

LELAND, J. *Commentarii de Scriptoribus Britannicis*, ed. A. Hall (2 vols., Oxford, 1709).

LELAND, J. *De Rebus Britannicis Collectanea . . .* (6 vols., London, 1774).

LEVETT, A. E. *Studies in Manorial History* (Oxford, 1938).

LEWIS, D. 'Notes on the Charters of Neath Abbey', *Arch. Camb.*, 1887, pp. 86–115.

LEWIS, E. A. 'A Contribution to the Commercial History of Medieval Wales', *Cymmrodor*, xxiv (1913), pp. 86–188.

LEWIS, E. A. 'The Development of Industry and Commerce in Wales during the Middle Ages', *TRHS.*, xvii (1903), pp. 121–73.

LEWIS, F. R. 'A History of the Lordship of Gower from the Missing Cartulary of Neath Abbey', *BBCS.*, ix (1938), pp. 149–54.

LEWIS, S. *A Topographical Dictionary of Wales* (3rd ed., 2 vols., London, 1843).

LEWIS, Saunders. *Braslun o Hanes Llenyddiaeth Gymraeg* (Cardiff, 1932).

LITTLE, A. G. 'Cistercian Students at Oxford in the Thirteenth Century', *EHR.*, viii (1893), pp. 83–5.

LLOYD, J. E., ed. *A History of Carmarthenshire* (2 vols., Cardiff, 1935–9).

LLOYD, J. E. *A History of Wales* (2 vols., London, 1939).

LLOYD, J. E. 'The Welsh Chronicles', *Proc. Brit. Acad.*, xiv (1928), pp. 369–91.

LOVEGROVE, E. W. 'Llanthony Priory, Monmouthshire', *Arch. Camb.*, 1943, pp. 213–29; 1947, pp. 64–77.

LOVEGROVE, E. W. 'Valle Crucis Abbey; Its Position in Monasticism; the Men who Built It', *Arch. Camb.*, 1936, pp. 1–14.

LOWER, M. A. *The Chronicle of Battel Abbey* (London, 1851).

LOYD, L. C. *The Origins of Some Anglo-Norman Families* (Leeds, 1951).

LUNT, W. E. *Financial Relations of the Papacy with England to 1327* (Cambridge, Mass., 1939).

LUNT, W. E. *The Valuation of Norwich* (Oxford, 1926).

McKISACK, M. *The Fourteenth Century, 1307–1399* (Oxford, 1959).

MAHN, J-B. *L'Ordre Cistercien et son Gouvernement des Origines au Milieu du XIIIᵉ Siecle* (2nd ed., Paris, 1951).

MAHN, J-B. *Le Pape Benoit XII et les Cisterciens* (Paris, 1949).

MALDEN, H. E. 'The Possession of Cardigan Priory by Chertsey Abbey: A Study in Some Mediaeval Forgeries', *TRHS.*, 3rd ser., v (1911), pp. 141–56.

MARCHEGAY, P. *Les Prieurés Anglais de Saint-Florent Près Saumur* (Les Roches-Baritaud, Vendee, 1879).

MATTHEW, D. *The Norman Monasteries and their English Possessions* (Oxford, 1962).

MOORMAN, J. R. H. *Church Life in England in the Thirteenth Century* (Cambridge, 1955).

MORGAN, G. E. F. 'The Vanished Tombs of Brecon Cathedral', *Arch. Camb.*, 1925, pp. 257–74.

MORGAN, M. M. 'The Abbey of Bec-Hellouin and its English Priories', *Jnl. Brit. Arch. Assoc.*, v (1940), pp. 33–61.

MORGAN, M. *The English Lands of the Abbey of Bec* (Oxford, 1946).

MORGAN, M. M. 'The Suppression of the Alien Priories', *History*, xxvi (1941), pp. 204–12.

MORGAN, O. *Some Account of the Ancient Monuments in the Priory Church, Abergavenny* (Newport, 1872).

MORRIS, J. E. *The Welsh Wars of Edward I* (Oxford, 1901).

NASH-WILLIAMS, V. E. *The Early Christian Monuments of Wales* (Cardiff, 1950).

NEF, J. U. *Rise of the British Coal Industry* (2 vols., London, 1932).

NICHOLAS, T. *History and Antiquities of Glamorganshire and its Families* (London, 1874).

O'SULLIVAN, J. F. *Cistercian Settlements in Wales and Monmouthshire, 1140–1540* (New York, 1947).

OWEN, E. 'A Contribution to the History of the Premonstratensian Abbey of Talley', *Arch. Camb.*, 1893–4.

OWEN, G. D. 'The Extent and Distribution of the Lands of St. John's at Carmarthen', *Carmarthen Antiquary*, i (1941), pp. 21–9.

OWEN, H. *Old Pembroke Families* (London, 1902).

PARRY, T. *History of Welsh Literature*, transl. Sir Idris Bell (Oxford, 1955).

PEGOLOTTI, F. B. *La Pratica della Mercatura*, ed. A. Evans (Medieval Academy of America, xxiv, 1936).

PIERCE, T. Jones. 'Strata Florida Abbey', *Ceredigion*, i (1950), pp. 18–33.

PIRENNE, H. *Economic and Social History of Medieval Europe* (London, 1936).

PLATT, C. *The Monastic Grange in Medieval England* (London, 1969).

PORÉE, A. A. *Histoire de l'Abbaye du Bec* (2 vols., Évreux, 1901).

POWER, E. *The Wool Trade in English Medieval History* (Oxford, 1941).

POWER, E. 'Medieval Monastic Finance', *Ec.H.R.*, vii (1936), pp. 87–92.

POWICKE, F. M. *Ways of Medieval Life and Thought* (London, 1950).

PRITCHARD, E. M. *Cardigan Priory in the Olden Days* (London, 1904).

PRITCHARD, E. M. *The History of St. Dogmaels Abbey* (London, 1907).

RADFORD, C. A. Ralegh. *Ewenny Priory, Glamorgan* (London, 1952).

REES, W. 'The Priory of Cardiff and Other Possessions of the Abbey of Tewkesbury in Glamorgan', *South Wales & Monmouthshire Record Society Publications*, ii (1950), pp. 129–86.

REES, W. *South Wales and the Border in the XIV Century* (4 sheets, Southampton, 1933).

REES, W. *South Wales and the March, 1284–1415* (Oxford, 1924).

REES, W. J. 'Account of Cwmhir Abbey', *Arch. Camb.*, 1849, pp. 233–60.

RICHARDS, M. 'The Carmarthenshire Possessions of Talyllychau', in *Carmarthenshire Studies: Essays Presented to Major Francis Jones*, eds. T. Barnes and N. Yates (Carmarthen, 1974), pp. 110–21.

ROBERTS, G. *Some Account of Llanthony Priory, Monmouthshire* (London, 1847).

ROTH, C. *History of the Jews in England* (Oxford, 1941).

ROUND, J. H. *Family Origins* (London, 1930).

ROUND, J. H. *Studies in Peerage and Family History* (London, 1901).

ROYAL COMMISSION ON ANCIENT MONUMENTS IN WALES AND MONMOUTHSHIRE. *Inventories:* Radnorshire, 1913; Carmarthenshire, 1917; Pembrokeshire, 1925.

RUSSELL, J. C. *British Medieval Population* (Albuquerque, 1948).

RUSSELL, J. C. *Dictionary of Writers of Thirteenth Century England* (London, 1936).

SAYERS, J. 'The Judicial Activities of the General Chapter', *Jnl. Ecc. Hist.*, xv (1964), pp. 18–32.

SLICHER VAN BATH, B. H. *The Agrarian History of Western Europe, A.D. 500–1850* (London, 1963).

SMITH, J. B. 'The *Cronica de Wallia* and the Dynasty of Dinefwr', *BBCS.*, xx (1963), pp. 261–82.

SMITH, J. B. 'The Lordship of Glamorgan', *Morgannwg*, ii (1958), pp. 9–37.

SMITH, J. B. and O'NEIL, B. H. St. J. *Talley Abbey, Carmarthenshire* (London, 1967).

SNAPE, R. H. *English Monastic Finances* (Cambridge, 1926).

STENGEL, H. 'Handschriftliches aus Oxford', *Zeitschrift für französische Sprache und Litteratur*, xiv (1892), pp. 147–51.

STEPHENS, T. *The Literature of the Kymry* (2nd ed., London, 1876).

TALBOT, C. H. 'Cadogan of Bangor', *Cîteaux in de Nederlanden*, ix (1958), pp. 18–40.

TALBOT, C. H. 'A List of Cistercian Manuscripts in Great Britain', *Traditio*, viii (1952), pp. 402–18.

TALBOT, C. H. 'William of Wycumbe, Fourth Prior of Llanthony', *Trans. Brist. and Glouc. Arch. Soc.*, lxxvi (1957), pp. 62–9.

THOMAS, T. *The Antiquities of Whitland* [text in Welsh] (Llanelly, 1868).

USHER, G. 'Welsh Students at Oxford in the Middle Ages', *BBCS.*, xvi (1955), pp. 193–8.

VICTORIA COUNTY HISTORY OF ENGLAND: Gloucester, ii (London, 1907); Norfolk, ii (London, 1906); Somerset, i (London, 1906).

VISCH, C. de. *Bibliotheca Scriptorum Sacri Ordinis Cisterciensis* (Duaci, 1649).

WADE-EVANS, A. W. 'Pembrokeshire Notes', *Arch. Camb.*, 1935, pp. 123–34.

WALKER, D. 'The Medieval Bishops of Llandaff', *Morgannwg*, vi (1962), pp. 5–32.

WARNER, G. F. *Catalogue of the Manuscripts and Muniments of Alleyn's College of God's Gift at Dulwich* (London, 1881).

WARNER, G. F. and GILSON, J. P. *Catalogue of Western Manuscripts in the Old Royal and King's Collection* (4 vols., London, British Museum, 1921).

WELCH, C. E. 'An Early Charter of Ewenny Priory', *NLWJ.*, x (1957–8), pp. 415–6.

WILLIAMS, A. H. *An Introduction to the History of Wales* (2 vols., Cardiff, 1941–8).

WILLIAMS, D. H. 'Fasti Cistercienses Cambrenses', *BBCS.*, xxiv (1971), pp. 181–229.

WILLIAMS, D. H. 'Grace Dieu Abbey: an Exploratory Excavation', *Monmouthshire Antiquary*, iii (1970–1), pp. 55–8.

WILLIAMS, G. 'Neath Abbey' in *Neath and District: a Symposium*, ed. Elis Jenkins (Neath, 1974).

WILLIAMS, G. *The Welsh Church from Conquest to Reformation* (Cardiff, 1962).

WILLIAMS, G. *An Introduction to Welsh Poetry from the Beginnings to the Sixteenth Century* (London, 1953).

WILLIAMS, S. W. 'The Cistercian Abbey of Cwmhir, Radnorshire', *Trans. Cymm.*, 1894–5, pp. 61–98.

WILLIAMS, S. W. *The Cistercian Abbey of Strata Florida* (London, 1889).

WOOD, S. *English Monasteries and their Patrons in the Thirteenth Century* (Oxford, 1955).

WOOD-LEGH, K. L. *Studies in Church Life in England under Edward III* (Cambridge, 1934).

WORMALD, F. and WRIGHT, C. E. *The English Library before 1700* (London, 1958).

(b) UNPUBLISHED DISSERTATION

OWEN, G. D. 'Agrarian Conditions and Changes in West Wales during the Sixteenth Century' (University of Wales Ph.D. thesis, 1935).

BIBLIOGRAPHY

PLATE I   Chepstow Priory: the Romanesque nave.

PLATE II   Llanthony Prima Priory from the north-west.

PLATE III   Ewenni Priory: south transept with founder's tomb.

PLATE IV   Neath Abbey: aerial view from the west.

NOTES ON THE ILLUSTRATIONS

FRONTISPIECE

This fine wooden effigy, the face of which is probably a portrait, has been assigned by Alfred C. Fryer to the early fourteenth century (*Archaeologia*, 61, 1909, pp. 503, 539). It may be attributed, therefore, either to John de Hastings, lord of Abergavenny, who died in 1313, or to his son of the same name who succeeded him and died in 1325. The latter is known to have been a particularly conscientious patron of the priory.

PLATE I

The parochial nave of the priory church of Chepstow, described by E. A. Freeman as 'the nearly perfect nave of no contemptible Norman Minster', was built about 1120 (A. W. Clapham, *English Romanesque Architecture*, ii, p.56).

PLATE II

The benefactions made at the end of the twelfth century by the priory patrons, Hugh de Lacy and his son, Walter de Lacy, from their newly-won possessions in Ireland, enabled the priory church and conventual buildings to be completely rebuilt. The work of rebuilding was begun about 1175 and completed about 1230.

PLATE III

At Ewenni the monastic part of the priory church, of which the transepts formed part, is of two dates. The work up to, and including, the heavy string course with chevron moulding belongs to the church which was built for the newly-established conventual community about 1141. The work above the chevron string course represents a rebuilding and heightening of the church which took place at the end of the twelfth century. The south transept houses *inter alia* the tombstones of the founder, Maurice de Londres, and of later patrons, William de Londres and Hawise de Londres (d. 1274).

PLATE IV

The church of Neath Abbey, like that of Tintern, was completely rebuilt in the last quarter of the thirteenth century but only its broken shell remains. The lay-brothers' western range has fared better and dates from between 1170 and 1230. Part of the domestic buildings of the abbey, including a fine vaulted undercroft which is virtually intact, were incorporated into an Elizabethan mansion built by Sir John Herbert at the end of the sixteenth century.

INDEX

Aberafan, church, 267.
Aberconwy, Cistercian abbey of, 26; abbots of, 115, 118, 127, 129 and n.114, 212, 223, see also John; compensated for war damage, 214; grange lands of, 259 n.146; move to new site at Maenan, 180; register and chronicle of, 155 n.81, 260.
Aberffraw, princes of, 195.
Abergavenny, castle, chapel of, 13. church, 276; vicarage of, 279. dean and deanery, 110, 172, 276. Benedictine alien priory of, 12, 13, 14, 17, 40–1, 56, 58, 59, 107 n.24, 279; annals of, 196; assessed value of in 1291, 274; condition of in 1320, 109–12; custody of during vacancy, 200; foundation of, 13, 270; income of, 43, 94, 110; monumental effigies at, 196; number of monks at, 43, 110, 111, 269; patrons of, 195–6; priors of, see Gastard, Fulk; Henry de Abergavenny; Richard of Bromwich; recruitment of monks at, 40–1; service books of burnt, 145 and n.35; seized as alien priory, 221; size of arable estate of, 57, 273; spiritual income of, 276; visitation of, 109–12.
Parliament of, 227.
Abergwili, church, 95, 186.
Aber-miwl, grange, 205–6, 260.
Abernant, chapel, 95; church, 277.
Abraham, abbot of Neath, 124.
Abraham, archbishop of Armagh, 189.
Acle, manor, 255, 266 and n.175.
Adam of Carmarthen, abbot of Neath, 246.
Adam of Llandeilo Porth Halog, dean of Upper Gwent, 200.
Adam de Orleton, bishop of Hereford, 43, 94, 109–12, 177.
Adam de Roch(e), 20, 270.
Aeron, vale of, 38, 72.
Afallennau, 158.

Afan, lords and lordship of, 76, 183, 197, 245, 248.
river, 23, 56, 71, 80.
fisheries, 23.
Agmondesham, church, 264.
Agnes, wife of Bernard Neufmarché, 14.
Ailred, abbot of Rievaulx, 48, 97.
Alaythur, sons of, 213.
Alberic, abbot of Cîteaux, 18.
Albert of Cologne, archbishop of Armagh, 208.
Aldgate, Augustinian priory of Holy Trinity, 30.
Alexander II, pope, 17.
Alexander III, pope, 173.
Alice de Putangle, 61.
alien priories, 94, 100; seizure of, 221–2, 233, see also Abergavenny, Chepstow, Goldcliff, Llangenydd, Monmouth, Pembroke, St. Clears.
Alis, Philip, 40.
brother of, Ralph, 41.
almoner and almonry, 61–2, 103, 207–9.
almsgiving, 82, 175, 185, 207–9.
Alrewas, 224.
Alschave, 247.
Alvington, chapel, 185.
manor, 266.
Amiens, Premonstratensian abbey of St. Jean, 37, 132, 271.
Anagni, Benedictine abbey of St. Mary de Gloria, 279.
Anchorite, Book of the, 52.
Andrew, sub-prior of Pembroke, 107.
Aneirin, Book of, 156, 157.
Anglesey, 82, 190.
Anhuniog, 72; grange, 260 n.150.
Anian, bishop of St. Asaph, 212.
Annales Cambriae, 87.
annals, monastic, 147–50.
Anselm, St., 10, 30.
Anselm of Laon, 150.
appropriation of churches, 60–1, 91, 169–73, 174, 176–80, 264–7.
arable farming, 53, 56, 57–8, 62, 70, 72, 78–83.